St Francis of Assisi

THE LEGEND AND THE LIFE

MICHAEL ROBSON

OFMConv

GEOFFREY
CHAPMAN

To my mother

Geoffrey Chapman
A Cassell imprint
Wellington House, 125 Strand, London WC2R 0BB
PO Box 605, Herndon, VA 20172

First published 1997

British Library Cataloguing-in-Publication Data
A catalogue record for this book is available from the British Library.

ISBN 0-225-66736-3

Typset by BookEns Limited, Royston, Herts.
Printed and bound in Great Britain by
Redwood Books, Trowbridge, Wilts.

Contents

Contents

Contents

Introduction

St Francis of Assisi (1181/82–1226) captivated his contemporaries and his life has been celebrated in prose, verse, art, music and film. The first biography, the *Vita prima,* was compiled by one of his followers, Thomas of Celano, at the instigation of Gregory IX in association with the ceremonies of canonization on 16 July 1228. Francis, one of the two patron saints of Italy, has never ceased to fascinate succeeding generations. He remains one of the most attractive saints, whose appeal is not confined to the Catholic Church or even Christianity. Each year millions of people from different religious traditions and none visit his last resting place in the basilica of San Francesco in Assisi. In an age which fosters ecumenism and has recently recovered a growing concern for the sacredness of God's creation he becomes an even more influential figure. His life proclaims the spiritual nature of God's creation, whose aspirations cannot be entirely satisfied by material benefits along with the pursuit of wealth and security. While he divested himself of his material goods, his security was rooted in his dependence upon his Creator for the development of his qualities and gifts. He was a paradoxical figure. Though he attended a school run by the canons of San Rufino in Assisi and his grasp of grammar was not always sure, Thomas of Celano proudly announces that the saint had already worked great miracles in France, where the king and queen and all the great ones run to kiss and venerate the pillow which he had used in his sickness. The most wise and learned men of the world, gathered at the University of Paris, humbly and most devoutly venerated, admired and honoured Francis, an unlettered man and the friend of true simplicity and complete sincerity.

By the evening of 3 October 1226, the date of Francis's death, his followers were growing at a spectacular rate and spreading throughout Christendom following an ideal which caught the popular imagination. Francis was happy to share his vision with men and women, regardless of their social background. Among those who followed him were bishops and knights, monks and merchants, scholars and labourers. Within a decade of Francis's death the friars' ranks included one of the most distinguished theologians of his era, Alexander of

Hales, who renounced his wealth and security to don the friars' habit at Paris. He continued his lectures as the first Franciscan master of theology, thereby incorporating the friars' school within the University of Paris. This dimension of the friars' ministry demonstrates the manner in which Francis's spirit was carried into all parts of society, excluding no one. In the thirteenth century the Franciscans were part of the landscape of Christendom and were found in hermitages, where they pursued the contemplative vocation to which all are called, and in the burgeoning cities of western Europe, where they applied the ethics of the New Testament to new commercial centres. In an attractive and cogent manner they brought the Gospel to life and reinforced its simple message of communion with God and their neighbour. They were engaged in alleviating the sufferings of the weaker members of society, the sick and the impoverished. Their presence in the ancient university cities carried the Gospel to the community of masters and students and the friars' own theological studies had a twofold root in the pastoral ministry and the quest for personal sanctification. Their missionary enterprises sprang from the imperative that the Gospel should be preached to all peoples. This conviction carried Francis into the heart of the Muslim camp at Damietta where he entered into dialogue with Islamic leaders. In the thirteenth century the friars set out with bare feet to proclaim the Gospel in north Africa and China and to promote ecumenical conversations with the separated Christians of the Greek Church. While the visible remains of the vast network of medieval friaries in England are few, the name Greyfriars survives in the names of streets in many old cities and towns.

Some introductory remarks on medieval hagiography are required in order to interpret the plethora of medieval biographers of Francis. The biographies of St Antony the Abbot (251–356) by St Athanasius and St Martin of Tours (*c.* 316–97) by Sulpicius Severus were revered as the classical models for the composition of a saint's life. The influence of these standard texts can be glimpsed in the earliest biographies of Francis, whose virtues associated him with the apostles and their mission. Thomas of Celano makes a comparison between Francis and St Martin. Francis's influence and power were increased in his death, with the succession of miracles accomplished at his tomb in his native Assisi. Franciscan hagiography presented Francis as the vehicle of God's grace in a world which offered new opportunities for prosperity and wealth. One of the four scenes depicted above the high altar in the lower basilica of San Francesco in Assisi shows the saint, adorned in a splendid dalmatic, being manipulated by strings from heaven. Thus Francis was a man through whom God worked out his plan in the early thirteenth century. The same presuppositions drive the medieval biographies of Francis, who becomes the embodiment of the individual intent solely on communion with his Creator and fellow creatures. This has the effect of producing a rather idealized portrait of a man who experiences little difficulty or hardship. Such assumptions do violence to truth and this is illustrated by the polarized account of the tussle between the spirit of the Gospel and that of society, represented by the saint and his father. Another aspect of the biographies of the founder is the way in which his teaching is applied to contemporary conditions in the fraternity, as the ninth chapter demonstrates.

Outstanding figures attract a great deal of attention, and their friends and disciples are anxious to ensure that a balanced account of their lives passes to posterity. A recent example of this concern is the desire of Professor Christopher Brooke, Drs Roger Lovatt and David Luscombe and Abbot Aelred Sillem to supplement Adrian Morey's *David Knowles: A Memoir*.[1] Francis had been in his tomb for less than two decades before the friars felt the need to enlarge the portrait already published in the *Vita prima*. As the battle for his soul and heritage intensified so the biographies started to mirror the authors' own understanding of Francis's ideals and their contribution to the contemporary Church and society; from the middle of the thirteenth century the biographers became increasingly polarized and friars offered portraits of the saint reflecting their own views about how the fraternity should develop. The tensions between the institutional accounts and the more polemical interpretations are barely concealed. In his survey of the partisan elements which have infected early Franciscan hagiography Professor C. H. Lawrence observes that anyone who sets out to describe the saint must recognize that the enterprise is subject to severe limitations.[2]

A brief introduction to two of the sources is in order, however, because they have a bearing upon the projected image of the saint. While the *Vita prima* was composed to announce the grace of God in the life of Francis, who was being presented to the world as an exemplary Christian, the biographies of the 1240s were largely concerned with the heritage of the saint. After the general chapter of 1244 there was an appeal to the friars who had known Francis to send in their reminiscences and anecdotes. Leo, Rufino and Angelo, the saint's early companions, compiled their own recollections of the saint, emphasizing his love of poverty and simplicity. Their accounts harked back to the halcyon days of the fraternity and were critical of some more recent developments in the observance of poverty and buildings. Questions of discipline and the preservation of poverty were to the fore and the development of schools and the use of books were treated with a tangible unease. These materials were employed selectively by Thomas of Celano's *Vita secunda*, which was concerned both with an interpretation of the founder's teaching and with the friars' place in the contemporary Church where they had many eloquent and powerful critics. The cautious and apologetic tone strips the biography of the freshness and informality which informed the recollections of Francis's early companions. The portrait is frequently stiff and circumspect, as in the 'official' assessment of Francis's dealings with St Clare and the sisters at San Damiano. The *Vita secunda* lacks the vitality and charm of the *Vita prima* and signals the birth of the institutionalized portrait of the saint. St Bonaventure built on the well-laid foundations of Thomas of Celano. While these biographers provide the framework for the saint's life, they underline the tensions between hagiography and historiography. Hagiographical texts were more concerned with edification and apologetics than with the level of detail required by the historian and thus their value as witnesses to historical events calls for some deconstruction, which will appear regularly in the ensuing study.

This study is concerned primarily with a portrait of Francis and his interaction with major figures and images. It is not my intention to provide a biographical picture of Peter Bernardone, Bishop Guido II, Innocent III, Cardinal Ugolino, Anthony of Padua and Clare of Assisi. They are examined in terms of their relationship with Francis. Neither is this the place for an appraisal of the complicated relationship between the early biographies. Numerous specialist studies on Francis address the knotty problems such as the historiographical 'Franciscan question' and I am happy to associate myself with the conclusions reached by Professor R. J. Armstrong OFMCap.[3]

The principal events in Francis's life have been explored through his interaction with major players and ideals. These encounters and influences illuminate certain areas in his life and provide a proper context for some of the momentous decisions which he took. The chapters on the key people in Francis's life point to different dimensions of his personality and teaching, revealing the influences on his life and fraternity. I have adopted a thematic approach, which does not adhere strictly to the saint's chronology, and in this I keep company with some of the early biographers, such as the *Vita secunda*, which assembles Francis's teaching on a variety of issues, such as poverty. The chronological table on pp. xx–xxvi, however, provides a point of historical reference to the major events in the saint's life and the emergence of his fraternity. There is, moreover, a steady progression from Francis's decision to base his life primarily on the Gospel to his call for the whole of creation to unite in praise of its Creator.

The first three chapters, dealing with Peter Bernardone, Bishop Guido and Pope Innocent, represent the early phase in Francis's new life. Peter Bernardone symbolizes Francis's family, though the first chapter takes into account the claims advanced by R. C. Trexler.[4] This chapter considers the origins of Christianity in Assisi and the influence of the martyred bishops. In the second chapter Bishop Guido, perceived as the vicar of San Rufino, provides Francis with protection, encouragement and sound advice at crucial stages in the fraternity's infancy. Francis's collaboration with the local bishop paves the way for the third chapter's treatment of his dealings with Innocent III and his participation in the papal programme of reform enshrined in the canons of the Fourth Lateran Council in 1215.

Chapters 4 to 6 locate the friars' ministry within the mission of the papal reforms flowing from the recent Lateran Council. The fourth chapter examines

Francis's decision to adopt a life of evangelical poverty, which became the hallmark of the fraternity. Thus, the friars' espousal of evangelical poverty became the emblem of the fraternity. The fifth chapter, dealing with Cardinal Ugolino, reflects the way in which the friars were making the transition from a small fraternity, based in Umbria, to an international brotherhood, which was present throughout Christendom. Francis's friendship with the cardinal was of the highest importance for the survival and growth of the fraternity. St Anthony of Padua has been included among the major figures not because the sources suggest that he had a great deal of direct contact with the founder, but because of his role in the evolution of Franciscan theology, which helped to turn the friars into such persuasive and powerful preachers.

No study of Francis could omit an analysis of his friendship with Clare, who mirrored his thirst for communion with God and so valiantly upheld his ideal of evangelical poverty. This vital friendship is examined in the seventh chapter. The series of 'conversion' events led Francis to the conviction that he should communicate to his contemporaries the liberating and enriching good news of the Gospel, and the methods which he chose are considered in the eighth chapter. The saint's death and his continuing influence over the fraternity, with the constant calls for reform and renewal based on the witness of the founder, form the last chapter, in which Francis takes his place among the saints of his native city. Just as the first chapter opens with a brief account of San Rufino directing the church of Assisi from his shrine in the cathedral, the book concludes with a brief examination of Francis, the new saint, governing and guiding his fraternity from the tomb in the basilica. The chapter on Cardinal Ugolino's communications with Francis illustrates the preference for themes rather than strict chronology, beginning with their meeting at Florence in 1217 and concluding with an account of how Ugolino, now as Gregory IX, employed the friars for various missions in the 1230s.

The study starts with an examination of the Christian origins of Assisi and the way in which the martyred bishops of the city, especially San Rufino, continued to play a significant part in the religious, social and civic life of the city in performing miracles. The martyrs' ideals impinged upon Francis who sought martyrdom and nurtured a deep reverence for the saints' relics. The connection between the patron saint and the bishop of Assisi identifies the source of spiritual authority in Assisi. Thus Guido was perceived as the vicar of the saint, whose spiritual authority he exercised. This was Francis's perception of a prelate whose intervention was benevolent at certain key stages in the evolution of the order and without whose help the friars would not have been entertained outside Assisi. A similar relationship, though with some major differences, shaped Francis's outlook on the papacy and his thirst for approval. The pope was identified as the vicar of St Peter and, more importantly, as the vicar of Jesus Christ. There was no higher spiritual authority in Francis's world. The last chapter returns to the theme of the sacred power associated with the saint's shrine and focuses on Francis's continuing responsibility for the fraternity. As the order became part of the ecclesiastical fabric, the figure of Francis was invoked either to approve or to castigate the policies pursued by his followers. His remained the moral authority within the fraternity in both life and death. Just as San Rufino was the dominant figure in the life of Christians in Assisi, so Francis remained the source of spiritual authority both in life and death as he presided over the fraternity which he guided from the tomb.

Like so many people, as a small boy I was introduced to Francis through the portrait of his gentle exhortation to the birds. With the passage of time the fascination steadily increased and brought me to the order of Friars Minor Conventual, a noble tradition within the regrettably fragmented Franciscan family. At the Franciscan Study Centre in Canterbury I first became acquainted with the wealth of the fraternity's devotional and theological heritage. Francis is too important a figure to be monopolized by any part of the order or the Church. His appeal is universal and his insights into our spiritual nature and a necessary detachment from an undue reliance on material things are accessible to all who strive to walk, however haltingly, in the footsteps of Jesus Christ.

Notes

1. C. N. L. Brooke (ed.), *David Knowles Remembered* (Cambridge, 1991), p. ix.
2. C. H. Lawrence, *Medieval Monasticism: Forms of Religious Life in Western Europe in the Middle Ages* (London, 2nd edn, 1989), pp. 244–5.
3. R. J. Armstrong (trans. and ed.), *Clare of Assisi: Early Documents* (New York, 1988).
4. R. C. Trexler, *Naked Before the Father: The Renunciation of Francis of Assisi* (Humana Civilitas, 9; New York, 1989).

Acknowledgements

The Revd Dr Bede Chaberski OFMConv, deserves my gratitude for kindly reading the last proofs of this book and making a number of valuable observations. Fr Alban McCoy OFMConv and Professor Joan Chittister OSB read earlier drafts of the text and made numerous helpful suggestions. Professor J. A. Watt's expertise on the history of the papacy in the Middle Ages gave me advice on the third and fifth chapters. The Revd Dr Michael MacCreath OFM read an earlier draft of the sixth chapter. Any errors of interpretation are entirely my own responsibility. I remain grateful to Mr Michael Walsh, Librarian of Heythrop College in the University of London, who invited me to embark upon this volume and gave much practical help throughout its writing.

Abbreviations

AF   *Analecta Franciscana* (Quaracchi, Florence and Grottaferrata)

AFH   *Archivum Franciscanum Historicum*

ALKG   *Archiv für Litteratur- und Kirchengeschichte des Mittelalters*, ed. H. Denifle and F. Ehrle (Berlin and Freiburg im Breisgau, 1885–1900)

Anon. Perug.   *L'Anonyme de Pérouse: Un témoin de la fraternité franciscaine primitive*, translation, introduction and notes by B. Beguin (Textes franciscains; Paris, 1979)

Assidua   *Vita prima o Assidua*, ed. V. Gamboso (FAA, 1; Padua, 1981)

Benignitas   *Vita del 'Dialogus' e 'Benignitas'*, ed. V. Gamboso (FAA, 3; Padua, 1986)

BF   *Bullarium Franciscanum*

BFAMA   Bibliotheca Franciscana Ascetica Medii Aevi

BFSMA   Bibliotheca Franciscana Scholastica Medii Aevi

BSFS   British Society of Franciscan Studies

Compilatio Assisiensis   *Compilatio Assisiensis dagli Scritti di fra Leone e compagni su S. Francesco d'Assisi* (Pubblicazioni della biblioteca francescana chiesa nuova – Assisi, 2), ed. M. Bigaroni (Assisi, 1992)

Dialogus   *Vita del 'Dialogus' e 'Benignitas'*, ed. V. Gamboso (FAA, 3; Padua, 1986)

FAA   Fonti agiografiche antoniane

LM   Bonaventure, *Legenda maior S. Francisci* in AF, 10, pp. 555–652

LSC   *Legenda Sanctae Clarae Virginis*, ed. F. Pennacchi (Società internazionale di studi francescani in Assisi; Assisi, 1910), trans. in *Clare of Assisi: Early Documents*, trans. R. J. Armstrong (New York, 1988), which also includes a translation of Clare's letters

LTS   'Legenda trium Sociorum Edition critique', ed. T. Desbonnets in AFH, 67 (1974), pp. 38–144

MGH SS   Monumenta Germaniae Historica, Scriptores

MOPH   Monumenta Ordinis Fratrum Praedicatorum Historica

NMT   Nelson's Medieval Texts Series

NV   *Nova vita di San Francesco*, by A. Fortini (Milan, 1926)

OMT   Oxford Medieval Texts

PG   Migne, Patrologia Graeca

PL   Migne, Patrologia Latina

Process   Z. Lazzeri, 'Il Processo di canonizzazione di S. Chiara d'Assisi' in AFH, 13 (1920), pp. 403–507, translated in Armstrong, *Clare of Assisi: Early Documents*

Raymundina   *Vite 'Raymundina' e 'Rigaldina'*, ed. V. Gamboso (FAA, 4; Padua, 1992)

Rigaldina   *Vite 'Raymundina' e 'Rigaldina'*, ed. V. Gamboso (FAA, 4; Padua, 1992)

RS   Rolls Series

Scripta Leonis   The Writings of Leo, Rufino and Angelo Companions of St Francis, ed. R. B. Brooke (OMT; 1970, reprinted with corrections in 1990)

1 C   Thomas of Celano, 'Vita prima S. Francisci' in AF, 10 (1926–41), pp. 1–117

2 C   Thomas of Celano, 'Vita secunda S. Francisci', in AF, 10, pp. 127–268

3 C   Thomas of Celano, 'Tractatus de miraculis B. Francisci', in AF, 10, pp. 269–330

Glossary

Bernard of Quintavalle a man of some wealth who was attracted by Francis's behaviour after his conversion. Fascinated by Francis's teaching, he invited him to his house and announced that he wished to renounce his possessions, following the Gospel in a literal manner. Francis accepted him as a companion and disciple. They went to the church of San Nicola in Assisi, where they had the book of the Gospels opened thrice at random. In the piazza commune he renounced his possessions and joined Francis. Regarded as Francis's first disciple, he was chosen to lead the small band of friars to the papal court in search of Innocent III's approval. He later settled in Bologna. Towards the end of his life he was a member of the same community as Salimbene, the celebrated chronicler, and related to him many stories about the founder. In death he acquired a reputation for sanctity and was buried near the sarcophagus of the founder in his basilica in Assisi.

Bonaventure born between 1217 and 1221 at Bagnoregio, near Viterbo. He believed that he was healed from a dangerous illness in his childhood through the intercession of St Francis, to whom his mother made a vow. He was a student in the faculty of arts in the University of Paris and was attracted by the birth and growth of the community. He was clothed in the friars' habit at Paris about 1243 and then embarked upon the study of theology under the direction of Alexander of Hales and Jean de la Rochelle. He attained the rank of master and became one of the most influential theologians of the Middle Ages. He produced a variety of treatises on philosophical and theological subjects as well as works of devotion and sermons. On 2 February 1257 he was elected as minister general of the order and pursued a policy of reforms, calling the friars back to a more faithful observance of the Rule. On 28 May 1273 he was elected cardinal bishop of Albano and was instrumental in the measures to seek reunion with the Eastern Church. He died at the Second Council of Lyon on 15 July 1274 and was buried in the friars' church there. He was canonized in 1482 and declared a doctor of the Church in 1588.

Elias a native of Assisi, who admired Francis a great deal and joined the fraternity in its first decade. By 1217 he had become the minister provincial in the Holy Land, where he received Francis and played a prominent part in the life of the fraternity throughout the 1220s. He accompanied Francis during the last phase in his life and was instrumental in the plans for the safe return of Francis to Assisi. He informed the friars of Francis's death and confirmed the unprecedented miracle of the stigmata. Afterwards he devoted his energies to the construction of a basilica in honour of the saint. His clandestine translation of Francis's remains to the new basilica in Assisi and the appalling behaviour of his supporters during the general chapter of 1230 aroused indignation among the friars. Expressions of penitence led to his rehabilitation and in 1232 he was elected as minister general. His plans for the fraternity were grandiose. Within five years his policies and his own conduct were causing first adverse comment and then concerted opposition, especially in the provinces of France, Germany and England. In 1239 Gregory IX deposed him at the general chapter. In the period following his deposition he flouted the order's constitution by making unauthorized visits to the Poor Clares and subsequently joined Frederick II. He was reconciled with the order towards the end of his life. His fall from grace was reflected in the later biographies, some of which accused him of losing the Rule, which Francis had compiled. Leo, Rufino and Angelo portray him in negative terms as one who strove to frustrate Francis's teaching, frequently linking him with the ministers provincial who opposed the saint.

Giles of Assisi after hearing of Bernard of Quintavalle's decision to renounce his possessions and join Francis, Giles did the same on St George's day, 23 April 1209. Clothed in the friars' habit, he went on pilgrimage to the shrines of St Michael the Archangel at Monte Gargano in Apulia, St James at Compostela, St Nicholas at Bari, the shrines of Rome and the Holy Land. Francis then sent him to the hermitage at Fabrione in the March of Ancona. Having attended Francis in his last illness, Giles moved to the hermitage at Cetona, close to Chiusi. He was venerated as a very cheerful companion of the founder, a mystic and a contemplative. Later he moved to Monteripido, near Perugia, which he made his home from 1234. He remained in close contact with Clare. He was critical of some developments in the fraternity and lamented the growth of schools. He was venerated by the citizens of Perugia, who guarded his dying body to ensure that he remained there and was not carried back to Assisi. He died on 23 April 1261 and some of his sayings have survived with the title *Golden Sayings of Brother Giles*. Brother Leo, who survived him by nine years, regarded him as a saint and wrote his life, which has been edited and translated by Rosalind Brooke.

Jacques de Vitry historian and preacher of the Crusade, he had studied at Paris and was an important witness to the development of religious life among women.

He compiled the life of Mary of Oignies and secured papal recognition for the Beguines in 1216. His letters offer an invaluable insight into the fifth Crusade. He was the bishop of Acre (1216-28) and then the cardinal bishop of Frascati (1228-40). He reported on the impression being made by the Humiliati, the Beguines and the Franciscans. He recounts the circumstances of Francis's visit to the Crusaders' camp and the enormous impact which he had; even clerics in his household queued up to join Francis. His writings capture the excitement generated by Francis and his followers in the years following the Fourth Lateran Council and their contribution to the renewal of the Church. In 1225 he returned to the West and was associated with Gregory IX.

John Pecham he entered the order at Oxford in the middle of the thirteenth century and studied at Paris, where he came under Bonaventure's influence and duly incepted in theology. He was the eleventh lector at Oxford and lector at the papal court, producing numerous philosophical and theological treatises. He was a very effective apologist in the friars' disputes with the secular masters and the Dominicans, producing several treatises which explained the friars' vocation and apostolate in the 1260s and 1270s. He wrote a *Commentary on the Rule of Saint Francis*, which appears among the writings of Bonaventure, to whom the treatise was subsequently attributed. A biography of St Anthony, the *Benignitas*, is attributed to him. He was the ninth minister provincial in England *c.* 1275-79 and became the only Franciscan archbishop of Canterbury (1279-92). He died on 8 December 1292 and was buried in his cathedral, although his heart was buried in the Greyfriars at London. Miracles were attributed to him.

Jordan of Giano a native of Umbria and one of the most important witnesses to the early life of the order. He accompanied Caesar of Speyer in the re-launching of the mission to Germany, where he spent the remainder of his life. He was an eyewitness to the friars' successful settlement in Germany and records the expansion and development of the fraternity, with the formation of a second province and custodies. He also was a reliable guide to events both in Germany and Italy. He explains the troubled events which led to the appointment of Cardinal Ugolino as protector of the order and was an invaluable witness to the divisions within the order in the 1230s and the mounting opposition to Elias as minister general: the events leading up to the deposition of Elias at the general chapter of Rome in 1239. The chronicle comes to an end in the early years of Bonaventure's term as minister general.

Matthew Paris the historian and chronicler of St Alban's abbey, who commented on the arrival of the Franciscans and Dominicans in England, noting their sterling work as preachers. Despite his profound admiration for Francis and his early respect for the friars, he criticized the friars for collecting money for the Crusades. He fulminated against their practice of accepting the vows of those who wished to go on the Crusades and, almost immediately, redeemed their vows in return for the payment of money. He was very critical of the friars' retreat from the high standards established by their founder and their high-handed behaviour towards the monastic orders. He compiled the lives of some saints, including St Edmund of Abingdon.

Ortolana born of noble stock, she was the mother of Sts Clare and Agnes. Accompanied by Pacifica di Guelfuccio of Assisi, she had travelled to the Holy Land, the shrine of St Michael the archangel at Gargano, Apulia, and the tombs of the apostles in Rome. Instructed by a divine message, she gave the name of Clare to her first daughter. Clare and Agnes settled at San Damiano, where they were eventually joined by their sister, Beatrice. Ortolana, too, entered the community at San Damiano and Clare entrusted some of the sick to her prayerful intercession. Both Clare and her mother blessed a young boy from Perugia, who was restored to health; mother and daughter attributed the miracle to each other. She was renowned for her humility and seems to have died at San Damiano before 1238.

Robert Grosseteste born about 1175, he became a member of the household of Hugh Avalon, bishop of Lincoln (1186–1200). Afterwards he became a master of arts and then theology at Oxford, where he developed an interest in the newly recovered Aristotelian texts and the writings of the Fathers of the Greek Church, eventually producing translations and commentaries on their texts. By 1230 he was already a senior figure in the University of Oxford when he accepted the invitation from the minister provincial, Agnellus of Pisa, to teach theology to the friars there. He remained in the friars' school until 1235, when he was appointed bishop of Lincoln. He wished to have both Franciscans and Dominicans with him to assist him in running the largest diocese in England. While he preached to the clergy, they preached to the laity and heard their confessions. While he did not shy away from necessary criticisms of the friars, he was one of their staunchest supporters, who commended their work to Gregory IX and the bishops of England. He died on 9 October 1253 and left his books to the friary at Oxford.

Salimbene born on 9 October 1221 at Parma, this member of an aristocratic family was received into the order by Elias on 4 February 1238, despite strong opposition from his father. Nonetheless, he lists twelve faults of Elias as minister general, believing that the promotion of theological studies was his only positive contribution to the welfare of the order. He lived in the same community as Bernard of Quintavalle, but he had travelled widely in Italy and France, where he seems to have known many of the leading friars in the middle of the thirteenth century. His minister provincial sent him to study in Paris, where he spent only a week before settling at Hyères; there he heard the lectures of Hugh of Digne on the speculation of Abbot Joachim of Fiore. He wrote a number of books, the most famous of which is his chronicle, which is an invaluable source for the history of the order to the year 1288. He probably died in 1289.

Thomas of Eccleston an Englishman who had studied in Paris, where he witnessed the increase in the fraternity. He joined the fraternity in England and studied at Oxford under Robert Grosseteste and later lived in London. He became the historian of the fraternity in England and recounted many anecdotes about the privations and virtue of the first friars in England. His account of how the friars settled in England serves as one of the major sources for historians of the order between 1220 and 1258. His account of the deposition of Elias is of particular importance. His chronicle is thematic rather than strictly chronological. He was proud of the English province's prowess in studies and delighted in rehearsing the fame of its theologians called to teach in France, Germany, Italy and the papal court. He was also acutely aware that learning could threaten the humble spirit and the poverty of the friars. As the fraternity settled in England, he hankered after the level of observance exhibited by the first friars. His chronicle ends with the election of Bonaventure and this may indicate that he died shortly after 1257.

Chronology for the birth and growth of the fraternity

1181/82   birth of Francis in Assisi. At his baptism he was named John, but on his father's return to Assisi his name was changed to Francis.[1]

1187   conquest of Jerusalem by Saladin. Two years later the third Crusade was launched.

1193/94   birth of St Clare in Assisi.[2]

c. 1195   birth of St Anthony in Lisbon. At baptism he was given the name of Ferdinand, which was changed to Anthony on becoming a friar.[3]

1198, 8 January   Innocent III elected pope.

1198, spring   the Rocca, Duke Conrad of Urslingen's fortress in Assisi, sacked by the people of Assisi.

1199–1200   civil war in Assisi; destruction of the castles of the feudal nobles, some of whom sought asylum in Perugia.

1202, November   war between Assisi and Perugia. Francis was captured at the battle of Collestrada and then imprisoned in Perugia.[4]

1204, April   the sack of Constantinople during the fourth Crusade.

1204   Bishop Guido II appointed to the diocese of Assisi.

1204   Francis was ill for a prolonged period.[5]

1204, end of, or early 1205   Francis set out for war in Apulia, but returned after a vision and a message in Spoleto.[6]

1204/05, unspecified dates   Francis's encounters with the pauper in his father's shop,[7] the poor knight[8] and the paupers at St Peter's tomb.[9]

1205/06, unspecified date   Francis met a leper in the plain below Assisi. His prejudice was mastered and he served the lepers.[10]

1205, late or 1206, early   an increasingly disenchanted Francis sold his father's cloth in the fair at nearby Foligno.[11]

1205/06   Francis's two periods of residence at San Damiano interspersed with a period of confinement in his father's house.[12]

1206, early   Francis brought before the episcopal tribunal.[13] He then returned to San Damiano.[14]

1206–08   at San Damiano Francis was instructed to repair the church; he subsequently restored the chapels of San Pietro and Santa Maria degli Angeli at the Portiuncula. During this period he lived as a hermit.[15]

1208, probably 24 February Francis attended Mass at the Portiuncula and his life was changed by hearing the Gospel passage in which the apostles were commissioned to preach.[16]

1208, spring Francis, who had begun to call people to penitence, was joined by Bernard of Quintavalle and Peter Catanii. Other recruits arrived in the course of the next year.[17]

1208, March/April Francis had the book of the Gospels opened thrice at the church of San Nicola in Assisi.[18]

1209/10 Francis compiled his Rule and went to Rome in search of papal approbation. Discussions with Cardinal John of St Paul, the bishop of Santa Sabina. Initial papal approval granted. At the conclusion of the visit Innocent III authorized Francis and the friars to preach penance.[19]

c. 1210 Anthony became an Augustinian canon at Lisbon.[20]

c. 1211 Francis went to Dalmatia.

1211/12, Palm Sunday Clare left home to devote herself to the Gospel according to Francis's teaching.[21]

c. 1212 Anthony transferred to the Augustinian canons in Coimbra.[22]

1212 the recovery and translation of the relics of San Rufino in Assisi's cathedral.

1213, 19-29 April Innocent III proclaimed the fifth Crusade.

1213, 8 May Count Orlando gave Francis the mountainous hermitage of La Verna in Tuscany.

c. 1213-15 Francis travelled to Spain en route to the Holy Land.

1215, October St Dominic, accompanied by Fulk, bishop of Toulouse, sought papal approval for his band of followers. Innocent III directed Dominic to adopt one of the Rules.

1215, 11-30 November Fourth Lateran Council promulgated a programme of renewal within the Church; Francis and Dominic may have attended.

1215/16 Clare received the privilege of poverty from Innocent III.[23]

1216 Francis's restoration of Assisi's former cathedral, Santa Maria Maggiore.[24]

1216, 16 July death of Innocent III at Perugia, where Francis visited him.[25]

1217, 5 May general chapter at the Portiuncula and missions to France, Germany, Hungary and Spain and some parts of Italy. Francis left for France, but Cardinal Ugolino persuaded him to return to Umbria.[26]

1217, 15 August a meeting of Dominicans at which it was decided that the friars would concentrate on Toulouse, Spain and Paris. Dominic proceeded to Rome.

1219 general chapter launched mission to Morocco.

1219 Cardinal Ugolino published his constitutions for the Poor Clares.[27]

1219, 11 June Honorius III recommended the friars to the bishops.[28]

1219, 29 August   the battle for Damietta, which the Crusaders had been besieging from August 1218 until September 1219. Francis had visited their camp before the battle and went to the Sultan's camp.[29]

1220, 16 January   first martyrs killed in Morocco.[30]

1220, spring or early summer   Anthony received into the fraternity at Coimbra.[31]

1220, spring or early summer   Francis returned to Italy and secured the appointment of Cardinal Ugolino as protector of the fraternity.[32]

1220, 22 September   Honorius III's *Cum secundum* established the novitiate year for the Franciscans.[33]

1221, Pentecost   Rainerio Capocci, the cardinal deacon, attended the general chapter with several other bishops and religious.[34] The chapter launched a second mission to Germany under the leadership of Caesar of Speyer.[35] Anthony attended the general chapter and then proceeded to a hermitage at Monte Paolo in northern Italy.[36]

1221   composition of the first Rule.[37]

1221, 5 August, approximately   the first party of Dominicans landed at Dover.

1221, 6 August   death of St Dominic at Bologna, where his funeral was attended by Cardinal Ugolino.[38]

1222, 15 August   Francis preached in Bologna.

1223, 29 November   Honorius III approved the Franciscan Rule.

1223, 24/25 December   Christmas crib at Greccio.[39]

1223/24   Francis invited Anthony to teach theology at Bologna.[40]

1224, 10 September   Franciscans landed at Dover.[41]

1224, about 14 September   Francis received the stigmata at La Verna.[42]

1225, spring   the ailing Francis was lodged at San Damiano for six weeks, when he composed *The Canticle of Brother Sun* and another canticle for the sisters.[43]

1225, July   Francis went to Rieti to receive treatment for his eyes. There he met Ugolino and the papal court.[44]

c. 1225   Anthony was teaching theology at Montpellier.[45]

c. 1226   Anthony preached, disputed and taught at Toulouse.[46]

1226, April   Francis in Siena for further treatment.[47]

1226, late summer and early autumn   Francis was lodged in the bishop's palace in Assisi.[48]

1226, September   Francis returned to the Portiuncula to die.[49]

1226, 3 October   in the evening Francis died.[50]

1226, 4 October   burial of Francis in the church of San Giorgio. Miracles were soon recorded as having taken place at the tomb.[51]

1227, 19 March   Cardinal Ugolino was elected as pope with the name of Gregory IX.

1228, 29 March   Gregory IX granted an indulgence of 40 days to those who assisted in the construction of the new basilica to be built in honour of Francis.

1228, 30 March   the piece of land on the 'hill of hell' was given for the use of the friars and the construction of an oratory or church to receive the saint's body.

1228, 16 July   Gregory IX canonized Francis in Assisi.[52]

1228, 17 July   Gregory laid the foundation stone for the new basilica to be built in Francis's honour.[53]

1228, 30 July   death of Bishop Guido II.[54]

1228, 17 September   Gregory IX reissued the privilege of poverty for the sisters of San Damiano.[55]

1228-29   Thomas of Celano composed his first biography of the founder, the *Vita prima*, at the instigation of Gregory IX.[56]

1228-29   the excommunicated Emperor, Frederick II, led a successful campaign to Acre and regained Jerusalem, Bethlehem and Nazareth.

1229/30   Robert Grosseteste, one of the most distinguished masters in the University of Oxford, was engaged to teach theology to the friars in that town.[57]

1230, 25 May   translation of Francis's remains to the new basilica in Assisi and the general chapter.[58]

1230, 28 September   Gregory IX, whose intervention had been enlisted by the friars, issued *Quo elongati*, the first papal interpretation of the Franciscan Rule.[59]

1231, 13 June   death of Anthony at Arcella, near Padua.[60]

1232, 30 May   canonization of Anthony and the composition of the first biography, the anonymous *Assidua*.[61]

1232-35   Julian of Speyer's biography of Anthony of Padua.

1234, 3 July   Gregory IX canonized St Dominic.

1236, late summer   Alexander of Hales, one of the regent masters in theology at the University of Paris, became a Franciscan and continued his teaching in the friary at Paris.[62]

1237, 5 April   *Confessor Domini*, by which Gregory IX defended the truth of the stigmata.[63]

1237, 6 April   *Quoniam abundavit iniquitas*, in which Gregory IX stated that the Franciscans were founded to spread the Gospel, especially in preaching against heresy and hearing confessions.[64]

1239, Pentecost   deposition of Elias and the election of Albert of Pisa at the general chapter in Rome.[65]

1240-41   the compilation of the *Anonymous of Perugia* by John of Perugia.

1241, 22 August   death of Gregory IX.

c. 1241   the general meeting of definitors at Montpellier called for the establishment of a commission in each province to discuss vexed matters of observance.[66]

1244   Crescentius da Iesi, the minister general, asked the friars to send in their recollections of the founder.[67]

1245 the first Council of Lyon, which was preceded by mounting opposition to the friars and some speculation that they might be suppressed.

1245, 14 November the publication of Innocent IV's *Ordinem vestrum* regarding the interpretation of the Rule, going beyond the terms laid down in Gregory IX's *Quo elongati*.[68]

1245-46 the anonymous *Dialogus* composed on the lives of holy friars and incorporated materials on the life of Anthony of Padua.

1246 Leo, Rufino and Angelo compiled their reminiscences of the founder, the *Scripta Leonis*.[69]

1246, July John of Piancarpino arrived at the court of Great Khan Guyuk, the grandson of Chingis Khan, as an emissary of Innocent IV.

1247, 6 August Innocent IV composed a Rule for the Poor Clares.[70]

1246-48 the compilation of Thomas of Celano's second biography of the founder, the *Vita secunda*.

1250 the compilation of Thomas of Celano's collection of the miracles at Francis's intercession.

1252, 16 September at Perugia the cardinal protector approved Clare's Rule.[71]

1253, 9 August at Assisi Innocent IV approved the Rule of Clare.[72]

1253, 11 August death of Clare at San Damiano.[73]

1253, 12 August burial of Clare in San Giorgio, Assisi.[74]

1253, 18 October Innocent IV initiated the process of Clare's canonization.[75]

1253, 24-28 November Bartholomew, bishop of Spoleto, presided over the depositions of the witnesses to Clare's canonization.[76]

1254, Pentecost general chapter at Metz suspended provisions of *Ordinem vestrum* which exceeded the terms of *Quo elongati*.[77] This decision was confirmed by the general chapter of 1260 which forbade the use of Innocent's interpretation of the Rule where it conflicted with the earlier ruling.[78]

1255, 15 August canonization of Clare.[79]

1257, 2 February Bonaventure elected as minister general in succession to John of Parma.

1257, 23 April Bonaventure's first letter to the order listed ten major failings of the friars and called for reform. He was commissioned to produce a biography of the founder.[80]

1260, Pentecost the general chapter at Narbonne produced the earliest extant constitutions of the fraternity.[81]

1261, 23 April the death of Giles, the third companion of Francis, in Perugia.[82]

1263, Pentecost Bonaventure, the minister general, presented friars at the general chapter at Pisa with copies of his biography of the founder, the *Legenda maior*.

1266, Pentecost the general chapter at Paris adopted the *Legenda maior* as the authoritative biography of the founder and ordered the withdrawal of all earlier biographies.[83]

c. 1280   the composition of the *Benignitas*, a life of Anthony of Padua, attributed to John Pecham.

Notes

1.   1 C, nn. 1-2; 2 C, nn. 3-4; LM, c. 1; LTS, c. 1.
2.   LSC, n. 1.
3.   Assidua, c. 2.
4.   2 C, n. 4; LTS, c. 2.
5.   1 C, n. 3.
6.   Ibid., nn. 4-5.
7.   Ibid., n. 17; Anon. Perug., c. 1, n. 4ab; LTS, c. 1.
8.   2 C, n. 5.
9.   Ibid., n. 8.
10. *Opuscula Sancti Patris Francisci Assisiensis*, ed. C. Esser (BFAMA, 12; Grottaferrata, Rome, 1978), pp. 307-8; 1 C, n. 17; 2 C, n. 9.
11. 1 C, n. 8; Anon. Perug., c. 1, n. 7bc.
12. 1 C, nn. 8-12; Anon. Perug., c. 1, n. 7c.
13. 1 C, nn. 14-15; 2 C, n. 12; Anon. Perug., c. 1, n. 8b; LM, c. 2, n. 4; LTS, nn. 19-20.
14. Anon. Perug., c. 1, n. 8c; LTS, c. 7.
15. 1 C, nn. 18-21; 2 C, nn. 10, 13; LM., c. 2, nn. 7-8.
16. 1 C, nn. 21-22; LM, c. 3, n. 1.
17. 1 C, nn. 24-25.
18. 2 C, n. 15; Anon. Perug., c. 2, n. 10.
19. 1 C, nn. 32-34; 2 C, nn. 16-17; Anon. Perug., c. 7, nn. 31-36; LM, c. 3, n. 3; LTS, c. 12; Salimbene de Adam, *Cronica*, ed. G. Scalia (Scrittori d'Italia, 232-233; Bari, 1966), p. 421.
20. Assidua, c. 3.
21. LSC, n. 8.
22. Assidua, c. 3.
23. LSC, c. 14.
24. M. Faloci-Pulignani, 'Il più antico documento per la storia di San Francesco', *Miscellanea Francescana*, 2 (1887), pp. 33-7.
25. Thomas of Eccleston, *Tractatus de adventu fratrum minorum in Angliam*, ed. A. G. Little (Manchester, 1951), p. 95.
26. *Chronica Fratris Jordani*, n, 3, ed. H. Boehmer (Collection d'études et de documents sur l'histoire religieuse et littéraire du moyen âge, 6; Paris, 1908), pp. 3-4; 1 C, nn. 74-75; *Compilatio Asssiensis*, c. 108.
27. R. J. Armstrong (trans. and ed.), *Clare of Assisi: Early Documents* (New York, 1988), pp. 87-96.
28. BF, I, p. 2.
29. 2 C, n. 30; 1 C, n. 57; LM, c. 9, nn. 6-9; G. Golubovich, *Biblioteca Bio-Bibliografica della Terra Santa e dell'Oriente Francescano*, I (Quaracchi, Florence, 1906), pp. 36-7.
30. *Chronica Fratris Jordani*, n. 7, p. 7.
31. Assidua, c. 5.
32. 1 C, nn. 73-74, 99-101; 2 C, nn. 23-25; *Chronica Fratris Jordani*, nn. 12-14, pp. 11-15.
33. BF, I, p. 6.
34. *Chronica Fratris Jordani*, n. 16, pp. 16-17.
35. Ibid., nn. 17-18, pp. 17-21.
36. Assidua, cc. 6-8.
37. *Chronica Fratris Jordani*, n. 15, p. 15.
38. Jordan of Saxony, 'Libellus de principiis Ordinis Praedicatorum' in MOPH, ed. M. H. Laurent, 16 (Rome, 1935), nn. 92-96, pp. 69-71.
39. 1 C, nn. 84-87; LM., c. 10, n. 7. Cf. *Compilatio Assisiensis*, c. 14; and E. A. Armstrong, *Saint Francis: Nature Mystic: The Derivation and Significance of the Nature Stories in the Franciscan Legend* (Berkeley, 1973), pp. 133-42.
40. *Opuscula Sancti Patris Francisci Assisiensis*, p. 95; 2 C, n. 163; Benignitas, c. 13, n. 2.
41. Thomas of Eccleston, *Tractatus de adventu*, p. 3.
42. 1 C, nn. 91-95; LM, c. 13.
43. *Compilatio Assisiensis*, c. 83.

44. 1 C, n. 99.
45. Benignitas, c. 17, n. 3.
46. Ibid., c. 16, c. 6; Bartholomew of Pisa, 'De conformitate vitae Beati Francisci ad vitam Domini Iesu' in AF, IV (Quaracchi, Florence, 1906), p. 338.
47. 1 C, n. 105.
48. *Compilatio Assisiensis*, c. 4.
49. 1 C, nn. 105-108.
50. Ibid., nn. 109-11; 2 C, n. 215.
51. 1 C, n. 121.
52. Ibid., nn. 125-26.
53. LTS, n. 72.
54. M. Faloci-Pulignani, 'Il messale consultato da S. Francesco quando si convertì', *Miscellanea Francescana*, 15 (1914), pp. 33-43; A. Brunacci, 'Il messale consultato da San Francesco all'inizio della sua nuova vita', *San Francesco Patrono d'Italia*, 58 (1978), pp. 80-8; G. C. P. Voorvelt and B. P. Van Leeuven, 'L'evangéliaire de Baltimore', *Collectanea Franciscana*, 59 (1989), pp. 261-321.
55. Armstrong, *Clare of Assisi: Early Documents*, pp. 103-4.
56. 1 C, prol., n. 1.
57. Eccleston, *Tractatus*, p. 48.
58. LM, c. 15, n. 8.
59. Eccleston, *Tractatus*, pp. 65-6; H. Grudundmann, 'Die Bulle "Quo elongati" Papst Gregors IX' in AFH, 54 (1961), pp. 3-25, 20-1.
60. Assidua, c. 17.
61. Ibid., c. 29.
62. *Hugh of Digne's Rule Commentary*, ed. D. Flood (Spicilegium Bonaventurianum, XIV; Quaracchi, Grottaferrata, 1979), p. 187; Bonaventure's 'Epistola de tribus quaestionibus ad magistrum innominatum', ed. F. M. Delorme, 'Textes franciscains', *Archivo italiano per la storia della pietà*, 1 (1951), pp. 179-218, 216.
63. BF, I, p. 214. Two other bulls, addressed to the bishop of Olmütz and the Dominicans a week earlier, condemned those who called the miracle into question.
64. Ibid., p. 214.
65. Eccleston, *Tractatus*, pp. 67-9.
66. Ibid, p. 71.
67. 2 C, n. 1.
68. BF, I, pp. 400-2.
69. *Scripta Leonis*, pp. 86-9.
70. Armstrong, *Clare of Assisi: Early Documents*, pp. 109-21.
71. Ibid., pp. 61-2.
72. Ibid., pp. 76-7.
73. LSC, n. 46.
74. Ibid., nn. 47-48.
75. Armstrong, *Clare of Assisi: Early Documents*, p. 125.
76. Ibid., p. 125.
77. Eccleston, *Tractatus*, p. 42.
78. F. M. Delorme, ' "Diffinitiones" Capituli Generalis O. F. M. Narbonensis (1260)' in AFH, 3 (1910), pp. 491-504, 503, n. 13.
79. LSC, n. 62.
80. *S. Bonaventurae opera omnia*, VIII (Quaracchi, Florence, 1898), pp. 468-9; D. V. Monti, intro. with trans., *Works of Saint Bonaventure: Writings concerning the Franciscan Order*, V (New York, 1994), p. 137, points out that virtually all modern studies state that the *Legenda maior* was commissioned by the general chapter of Narbonne. No such decree survives among the documents of that chapter. Monti believes that the decree seems to have emanated from the general chapter of 1257 in Rome.
81. M. Bihl, 'Statuta generalia Ordinis edita in Capitulis generalibus celebratis Narbonae an. 1260, Assisii an. 1279 atque Parisiis an. 1292. (Editio critica et synoptica)' in AFH, 34 (1941), pp. 13-94, 284-358.
82. *Scripta Leonis*, pp. 307, 348-9.
83. L. Di Fonzo, 'L'Anonimo Perugino tra le fonti francescane del sec. XIII. Rapporti letterari e testo critico', *Miscellanea Francescana*, 72 (1972), pp. 117-483, 247, n. 49.

1

~~~~~~~~~~~~~~~~~~~~~~

Peter Bernardone

> Still a youth, he [Francis] ran into strife with his father for a lady ... and before his
> spiritual court *et coram patre* he was joined to her[1]

St Francis was born in 1181 or 1182 at Assisi, an Umbrian city with a long and
noble Christian tradition stretching back to the early third century. The first
bishops of the city had been martyred and the medieval city looked back to its
Christian origins with a mixture of piety and local pride. Francis and many of his
first companions, including Clare, were baptized in the cathedral and reared on
accounts of the martyrs of their city. These legends played some indirect part in
inspiring the renewal of religious life, which began with Francis. Tradition
records that Francis was the son of a cloth merchant, Peter Bernardone, whose
trips to French markets were numerous; a love of France was communicated to
the young Francis. After the war between Assisi and Perugia at the beginning of
the thirteenth century he passed through a period of transition, which was as
painful to him as it was puzzling to his family and friends. The flamboyant youth
had given way to an introspective adult who turned his back on the city and
haunted the countryside, with its grottoes and wayside churches. During this
period Francis encountered a leper and was brought face to face with prejudice
and the divisions within society. He was being groomed to take over the family
business and his increasing eccentricity was becoming a source of gossip,
embarrassment and disgrace to his father. The period of disillusionment and
detachment from his earlier lifestyle culminated in the illegal sale of his father's
cloth in the fair at Foligno. His resolution to turn his back on his profession
dismayed his uncomprehending father, leading to a period of estrangement.

CHRISTIANITY AND MEDIEVAL ASSISI

In medieval Umbria there was little detailed knowledge about the martyrs' lives,
except the fact that they had been put to death during the bouts of persecution to
eradicate Christianity. San Rufino, who was martyred about 238, was the
principal patron saint of Assisi and a powerful presence in the city and diocese.
The account of his heroic death passed into the oral history of the city and was

known to the young Francis and Clare, who were taught from their earliest years to pay due respect to him at his tomb in the basilica of San Rufino. Francis's participation in the liturgical celebrations of the martyrs' feasts formed the context for his own spiritual development and undoubtedly communicated values, such as the thirst for martyrdom and a profound reverence for saints' relics.

The martyred bishops of Assisi

There was no early and reliable documentation regarding the establishment of Christianity in Umbria. The existence of a number of martyrs is attested by the chapels and churches constructed over their tombs. R. Brown remarks that authentic evidence of the cult of the local martyrs in Assisi, Foligno and Spoleto appears first in the tombs, chapels, and churches, and later in liturgical calendars.[2] The more substantial accounts of the saints' lives, the *passiones* of Assisi's martyrs, were generally compiled in later centuries when the need to record the glory of the city's martyrs was more keenly felt. Many medieval cities boasted of their shrines and the saints' legends. The miracles at the martyrs' tombs offered the citizens reassurance that the saints were actively still working on their behalf.

The first martyr who laboured in Assisi was San Feliciano, portrayed as the father of Christians and athlete of the Lord.[3] He preached first at Foligno, then at Spello, Bevagna, Perugia and Assisi; two fourteenth-century manuscripts record his activity in Assisi.[4] He was unable to make many converts and he was eventually expelled from the city. Before taking his leave, he called together the Christians of the area on the hill above San Damiano and exhorted them to remain steadfast in times of trial. Finally, he fixed a huge cross in the ground and then left the city. When the wooden cross eventually disintegrated, the people of Assisi built a little chapel on the site. He was the first bishop of Foligno and was martyred at the age of 93 under Decius about 249–251.

San Rufino was the first bishop of Assisi and also the principal patron of the city. Oral tradition situated his martyrdom in the territory of Costano, on the Chiagio river, where, having refused to offer sacrifice to the pagan gods, he was drowned. In the middle of the eleventh century St Peter Damian devoted a homily to the miracles worked by this martyr and composed two hymns in his honour. He also referred to the recent recovery of the martyr's *passio*. San Vittorino was venerated as the second bishop of Assisi and as the co-patron of the city. His martyrdom occurred in the middle of the third century.[5] An ancient tradition located his martyrdom on the river Tescio. His body was preserved in a Benedictine monastery until *c.* 1000, when it was removed to the church of San Pietro inside the city walls. Frescoes in that church, the earliest from the twelfth century, testify to the loyalty of generations to the martyred bishop. Vittorino was portrayed in a white chasuble and red mantle, wearing a mitre and carrying his pastoral staff.[6] San Savino, the third bishop of the Roman period, was commemorated by the part of the commune which has borne his name since the first Christian centuries.[7] Tradition attributes to Savino the foundation of the first cathedral, Santa Maria Maggiore, also known as Santa Maria del Vescovado, which was built over the ruins of the temple of Jove.[8] Savino was arrested in Assisi along with his deacons and then taken to Spoleto where he was martyred. He had been so brave under torture that he came to be considered the protector of those who went to face up to war.[9] A short distance from Spoleto there was a basilica dedicated to San Savino, erected over the site of his burial. Men came from all parts of Italy to pray at the shrine before going off to war.[10]

Eleventh-century renewal of devotion to San Rufino

The eleventh-century revival of the cult of San Rufino in Assisi had a divisive and unlikely beginning in a titanic battle of wills between Bishop Ugone and the church of San Rufino. The bishop was anxious to claim an important relic of the patron saint for the cathedral of Santa Maria Maggiore, while there was growing support for the church dedicated to San Rufino in the heart of the medieval city; by the early thirteenth century San Rufino was securely established as the city's cathedral. The episode, narrated by Peter Damian, illustrates the authority and power of the patron saint, whose wishes overshadowed those of his vicar, the bishop of Assisi. During the invasions of the Dark Ages, the martyr's body was carried within the walls of Assisi, leaving the pagan sarcophagus at Costano, the site of his martyrdom. There arose a heated and acrimonious dispute concerning the competing claims for possession of the sarcophagus. In the ensuing arguments blows were struck, but the patron intervened to protect his people, preventing bloodshed so successfully that not a single man was wounded. While about sixty of the bishop's followers were unable to carry the sarcophagus to the cathedral, seven men succeeded in transporting it to the church of San Rufino. Those advancing the claims of the church of San Rufino were exultant and interpreted their triumph over the bishop as the will of God and the martyr.

Ugone was still not satisfied and the intervention of the saint was needed to wear down his opposition. Two men approached him with a message from the martyr. The first was a priest who notified the prelate that, if he did not wish to offend the martyr, he should not demand reparation from the people and should give them his blessing. He acted as a messenger for the martyr whose will was that the sarcophagus should be carried to his church so that his body might rest there. The bishop still hesitated to accept such testimony. But on the same day a man who had been crippled proclaimed that he had been healed by the intercession of the martyr, who had commanded him to repeat to the bishop the message announced earlier by the priest. At last Ugone abandoned his doubts and opposition, accepting the two men as messengers of the martyr. He acted on San Rufino's instructions and made a pact with the people.

The bishop's capitulation was followed by a series of miracles, some of which are described briefly and others more fully; Peter Damian creates the impression that the miracles were numerous. Further confirmation of the martyr's involvement in the dispute came when it became known that, on the day that Ugone received the two messengers from the martyr, two blind men received their sight at the saint's altar and a cripple was enabled to stand up and was restored to health. The spate of miracles was linked with Ugone's resolve to erect a large church, which he accomplished. Then he had the body of the martyr placed in the sarcophagus, and consecrated an altar over it in the presence of a large crowd of people from the entire diocese. Afterwards many people received their sight, some were freed from devils and others were released from various sicknesses. The flow of miracles stimulated a search for fuller information about the martyr, though Peter Damian attributes the recovery of the account of the martyr's life to divine revelation.

A. Fortini believes that it must have been Assisi's merchants travelling to the fair in Troyes who, towards the middle of the eleventh century, brought back an account of the events in that city which made a deep impression on Assisi. Troyes also had its martyr, St Patroclus, over whose tomb there was a small oratory served by a cleric; the martyr received little respect in the region, because there was no biography on hand. Gregory of Tours comments that it was the custom of untutored men to venerate more carefully those saints whose struggles were recorded. The relative neglect of the martyr came to an end when a stranger arrived and presented an account of the martyr to the cleric, who copied it and disseminated it. The discovery of the *passio* stimulated the growth of a cult.[11] On learning of this, the people of Assisi nursed a similar ambition to obtain the text of the martyrdom of their own patron saint.[12] In two manuscripts, one from Perugia, written at the end of the eleventh century, and the other from Spello, Maurino described the recovery of the highly prized text. Already an old man, he felt that he could not close his eyes without first learning the acts of that glorious martyrdom. Having wandered all over Campania anxiously in search of information, he reached Anagni, where he met a monk, named George, whom he persuaded to consult the ancient manuscripts in order to copy the life of the martyr.

After the building of the new basilica there was a thorough investigation into the date of San Rufino's martyrdom. The anniversary of the dedication of the first church was celebrated on 3 August. But when the account of the saint's life and martyrdom had been recovered,[13] Ugone ordered that the saint's feast day be celebrated on 11 August, the anniversary of his martyrdom, along with the older feast. The feasts of the dedication of the cathedral and the martyrdom of San Rufino were still being celebrated with solemnity in the early thirteenth century.[14] The lives of the saints written in the Middle Ages often deal with the punishment meted out to those who neglect to celebrate feast days. The misfortunes which befell those who withheld the honour due to Assisi's martyr were explained by Peter Damian. Fires blazed up in their houses and fields and eventually they realized that the flames were a punishment for their arrogance. They rushed to the church of the martyr and threw themselves in front of the altar. Immediately the fires were extinguished, and they returned to Isola safe and sound.[15] Less than two centuries later, Thomas of Celano describes the fate of those who opposed the feast day of Francis.[16]

Christian observance in medieval Assisi

The *passiones* of the local saints of Assisi provided documentary evidence of the city's noble tradition within Christendom. The church of medieval Assisi had reason to be proud of the martyrs whose blood had planted the seed of the Gospel on their soil. In addition to the martyred bishops, there were other unnamed men and women who had been executed for their faith in the teaching of Jesus Christ. The feasts of the local saints provided the citizens with an opportunity to express their fervour and admiration as well as their artistic flair and imagination. For example, the feast of San Vittorino was celebrated in Assisi by the Company of San Vittorino or the *Compagnia del Bastone*—a name given from the fact that the leader carried a raised staff to show his office. On the day of his election those in the company swore to obey him by touching this staff. Meetings were held in the church of San Pietro in Assisi, behind the altar that enclosed the bones of the martyr. From a reading of episodes related by Thomas of Celano and the *Legenda trium sociorum*, along with evidence in some documents in the Assisi archives, Fortini concludes that Francis was the leader of this group and that he was at the head of the boisterous group that would burst on to the piazza on the evening of 13 June, his feast day. People thronged the piazza, avid to relive the story. At a signal from the leader the drama unfolded as young men and women threw themselves into the holy and warlike dance. The martyr appeared before a crowd of idolaters, and proclaimed the glory of Jesus Christ. The power which the bishop invoked was sufficient to loosen the tongue of a mute boy and open the eyes of a man born blind. Vittorino was taken before the Roman prefect and disdainfully refused to offer sacrifice to the pagan gods. The bystanders rose up, muttering imprecations, and loudly demanding his execution. The bishop walked towards his martyrdom, knelt and laid his head on the executioner's block. The pious women came silently by night, lifted the precious corpse, wrapped it in linen sheets, carried it away to protect it.[17] Francis's participation in the celebration of the martyr's feast provided him with ample opportunity to reflect upon the integrity and courage of the first martyrs of Christian Assisi. Such a celebration may have been at the root of his desire to imitate the martyrs of the early Christian era.

In contrast to the halcyon days of the third and fourth centuries, with their martyrs, some of the early biographies paint an unattractive picture of life in medieval Assisi and complain about the level of Christian observance. Indeed, the ancient city's notorious reputation was mentioned by the dying Francis on taking his leave of the city for the last time. It was well known in the locality that the city had once been the resort and home of wicked and evil men.[18] A bleak picture of Christian observance in that medieval city was painted by Thomas of Celano, the saint's first biographer. The fact that Christian values were ignored and that the vanity of the world had made inroads in Assisi, resulting in a nominal Christianity, was lamented. The negligent manner in which children were educated from the cradle onwards in a dissolute way was deplored. Another gloomy image was drawn from the vision of Sylvester, a secular priest from the city. In his sleep he observed that the whole city was caught in the coils of a huge serpent, whose sheer size threatened to devastate the whole area. Then he saw a golden cross issuing from the mouth of Francis; its top touched the heavens and its extended arms encircled both parts of the world in their embrace. The serpent was completely vanquished at the sight of the cross of gold. Filled with compunction at the sight, Sylvester decided to throw in his lot with the friars, realizing that the vision was a divine revelation; after he had seen it a third time, he informed Francis and the friars about it.[19]

Such a negative account of the abdication of parental responsibility in medieval Assisi enabled the biographer to emphasize the goodness and attractiveness of the saint and the burning need for repentance in the city and the region. This impression was corroborated by the account of Sylvester's vision, which again focuses upon the saint's role in warding off the destruction threatened by the serpent, with all its obvious allusions to the fall of humanity narrated by the book of Genesis. These accounts, however, were less than flattering to the citizens of Assisi who cherished Francis, their saint, and provided the friars with a great deal of material support. A note of caution about placing undue weight upon the hagiographical details is sounded by Lawrence, who believes that Thomas of Celano compromised his credibility by composing the *Vita secunda* about 1246–48; on important issues this fails to square with the earlier biography. The selection of the material for the second work reflects the pressure of later events. There were significant omissions and changes of contour and also perhaps the need to placate lay opinion in Assisi. His attack upon parental mores in the city was prudently dropped from the second biography.[20]

The biographer's criticisms of contemporary life had a clearly defined purpose: to draw a sharp distinction between the saint and the society which he strove to reinvigorate. Despite the hagiographical exaggerations, it remains an indisputable fact that Francis's own behaviour offered some support for such critical views of life in medieval Assisi. Francis did not feel that the pursuit of sanctity was as accessible in the city as it was outside it. The gradual evolution of his vocation draws attention to the conventions which obtained in the city. The perennial tension between the norms of society and the principles of the Gospel was conspicuous in his change of life. This was illustrated by the treatment meted out to lepers and paupers. Francis was gradually coming to the conclusion that the incisiveness and vitality of Jesus' message could be effectively blunted by the various layers of interpretation and accommodation. This may account for his own very literal approach to the Bible which remained with him until his dying moments. The conviction led him to describe the conventions of society as one of humanity's enemies by which people were deceived.[21] The rules and regulations devised by cities were not always primarily influenced by the Gospel. The saint's conversion led him to go beyond the customs of society, even one which purported to be Christian, and to weigh the demands of the Gospel in a more independent manner. Indeed, his vocation led him in a traditional direction because he withdrew from the city of his birth into the countryside and this implied a criticism of the values which regulated society. Despite the new form of religious life which he ushered in, Francis felt that the Gospel was calling him to abandon his earlier lifestyle and to concentrate on the poor and the marginalized as he awaited further guidance on his own future. Moreover, the conventional hagiographical criticisms of contemporary society must be balanced by the recognition that this small Umbrian city gave the Church two of the most attractive and influential saints in the Middle Ages in Francis and Clare, whose early followers were natives of Assisi and other Umbrian cities and towns.

FRANCIS'S FAMILY

The *Vita prima* opens with a withering denunciation of parental irresponsibility in general and then proceeds to single out Francis's parents, who had brought him up from his earliest years proud of spirit in accordance with the vanity of the world. This bad example produced its own predictable and lamentable results: Francis became for a long time even more proud and vain. The way in which contemporary parents educated their children was bemoaned. Neither was the environment congenial to independence and goodness, because the pressure on young people to conform to prevailing tastes was so strong. The denunciation closes with the biblical image of a corrupt tree, which grows from a corrupt root. While Clare's mother engaged in conventional acts of piety, there is no indication that Francis's parents had such devotional tastes and pious practices, however much the *Vita secunda* tries to correct the earlier impression of Francis's mother, Pica. The failure of Francis's parents to instil wholesome values which were based on the Gospel is evident in the description of his prodigal youth. The *Vita prima* comments that such a start in life offers sons and daughters little hope of emerging unscathed from adolescence. Once they have become the slaves of sin by a voluntary servitude, they make themselves instruments of wickedness. Their lives and their conduct declare them to be Christians in name only and the decadent environment erodes their sense of shame.

Francis was born when his father was away from home on business. Trexler argues that Peter was Pica's second husband.[22] Henry d'Avranches states that Francis, already corrupted by the training of his avaricious father, followed the money changers. Having been taught to deceive, he made a great deal of money. He was a peddler, deceitful and violent.[23] The image of the money changers in the Temple shapes the hagiographers' perception of Francis's commercial activities: he was absorbed in making money.[24] Lawrence provides a historical context for such comments about Peter's commercial activities and explains that a long tradition of hagiographical writing associated noble birth with virtue and trade with villainy. These notions were reinforced by the Church's prohibition of usury and its censure on the making of profit. Despite the changing economic conditions of the early thirteenth century, the disparagement of merchants continued to be a commonplace in monastic hagiography. The persistence of this form of snobbery was demonstrated by the portrait of Peter Bernardone in the *Vita prima*.[25]

Peter's influence in Assisi was such that it deterred the impoverished priest at San Damiano from accepting the money which Francis attempted to thrust into his hands on his return from Foligno; G. Fortini speculates whether Peter's origins were Jewish.[26] In contrast to the charge that there was a high level of nominal Christianity in the city, Francis was presented as the genuine Christian, who took the Gospel to heart, the very incarnation of the dominical instruction: he was not a deaf hearer of the Gospel,[27] which became his rule of life, as Thomas of Celano never tires of reminding his readers. A. Mockler takes issue with the hagiographers' negative portrait of Peter and concludes that on any view of human relations it was the father who behaved well and even overindulgently, putting up with his son's extravagances.[28]

Despite his general denunciation of both parents, the biographer later softens his remarks about Pica and concedes that she did not always agree with her husband's treatment of Francis. Henry d'Avranches contrasts Pica favourably with Peter and presents her as virtuous, upright and kind; in the *Vita secunda* she was styled as the friend of all goodness. This portrait was so altered that Pica was awarded a place in the New Testament gallery, where she was revered as a contemporary St Elizabeth. This association with the mother of John the Baptist indicates that the biographer located Francis within the prophetical tradition. Because the friars were becoming increasingly anxious to exalt their saint and to emphasize parallels with the life of Christ, Pica was clothed in nobility of spirit and purity of soul. Pica resembled Elizabeth in giving her son a name and in prophesying that he would become a son of God. The parallel was extended to claim that Francis had a strong devotion to St John the Baptist. This is a topos, a common feature, in the lives of many saints: the mother is the source of virtue, while the father is devoid of compassion and understanding. No such hagiographical reprieve was granted to Peter, who was consistently styled as an avaricious merchant bereft of any finer paternal feelings for his son.[29]

Wealth of Peter Bernardone

The desire to extend trading links between western Europe and the East was one of the reasons why the merchants of the great trading cities of Italy were prepared to support the first Crusade.[30] L. K. Little comments on the revolutionary expansion of commerce, including the mobility of peoples as well as spices, fish, cloth, wine and iron. In the 1070s Gregory VII referred to the many Italian merchants who went to France. In 1127 there were Lombards at Ypres and in 1190, when the Genoese planned to take the Duke of Burgundy on Crusade, part of the arrangement specified safe conduct for Genoese merchants passing through Burgundy on their way to Champagne; the same promise had been made a little earlier to the merchants from Asti. There were Milanese merchants at the fairs in 1172, while this steady procession of Italians to northern Europe included a greater proportion of Tuscans during the thirteenth century.[31] Economic links between England and France remained strong in the twelfth century and English merchants continued to frequent the international fairs of Champagne.[32] D. Waley states that much Italian trade was concerned with the interchange by land of grain, oil, wine, salt and other foodstuffs and of the cheaper textiles and products of local artisans. Nonetheless, there was a long-distance exchange, particularly by sea, of valuable commodities, such as spices, dyes and high-quality textiles. Ultimately, the wealth and way of life of most of the largest cities came to be bound up with international trade and finance.[33]

A. Fortini attests that by the end of the eleventh century merchants from Assisi had already established important connections with France and a century later their activity assumed enormous importance. The fair in Champagne, the most famous of all fairs from 1150 to 1300, was an international market for the exchange of goods between the peoples of the Mediterranean and the North Sea. Merchants from France, Flanders, Germany, England, Catalonia, Spain, Languedoc and Provence, as well as Jews, Samaritans and Levantines assembled there. There was an influx of Lombards, Piedmontese, Genoese, Bolognese and Romans. Such multitudes had a common goal: profit, which drove them to leave their houses, venture forth on unsafe roads, travel for weeks and months, fight against armed gangs holding mountain passes, deal with tolls and ransoms, clamber up mountain peaks and sail on frail boats on which they braved tempests and attacks by pirates.

The insatiable drive for the finest materials in the markets of France was described by Bernard of Clairvaux. He remarks that some people made the rounds of all the cities and passed through every centre of commerce, inspecting markets. Shops were scrutinized and they had the whole stock brought out. Huge bolts of cloth were unrolled for them, fingered and held up to the daylight for inspection; what was coarse and faded was firmly rejected.[34] A. Fortini explains that Peter Bernardone went to the fair in Champagne to buy the finest French and Flemish fabrics and other textiles woven in Flanders, Holland, England and Brabant. According to the term used in the statutes of Assisi, he would become a *franciarlo*, a merchant specializing in the sale of *panni franceschi*. It is probable that he, following the usual custom of joining other merchants to make the trips under the command of an appointed leader, went with the Tuscan caravans, particularly those from Florence. Assisi was well situated for the commercial traffic, because it was on a road that linked Rome and France, the Via Francesca, which was mentioned in an eleventh-century document. This road went along the foot of the hill and so was called the road at the base of the mountain.[35] From the time of the Frankish kings the dependants of the manors had gathered in the piazza to sell their crops and small necessities. Later a permanent market was established with shops, warehouses, commercial displays and the offices of notaries. The piazza in the medieval period was also called the market, a term first mentioned in an Assisian document of 1093.[36]

Peter took advantage of the new and ever growing mercantile trade. One of the characteristics of the period was the feudal lords' widespread conversion of land into moveable goods, which could then more easily be changed into cash. At the same time the merchants, both through expropriation of the land of their debtors and through the desire for investment to offset the necessary commercial risks, were acquiring great estates. Peter's extensive holdings on Assisi's mountain and plain were catalogued in the local records: in Campagna, a large strip of land on Mount Subasio, the olive groves of Val Canale, the field of San Martino d'Argentana, Rigo Secco, Fontanelle and the watery field of Gorghe towards Foligno.[37] Trexler argues that, even if Peter were the rich merchant described in the biographies, the house in which he lived and the capital that financed his activities could have come from his wife.[38] Peter undertook numerous journeys and was absent when Francis was born and when Pica released their son from his domestic incarceration; his absence on other occasions was noted by the biographers. He may have been away from home for shorter periods as well in trying to establish or strengthen business connections in the locality. Francis's training in the world of commerce showed him the level of enterprise required for success in trade and he was aware of the single-mindedness necessary to achieve this.

Francis undoubtedly accompanied his father on some journeys to markets in France to purchase cloth; in his early twenties he may have been permitted to travel to France alone on behalf of his father. Peter's anecdotes about his visits to

France or Francis's own time in that country enkindled a profound love for France. In happier times Francis may well have taken up the reins of the family business during his father's absence. A degree of liberty was obviously extended to him and this enabled him to take cloth from the family shop in Assisi to the fair at Foligno without any apparent explanation before setting out. His father had probably made him responsible for the sale of cloth in the local markets and the strength of Peter's reaction may have arisen from what he regarded as Francis's breach of trust. The wound was all the deeper because of an assumption that the family business would have been taken over in due course by Francis and the dispute about the stolen cloth may have been a symbol of Francis's independence. One of the major moments in Francis's conversion was located in the family shop which prefigures his later conflict between the values of the market place and the Gospel. He came to a realization of the power of wealth and goods with their security and began to react against the itch to accumulate wealth. From that moment he could find neither contentment nor fulfilment in the role which he had hitherto played.

Francis acknowledged the single-minded dedication of the merchant and this image helped to shape his views on the friars' responsibility to make the Gospel incarnate in both their words and deeds. Numerous references were made to the profession which Francis took up and he is frequently portrayed as a merchant. Bonaventure remarks that once Francis had got a slight knowledge of reading and writing, he was given a job in the lucrative trading business.[39] He was a merchant by trade, the dispenser of the opulent vanities of the world,[40] and was accustomed to seeing in his home piles of cloth to be sold. These comments imply that Francis was being groomed to succeed his father in the family business. Although the biographers show that Francis withdrew from society, they also pointed to elements of continuity. Thus, in the period following his conversion, Francis was styled as a happy merchant and a prudent businessman.[41] When preaching on the feast of St Francis in the friars' church in Pisa in the 1260s, Frederick Visconti, the archbishop of that city, reported being present at a sermon delivered by the saint four decades earlier in Bologna. Reminding the congregation that Francis had been a wealthy merchant, he told the merchants that in the saint they had an intermediary with God. It is one of the ironies of history that Francis, who so resolutely turned his back on the world of commerce, was honoured as the patron and protector of merchants in Pisa.[42]

Francis's youth

The commercial prosperity enjoyed by the Bernardone family bestowed many benefits upon Francis, who grew into something of a pampered and fastidious youth; he was not short of money to lavish upon food and drink. The evidence provided by the hagiographers draws attention to Francis's flamboyant character, but this may have been exaggerated in order to emphasize the sacrifices of a life of voluntary poverty in imitation of Jesus Christ. His early life was perceived in terms of the prodigal son, the classical example of repentance: the adolescent Francis was, according to his first biographer, accustomed to dress in fine garments[43] and up to his twenty-fifth year he squandered and wasted his time miserably, outdoing all his contemporaries in vanities; he was more abundantly zealous for all kinds of foolishness. He won the admiration of all and strove to outdo the rest in the pomp of vainglory, in strange doings, in idle and useless talk, in songs, in soft and flowing garments. From his youth he had been frail and delicate in physique and had been pampered; he had lived delicately and he was used to luxury.[44] He was intent on games and songs and day and night he roamed about Assisi with his companions. He was a spendthrift, and all that he earned went into eating and carousing with his friends.[45]

Despite critical remarks about Francis's upbringing, his qualities did not escape the biographer. He possessed a deep-rooted compassion for the poor and instances of his generosity were carefully recorded. Some concern was shown lest he appear to be mean, an accusation deflected by the focus upon his innate generosity. He was styled as the helper to those who had nothing, and habitually showed compassion to the afflicted. There were more direct foretastes of the saint's future ministry among the poor in his concern to alleviate the suffering of those who had became the victims of the economic benefits enjoyed by the wealthy. Sometimes he remained in the house alone with his mother while his father was away on business. On these occasions he would heap the tables with loaves, for both lunch and dinner, as though for the whole family. One day his mother asked him why he prepared so much bread, and he replied that he wished to distribute the loaves to those in need because he had promised always to give alms to anyone who begged from him in God's name.[46]

TROUBLED RELATIONS BETWEEN ASSISI AND PERUGIA

Francis's training in the world of commerce was interrupted by a fresh outbreak of hostilities between Assisi and Perugia. The turbulence of urban life in late twelfth- and early thirteenth-century Italy seeps into a variety of Franciscan sources and the hagiographical tradition. The civil war in Assisi was extended to include Perugia, which provided assistance to the nobles of Assisi. The conflict between the two cities forms the background to Francis's period of uncertainty, his radical change of direction and the inception of his new fraternity. Assisi's foe from time immemorial was Perugia, a stronger and more powerful neighbour. The intensity of the local rivalry appears also in the lives of the local saints, manifesting itself in some of the least likely situations. It is one of the ironies of Umbrian history that the bodies of Francis and Clare, the champions of the poverty which they discerned in the Gospel, were defended by armed guards lest they be spirited away to Perugia.

Along with several communities in eleventh-century western Europe, the people of Assisi set about rebuilding their cathedral which symbolized its civic and diocesan identity and pride. The spate of miracles at the tomb of San Rufino inspired the citizens to build a new cathedral in his honour. Using the wood of the forests and the stones from the ruins that surrounded them, they built the new cathedral. This flurry of civic pride and activity, however, attracted the attention and jealousy of their hereditary rivals. Peter Damian records the local oral tradition that San Rufino intervened to champion the Assisians' cause and subdued their powerful neighbours, who were eventually obliged to bend to his will. As in the controversy over his sarcophagus, the martyr expressed his wishes without any ambiguity. While the men of Assisi were preparing to carry some oak to the church, they were ambushed. The beam was seized by the Perugians, who were intent on carrying it to their own city. When they were only a mile from Perugia, the beam suddenly seemed to be made of lead. Placing it on the ground, they discussed what they might do and additional help was enlisted; teams of oxen were engaged. The efforts of men and the oxen achieved nothing; they then realized that they had committed sacrilege. Turning their oxen towards Assisi, they restored the great beam to the martyr.[47]

The social divisions within medieval Assisi were reflected in early Franciscan hagiography. Leonard, who had joined the fraternity, recollected that his parents were superior to the Bernardone family and noted that Francis, who was sick, was riding a donkey, while he trudged along beside him.[48] As an adolescent Francis probably took part in the sack of the Rocca Maggiore in 1198, toppling the symbol of an odious Germanic oppression in medieval Assisi; the early biographies, however, make no reference to it. At the beginning of the thirteenth century Francis was sufficiently involved in local politics to fight with his peers against the feudal lords, who found support from Perugia. The biographers provide no detail regarding the battle nor Francis's part in it. They disclose only that he was captured at Ponte San Giovanni, between Assisi and Perugia, and endured the squalors of prison in Perugia. This was the first crisis in his young life where he became acquainted with the limitations of his own powers. The *Legenda trium sociorum* records that he was imprisoned among the nobles on account of his distinguished bearing. His future ministry of gentleness and reconciliation was, however, anticipated by his patience towards a proud and overbearing knight who was shunned by all the other captives.

During the seemingly interminable days of captivity Francis's mind frequently turned to the question of what he would do on his release. Thomas of Celano sees the first expression of Francis's vocation in his period of captivity and contrasts the depression and sorrow of most prisoners with the saint's indifference and gaiety. Francis was depicted as rejoicing in the Lord and laughing at his fetters, which would soon be shattered by his conversion. The first biographer anticipates the freedom and confidence of the later years by attributing to Francis the claim that he would be venerated as a saint. This hagiographical exaggeration was exposed by the fact that within a short period of his release Francis was dismissed as a madman. In prison, a symbol which the biographers delighted in exploiting, he had time on his hands and it was natural for a young man in his early twenties to assess the values which had hitherto guided him and the economic factors which had contributed to the state of civil war in Assisi. He reflected upon the values of the urban communities and the divisions which were becoming more conspicuous in his native city. This prolonged period of imprisonment seems to have brought to an end the sectarian instincts which led him into the war. On release his actions reflected a greater compassion and reconciliation, exemplified in his response to the poor knight and his greeting of peace to all whom he encountered. During his time as a prisoner Francis, who had hitherto seemed impregnable, had to learn a bitter lesson that in some situations he was powerless to change his circumstances and that major decisions regarding his life rested with others. For the first time in his young life the disturbing notion of human dependence reared its unattractive head and began to impinge upon him. The biographers rightly treat this period of incarceration as a stepping stone on the way to conversion and the change in his outlook was already beginning. It is probably true that he emerged from prison as a changed man who was in the process of formulating a more critical attitude towards the norms of life in medieval Assisi, even though his military aspirations remained strong.

The perennial tensions between the two neighbouring Umbrian cities surface in Francis's words of reproof to some knights who disrupted his preaching. On this occasion his preaching was intended to stave off the punishment arising from Perugian aggression. While he was addressing a large crowd in the piazza at Perugia, the knights, bearing their arms, began to disport themselves, riding their horses through the public square. Although those listening to the sermon berated them, the knights refused to desist. Francis then turned to them and fervently declared that they should listen to what God was saying through him. They were reminded that God had exalted them, making them greater than all their neighbours, for which they ought all the more to remember their Creator. This realization should make them more humble towards the omnipotent God and their neighbours. They laid waste their neighbours' property and killed many. They were admonished to repent and make satisfaction. Francis prophesied that, if they continued to abuse their powers, they would be engulfed by internecine strife. In such a civil war they would suffer a far greater loss than their neighbours would be able to inflict upon them. The consequences of disregarding the saint's admonitions were illustrated by the divisions which engulfed the population of the mighty city. A few days later a quarrel ensued between the knights and the people. The people drove the knights from the city and, in response, the knights, with the help of ecclesiastics, laid waste many of their fields, vineyards and trees. The people retaliated by doing the same to the knights' properties.[49]

In later years the centuries of strife between Assisi and Perugia were to play a central role in the discussions concerning the burial places of Francis and Clare. These decisions acknowledged the superior military might of Perugia and the real fear that the bodies of the new mendicant saints would be carried from Assisi. The saints' bodies were cherished for both devotional and commercial reasons. It is probable that Francis fully realized that the practice of the theft of relics, in which even future saints like Hugh of Lincoln indulged, made it impossible for him to be buried at the Portiuncula. A similar process was invoked with the death of Clare 27 years later, when the *podestà* posted a squadron of soldiers at San Damiano and a crowd of armed men kept careful guard night and day to prevent the loss of the precious treasure.[50] Her body, too, was carried inside the city walls for burial. In each case it was necessary to ensure that the saints were not buried at churches in the countryside, where they could not be defended. Thus the shrines of Francis and Clare were safely located within the ancient city of Assisi in secure sanctuaries. Within a few years, in the spring of 1261, the roles were reversed and there were fears in Perugia, where Giles, one of Francis's first companions, lay dying. On his death bed the contemplative friar was guarded by armed citizens, lest he be carried back to Assisi for burial.[51] These questions will be explored more fully in the last chapter.

MILITARY AMBITION THWARTED BY SICKNESS

While the experience of prison was undoubtedly a stage in Francis's response to his vocation, it did not bring his military aspirations to an end. Military images persisted in his dreams and he continued to seek to win fame as a celebrated knight. On his release he persevered with his scheme to become a knight in Apulia. There is abundant evidence that his progression towards a new vocation was slow and halting, subject to certain doubts which persisted throughout his life, though with diminishing force. When he was freed from prison, he did not seek the service of God above everything else, as his biographers indicate. His military aspirations remained intact and he was intent on becoming a knight.

The process of reorientation continued in the form of a debilitating illness, which none of the early biographers identified. Protracted sickness brings us all face to face with the uncertainty and frailty of life and teaches us to treasure the blessing of good health. It makes us realize that, however powerful or influential, we are dependent creatures. The symbol of sickness, with its power to frustrate ambitions, was no stranger to the hagiographical tradition, where it was employed to herald a change of direction and at times it was used to subordinate the individual's wishes to God's plan. Even aspirations for virtue were not necessarily guaranteed to meet with success, because sickness frustrated the desire for martyrdom cherished by both Francis and Anthony of Padua[52] and in both cases this paved the way for an unexpectedly rich development.

Imprisonment and illness did little to check Francis's military ambitions. Thomas of Celano argues that the change was taking place slowly and that he was still firmly wedded to some of his old ideals. Francis decided to accompany a nobleman from Assisi who was preparing himself to go to Apulia in search of wealth and fortune. His ambition was to win knighthood and after he had made the necessary preparations in a lavish manner, he hurried on to gain military renown. The biographer regarded Francis's illness as an important stage along the road to conversion, stating that our stubbornness is broken by such experiences of infirmity. This realization reinforced some of the resolutions which Francis had made during his stint as a prisoner. By depicting sickness in this manner Thomas of Celano's outlook reflects the teaching of some medieval theologians that sickness was one of the consequences of the rebellion by Adam and Eve. Illness, another symbol of incarceration, confined Francis to the house for a lengthy period in which he began to assess aspects of his former lifestyle and to ponder a somewhat different future; his health seems to have collapsed. Eventually he was able to move around the house with the aid of a cane and then he began to venture outside again. On his return to society it was clear that he was passing through a period of immense change in his life. He went outside one day and began to look about at the surrounding landscape with great interest. But the beauty of the fields, the pleasantness of the vineyards and whatever else was beautiful to look upon, no longer stirred him. He was aware that a change was taking place, but he was at a loss to understand or explain it. The biographer states that the saint tried to escape the hand of God, and, forgetting for a while his correction by his divine father, he still looked forward to accomplishing great deeds of worldly glory and vanity.

Shortly before setting out he was given a vision in which it seemed that his whole home was filled with the trappings of war, namely, saddles, shields, lances and other things. He wondered what the vision meant because he was unaccustomed to seeing such things in his home, but rather piles of cloth to be sold. He was told that all these arms would belong to him and his soldiers. The dream, whose message was clarified only later, was interpreted in a literal manner and it did nothing to deflect him from quest for knighthood. The next morning he arose with a glad heart and felt sure that the journey to Apulia would be successful. In a second vision a more direct question was put to Francis: should he serve the servant or the lord? When he indicated the latter, he was asked why he had spent so long in the service of the servant. Changed in mind, but not in body, he refused to go to Apulia and was directed to return to Assisi where the fulfilment of the dream would be given; he prophesied that he would do great and noble things in his own homeland. The two decisive dreams signalled the end of Francis's military ambitions, even though the biographers continued to exploit this imagery. They had prevailed upon Francis to abandon his own long-held ambitions and from that point he conceded the initiative to a divine force, which he grasped imperfectly. Only then did his new vocation begin to flower. Hitherto, he had shaped his own life and pursued his own goals. On the rubble of his shattered aspirations God began to raise up one who not be merely a local hero, but one of the most famous figures in the western world. Francis's unexpected return to Assisi became a talking point, especially because he had gone home as a different, perhaps shaken, figure. His dreams of becoming a knight yielded to a prolonged period of uncertainty in which he struggled to divine the way forward.

Francis, who had finally been weaned from his military ambitions, entered into a lengthy period of waiting; it lasted for two years, although there were some pointers visible to him. Because he had so little understanding of the forces which were taking hold of his own life, it is scarcely surprising that his family and friends were even more perplexed. One of the simpler explanations was that he had fallen in love and that he wished to marry. When friends put the question to him, he replied in his typically flamboyant manner by saying that he would take a more noble and more beautiful spouse than they had ever seen: he prophesied that his spouse would surpass all others in beauty and excel all others in wisdom. Such a declaration was seized on by the biographers, who were happy to interpret this as a prediction of Lady Poverty, his feminized ideal, and the fraternity which would gather around him.[53]

Thomas of Celano's description of Francis's conversion was shaped by the parable of the prodigal son (Luke 15:11-32). As he yearned for a more satisfactory lifestyle Francis began to discard his former habits. The *Vita secunda* gives a somewhat sour account of his dealings with his friends in the transitional phase. Because Francis had been the leader of a band of young men in vain pursuits, his friends invited him to their social banquets which always served their wantonness and buffoonery. The biographer suggests that Francis's choice as their leader was based on his liberality and his generosity in footing the bill; they gave him obedience so that he might feed them. Mindful of the obligations of courtesy, he prepared a sumptuous banquet, doubled the dainty foods. Filled to vomiting with these things, they defiled the streets of the city with drunken singing. The future saint followed them, carrying a staff in his hand, as the master of the revels.[54] Such a concentration upon Francis's magnetic appeal and his leadership qualities was no doubt given due emphasis as a harbinger of his future role as the animator and guide of an enormous and rapidly spreading fraternity, which gave him obedience.

Francis was depicted as very rich and prodigal. He was a squanderer of his possessions, a cautious businessman, but a very unreliable steward. His faults were attributed to his parents, who were given none of the credit for his attractive qualities. Despite his upbringing and the excesses of his youth, the biographers nonetheless refer to certain qualities which pave the way for the later conversion. He was neither avaricious nor a hoarder of money; he was a very kindly person, easy and affable, even making himself foolish because of it; these characteristics attracted many, including the promoters and perpetrators of evil and crime. In sentences teeming with biblical allusions, his first biographer reports that Francis was overwhelmed by a host of evil companions. Proud and high-minded, he walked about the streets of Babylon until God rescued him. After his early diffidence and loss of nerve Francis become a prophetical voice to a society that had deviated from the teaching of the Gospel. The biographers' bleak picture of the life and customs of early thirteenth-century Assisi is in marked contrast to the portrait of the saint who appears all the stronger in proffering salutary advice to the people and mapping out the route to salvation. The first biographer maintained that Umbrian society had grown careless about the teachings of the Gospel, with apathy and indifference constituting a formidable challenge to the saint.[55] His meeting with a leper on the plain below Assisi provided him with some clues about the next stage in his pilgrimage.

FRANCIS AND THE LEPER

At the root of medieval hagiography was the tension between society and Christianity and one of the objectives of the biographer was to demonstrate that the values and customs of society bedevilled the attempt to live according to the teaching of Christ. Local records in Assisi, however, do offer strong support for this conventional interpretation and specify some of the maladies besetting society at the beginning of the thirteenth century. For instance, there were ideological and economic struggles which eventually resulted in the civil war. On the margins of society were the poor, the victims of financial policies, and the lepers, whose physical proximity struck nausea and terror into the hearts of many. A society which purported to be Christian took active measures to protect itself from the deadly disease of leprosy and banned lepers from the city, offering them no protection from attack. These divisions were instrumental in the evolution of Francis's conversion and they undoubtedly stimulated the role of the friars in fomenting peace within and between the neighbouring cities in Italy.

Just as AIDS became the scourge of the western world in the late 1980s and early 1990s, medieval men and women were terrified of leprosy, a disease which forced the individual to withdraw from society, leaving his family and goods. The disease was treated by some medieval theologians as a symbol of sin which excludes the victim from society.[56] Nonetheless, some provision was made for the afflicted and leper houses were built. M. Rubin explains that they were, however, usually located beyond the town boundaries, often near springs and rivers. Thirteenth-century French legislation reflected that it would be dangerous to keep the leprous with the healthy and accordingly leper houses were built outside the towns. The leper hospital in Cambridge was situated some two miles away from the centre of town, beyond the Barnwell precinct.[57] In Assisi the leper hospital was established near the church of Santa Maria Maddalena, halfway between Rivo Torto and the Portiuncula—clearly a safe distance from the city. Lepers lived on the margins of society, a group of people awaiting death. The statutes of the commune were harsh and required the *podestà* to make a scrupulous search for lepers in the city and in the region within a month of taking up office. Any leper, male or female, living in the city or in the countryside, was to be hunted out from these places, and from the *castelli* and from the *ville*. The syndics of the cities and the castellans of the castles were obliged to take care to bring charges against lepers. The leper who risked entering the city was left to the mercy of the crowd, which hunted him down. The statutes declared that:

> no leper may dare to enter the city or walk around in it, and if any one of them shall be found, everyone may strike him with impunity.[58]

Another prejudice against lepers was that they were greedy for money.[59]

The sight of lepers horrified the young and fastidious Francis, who had been brought up to enjoy comforts and luxuries in the home of a prosperous merchant. The disfiguring marks of the disease were described by Thomas of Celano: all the leper's limbs were swollen and enlarged and, because of the distension and puffed-up condition of his veins, his vision was impaired and he was unable to walk.[60] Francis gives his own account of the momentous meeting with the leper in the plain below Assisi, an event which convinced him that his instincts were capable of distorting the Gospel. Suddenly he found himself face to face with a leper and in a flash it dawned on him that his normal reaction was rooted in selfishness and prejudice rather than charity and compassion. He came to realize that there were areas of his life which called for reassessment and a greater openness to the spirit of the Gospel. Medieval Assisi distanced lepers from the city and Francis had been brought up to accept this segregation of humanity. His expanding vision was beginning to combat prejudice and to incorporate the whole of creation. His *Testament* gives an invaluable insight into his frame of mind as he prepared to die. More importantly, it reveals his own understanding of the process of his conversion. While there were several events in the clarification of his new vocation, this was the one which was the most vivid to him:

> the Lord granted me, Brother Francis, to begin to do penance in this way: While I was in sin, it seemed very bitter to me to see lepers. And the Lord himself led me among them and I had mercy upon them. And when I left them that which seemed bitter to me was changed into sweetness of soul and body.[61]

His conviction was that his conversion took place at the divine instigation and that God had led him to do penance, transforming what had hitherto filled him with a sense of nausea into sweetness. His perception of the world had been distorted by sin, a condition in which he was concerned primarily with himself, and this had robbed him of compassion for the suffering of the social outcast. He believed that, just as God led him to do penance, so he also guided him into the lepers' midst and this may account for the time which he spent among them, exhorting his followers to do the same. This was a seminal experience for the complete conversion of life on which he now embarked, a vocation characterized by the universal fraternity.

Francis's view of the pivotal meeting was also quoted in the *Vita prima*, which provided fuller details of the event. The sight of lepers was so loathsome to him that he would look at their houses only from a distance of two miles; and he would hold his nostrils with his hands. The crucial meeting occurred during the period in which he was seeking a new direction. Nonetheless, his instinctive reactions to the sight of lepers persisted. Only the power of God's grace enabled him to master his normal feeling of abhorrence at the sight of lepers. He received strength which enabled him to restrain his instinct to flee. A new energy was at work in him: instead, his newly attained self-mastery was displayed by the kiss which he gave to the somewhat startled leper. From that moment the recollection of his earlier behaviour filled him with remorse; the biographer speaks of him despising himself until he attained perfect mastery over himself.

The account of this momentous meeting was clothed in a more theological form in the *Vita secunda* where the biographer displays some signs of theological training. A religious spirit was taking hold of Francis and he began to spend more time in solitary places, which were deemed more conducive to prayer; the process was purgative. The sight of lepers had been abhorrent to him, who had been brought up with a strong interest in the finer things of this life. On the plains below Assisi he unexpectedly came across a leper and seems to have experienced the customary reaction. Nonetheless, by this stage he was resolved to respond in a more constructive manner and, getting off his horse, he prepared to kiss the leper, who stretched out his hand for money. The leper was perhaps amazed by this gesture, receiving both money and a kiss. On remounting his horse, Francis looked all around him. Though the plain was open on all sides, he could not see the leper anywhere. Filled with joy and wonder, he was determined to do the same a few days later. At the leper colony he gave each of the lepers some money and kissed them on the hand and mouth. The narrative concludes with the words 'Thus he exchanged the bitter for the sweet, and manfully prepared himself to carry out the rest'. His first meeting with the leper radically altered his life and afterwards he went to live with the lepers whom he served. This radical change in his behaviour was treated as a restorative activity because his biographer remarks that by washing away all their foulness, he wiped away also the corruption of his own ulcers. He gave the lepers some money, he kissed them on the hand and mouth.

Recognizing that his inherited set of values had played him false and that it had closed his eyes to the demands of the Gospel, especially in the form of suffering humanity, Francis began to cast around for a new lifestyle which would embrace those whom the local society had effectively marginalized. In his penitential life his perception of society was henceforth to be shaped solely by the Gospel and excluded no one: lepers, the poor, the wealthy, and former opponents in local politics and warfare, were among the friars' first benefactors; men from these social categories would soon be clothed in the friars' habit. The enthusiasm with which Francis undertook this work among the lepers was due partly to an unshakeable conviction that God had led him upon the lepers and partly to an awareness that the Gospel and grace should inform and sustain human interaction and that equality should obtain, regardless of economic status. Friars worked in the lepers' houses[62] and the Rule of 1221 stipulates that they should be glad to live among the social outcasts, and in this context lepers were specifically mentioned. Francis envisages friars begging alms for lepers in urgent need and from the beginning of the fraternity he wanted them to stay in leper hospitals.[63] On another occasion he was entertained at a leper hospital at Trevi.

Francis's immediate response to the encounter with the leper was to leave the city and commit himself to the needs of the social outcasts. The medieval city offered protection from the marauding armies, robbers and wild animals. It was a place of security and some comfort. Francis's declaration that he had left the world does not suggest any criticism of what God had created; instead, he rejected those values which were out of sympathy with the Gospel. His conclusion that his former lifestyle had failed to satisfy him meant that a new start had to be made. At that stage he appears to have had little idea of where that decision would lead him, but it was clear that his former security had to be abandoned in order to entrust himself to the divine providence described in the Gospel. Like the prophets of the Old Testament, he was entering the desert and making a new beginning in his life, learning to respond more wholeheartedly to the divine voice. Our radical decisions are based upon an act of faith and carry with them a large element of risk: the future cannot be guaranteed, however good and noble our aspirations. Moments of doubt and uncertainty often accompany the pilgrimage into the unknown. Francis, too, must have had his moments of anxiety and trepidation, but in the interim he was content to minister to those rejected by the urban centres as he awaited further guidance from God.

Francis's *Testament* contains some phraseology which reflects the traditional vocabulary of religious life, which brought with it a rejection of the earlier lifestyle and a retreat from the cities to the desert or the monastic enclosure. He announced that, following his providential meeting with the leper, he lingered for a little while and then left the world. The *Vita secunda* speaks about Francis leaving his parents for the sake of poverty.[64] Commercial values had been sacrificed on the altar of the saint's desire for communion with his Creator.[65] The language was traditional and so was the initial intention because he had turned his face from the city; at the time of the experience with the leper, he seems to have had no thoughts about re-entering society. The self-mastery which he attained needed continual affirmation, as the account of his dealings with the leper whom James brought to the Portiuncula shows.[66] Peter Catanii was Francis's vicar in 1220 and this helps to date the event, revealing that over a decade after the decisive meeting with the leper Francis's old habits were capable of reasserting themselves. Lepers at San Severino in the Marches of Ancona and Fano were among the numerous beneficiaries of Francis's intercession and feature in the collection of miracles appended to the first biography.[67]

BEGINNINGS OF A VOCATION

Peter Bernardone was allotted a negative function in the early biographies, seeking to frustrate his son's laudable aspirations. He was cast in the role of a brutal and insensitive figure who was determined to subdue Francis, who was becoming something of a fanatical figure. Resisted by his son, his only interest was the recovery of his money and in his exasperation he delated him to the civic and ecclesiastical authorities. The hagiographers polarized the figures of father and son and it was not in their interests to reveal the sunnier side of Peter's nature. His greed was contrasted with Francis's desire to serve God alone and this comparison prepared the ground for the life of evangelical poverty which Francis subsequently embraced. The early biographers sketched the conflict between father and son in terms of cupidity and voluntary poverty in imitation of the Gospel. While the imagery was appealing to the hagiographical tradition, Francis's ideas about poverty were not yet mature. It is true that Francis was no longer satisfied by material things, but his decision about a life of voluntary poverty in imitation of Jesus Christ was not clarified until he attended Mass at the Portiuncula and opened the book of the Gospels. The hagiographical portrait of Peter needs to be purged of all exaggeration and distortion to show that what was happening was an event which brought sadness to the Bernardone family, which was on the brink of breaking up. Moreover, Peter was unable to deal with Francis's growing religious idealism, which others interpreted as eccentricity or madness.

Withdrawal

Francis's dream about arms effectively sounded the death knell of his military ambitions and from that time he became increasingly determined to subjugate his own wishes to God's will. He set about this task by turning his back on his normal activities in order to develop deeper communication with his Creator and to rectify his dealings with his neighbour. Leaving behind the bustle and tumult of the city, he desired a more reflective life. His biographer reports that, like a prudent business man, he had discovered the treasure hidden in a field (Matthew 13:44-46). Educated in accordance with the norms and conventions of that society, he had embarked upon a life of trade, a spiritual commerce. The conversion experiences, however, pronounced the values of the market place to be defective in terms of satisfying human aspirations, running the risk of disfiguring the created order. Divine compassion and mercy rescued Francis from the pitfalls of urban life, bestowed a greater dignity upon him and sent him back to society with a plan for its spiritual rejuvenation.

Laying aside his secular ambitions, Francis embraced a more meditative life and increasingly looked towards the Gospel for instruction. With a vague idea about his future he set about the grand gesture which would demonstrate his alienation from the plan marked out for him by his father. He rode to the market in Foligno with some fine cloth. Was he intent on a spectacular gesture of renunciation? Or was he primarily intent on raising money for the restoration of San Damiano? My own instinct tends towards the latter. At the fair he sold everything, as usual, though on this occasion he even sold the horse. The sale of the horse may have betokened his fundamental break with the past and inspired the subsequent prohibition on the friars riding horses, a symbol of wealth. His gestures had a spontaneous quality because on his journey back to Assisi he wondered what he should do with the money. Little uncertainty about what he would do next or how he would explain himself to his father was allowed to survive the editorial scissors. Instead, the biographer's imagery and language imply that the flight from society had already occurred and that Francis's only concern was how best he might serve Jesus Christ. The events at Foligno contain elements of an act of renunciation, though perhaps Francis's appearance before the episcopal tribunal was a more attractive candidate. The *Anonymous of Perugia* makes no mention of the theft from the family business and records that, when Francis was travelling back from Apulia, he stopped in Foligno and sold his horse and clothes.

Francis at San Damiano

Francis was a changed man on his return to Assisi. No longer would he return to his parental home in the heart of Assisi. On his way back to the city he pondered on the new direction which his life was taking. The life of commerce had been discarded in favour of his commitment to the dictates of the Gospel. A new phase of his life had been ushered in as he enlisted in the service of another lord, far more powerful and good than any feudal lord whom he had encountered. He had become a new soldier and athlete of Christ entering San Damiano with the intention of doing battle on behalf of his new master, emphasizing his attachment to the Gospel. At the dilapidated rural church Francis found a poor priest, named Peter, whose hands he kissed with great faith, offering him the money which he had with him. The priest was astonished and puzzled by the reckless young man's behaviour. Aware of Francis's reputation in the city, he was reluctant to believe his ears; the offer of money was spurned. In the end Francis was allowed to remain there, but out of fear of Peter Bernardone, the priest did not accept the money. In this way Francis became an oblate and passed under ecclesiastical jurisdiction; this decision freed him from the authority of his family.

Francis hurled the coins into a window, perhaps as a symbol of his alienation from the values of the market place. At this stage his thoughts were fixed on the restoration of the chapel and the money raised at the fair was a means of achieving this end. Hitherto there was little evidence that Francis had decided to turn his back on money. The biographers seized on the moment when he dismissively put this money on the windowsill as the seed of his later vocation to a life of voluntary poverty in imitation of Jesus Christ and the apostles. The subsequent dispute with his father reinforced the sense that money created and sustained divisions. A consciousness that material things were potentially intrusive and divisive remained with Francis throughout his life. The way in which an undue attachment to inherited wealth and possessions was capable of imperilling the soul and polluting human relations was illustrated by the image of the dying rich man surrounded by relations awaiting their inheritance.[68]

Thomas of Celano interpreted Francis's return from Foligno as a root of his decision to turn his back on material advantage. Sketching the rift between father and son, he was determined to expose Peter's love for Francis as limited and carnal; he implied that Peter's affection was contingent upon filial subservience. There was no paternal effort to understand the ill-defined ideals to which Francis had pledged himself. Hagiographical models persuaded Thomas of Celano to depict Peter's protest at San Damiano within the context of a tussle between an aggressive father, goaded only by the love of money, and the servant of God. The image enabled the biographer to regard Peter as one who went about the place like a persistent spy, wanting to learn what had happened to his son. Something of Peter's agitated state of mind was, however, captured by the concession that he was exceedingly troubled at the sudden turn of events. Calling his friends and neighbours, he hurried to San Damiano where Francis was brought face to face with his own frailty, taking fright when he heard the threats of those pursuing him; he hid himself in a secret pit which he himself had prepared for just such an emergency. His fear was such that he remained hidden there for a month, even taking his meals there.[69] Events proved him to be a raw recruit to the Gospel and showed how he capitulated at his very first test. However, in his weakness he found the means of his recovery and learned to rely less on his own self-confidence and strength. While he had manifestly failed his first test, a constructive interpretation was given by his biographer, who reported that he devoted himself to prayer and fasting, paving the way for the attainment of self-mastery.

Images of martyrdom

In the Middle Ages martyrdom was perceived as one of the clearest demonstrations of sanctity. It was the form of death by which men and women identified themselves most closely with the events of the crucifixion. The bishops venerated in medieval Assisi were martyrs and in the late twelfth and early thirteenth century the cult of martyrdom was very powerful, especially when new martyrs were shedding their blood for Jesus Christ in the crusading territories. A chronicle of the first Crusade reports that among those cut down by the enemy was a priest celebrating Mass and that those who died in a siege were treated as martyrs.[70] Francis had attended school at San Giorgio, a saint who enjoyed much popularity among Crusaders. He also nurtured a strong devotion to St John the Baptist. This motif was prominent in early Franciscan literature and the desire for martyrdom took Francis to Syria. Clare, too, nurtured a strong desire to give the ultimate proof of her love for Christ and the accounts of the protomartyrs of the order in Morocco accentuated her desire for martyrdom[71] and drew Anthony of Padua to the fraternity. Indeed, his early biographers felt constrained to explain why this wholesome desire was not realized.[72] Thomas of Celano believed that there was a continuity in Francis's life and that he, who had previously sought glory as a knight, became the valiant soldier of Christ on whose behalf he rode into battle. The events following his return from the market in Foligno, when he was initially cowed by his father and then mastered his fear, chart the victory of the saint who had been subjected to a searching examination. A quotation from the Office of St Martin of Tours shows that even though he did not lose his life in persecution, Francis was not deprived of the martyr's palm.[73] While his period in hiding issued in a new strength and confidence in God, the battle was not over; there would be other situations in which weakness was confronted. For instance, his nerve failed him not long afterwards when he went to beg oil for the lamps at San Damiano. Seeing a large group of men before the house which he wished to enter, diffidence mastered him and he withdrew, though he later bemoaned his weakness.[74]

Chastened by his earlier failure, Francis emerged from his hiding place with a new resolve and determination to do battle for Christ. With renewed confidence he took the road to Assisi, where he began to accuse himself severely of laziness and cowardice. Witnessing the change in his conduct, his former companions reviled him, shouting out that he was mad and demented; they threw the mud of the streets and stones at him. They saw that he was changed from his former ways and had become greatly emaciated; everything that he did was attributed to exhaustion and madness. Francis was deaf to all these taunts and his experience was interpreted by Thomas of Celano as a wicked persecution of the young man intent on virtue. Nonetheless, on more than one occasion the biographer concedes that Francis was thought to have taken leave of his senses.[75]

The insults heaped upon Francis brought humiliation upon the proud name of Bernardone in Assisi; the mere suggestion that his son was insane filled Peter with shame and indignation. Peter was not alone in believing that his son had undergone some kind of psychological trauma, as the noise and shouting in the streets of Assisi seemed to confirm. The reaction of many of the citizens of Assisi confirmed the view taking shape in Peter's mind, that his son, following his bout of illness, had gone too far and had lost his sense of perspective. But for Thomas of Celano this was further proof of paternal intransigence. In an extraordinary passage the *Vita prima*, bristling with biblical imagery, proclaims that, when Peter heard the name of his son mentioned and understood the commotion, he immediately arose to destroy him. He reacted with savagery and became a dark-minded persecutor of the 'elect of God', displaying only severity instead of sympathy for his son. This is presented as a clear conflict between the values of the market place and the Gospel and in the ecclesiastical version Peter's faults were magnified so that he became the very antithesis of his son's pure love of apostolic poverty. With no regard for moderation, he rushed upon him like a wolf upon a sheep, and looking upon him with a fierce and savage countenance, he laid hands upon him and dragged him shamefully and disgracefully to his home.

At first Peter used words and then blows and chains. He mercilessly locked Francis in a dark place for several days in a vain attempt to bring him to submission and obedience. There can be little doubt that Peter was completely bewildered by his son's behaviour, which occasioned gossip and scandal in the small city and also led to the expropriation of commercial assets. According to feudal ideas, the father, as the head of the family, enjoyed absolute control over the household; children were his to deal with as he thought best and his own ideas and needs were the sole directing force.[76] The communal statutes authorized a father to imprison a son who had squandered the family assets. Guilty sons must be imprisoned at the request of two near relatives and might not be released until such time as it would please the members of their family.[77] Imprisonment serves as another topos in the conversion of the saint, first during the civil war, then at San Damiano and at home. The biographers treat this as the last act in Francis's emancipation; his liberation was at hand and then the work of God could begin. Francis's reappraisal of life was teaching him the ultimate source of authority and convincing him that he had to reject filial subservience in order to obey the Gospel to the letter. M. de la Bedoyère voices a pious view in remarking that it is hard to forgive Peter's brutality and stupidity, but concedes that his behaviour suggests that the real Francis was a far odder and more difficult person than the pious streamlining traditions of hagiography allow.[78]

While Peter was away on business, Pica attempted to dissuade Francis from his decision to turn his back on the commercial world. However much Thomas of Celano eulogizes her in the *Vita secunda*, his earlier biography affirms that she took her husband's part in attempting to win over her son. Only when everything else had failed, did she release him from his prison. The biographers depict Francis as a confessor emerging from his spell of captivity with the resolve of returning to the service of Christ. His experiences imparted new confidence to him and he gave thanks to God. His release and display of new-found boldness generated a great deal of comment and speculation in Assisi. He had stolen a march on his doubly outraged father. In contrast, not finding Francis at home, Peter upbraided his wife for her part in the release. Then, raging and blustering, he ran to San Damiano hoping that if he could not recall him from his ways, he might at least drive him from the province,[79] a measure for which the communal statutes made provision.[80]

By this stage Francis was learning to place his trust in God from whom he was drawing new strength. Fear of his father had earlier reduced him to cowardice; instead his fears were given a new focus and were directed towards God. The struggle was located in the traditional battle between grace and the secular spirit. Francis, having escaped from a material perception of the world, heard the hustle and bustle of the arrival of his carnally minded father. Like one of the heroic martyrs of Assisi in the third or fourth century, he joyfully and confidently went forth to meet his father, heralding his indifference towards whatever punishments his father might inflict upon him; no longer were his father's chains and blows to be feared. This is the language of the martyrs in their defiance before their persecutors: he declared that he would joyfully endure any punishment for the name of Jesus Christ. A fortified Francis gloried in the idea of enduring suffering for the name of Christ.

The hagiographers exaggerate the contrast between the lure of the market place and the dictates of the Gospel, portraying Peter as an avaricious merchant, motivated primarily by the urge to accumulate wealth. With all the censoriousness that he could muster, the biographer declares that Peter's abiding concern was the recovery of his money. No tinge of sadness at his ruptured relations with his son was permitted to Peter. Therefore, when the money was found in the dust of the windowsill, the fury of his raging father was extinguished a little and the thirst of his avarice was somewhat allayed by the warmth of the discovery. The opposite disposition animated Francis, who wished to use the money to feed the poor and repair the buildings at San Damiano. There is a stark contrast between the father intent on regaining his money and the penitent who sought only the liberating values of the Gospel, particularly alienation from money which had precipitated the rift. The report of the cold greed displayed by Peter on his second visit to San Damiano was magnified to form an unfavourable comparison with his son who was about the embark upon a life of voluntary poverty. Thomas of Celano grandly announces that by this stage Francis hated money and could not be misled by any aspect of good in it. Nonetheless, his two biographies cite instances of Francis's continued use of money; it is probable that his scruples about touching money belong to the period after the Mass at the Portiuncula and the opening of the Gospel at San Nicola.

CONCLUSION

Christian Assisi was proud of its lengthy tradition, which had begun with the heroic witness of the martyred bishops of the city. As a man who fought for his city Francis was brought up on the legends of San Rufino and San Vittorino. His thirst for martyrdom and his reverence for relics may have had their roots in the traditions of his native city. One of the traditional signs of the saint's peculiar indifference to worldly matters was his abandonment of family and kin. Luke 14:26 has been interpreted rather narrowly by some Franciscan biographers, who firmly believed that the Gospel demanded such a renunciation of parents.[81] Such an evangelical model may have sustained Francis throughout his conflict with his father. In his time at San Damiano he visited the chapel dedicated to San Feliciano, who had gathered the handful of converts there to address them for the last time. Did Francis envisage his own personal reform as a continuation of the mission of the martyred bishop of Foligno, who had brought Christianity to Assisi? The first biographers treated Francis as a new martyr and this led them to exaggerate the strains between him and his father, who personified the customs of Assisian society. They emphasized the radical break which he made with his family, establishing this as the model to be copied by all who take the Franciscan habit; the *Vita secunda* contains several anecdotes of friars who failed to make a complete break with their families.[82]

Francis's decision to make the Gospel his pattern of life was located in the context of liberation from the conventions of society, which were personified by his father. In early Franciscan hagiography Peter, a man bereft of virtue and cast in an extremely uncomplimentary role, was allotted the task of conducting a searching examination of his son's resolve to follow Christ literally. He mirrors the spirit of society, which is continually in tension with the teaching of the Gospel. He was a caricature of the forces ranged against Christianity, the embodiment of the vices of a society preoccupied with the accumulation of material wealth and indifferent to the plight of those marginalized in economic terms. The biographers' primary concern was to chronicle the way in which Francis responded fully and generously to the call of the Gospel and Peter was incidental to the principal theme. The biographers do not raise the question of a reconciliation between Peter and Francis; such materials may have been regarded as subverting the initial gesture of renunciation. In the 1050s St Anselm quarrelled with his father before crossing the Alps and his father, too, played no further part in Eadmer's biography. Nonetheless, additional materials in manuscript form leave the door ajar.[83] The biographers' silence does not necessarily preclude the possibility of a reconciliation between Francis and Peter and their relationship *cannot* be understood solely in the terms of the hagiographical evidence. While they treat Peter as an obstacle to Francis's spiritual aspirations, they grant a more central and paternal role to Bishop Guido, to whom we now turn.

Notes

1. Dante, *The Divine Comedy*, 3: *Paradiso*, XI, 58-63, ed. and trans. J. D. Sinclair (Oxford, 1971), pp. 164-5.
2. R. Brown, *The Roots of St Francis: A Popular History of the Church in Assisi and Umbria before St Francis as Related to his Life and Spirituality* (Chicago, 1982), p. 75. Cf. J. M. H. Smith, 'Oral and written: saints, miracles, and relics in Brittany, *c.* 850-1250', *Speculum*, 65 (1990), pp. 309-43, 313, 338, comments that all the lives of the Breton saints under examination were written hundreds of years after their subjects' putative lifetimes. It is impossible to trace the developments of the cult of the Breton saints *ab origine.* Indeed, most Breton saints never had a written life at all.
3. A. Fortini, *Assisi nel medioevo* (Rome, 1940), p. 33.
4. Ibid., p. 72, n. 5. Cf. M. Faloci-Pulignani, 'La passio S. Feliciani e il suo valore storico', *Archivio per la storia ecclesiastica dell'Umbria*, 4 (1917), pp. 137-274.
5. Fortini, p. 47.
6. NV, I, pt. 1, pp. 17-18, n. 1.
7. NV, II, pp. 284-5.
8. Fortini, *Assisi nel medioevo*, p. 35.
9. Ibid., pp. 35-41.
10. Paul the Deacon, *Historia Langobardorum*, lib. 4, c. 16, lib. 6, n. 58 (MGH SS; 1878), pp. 121-2, 186.
11. Gregory of Tours, *Liber in gloria martyrum*, lib. 1, c. 63 (MGH SS; 1885), p. 531. Salimbene, *Cronica*, ed. G. Scalia (Scrittori d'Italia, 232-33; Bari, 1966), pp. 304-5, testifies that there were many Lombard and Tuscan merchants at the market in Troyes which lasted for two months and the same was true of Provins in 1247.
12. NV, I, pt. 1, p. 49.
13. A. Brunacci, 'Leggende e culto di S. Rufino in Assisi', *Bollettino della Deputazione di Storia Patria per l'Umbria*, 45 (1948), pp. 5-91, 81-2.
14. NV, III, p. 592.
15. Peter Damian, *Sermo 36* in *Corpus Christianorum, continuatio mediaevalis*, 57, ed. J. Lucchesi (1983), pp. 217-22. Cf. NV, I, pt. 1, pp. 62-3.
16. 3 C, nn. 95-108. Similar incidents are recounted in the life of St Anthony, *Benignitas*, c. 23, nn. 1-7.
17. NV, v. 1, pt. 1, pp. 167-8.
18. *Compilatio Assisiensis*, c. 5.
19. 2 C, n. 109; LM, c. 3, n. 5.
20. C. H. Lawrence, *Medieval Monasticism* (London, 1989), p. 244; Lawrence, *The Friars: The Impact of the Early Mendicant Movement on Western Society* (The Medieval World; London, 1994), pp. 27-8.
21. *Opuscula Sancti Patris Francisci Assiensis*, ed. C. Esser (BFAMA, 12; Rome, 1978), p. 111. He teaches that sin springs from the flesh, the world and the devil. *S. Bonaventurae opera omnia*, V (Quaracchi, Florence, 1891), p. 232, suggests that all temptation arises from the world, or the flesh or the devil. This shows that some of Francis's ideas were not very far removed from the teaching of the scholastics.
22. R. C. Trexler, *Naked before the Father* (Humana Civilitas, 9; New York, 1989), p. 25.
23. Henry d'Avranches, 'Legenda S. Francisci versificata' in AF, 10, pp. 408-9.
24. LTS, n. 2.
25. C. H. Lawrence (ed. and trans.), *The Life of St Edmund by Matthew Paris* (Oxford, 1996), p. 5.
26. G. Fortini, *Francesco d'Assisi Ebreo?* (Assisi, 1978).
27. 1 C, n. 22.
28. A. Mockler, *Francis of Assisi: The Wandering Years* (Oxford, 1976), p. 37.
29. 1 C, n. 13; Henry d'Avranches, p. 408; 2 C, n. 3.
30. R. Hill (ed.), *The Deeds of the Franks and the Other Pilgrims to Jerusalem* (NMT; 1962), republished in OMT (1972), p. xxiii.
31. L. K. Little, *Religious Poverty and the Profit Economy in Medieval Europe* (London, 1978), p. 12.
32. C. H. Lawrence, *The Life of St Edmund by Matthew Paris*, p. 11.
33. D. Waley, *The Italian City-Republics* (London, 3rd edn., 1988), p. 5.

34.   *S. Bernardi opera*, III, ed. J. Leclercq and H. M. Rochais (Rome, 1963), p. 102.
35.   NV, I, i, pp. 45-7.
36.   Ibid., I, i, p. 43.
37.   Ibid., I, i, pp. 142-6.
38.   Trexler, *Naked before the Father*, p. 25.
39.   LM, c. 1, n. 1.
40.   Anon. Perug., c. 1, n. 3b.
41.   1 C, nn. 5, 6, 9.
42.   L. K. Little, *Religious Poverty*, pp. 216-17.
43.   1 C, n. 16.
44.   *Compilatio Assisiensis*, c. 50; 2 C, n. 13, states that such luxury was opposed to the goodness of nature.
45.   LTS, n. 2.
46.   Ibid., n. 9.
47.   Peter Damian, n. 12, pp. 221-2.
48.   2 C, n. 31.
49.   *Compilatio Assisiensis*, c. 75.
50.   LSC, n. 47.
51.   'Chronica XXIV generalium ordinis minorum' in AF, III (Quaracchi, Florence, 1897), p. 113.
52.   Dialogus; 1 C, nn. 55-56.
53.   1 C, nn. 4-7; 2 C, n. 6.
54.   2 C, n. 7.
55.   1 C, nn. 36-37.
56.   *S. Bonaventurae opera omnia*, VII (Quaracchi, Florence, 1895), p. 434.
57.   M. Rubin, *Charity and Community in Medieval Cambridge* (Cambridge Studies in Medieval Life and Thought; Cambridge, 1987), pp. 106-7, nn. 38-40.
58.   A. Fortini, *Francis of Assisi*, translated from NV by H. Moak (New York, 1981), pp. 210-11; NV, I, pt. 1, p. 271.
59.   1 C, n. 103; 2 C, n. 66.
60.   1 C, n. 146.
61.   R. J. Armstrong and I. C. Brady, *Francis and Clare: The Complete Works* (The Classics of Western Spirituality; New York, 1982), p. 154.
62.   1 C, n. 39.
63.   *Opuscula Sancti Patris Francisci Assisiensis*, pp. 258-60; *Compilatio Assisensis*, c. 9.
64.   2 C, n. 55.
65.   *Opuscula Sancti Patris Francisci Assisiensis*, p. 120.
66.   *Compilatio Assisiensis*, c. 64.
67.   1 C, n. 146.
68.   *Opuscula Sancti Patris Francisci Assisiensis*, pp. 66-7, 126-7.
69.   1 C, n. 10.
70.   Hill, *The Deeds of the Franks and the Other Pilgrims to Jerusalem*, pp. 4, 17, 40.
71.   R. J. Armstrong, *Clare of Assisi: Early Documents* (New York, 1988), pp. 151, 153-4, 165.
72.   Julian of Speyer, *Officio Ritmico e Vita Secunda*, ed. V. Gamboso (FAA, 2; Padua, 1985), c. 2, n. 8, pp. 398-9; Benignitas, c. 4.
73.   LM, c. 9, n. 9; Benignitas, c. 6, nn. 1-2.
74.   2 C, n. 13.
75.   1 C, nn. 10-14; 2 C, n. 4, when Francis's companions in the jail at Perugia deemed him insane and demented.
76.   H. S. Bennett, *The Pastons and their England* (Cambridge, 1922), pp. 78-9.
77.   NV, I, i, p. 285; ibid., II, pp. 230-1.
78.   M. de la Bedoyère, *Francis: A Biography of the Saint of Assisi* (London, 1962), p. 65.
79.   2 C, n. 12; 1 C, n. 13.
80.   NV, I, i, p. 288.
81.   Rigaldina, c. 3, nn. 2, 8, pp. 514-15, 518-19.
82.   2 C, nn. 80-81.
83.   M. Robson, 'Saint Anselm and his father, Gundulf', *Historical Research: The Bulletin of the Institute of Historical Research*, 69 (1996), pp. 197-200.

2

Bishop Guido II of Assisi

Frequently Francis used to go to the bishop of Assisi for advice[1]

In search of the freedom to follow the Gospel in a more satisfactory manner Francis chose a path which brought him into collision with his family's plans that he should be groomed as a successful merchant. The dispute with his father led him into closer contact with a very unlikely ally, the wealthy and litigious bishop of Assisi, Guido II, who played a central role in the evolution of the fraternity. Guido emerged as a prelate supportive of a young man with the highest spiritual aspirations and his contribution has not always received sufficient acknowledgement from historians. Moreover, he was a paternal figure, offering guidance and encouragement to Francis. As bishop of Assisi he was the visible representative of an ancient and venerable tradition, which was recognized and respected by Francis, Clare and their first followers. Guido arrived in Assisi in the aftermath of the civil war, and the early years of his episcopate were marked by further plans for building in the cathedral. In 1212 he presided over the discovery of San Rufino's bones and their translation and this recovery of the martyr's bones was accompanied by further miracles, recorded in full by Guido.

Guido witnessed the early manifestations of Francis's vocation and lived to see, and probably participate in, the ceremonies of his canonization in Assisi on 16 July 1228. He died two weeks after his friend was formally raised to the altar of the saints. He was a unique witness to the origins of the Franciscan order and a key figure in its earliest years. He was one of the few people whom Francis consulted about his wish to live in the manner of Jesus Christ and the apostles. His first public intervention was in the dispute between Francis and his father and afterwards he arranged for Francis to return to San Damiano, which he subsequently placed at the disposal of Clare and Agnes, her sister. A more positive view of the relations between the bishop and the saint is replacing P. Sabatier's belief that Guido played a somewhat negative role in the evolution and development of Francis's vocation.[2] For instance, J. M. Powell treats Guido as a strong supporter of Francis's work.[3] His was a benevolent and practical role in the early years of Francis's vocation and the formation of his fraternity. He acted as a mediator in Assisi when there were some hard feelings about the friars' practice of seeking alms. Another contribution, this time in Rome, was decisive because he introduced Francis to a reforming cardinal, John of St Paul. The cardinal held a series of interviews with Francis and then steered the fraternity through some curial opposition and obtained papal approbation. Guido was a witness to at least two of Francis's miracles and his involvement in the origins of the Poor Clares was equally significant. In the early days of the fraternity his support, advice and encouragement were crucial. Francis himself regarded Guido as the divine mouthpiece and cited this as a reason for his deep respect for the members of the hierarchy.

EPISCOPAL APPEAL AND FRANCIS'S RENUNCIATION

An exasperated Peter Bernardone was reduced to approaching the civic authorities in order to bring his son to heel. His demand for full restitution carried sufficient weight for action to be taken. Enquiries were made and a summons was delivered to Francis, who flatly rejected it on the grounds that he was no longer under the jurisdiction of the civil authorities. When the messenger returned to the city with news of his meeting with Francis, the consuls did not wish to proceed further and acknowledged the validity of the new claim. Peter was advised that, because his son had already entered ecclesiastical service, he was no longer subject to their jurisdiction. No further satisfaction was to be had from the civic authorities and so Peter made the short journey to the *vescovado*, the episcopal residence, where he laid his accusation before Guido. Indeed, his knowledge of the prelate encouraged him to take an optimistic view of his chances of success; he was inclined to believe that Guido would be very much in sympathy with a businessman whose assets had been squandered in this manner. Mockler argues that Guido was much of a muchness as far as character went with Peter. If Francis chose him as a father-substitute, it was not for his personal qualities but for his position.[4] It is, however, equally feasible to believe that there was also a much more positive dimension to the character of Guido, who may already have held some communications with Francis. The decision to have the case referred to the bishop ensured that the complaints would be examined in the presence of one of the most powerful figures in the city, a man whose decision would bind both father and son. The exchanges between father and bishop were not recorded, though the former must have spent sufficient time at the episcopal curia to give his version of the events. Trexler believes that Peter's indignation may have arisen from a consciousness that Francis's resolve to turn his back on society meant that the Bernardone name and estate would end with him.[5]

Francis's response

There was no doubt that Francis was now in the service of the Church and lived in a place subject to the bishop. Imperial diplomas and papal bulls issued in the previous two centuries spoke clearly on the matter. The bull of Innocent III (1198-1216) issued nine years earlier forbade anyone to cite a priest or any person resident on episcopal lands without the ordinary's consent: the penalty for violation was excommunication.[6] This case provided Guido with an opportunity to assert himself against the growing pretensions of the commune. In the biographies there is a contrast between the speed with which Peter sought legal redress and the promptness and confidence with which Francis agreed to go before the bishop. He now confidently cast himself upon the Church, a more appropriate arbiter of evangelical aspirations than Peter. Francis accepted the summons to present himself before the bishop. In somewhat conventional hagiographical language the *Legenda trium sociorum* records that Francis willingly consented, because he regarded the bishop as the father and lord of souls. His agreement to have the dispute settled in the bishop's presence may have arisen from both his new ecclesiastical status and the basis of his own informal consultations with Guido in the period preceding his public clash with his father. The early biographers do not indicate whether there was a private meeting between Guido and Francis before the public hearing.

Despite the excesses in his defence of his rights and privileges, Guido, as the vicar of San Rufino, was the custodian of Christian ideals within the city. While the biographers proclaim that he received Francis joyfully, the bishop was not disposed to draw a veil over his failings. The charge brought by Peter was a serious one and an appropriate response was required. The nature of the hagiographical evidence is such that there is no indication of compunction on Francis's part, no feeling that he had acted badly or sadness that his dispute with his father was escalating by the hour. The received, but inadequate, portrait is of a young man who was being hounded by his merciless father. Thomas of Celano implies, however, that there was a certain sympathy between the young man and the pastor and he granted Guido's words an objectivity which was generally denied to Peter. As the defender of Christian ideals, Guido castigated Francis for conduct which had greatly disturbed and scandalized his father. In addition, Francis was left in no doubt that any plan to serve God should have a better beginning: the Church should not benefit from stolen goods and the money which Francis had earmarked for the restoration of San Damiano should be returned to its rightful owner. In short, the idealistic Francis was rebuked by the bishop for behaviour which brought no credit upon him or the Church.

The *Munich Legend* reports that Francis went to the bishop because he was unsure about his right to dispose of the money which he had received at Foligno. In this account Francis had sold his goods with the intention of applying some of the money for the restoration of the church and giving the rest to the poor. When Peter tried to seize the money from him, Francis carefully considered how he might get rid of it licitly. Accordingly he approached Guido and resigned both his money and his clothes; there is no indication that Peter was present. Francis gave the money to the bishop because he was unsure what to do with it.[7] Trexler interprets this later text as an indication that Guido informed Francis that these goods had been obtained illegally, drawing attention to the more complex notion of restitution prevailing at that time. Some theologians and canonists were in fact discouraging ecclesiastics who came into possession of such uncertain usury from using it for church building. If anything, they favoured a distribution to the poor as an alternative and Guido's judgement fits into this constellation of disputed legal questions concerning restitution. From these few words in the sources about illicitly gained goods also sprang the question of whether Francis had sinned in having possession of such goods.[8]

The *Vita secunda* discloses that Francis acted on Guido's command and implies that he immediately returned the money to his father and the *Vita prima* reports that Francis did not delay, acting immediately. Had Francis planned this gesture or was it purely spontaneous? The event certainly caught the attention of those present. With the benefit of hindsight Thomas of Celano believes that Francis's enthusiasm and fervour moved Guido, who arose to cover his nakedness. The bishop was credited with the insight that this gesture was deeply significant and, even though he did not fully comprehend what was happening, he pledged himself to give Francis as much assistance as he could. Francis, by turning his back on his father, acted on the advice imparted to the rich young man and embarked upon a life of fidelity to the Gospel. While Bernard of Quintavalle, Giles and Clare of Assisi could all point to moments at which they publicly renounced their former way of life, this was not the case for Francis. Perhaps for this reason his biographers seized on the events before the episcopal tribunal and converted them into the symbol of his transition from the norms of society to those of the Gospel. While the events at the fair in Foligno serve as a signpost to Francis's future intentions, the scene enacted before Guido marked the public beginnings of Francis's resolve to commit himself to the Gospel.

The biographies of the later thirteenth century emphasize Francis's absolute confidence in God and his indifference to any punishment from his father. For instance, Bonaventure, anticipating later decisions by the saint, speaks of him as one driven by genuine love for poverty and observes that he was more than ready to comply with his father's request. When he had divested himself of his fine clothes, he was found to be wearing a hair shirt, the badge of asceticism which Thomas of Celano had not mentioned. Bonaventure's additional information tends to mar the gesture of Francis returning all his clothes to his father. Indeed, the earlier biographies paint so unattractive a picture of Peter that the merchant would hardly have known what a hair shirt was, never mind any hint that he had supplied his wayward son with one. This display of piety, continues Bonaventure, led Guido to embrace Francis, perhaps denoting the Church's blessing upon him. This section of the *Legenda maior* concludes with the reflection that Francis, now the servant of the most high king, stripped himself of all that belonged to him in order to follow the Lord whom he loved. By returning his clothes to his father he sought to identify himself with his divine master who became poor and naked on the cross for the redemption of the human race.

Guido commanded his servants to bring some old garments. Francis received an old tunic which belonged to one of the bishop's farm hands and this was gratefully accepted. This event assumed a mystical significance in Bonaventure, who implies that the bishop provided Francis with a habit symbolizing his withdrawal from society. A cross was drawn on the garment by Francis who made it a worthy garment for a man who was crucified and a beggar. He stripped off all that belonged to him in order that he might follow Jesus Christ, who hung naked upon the cross. He was armed with the cross, the means of salvation which would enable him to escape from the shipwreck of the world.[9] The event may be viewed in terms of Francis's adoption of a new form of life and his espousal of Lady Poverty with the bishop there in his capacity to bless and sustain.

The significance of Francis's decision

In the hagiographical tradition saints are depicted as the embodiment of fidelity to the Gospel. Following the dream about arms, Francis had begun to spend a growing amount of time in solitude, addressing his divine father in prayer and bewailing aspects of his earlier behaviour. His decision to turn his back upon a comfortable, possibly lucrative, future as a cloth merchant in Assisi consigned him to an uncertain future in which he proposed to follow his own vocation, though he seems to have had little idea where that would lead. Thomas of Celano establishes a causal connection between Francis's renunciation of his father's authority and his freedom to become a servant of God, restoring the three churches and preparing the way for his hearing the Gospel at the Portiuncula. Thus, the act of removing his clothes and handing them over to his startled father denoted a break with his former way of life and his relationship with commercial society in Assisi. His fine clothes were discarded and he began to rise above the social divisions of society, exemplified by his grateful acceptance of the tunic of a farm hand. The fundamental change in Francis's life was mirrored by his clothing: fine clothes were returned to Peter and Francis received the tunic of a farm hand, a foretaste of the poverty which he would embrace more fully at a later date.

There are several instances of the motif of nudity in the biographies of Francis, whose appearance before the bishop provides one of the most famous examples.

By casting off his clothes Francis proclaimed the renunciation of his birthright and all claim to paternal support. His nakedness primarily associated him with the imitation of Christ, whose mode of redemption was being considered more closely by Francis as a symbol of self-emptying. He was considering how best he might enter more deeply into the redemptive process, meditating upon the poverty of the incarnation and the cross, regardless of the conventions of society. In addition, he had turned his back upon the quest for wealth and security and his nakedness at the episcopal tribunal signified his new vulnerability and uncertainty. Scenes of nudity accompany instances in which he reaffirmed his resolve to walk with Christ and to reject whatever was contrary to the Gospel. They also point to the poverty which he would voluntarily embrace. Francis believed that the Son of God had chosen a life of poverty and he felt impelled to do the same.

The process of Francis's conversion had a decidedly scriptural character and the divinely inspired Word of the Bible provided him with his key to the future; this immense reverence for the Scriptures remained with him until the last moments of his life. Accordingly, his conversion was seen as a fulfilment of a petition in the Lord's Prayer whereby he announced that henceforth he could freely call God his father in heaven (Matthew 6:9), instead of Peter Bernardone, whom he had hitherto recognized as his father. Francis proclaimed that hereafter he would take direction from the highest authority, his celestial father. This was a confession that God was the source of all authentic life and that everything else was subordinate. Francis had concluded that subjection to Peter was undermining his wish to live according to the Gospel. In contrast, his absolute dependence upon his divine father was manifested in his renunciation of his birthright and in a deeply symbolic gesture he returned both his money and his clothes to his father. The act proclaimed his confidence in the divine providence which Jesus Christ had revealed in the Gospels. The scene was also the fulfilment of the dominical precepts to call no one father but God and to leave everything in order to follow the Son of God.

Francis is described as trampling worldly things under his foot.[10] The scene enacted before the bishop was Francis's passage from his father's jurisdiction to that of the Church. The image denotes a fundamental break with the past and the desire to identify with the crucified Christ and teems with baptismal symbolism. Mindful of that nakedness on the cross, Thomas of Celano invokes the authority of Gregory the Great, who speaks of the faithful Christian wrestling nakedly with his naked adversary, and having cast aside everything that is of this world, to think only about the things of the Lord.[11] In this classical act of renunciation Francis was shown to be rising above even the strongest ties of blood. He underwent a test for his divine teacher and abandoned himself to divine providence.

Artistic images of episcopal protection

The hagiographical tradition of the act of renunciation is supplemented by celebrated works of art in Franciscan churches. One of the 20 scenes from Francis's life painted by Barone Berlinghieri in the Bardi chapel at Santa Croce in Florence shows Francis standing beside Guido as he returned his clothes to both Peter and Pica. This picture lacks some of the passion and anger which were introduced into the school associated with Giotto. By the end of the thirteenth century Francis's act of renunciation served as a major event in his life and relations with his family were subjected to the same level of exaggeration, which mars the dependability of the hagiographical evidence. As Pica withdrew from the scene, some of the more celebrated artistic depictions dwell upon the tension between father and son. Peter was presented as one devoured by a disfiguring anger. The Giotto school's renunciation in the chapel at Santa Croce was much more confrontational. An enraged Peter was being restrained by friends and neighbours as he bore down upon his virtuous son, who was being protected by the bishop. In the cycle of frescoes in the upper basilica of San Francesco in Assisi the saint, whose nakedness was covered by the episcopal mantle, responds to a hand protruding from the skies. The fresco captures the way in which Francis bows to and collaborates with the divine will, an event which became a paradigm for the process which leads Francis into the service of his divine master. A wrathful Peter menaces his fearful-looking son in the painting by Sassetta for the church of San Francesco in Borgo San Sepolcro. Peter strains to lay hands on his son. The primary aim of these artists was to portray the conversion of the saint and to underline the radical nature of the decision which enabled him to become one of the most celebrated saints in the western Church.

The artistic accounts of the dramatic dispute between Francis and his father accord a more central role to Guido. The episcopal mantle, which was draped around Francis, has become a symbol of the sympathy and protection which were extended to the saint. Peter emerged as a man driven by a love of material pleasures, the personification of the greed which marred the activities of the market place. His own success in trade and his frustrated ambitions for his son combined to undermine the paternal bond with his son. While Peter was presented as a man wanting in paternal affection and guidance, Guido filled that vacuum admirably, providing Francis with correction, encouragement and guidance at a crucial stage in his life. Although the bishop was somewhat belligerent in the defence of his rights, he was also instrumental in one of the greatest experiments in Christian living in the Middle Ages and two people from his cathedral city were formally canonized. A. Fortini notes that in that hour of great decisions Guido was touched by Francis's ardent appeal and answered it with a magnificent gesture, one that remains as a symbol of the authenticity of his priestly calling. The greatest glory in the varied and stormy lives of the bishops of

Assisi was Guido's act.[12] Francis's confidence in Guido's advice and direction was rooted in the role which bishops played in the life of their dioceses. Whatever his own shortcomings, Guido exercised an authority which stretched back to San Rufino and the other martyred bishops of Assisi. He represented a tradition which was always more powerful than his own flaws and failings. This was a crucial element in Francis's own perception of his dealings with the bishop of Assisi.

GUIDO AS THE VICAR OF SAN RUFINO AND PATRON SAINTS OF ASSISI

Until recently three huge statues stood behind the high altar of the cathedral of San Rufino in Assisi. Rufino, the principal patron of the diocese, towered above Francis and Clare, who were placed on lower plinths to left and right. This arrangement symbolized the relationship between the origins of Christianity in the city and its medieval flowering in the mendicant movement. Francis, who was nurtured on the legends of the heroic martyrs of Assisi, would have recognized the appropriateness of the eminent position accorded to the first bishop and martyr of Assisi, thereby locating himself within the Christian traditions of his native city. The bishops of medieval Assisi were identified with the origins of Christianity in the city and associated themselves with their martyred predecessors. They signed themselves as the vicars of the martyred bishops such as Rufino, Vittorino and Savino, who had established and consolidated Christianity in the ancient Umbrian city. They regarded themselves as the custodians of the spiritual and temporal patrimony of the diocese and invoked the martyrs' authority.

Guido's role in the life of the fledgling Franciscan fraternity was initially rooted in the medieval understanding of the bishop's responsibility and authority, although the friars later came to regard him as a strongly supportive figure. The relationship between the bishop and the patron saint of his church was very complex, although it is not entirely foreign to the contemporary outlook, which attaches more power and influence to the office rather than the person who happens to be occupying it in a particular period. The prelate saw himself as answerable to God and the saint for the administration of his diocese. His responsibility towards the celestial patron was acutely felt, because he was required to conserve—and, where appropriate, enlarge—the patrimony of the saint. The imperative need to preserve intact the property, privileges and rights of a church or abbey caused much friction in the Middle Ages and provides the background to the protracted dispute about the primacy between the dioceses of Canterbury and York.

P. Brown explains that the prelate enters into his role as the visible patron beneath the invisible patron[13] and that between the third and sixth centuries in western Europe the power of the bishop tended to coalesce with the power of the shrine.[14] The shrine provided a localized presence where the saint exercised authority in the working of miracles. Peter Damian comments that places blessed by the possession of saints' relics are bits of heaven on earth.[15] The connection between the saint and the shrine was so close that medieval men and women spoke of going to visit the saint; this terminology appeared in early Franciscan hagiography. Bernard and Giles set out towards St James, that is, the shrine at Compostela.[16] In Assisi the majority of the miracles described by Peter Damian took place at San Rufino's tomb.[17]

One expression of the bond between the saint and the prelate was the title of vicar or substitute. Bernard of Clairvaux describes Innocent II as the successor of St Peter who would judge Peter Abelard for impugning the faith of Peter; the pope was exhorted to do no less than the great bishops, his predecessors, to eradicate heresy.[18] In Assisi, Bishop Ugone (1038-52) showed himself to be aware of the links between the origins of Christianity in the city and his own office. He was fired with zeal to promote a renewal of devotion to San Rufino and loved to sign himself Ugone, bishop and vicar of San Rufino.[19] The dealings between Innocent III and Francis were characterized by Bonaventure as the successor of the apostle Peter speaking to the poor of Christ.[20] Similar formulae were widely used in Assisi and elsewhere in the thirteenth century and survive to this day. When John Paul II celebrated the sacrament of confirmation in Liverpool Cathedral in the summer of 1982, Derek Worlock, the city's archbishop, articulated the medieval understanding by proudly proclaiming that St Peter had confirmed in Liverpool.

M. Chibnall points out that there was always a specially close relationship between the abbey and its patron saint or saints and charters recorded grants as gifts to the saints as much as to the monastery.[21] The responsibility borne by the bishop was felt as much in Assisi as elsewhere in medieval Europe. The relationship between the patron saint of a church and his vicar can be seen in St Anselm's prayer written for a bishop or an abbot to the unnamed patron saint of his church. The prayer expresses the source of authority and the nature of the relationship between the patron saint and the vicar entrusted with it:

> For I have undertaken to rule the church of God under you, ... So holy, blessed and good N, recognize me as in some kind of way your deputy, and always go before me with your counsel, and follow me with your help, ruling me, and the flock committed to me. For they are committed more to you than to me, and those who are committed to me are not taken away from you, but I am the more greatly committed to you. So what is enjoined upon me about them do you perform for me and for them. Do on my behalf what is enjoined upon me to do in your place.

The prelate was thus assured that God and the patron saint had ordered or permitted his appointment to the pastoral office. The saint was recognized as possessing more influence, knowledge and power than his vicar and he acted as the prelate's advocate.[22] This tradition was known to Thomas of Celano, who attributed to Francis an understanding of the spirit which informed the Anselmian prayer. In similar language, Francis styled himself as a little man and as the shepherd of the flock entrusted to him by God, the principal patron.[23] After his death the friars rapidly turned to him as the primary source of authority in the Franciscan cosmos, especially when it came to the vigorous defence of Lady Poverty.[24] John Pecham refers to the first patrons of the mendicant movement, the *primi patroni*.[25] This served as one of the most powerful assumptions of early Franciscan hagiography.

The recovery of the saint's relics was interpreted by the bishop as a mark of divine favour. The location of the bodies of the martyrs Protasius and Gervasius was revealed in a vision. Ambrose, bishop of Milan, comments on the particular favour bestowed upon him in his finding the martyrs' bodies.[26] Between late 1006 and early 1008 Fulbert of Chartres, bishop of Chartres, congratulated Leothericus, archbishop of Sens, on discovering holy relics; he thanked God for having chosen to reveal them in the latter's episcopate.[27] The rediscovery of San Rufino's body in 1212 was undoubtedly interpreted as a special mark of divine favour upon Guido, whose authority received a further fillip. While the early biographies of Francis make no mention of the first martyrs of Assisi, A. Fortini asserts that Francis used to go to the cathedral of San Rufino to offer his votive candle on the eve of the feast day.[28] The legend of San Savino was well known in Assisi in Francis's day and Fortini maintains that it was impossible to think that Francis, girding himself for a future that would depend upon his sword, would have neglected to follow this pious custom. He would certainly have invoked the protection of the martyr whom Assisi considered one of its principal protectors.[29]

Two passages in Thomas of Celano demonstrate that Francis's respect for the saints' relics and his admiration of the martyrs were deeply ingrained. First, attention was drawn to Francis's profound respect for the saints' relics, which probably sprang from his participation in the local cults of Assisi. During the transitional phase in his life Francis went on pilgrimage to the tomb of St Peter and one of the first things that he did, on receiving papal approval of the fraternity, was to return there to express his gratitude. Secondly, he had conceived a strong desire for martyrdom. He was burning intensely with the desire for holy martyrdom and wanted to set out for Syria about 1211; he made two further attempts to win the crown of martyrdom and taught the friars that they should always desire it.[30] Moreover, the more important saints in Francis's local and international cosmos were martyrs, from the martyred bishops of his native city to New Testament figures such as John the Baptist and St Peter, the prince of apostles. Such admiration for these figures was undoubtedly intensified by the fact that martyrdom was such a cherished ideal and was regarded as the most complete form of self-identification with Christ. His reverence was stimulated by the accounts of the contemporary martyrs who died in defence of the Holy Land. This ideal stirred figures like Francis, Clare and Anthony to seek martyrdom.

GUIDO'S DEFENCE OF HIS EPISCOPAL HERITAGE

Guido's responsibilities towards San Rufino and the other martyred bishops of the city were clear: he was entrusted with the saint's spiritual and temporal heritage and any erosion of the rights and privileges of his diocese would be to his immense discredit. To the best of his ability the conscientious prelate resisted such efforts. Respect for the ecclesiastical order was a normal ingredient in medieval hagiography, which was written for purposes of edification. Saints were model Christians and their lives were composed to foster a more conscious imitation of Jesus Christ within the Church; anything which smacked of subversion would have been rigorously excised. These communities were guided by bishops, who represented the patron saint of the church and commanded obedience. While various heretical movements threatened to subvert the role of the hierarchy, Francis was shown to be appropriately deferential to the pope, bishops and priests. Nonetheless, he did urge priests to behave in accordance with the immense dignity which was entrusted to them, particularly in their celebration of the Eucharist. Franciscan hagiography refers to the bishop of Assisi in a complimentary manner, especially because he was so instrumental in obtaining papal approval for the fraternity and had opened the pulpits of the city to its most famous son. These instincts were reinforced by the fact that the *Vita prima* was commissioned by the pope and by an awareness of the debt of gratitude which Francis and the first friars owed to Guido, without whose support the fraternity would not have gained initial papal backing.

When Guido II was appointed to the ancient see of Assisi, the diocese was then immediately subject to the papacy. S. J. P. Van Dijk and J. H. Walker portray him as one of the pope's close friends,[31] though no documentary evidence was cited in support of this intriguing claim. The early biographies pay little attention to the bishop of Assisi and focus on the spectacular growth of the order throughout Italy and thence to the rest of Christendom; the bishop's appearances were no more than occasional. The biographers painted on a larger canvas, recording the workings of God's grace in the life of Francis and his followers. Their commission was not interpreted in terms of recording each detail of the saint's conversion. Despite the biographers' respectful attitude towards Guido, his influence was broader and more decisive. Nonetheless, he, the vicar of San Rufino and the other martyred bishops of Assisi, was normally described in constructive terms: discreet and wise, the father and lord of souls;[32] a pious man;[33] and a pious and good man.[34] The early biographies do not concern themselves with the more bellicose and litigious side of Guido's personality manifested in his dispute with the *podestà*.

Despite the biographers' complimentary remarks about Guido, medieval bishops were expected to safeguard their heritage. The papal registers confirm that Guido was very active in this regard, even to the point of excesses or the breach of episcopal etiquette. From time to time the popes had occasion to bring Guido to book for various excesses. Such selective use of the materials shows that the biographers were not always very thorough and reliable in their report of the various details of Francis's conversion; their omissions were judicious and almost as interesting as the material which they included. It would have been very difficult for the first biographer to present the bishop, as well as Peter Bernardone, in a poor and negative light. Furthermore, Guido was an experienced and influential figure in promoting the cult of Francis.[35] This illustrates the care that should be exercised about a literal interpretation of the hagiographical evidence. There is a significant distinction between the writing of history, with its demands of scrupulous accuracy and impartiality, and hagiography, with its emphasis on grace, miracles and edification.

By the end of the twelfth century the bishop of Assisi was apparently the owner of half the property in the commune. The bull of Innocent III, promulgated on 26 May 1198 and addressed to Bishop Guido I, lists the churches, monasteries, lands and *castelli* which were under episcopal jurisdiction. It confirmed ancient privileges, some of which went back to Paschal II (1099-1118).[36] By the first decade of the thirteenth century the bishop had reached the highest point of his power and wealth; he seems to have been the strongest and richest feudal lord of the whole area. Avid for material goods and thirsty for power, Guido II did not hesitate to fight constantly for his power or for his riches against the magistrates of the commune who did not wish to bend to his will, and against monasteries that rebelled against his authority.[37]

Guido reacted vigorously towards those who challenged his authority, relying more on his imperious and violent temperament than on sanctions of a spiritual nature. His tendency was to attack rather than to be on the defensive. He came into conflict with many of the religious institutions of Assisi and its environs and his episcopate was full of disputes and litigation. Even the gloomy rooms of the leper hospital under the direction of the Crucifer Knights echoed with his shouts, as when in a noisy fight he attacked the clerics over some wine in their possession. The decretals of Honorius III (1216-27) reveal that Guido high-handedly took the wine away from them; and when they protested, he went to the Ospedale di San Salvatore delle Pareti and assaulted them. On 4 May 1224 Honorius wrote to the prior of St Mary in Spoleto about this dispute.[38] On several occasions he had recalled Guido to moderation and to the observance of the norms laid down by the councils. At times he also reproved the prelate for his greed, which had led him to make a scene even around the biers of the deceased over his right to a percentage of the payment for the obsequies. He got into a protracted quarrel with the Benedictine monks of Monte Subasio about his claim to jurisdiction over churches dependent on the monastery and the right to fees from funerals, the part which traditionally belonged to the bishop. A papal letter of 4 March 1217 contained the agreement between the abbey and the bishop after many altercations between the bishop and the abbey's procurators. Litigation was long and violent and there were many harsh arguments as a result of which Honorius took the opportunity to rebuke Guido for his never sated appetite for new income and revenues. A letter of 17 January 1222 from Honorius to Guido refers to the form and composition made between the latter and the monastery regarding offerings.[39] The beginning of the thirteenth century saw a revival of the tensions between the bishop and the canons of San Rufino. On 8 March 1217 there was a papal arbitration of this dispute.[40] Guido's name was no stranger to those employed in copying papal letters to prelates embroiled in litigation with their ecclesiastical neighbours.

A later illustration of Guido's disputes with clerics and civic officials emerges from the account of his dispute with the *podestà*, whom he subsequently excommunicated. The *podestà* retaliated by announcing a boycott of the bishop: the population of the city was ordered to have no commercial dealings with him. Reconciliation was provided by the ailing Francis and his followers. Moved by the canticle which the friars sang, Guido took the *podestà* in his hands, raised him up and confessed his own irascibility, even though his office required him to be humble; he asked the *podestà* to make allowances for him. They embraced and kissed each other with much graciousness and affection.[41]

BENEVOLENT EPISCOPAL INTERVENTION

Guido's vigilant defence of the rights, privileges and estates of the bishopric of Assisi identify him more with Peter Bernardone than with the evangelical ideals which so revolutionized the life of the young Francis. The rich and stubborn bishop was not at first sight likely to provide a young visionary with protection, sympathy and salutary advice. One of the ironies of Francis's life is the unexpected and crucial partnership which he struck with Guido. The two men were of vastly different backgrounds and this may have been a vital ingredient in their partnership, which was to blossom into friendship. While Guido's temper and violence did not recommend him to Francis, he did, however, stand in a venerable tradition which the saint understood very clearly. He occupied the place of the martyred bishop and presided over the diocese from San Rufino's tomb in the cathedral, exercising the martyr's spiritual authority within the city and diocese. In obedience to God and the patron saint, Guido was acutely aware of his own responsibility to promote higher standards of Christian observance. Whatever his personal blemishes, Guido was perceived as acting in the place of San Rufino. This was undeniably a pivotal factor in Francis's view of the episcopal office and he could not have considered any serious attempt to live in a

Christian manner without reference to the man whose office bound him so closely to the origins of Christianity in the cherished city of his birth.

Although early Franciscan hagiography glosses over the bishop's faults, it refers briefly to his qualities and that may be more than an ecclesiastical convention. Too little attention has been paid to the reforming instincts of Guido. He was a privileged witness to the aspirations of both Francis and Clare, but was undoubtedly just as foxed by some of Francis's plans as were other people. Such puzzlement does not turn him into a figure bereft of sympathy for Francis. No obstacles were placed in the path of the young man and, on the contrary, Guido gave Francis practical assistance, anticipating objections to come from less positive quarters, and steady support. Indeed, at a later stage, his benign interventions were absolutely vital for the fraternity's survival and development, as will be demonstrated by his role in the friars' visit to the papal court.

Even though the period of Guido's appointment to the diocese of Assisi coincided with a deterioration in the youthful Francis's health, he had undoubtedly attended Masses celebrated by the new bishop. In turn Guido had heard the talk about the merchant's son, who, despite poor health, still nurtured the ambition of becoming a celebrated knight. It was a matter of some discussion in the city that Francis had quite suddenly discarded his dream of becoming a famous knight and, instead, begun to haunt churches and show a heightened concern for the poor; such news may have reached the ears of the new bishop. Later reports of the transitional phase in Francis's life may have evoked some detached sympathy from Guido. Although Pica released Francis from his domestic imprisonment, the early biographies do not suggest that she recognized the forces which were at work in her son. With the exception of the unnamed friend who accompanied him to the places of prayer in the countryside, his other friends fell away. At a time when few seem to have comprehended what was driving Francis, understanding came from Guido. There is enough evidence to believe that Francis consulted Guido in the early period of his own vocation and in the formation of his fraternity. Guido had paved the way for Francis's return to San Damiano and gave him a message to the priest there.[42] During the formative period of his vocation Francis confided in him and, after his return from Rome, the only person whose advice he sometimes sought was Guido.[43]

Sabatier believes that Francis opened his mind to the bishop, who understood no more than others his vague and incoherent plans, filled with ideas impossible to realize and possibly subversive.[44] While Guido may not have grasped Francis's plans, this should not be interpreted as a sign of indifference, especially because the plans were not exactly clear to Francis. A more constructive view was taken by J. R. H. Moorman, who maintains that during the transitional phase in Francis's life the bishop was one of those who showed him some sympathy.[45] Francis was a visionary who possessed the insight to see to the heart of some questions, such as the inequalities which money created and sustained within society. However, some situations exposed him as a man with little flair for organization and on more than one occasion he acted in an impulsive manner. There was little thought given to how he might get back from Foligno, where he sold both the cloth and his horse, or what his next move would be. The priest's refusal to receive the proceeds of the sale at Foligno for the restoration of San Damiano seems to have left Francis puzzled and his courage failed him when his father hastened to San Damiano. In this early period he seems to have found a practical guide in Guido, who gave him advice and protection on several occasions.

L. Bracaloni speculates on the role played by the priest of San Damiano in the events leading up to the hearing before the bishop. The priest may have advised Francis about how to avoid trial in the secular court and in the interim he may have provided Guido with a strong testimonial on Francis's behalf or arranged for him to meet the bishop.[46] This attractive hypothesis offers one explanation for the positive position taken by Guido in the dispute between father and son. It is highly unlikely that the bishop behaved in a spontaneous manner without first familiarizing himself with the young man's background and aspirations, though he may have known Francis and his father already. It is conceivable that there may have been one or more meetings between Francis and Guido. The bishop was gradually convinced that, despite the dishonest use of his father's goods, Francis was struggling to respond to a new vocation and was not a fanatical figure.

Moorman notes that on the whole Guido appears as a wise and sympathetic father in God, with a real concern for this original and unconventional young man and a genuine desire to understand his idiosyncrasies and help him to fulfil his vocation whatever that might be.[47] Guido's role was also that of the person who enabled Francis to pass from subjection to his father to collaboration in the work of evangelization. The biographies project an image of authentic paternity: Peter had provided one form of fatherhood, whose limitations Thomas of Celano had clinically exposed; Peter's values had set Francis on a path that was liable to lead him away from union with his divine father. The incidents at San Damiano and the settlement of the dispute before the bishop confirm this impression, as Peter was seen to act without understanding and tolerance. Instead, he sought the expulsion of his son from the territory. There is sufficient information to show that Guido, the most unlikely of patrons, provided a much greater sympathy and assurance for the young zealot. L. K. Little interprets the scene enacted at the episcopal tribunal as a sign of Francis casting aside all the symbols of his social status, rejecting any material form of patrimony. He turned away from his father and took refuge with a new spiritual father; the old Francis had been definitively thrown off,[48] rather like a lifestyle that was publicly discarded. During the hearing of the complaints Peter's obstructiveness and cruelty were contrasted with the spirit of charity and guidance incarnate in Guido, who became Francis's helper. One father was spurned because his counsel was defective and another, who was the father of souls and whose advice was life-giving, was accepted. The latter, of course, prepared the way for the beginning of Francis's life of commitment to the Gospel.

INCIPIENT FRATERNITY

The first manifestations of Francis's new vocation had brought him into conflict with his father and he had been derided as a madman by the citizens, who were appalled by the change which had come over him. New direction was given to Francis by the Gospel which he heard during Mass at the Portiuncula on 24 February 1208; this will be more fully explored in the fourth chapter. The biographies show that this mandate to preach took Francis back into the city of Assisi, which then became the focus of his apostolate. The imperative contained in the Gospel was such that he felt obliged to discontinue his life as a hermit living in retreat outside Assisi and compelled to re-enter the city with a clarion call to repent and believe in the Gospel. This unexpected development paid immediate dividends. Francis's proclamation of the Gospel brought him new respect in Assisi, planted the seeds of the fraternity and the magnetic appeal of his earlier years returned with a new focus, the imitation of Jesus Christ. His first biographer tried to explain this by reporting that he seemed completely different from what he had been and the new element was attractive to young men in search of a programme for life. The combination of his preaching and his lifestyle served as a recruiting sergeant in Assisi. There is no evidence that Francis even considered the possibility of having companions or recruits, because in the early days aspirants sought him out for advice and asked to be admitted as his pupils. Fervour and joy marked his call to repentance and he preached with telling effect: his words were like a burning fire, penetrating the inmost reaches of the heart, filling the minds of his hearers with admiration. His sermons in war-torn Assisi began with a prayer for peace and a peaceful greeting was extended to those whom he met on the roads and lanes of the city and its environs. The result of his preaching was that many former enemies were reconciled and this ministry presages his talents as an instrument of reconciliation both in Assisi and beyond. The powerful persuasion of Francis's words made a profound impression upon the people of Assisi. No longer do the biographers speak of the abuse which had been heaped upon him. The tide had turned and thenceforth the early biographers set about charting the phenomenal growth of the fraternity. Francis was cast in the role of the master at the head of the first school of the friars which abounded in purity and disputed in the school of humility in which they became accustomed to sacrifice and hardship.[49] Within a short time of identifying his own vocation, he accepted the direction of a small band of zealous followers who were excited by his message and insights.

The *Vita prima* looks back upon the life of the founder of a rapidly expanding fraternity which was spreading into all parts of Europe and the Holy Land and with various missions to Muslim territory. The author speaks confidently about Francis as one who became the religious guide to a vast body of men. He seems to have had no doubt and the founder's wishes were exemplified by the prophecy that the order would grow, though in the *Vita secunda* the question of expansion was viewed as a mixed blessing, capable of jeopardizing the friars' simplicity and poverty. The question of whether Francis set out to establish a fraternity has been debated by Franciscan scholars. Part of the difficulty lies in the fact that his teaching, which could be implemented on 'a personal level', was not easy to 'institutionalize', as the history of the fraternity so ably demonstrates. The decision to accept companions and to become their mentor was a crucial one with wide-ranging implications for the history of the order. The biographers do not record any reluctance by Francis to accept the first recruits, although Leo and companions record his later misgivings at the growth of the fraternity in the 1220s.

Assisi provided the fraternity with its beginnings, its first recruits and also one its first challenges. While the friars' acts of renunciation caused admiration, the community's practice of begging for alms created a crisis in which Francis consulted Guido once more. As the number of friars was augmented there was a dispute about begging in Assisi. We have the accounts of the public renunciation of possessions by Bernard of Quintavalle and Giles of Assisi; the other recruits to the fraternity gave similar demonstrations. Such acts of renunciation drew gasps of admiration in the city, but also sowed the seeds of later discord. When these friars returned to the city seeking alms, there was some resentment and the finer theological points were lost on some citizens of Assisi; the outcome was that the supply of alms came perilously close to drying up. When the friars begged for alms in Assisi, they received very little else than reproaches at having left their own possessions to eat at the expense of others. This reaction caused the friars much suffering and they were persecuted by their friends, relations and the citizens, both rich and poor alike; they were derided as madmen and fools because at that time no one renounced his goods to beg from door to door. Just as Guido had dispensed sound advice at vital moments in the early stages of Francis's conversion, so the latter turned to him once more in the face of teething problems in the nascent fraternity. Francis approached Guido for advice and help to defuse the situation. Even the friars' families and others had begun to heap abuse on them, and the people in the city were reproaching them. Guido, who was presented as an exception to the general resentment towards the friars, discussed the issues with Francis and was satisfied with his reply.[50] While Franciscan hagiography was anxious to emphasize Francis's good relations with Guido, this example reveals that the bishop was not without sensitivity and did not attempt to impose his will on the incipient community; he seems to have been more anxious to assist than to control.

A later version also captures both the insight and the spirit of the reforms pursued by Francis. In their perplexity the friars turned to Guido, who received Francis with kindness. Guido, ever a practical and thoughtful pastor, was one of the first to point out the hazardous nature of the ideal which the friars had espoused; in the following decades that point was made over and over again by those who wished to temper the rigour of the Franciscan ideal. His opinion was that the absolute renunciation of possessions was a path fraught with dangers. He himself was the owner of vast estates whose income sustained him in his episcopal office. His own episcopate, littered with disputes involving local ecclesiastical institutions, illustrated the problems occasioned by wealth and the need to protect and increase it. Despite his admiration for Francis and his followers, he was sufficiently aware of the economy of religious houses and acutely conscious of the need for financial stability. His was a practical point to which Francis replied prudently that, if the friars had any possessions, they would also be forced to have arms to protect them. Francis reflected that possessions were a cause of disputes and strife, which would distract the friars from loving God and their neighbour, and on that account he refused to have possessions.[51] This is another example of the perspicacity of Francis, whose spiritual poverty was envisaged as an antidote to the greed arising from the new commercial life of the cities. Listening to Francis's response, Guido undoubtedly reflected on the discord and bitterness caused by disputes over his own land and income. We see Francis emerging as a perspicacious teacher, who had reflected much on the ills of contemporary society. Poverty was perceived as a way of emancipating himself from the disorders at work within the human community and his convictions were accepted by Guido who made no attempt to impose his own solution on the friars. This response illustrates Guido's patient and respectful attitude towards Francis and his inclination to allow him to develop his own ideals, even if there were many who criticized his solutions.

GUIDO AT THE PAPAL COURT

The earliest version of how the fraternity won papal approval appears in a matter-of-fact way in the *Vita prima*, as though the matter were routine with no hint of any opposition. The biographer writes that, when the fraternity began to increase, Francis wrote a form and Rule of life for his small band of followers, basing it on the texts of the Gospel, and went to Rome in search of papal approbation. The biographer's purpose was to proclaim the founder's sanctity and the birth of the rapidly expanding community of friars. He does not offer a blow-by-blow report of the various stages along the shark-infested waters leading to the approval of the Rule. He reports that Guido happened to be in Rome at this time, though there is no suggestion that he was there on the friars' business. In the life of a saint, however, this cannot have been a purely coincidental encounter; rather his presence there was entirely providential and absolutely crucial in setting in motion a train of events which culminated in papal approval. R. B. Brooke explains that without papal sanction the friars could not have spread widely among the faithful any more than could the other popular religious fraternities that resembled them in composition, poverty and preaching. That they fared differently from these was due to the wisdom and sympathy of Innocent III; for the granting of their request was no matter of course.[52]

The gradual admission of recruits to the fraternity raised the question of its status within the Church. What began as a small band of zealots was beginning to take on some of the trappings of religious life. At an early stage a form of commitment or profession was required of candidates for the fraternity. Did Francis consult Guido about the canonical ramifications of these forms of profession? Moreover, Guido could not be indifferent to the evidence of a new form of religious life in Assisi, however few the friars. The biographers relate that, when the friars eventually attained the biblical figure of twelve, Francis decided to seek the blessing of the vicar of Christ. While some very able and talented men in Assisi had joined the fraternity, the one man in the city who was most familiar with the working of the Curia in Rome was Guido. He would have left Francis in no doubt that the approval of the fraternity would not be a mere formality and that there would be tough questioning. Although Francis was capable of impulsive decisions, it is unimaginable that he did not take soundings from Guido before setting out for Rome, especially because the recent history of the papacy had shown some caution in the face of new religious institutions. An attractive hypothesis is that Francis discussed the matter at some length with Guido whose assistance he enlisted. Moorman points out that, alone in the great city of Rome, this little band of enthusiasts would have had small chance of achieving their purpose had Francis not, at this point, met Guido.[53] The evidence indicates that this prelate's role in the proceedings at Rome was central, even if the early biographers treat his presence there as coincidental.

W. R. Thomson comments that surely the friars soon discovered that access to the pope was not easily obtainable. They came to understand that prestigious friends were needed to improve their chances of success. Every day great prelates in silk and satin and fine robes, wearing velvet capes, entered the papal chambers and came out empty-handed, and everywhere there appeared notaries and procurators, prophesying frustration. He suspects that all this proved somewhat disturbing for Francis. Certainly Guido would have suggested to Francis that it was both opportune and necessary for him to be introduced to an influential member of the pope's inner circle.[54] The key player in this drama was Guido, whose contacts with the papal court set Francis on the right path. Moreover, his own circle may have advised him that the climate for Francis's petition was now more favourable than it would have been a few years earlier. J. E. Sayers relates that rumours must have been abroad of Innocent's dealings with the new religious groups and perhaps of his more liberal attitude.[55] Francis's petition was presented in a form which would have done much to allay any curial fears about its integrity and orthodoxy. It came with the strong endorsement of the diocesan bishop and one of the leading cardinals, who had held a series of conversations with Francis.

Francis's confidence in Guido paid off handsomely in his quest for papal approbation. The exaltation of Francis and the friars was a major theme in the *Vita prima*, which derives some propaganda value from what was presented as a chance meeting in which the bishop was immediately concerned lest the friars were about to leave his diocese. The prelate's admiration and affection for the friars were emphasized, though these would become more necessary than the biographer acknowledged in that context. The *Anonymous of Perugia* and the *Legenda trium sociorum* provide a fuller report than Thomas of Celano. Whatever the antecedents of the meeting in Rome, these three biographies unite in their assertion that Guido gave the friars practical assistance. Episcopal support and advice were freely promised and this took the form of the invaluable introduction which furthered the friars' cause and brought them ultimate success. Guido knew Cardinal John of St Paul, whom Celestine III (1191–98) had wished to have as his successor on the throne of St Peter.[56] This cardinal was a man of holiness and portrayed as dedicated to Christ's poor and inspired by the Holy Spirit. Moreover, he was known to be sympathetic to penitential groups and had a great deal of experience working among heretical groups in southern France.[57] Knowing that this cardinal would be a powerful advocate in the Roman Curia, Guido arranged for Francis to be received.

The *Vita prima*, the *Anonymous of Perugia*, and the *Legenda trium sociorum* testify to the favourable impression which the friars' lifestyle had made upon Guido. He was the one prelate whose advice and support were absolutely essential at so momentous a stage in the life of the fledgling fraternity. At this decisive moment in the history of the western Church everything hinged on Guido's response. His endorsement of the friars' lives and deeds was a condition of papal approval and without it there would have been no further progress. The support and recommendation of the local bishop were all the more important at a time when there was some suspicion within the Roman Curia about the proliferation of poverty movements, some of which found themselves at odds with the papacy, such as the Waldensians. The *Anonymous of Perugia* and the *Legenda trium sociorum* confirm that Guido spoke very favourably about the friars' contribution to the diocese of Assisi, explaining their ideals and persuading the cardinal to receive them. By the end of the discussions the cardinal had been convinced of the friars' qualities and invited them to meet him.

At crucial stages Guido made decisive interventions in Francis's life and there was none more vital than his presence at Rome when the friars arrived. His knowledge of how the Roman Curia operated and his good relations with curial prelates saved the day for Francis and the fraternity. His friendship with Cardinal John of St Paul, a man sympathetic to reform, provided the key to a meeting with Innocent III, before whom Francis was to lay his petition. He was able to assure that cardinal that Francis and his followers were a force for good in the diocese of Assisi and that convinced the cardinal that he should receive them. Were Guido's assistance restricted to this occasion alone, he would have earned for himself a place of affection in the history of the fraternity. But his contribution was much more pervasive.

GUIDO, FRANCIS AND CLARE

Francis's successful visit to the papal court will be explored more fully in the context of his dealings with Innocent III. On his return to Assisi he no doubt held several meetings with Guido, who wished to receive an account of the meetings with the cardinal and the pope. Francis was now authorized to preach repentance and the way in which this was to be accomplished in Assisi was a further matter for discussion. The outcome of these exploratory talks was that Guido made the necessary arrangements with the priests of Assisi for Francis to preach in their churches. These sermons in the city's churches provided the friars with the opportunity to introduce their fervent message to a larger group of men and women in Umbria. Guido's co-operation in throwing open the city's pulpits to Francis and his disciples played no small part in the diffusion of the saint's ideals in Assisi and beyond.

While Francis preached throughout his native Umbria, Assisi was the venue for many of his sermons either in churches or on the piazza. His first sermon was preached in the church of San Giorgio in Assisi, where as a child he had gone to school,[58] another fact which was ripe for the biographers to exploit. In this early period, while the friars were still dwelling at Rivo Torto, Francis delivered a series of Lenten sermons in the cathedral of San Rufino, spending the preceding evening in a garden belonging to the canons.[59] His were no ordinary sermons, but those fortunate to attend heard a man whose every word was supported by prayer and reflection. Moreover, his words carried fire and passion and stirred those present. One of those present at these stirring homilies was the young Clare, who was increasingly drawn to the message of evangelical purity propounded by this charismatic preacher.

Francis was initially the recipient of Guido's advice and practical help, but a friendship developed between the two men and there was a phase of growing collaboration in the years following the oral confirmation of the fraternity.[60] This interpretation is encouraged by the observation that they were accustomed to meet regularly on a friendly and informal basis. Francis's work in restoring churches did not come to a full stop at the Portiuncula. In 1216 he took an active part in the restoration of the old cathedral, Santa Maria Maggiore; a contemporary inscription, which leaves many questions open, identifies him with this renovation. M. Faloci-Pulignani depicts this as the oldest expression of Francis's special affection for the old cathedral and his association with Guido.

While early biographies of Francis reveal little about Guido, there are some suggestions that there was a degree of informality and ease about their meetings, which may have been regular. A miracle story concerning the efficacy of Francis's prayers confirms the development of a friendship between the two men who were accustomed to visit each other. Leo and companions report that Guido called on Francis at the Portiuncula and knocked on his door. When the door opened, he entered the cell. Knowing that Francis held him in friendship and affection, he proceeded unannounced and lifted the flap of the cell to call on him. As soon as he put his head inside, he was forcibly ejected by a spiritual force; the companions add that the bishop was unworthy to see the saint in prayer. He at once left the cell and went outside trembling and acknowledged his fault before the friars. Thomas of Celano adds that Guido was wont to make friendly visits to Francis at the Portiuncula.[61] While both versions reflect the hagiographical hierarchy in which saints were superior to bishops, they offer valuable documentary evidence for the friendship between the two men and indicate that their meetings were not confined to the early period when the saint was very much indebted to the bishop. These visits indicate that, whatever his disputes with the clergy and religious of the diocese, Guido was a prelate with interests in reform. His friendship with Francis lifts the veil on another side of his character. It is to his credit that he played a leading role in enabling Francis to gain papal approval for his fraternity. He was also instrumental in the vocation of another saint, the noble Clare of Assisi.

One of the fruits of Francis's good relations with Guido was the train of events leading up to Clare's profession. In the course of the prolonged and secret conversations which preceded her departure from home it is difficult to imagine that Francis did not turn to Guido for the necessary canonical help and authority, especially because the latter had already proved himself to be such an invaluable ally at the papal court. Had Guido already issued an indult for Francis to receive Clare's profession? It is highly unlikely that there was no canonical preparation for her profession. Furthermore, the early portraits of Francis emphasize his respect for and obedience towards bishops and lead me to think that he proceeded with the appropriate licence. His deepening friendship with Guido would have prevented him from acting unilaterally in this matter. Moreover, he would not have acted in a manner which would bring discredit upon the fraternity, whose own constitutional status was still to be settled; more than a decade was to pass before his Rule was approved by Honorius III on 29 November 1223. It is equally unlikely that Francis would have acted in a manner which might cause Guido some embarrassment. Francis and the friars cannot have proceeded alone in this sensitive venture which concerned Guido's own cathedral parish.

In the absence of such canonical preparations, would not Clare's family have been all the more convinced that they were in the right, and that she was involved in a canonically irregular situation? Because a powerful and well-connected family in the shadow of the cathedral was about to be incensed, the preparations had to be made with close attention to detail. Any canonical defect would have been seized on by Clare's distraught relations and there is no surviving record of a canonical challenge to her profession. The bishops' registers of medieval England contain numerous commissions for those delegated to receive vows of chastity and frequently the names of those making and receiving the vow were supplied. Guido would have had to give the appropriate permissions for the profession of vows.

Guido's involvement in these preparations provides an explanation for the remarkable event which took place during Mass on Palm Sunday when Clare uncharacteristically failed to go forward to receive the newly blessed palm. What was even more amazing was that Guido descended the steps of the altar and, advancing to Clare, presented her with the newly blessed palm.[62] Was this a spontaneous gesture on the part of Guido who was sufficiently conscious that Clare had not advanced to the altar? Might the gesture also be interpreted as a signal that all was set for her departure from home that night? There is some evidence that Guido was being drawn into the triangle. This hypothesis draws some support from his subsequent dealings with Clare and her sisters at San Damiano, where he seems to have collaborated with Francis to some extent.

A. P. Tini suggests that Guido played an active part in paving the way for the emergence of the second order.[63] While he had been unable to provide the first friars with a church,[64] he did place San Damiano at the sisters' disposal. After Clare's temporary sojourn at San Paolo and Sant'Angelo da Panzo she and Agnes were established at San Damiano at Francis's instigation.[65] Francis did not act alone in this matter because the sisters' stay at San Damiano depended upon Guido's consent. In the papal bull of 26 May 1198 San Damiano was not listed among the churches belonging to the bishop. However, documents in the cathedral archives indicate that the church came into the possession of Guido II, who then made it available for Clare and Agnes.[66] Tini describes Guido as the generous donor of this church, expatiating upon the holy friendship which bound the bishop and Francis.[67] Bracaloni refers to Bishop Guido's munificence in this matter.[68]

When Clare's asceticism brought about a deterioration in her health, the sisters at San Damiano eventually looked outside the cloister for assistance, enlisting the support of both Francis and Guido. They intervened and commanded her to eat half a roll on three specified days; the half roll weighed about one and a half ounces.[69] Francis and Guido probably met to consider

Clare's asceticism and her failing health. M. Carney notes that the presence of the bishop in this scene indicates that Clare was probably resisting the advice of Francis and the sisters. Francis clearly felt constrained to bring some higher authority to bear upon the situation; it would appear that such involvement preceded the appointment of Ugolino as cardinal protector. This command illustrates Guido's role in the early organization of the Poor Ladies, which began with the conferral of the palm branch, continued in the donation of San Damiano and expressed itself anew in this intervention to temper Clare's fasting.[70] Clare's needlework contributed to the liturgical life of the diocese, reflecting Francis's own high standards of respect for the Eucharist and everything pertaining to it. During bouts of sickness she had herself raised up in bed so that she could spin and make corporals with the linen, which she then sent to the churches around Assisi. She kept the corporals in cases lined with silk and had them blessed by the bishop.[71] She made more than 50 pairs of corporals[72] and, because she was ill from 1225 onwards,[73] some of them would have been blessed by Guido.

While the oral approval of Innocent III had given the friars some canonical security, the beginnings of the second order were even more fraught with uncertainty and insecurity, particularly prior to the appointment of Cardinal Ugolino. Moorman argues that Francis, perhaps in conjunction with the bishop of Assisi and Cardinal Ugolino, wrote out a form of life for the sisters at San Damiano, deriving some evidence for this hypothesis from the joint action of Francis and Guido in tempering Clare's fasting.[74] Following the death of Francis in 1226, Clare spent the remainder of her life struggling for the preservation of the Franciscan ideal, resisting a series of popes who wished to dilute her conception of absolute poverty. During the period following Francis's death she may have had further meetings with Guido, who had done so much to prepare the ground for the papal blessing of Francis's fraternity and its ideals.

FRANCIS'S RESPECT FOR BISHOPS AND PRIESTS

A salient feature of Francis's life was his profound respect for bishops and priests. While some religious in the twelfth century sought exemption from episcopal jurisdiction, Francis was determined to collaborate with the local bishops and not to work in areas where there was episcopal opposition.[75] The friars complained that sometimes the bishops were reluctant to allow them to preach in their dioceses, keeping them waiting for permission for several days. They suggested to Francis that he might consider petitioning the pope for a privilege. He replied angrily that the friars' humility and reverence should win over the prelates and he regarded the winning display of these virtues as much more useful than privileges to the friars. By abandoning all avarice and persuading the people to pay their dues, the friars would be asked by the clergy to hear their parishioners' confessions.[76] He instructed his disciples that, when the friars were offered land for a foundation, they should first approach the bishop, the father and lord of souls entrusted to him, among whom were the friars. This advice was issued because he believed that the friars' work of winning souls was the better accomplished in collaboration with the bishop and clergy. This profound respect appears to be connected with the beginnings of the saint's own conversion, when he was convinced that God had spoken to him through Guido, who had given him good advice and comforted him:

> at the beginning of my conversion, when I separated myself from the world and from my earthly father, the Lord put his word into the mouth of the bishop of Assisi, so that he advised me well in the service of Christ, and comforted me. Because of this and the many other excellent qualities I perceive in prelates I want to love and revere not only bishops but poor priests and consider them as my lords.[77]

This excerpt has a twofold significance. First, Francis believed that Guido had been the divine mouthpiece at a crucial stage in his own conversion and this would have deepened his respect; he had been firmly reminded of his own lapse from the norms of morality. He had reflected a great deal on the advice given to him by the successor of San Rufino and concluded that the bishop's intervention at various stages had been providential. Secondly, the medieval practice of placing more interest in the patron saint than in the prelate who temporarily filled his office may have been at least partially responsible for Francis's concentration upon the ecclesiastical office rather than the person who exercised it. Moreover, as he reviewed his life Francis may have concluded that in the early days Guido was one of the few who responded to him in a sympathetic manner, offering correction, encouragement, advice and friendship.

Francis's respect for the hierarchy was communicated to his followers, who were instructed not to preach in any diocese contrary to the bishop's wishes. On his death bed he reiterated this counsel, remarking that he would refuse to preach in the parish of the poorest priest without his consent. His practice on entering a city or diocese was to report to the bishop, a practice exemplified by his dealings with Cardinal Ugolino, legate of the Holy See in Tuscany, and the bishop of Imola.[78] At Terni the bishop of the city was present at his homily and at Osimo he was received by the bishop. It was his custom on entering a city or country to go to the bishops or priests.[79] While Thomas of Celano was anxious to draw parallels with the life of Jesus Christ, he reports that when Francis entered a city, the clergy rejoiced. It was common knowledge that Francis was fostering respect for the priests and their office at a time when there was strong criticism of them in other quarters. His intention was that the friars should provide assistance to the bishops and priests rather than competition; it is one of the regrettable aspects of the early history of the fraternity that friars came to be seen as rivals to the parochial clergy. Francis had firmly believed that friars were called to always love, honour and revere members of the hierarchy, especially because their own name required them to be humble in their example and work. The *Vita secunda* focused on the founder's good relations with bishops and demonstrations of his humility towards prelates at a time when some friars were beginning to deviate from the founder's intentions. Francis stayed with the bishop of Marsica and in his sickness he was lodged in the houses of the bishops of Rieti and Assisi.[80]

FRANCIS'S DEATH AND CANONIZATION

Guido was a central player in the plans hatched by the friars and the city's commune for the last days and burial of the *poverello*. He was undoubtedly kept informed of the deterioration in Francis's health. In view of this, he was involved in laying contingency plans for Francis to be nursed in the episcopal palace on his return to Assisi. These preparations were no doubt in place before Guido set out on pilgrimage to the shrine of St Michael in southern Italy.[81] Francis's health may have suffered a rapid deterioration in the period after Guido's departure. Nonetheless, the ailing Francis was lodged in the bishop's palace.

Two friars—Augustine, the minister provincial of Naples, and an unnamed friar of praiseworthy life—were privileged with a vision of the deceased Francis on the night of his death. The third person to whom Francis appeared was Guido, who was returning to Benevento. He greeted Guido as his father (*ecce, pater*), and announced that he was leaving the world and going to Jesus Christ. Guido wept copiously, grieving over the loss of Francis, whom he styled as his distinguished father. The fact that he had come to regard Francis as his father in God underlines the evolving nature of their healthy friendship. On his return to Assisi, he checked the details of Francis's death and then made known the saint's appearance to him.[82] Bonaventure adds that Guido investigated the matter carefully in Assisi and reached the conclusion that the saint had appeared to him at the time of his death.[83] Guido's emotional response to the news of Francis's death is a further indication of the bond of friendship between the two men. In similar fashion on the day of his death Anthony of Padua appeared to his friend, the celebrated Thomas Gallus, abbot of Vercelli.[84] Guido was the only person outside the order known to have received a communication from the saint on the evening of his own death. He returned to Assisi and made the first of his visits to the tomb of his friend in the small church of San Giorgio.

At an early stage miracles occurred at the tomb of Francis. In the excitement generated by the new cult Guido's experience was beneficial because he had presided over the rediscovery of the relics of San Rufino in 1212. This event caused a great deal of excitement in Assisi and even before the revelation there had been reports of miracles in the city: a German pilgrim, named Brocardo, sheltering in the hospital of San Rufino, had badly contracted hands and feet.

When he invoked the aid of the martyr, he was miraculously restored to health. A child in the *contado*, knocked down by an ox cart, escaped death. After the discovery of the relics the miracles could no longer be counted. The truth of the multitude of miracles was attested by Guido and the canons. All the details about the discovery of the bones of San Rufino are included in a 248-page passional of the cathedral, dating from the early part of the fourteenth century, but using material brought forward from an earlier time.[85] The careful documentation of the miracles occurring during the translation of San Rufino reflects the new criteria for the witnessing of miracles laid down in the revision of the process of canonization carried out by Innocent III.[86] For instance, in underlining the truth of the stigmata Thomas of Celano points out that a number of friars who witnessed Francis's wounds gave their evidence under oath.[87]

M. Goodich comments that the first stage in the process of canonization was the receipt by Rome of petitions from leading lay and ecclesiastical figures.[88] A fuller report of the process of postulation was furnished by the first biographer of Anthony of Padua and due attention was given to the role played by the bishop of Padua. Within a month of the death of Anthony of Padua the bishop of that city assumed a leading role in the steps leading to the speedy canonization.[89] No such detail was provided by Francis's early biographers. Just as Guido and the canons were careful to document the authenticated miracles in 1212, so 14 years later the same bishop was able to advise the friars on the importance of recording the details of miracles and recommending Francis to Gregory IX (1227–41). Moreover, on more than one occasion Guido had been an eyewitness to the miracles of Francis. As the miracles began to take place at the tomb in San Giorgio he may also have become an active promoter of the incipient cult and a powerful campaigner for Francis's canonization. As the prelate who had presided over the solemn translation of the relics of San Rufino, his experience was of immense value to the friars. Similarly he must have been prominent in postulating Francis's canonization. In addition, he was greatly aware of the spiritual and material advantages which another popular cult could bestow upon Assisi.

Just as Guido was obviously the principal witness at the papal court to the authenticity of the friars' vocation and helped them to gain the approval of Innocent III, so also his testimony was of the utmost importance in the process leading to the canonization. Despite the fact that the cardinal protector of the order had taken over many of the functions which he had initially shouldered, Guido was a major witness in the proceedings leading to the canonization, particularly given the extent of his knowledge of the saint. In addition to his virtually unrivalled knowledge of Francis and his order from the outset, he had also been personally involved in two miracles. Did his account of the miracle at the Portiuncula and his carefully recorded and verified account of the saint's appearance to him form part of the process of canonization? In enrolling Francis among the saints of the Church on Sunday 16 July 1228, Gregory IX announced that he had sought the advice of prelates. He himself had visited Assisi to pray at Francis's tomb and to discuss the canonization.[90]

Gregory IX also laid the foundation stone of the new basilica; A. Fortini maintains that this ceremony occurred on Monday 17 July 1228, that is, the day after the ceremony of canonization. Some days later the pope blessed the high altar in the cathedral of San Rufino. Thus the last phase in the rebuilding of the cathedral coincided with the beginnings of the new basilica in honour of Francis. The links between the roots of Christianity in Assisi and its medieval flowering in the Franciscan movement were symbolized in the completion of the work on the city's cathedral and the building of the basilica in honour of St Francis. Guido died only two weeks after the ceremonies of the canonization, the laying of the foundation stone of the basilica to be raised in Francis's honour and the consecration of the high altar in the cathedral. His death occurred on 30 July 1228 and his obituary was entered in a missal which was formerly at the church of San Nicola in Assisi, then passed, via Germany, to Baltimore. It is ironical that the missal which Francis and Bernard of Quintavalle consulted should be the one containing the obituary notice of the bishop who had given such vital support to the nascent fraternity.

CONCLUSION

Francis regarded Guido as the custodian of the spiritual authority of the martyred bishops of Assisi. He was conscious that Guido stood in a long line of bishops stretching back to San Rufino himself and his desire to observe the Gospel fully was located within the local community over which the bishop presided. While he did not neatly fit into the ecclesiastical structures of the Middle Ages, he was on good terms with Guido, who was an invaluable helper in the early stages of his religious life. On occasion he consulted Guido, whose gesture in covering him has passed into the history of Christian art. Moreover, Guido paved the way for Francis to return to San Damiano and was consulted by him on the teething troubles with the practice of begging for alms. His knowledge of the Curia paved the way for Francis and the friars to be received by a cardinal whose sympathy for reform was recognized and Cardinal John of St Paul then championed Francis's cause before the cardinals and his ringing endorsement of the friars' conduct was of the utmost importance.

Guido opened the pulpits of the city's churches to Francis, who preached first in San Giorgio and then in the other churches of the city. In the years following the initial approval of the friars' Rule and form of life Guido played a less central role as more powerful figures, like Cardinals John of St Paul and Ugolino, took a greater interest in the guidance of the fraternity. This period saw a friendship developing between the young visionary and the bishop, who had been obliged to rebuke him for his attitude to his father's goods. A miracle story about Francis's prayer reveals the level of friendship which developed between the two men. Their collaboration in the profession of Clare was essential and was also expressed in the decision to place San Damiano at the sisters' disposal and in the steps taken to temper Clare's asceticism. At the end of his life Francis was nursed in the bishop's palace in Assisi and the third person to whom he appeared after his death was Guido, whom he greeted as father. In the process leading to Francis's canonization Guido drew upon his own experience of the miracles worked by San Rufino in 1212; he and the canons had carefully recorded the events. He himself gave the details of two miracles concerning Francis for the process of canonization in which he was a key witness on account of his lengthy association and then friendship with Francis.

Appointed to the diocese of Assisi about 1204 in the aftermath of the civil war, Guido was a unique figure in the history of the Franciscan movement. He had witnessed Francis's first uncertain steps towards a life of obedience to the Gospel and had spoken to him a great deal in the first days of the fraternity and advised him on different points. Francis regarded him as a divine mouthpiece and his respect for members of the hierarchy seems to have stemmed from this conviction. By the time that Guido's lengthy episcopate ended on 30 July 1228, Francis was already acclaimed as the canonized founder of a vast army of zealous men intent on living according to the poverty and simplicity of Jesus Christ. In the days following that ceremony, Guido had seen Gregory IX lay the foundation stone of the basilica to be constructed in Francis's honour and consecrate the high altar at San Rufino. Guido recognized Francis as a young man aspiring to the ideals of the Gospels and gave him vital help at a crucial stage in the life of the nascent fraternity. His knowledge of the papal court provided Francis with the introduction to Cardinal John of St Paul, enabling him to secure the approval of Innocent III and make a contribution to the welfare of the universal Church.

Notes

1. Anon. Perug., c. 3, n. 17b.
2. R. Brown, *The Roots of St Francis* (Chicago, 1982), p. 189. Cf. L. Canonici, 'Guido II di Assisi. Il vescovo di san Francesco', *Studi Francescani*, 77 (1980), pp. 187-206; M. Robson, 'Assisi, Guido II and Saint Francis', *Laurentianum*, 34 (1993), pp. 109-38.
3. Cf. J. M. Powell, 'The papacy and the early Franciscans', *Franciscan Studies*, 36 (1976), pp. 248-62, 252.
4. A. Mockler, *Francis of Assisi* (Oxford, 1976), p. 76.
5. R. C. Trexler, *Naked before the Father* (New York, 1989), p. 27.
6. NV, I, i, pp. 289-90.
7. AF, X, p. 697.
8. Trexler, *Naked before the Father*, pp. 48-52.
9. LM, c. 2, n. 4.
10. 1 C, nn. 6, 18.
11. Ibid., n. 15; cf. 2 C, n. 214; Gregory the Great, *Homilarium in evangelia*, II, homilia 32, n. 2, in PL, 76.1233.
12. NV, 1, pt. 1, pp. 32-3.

13. P. Brown, *The Cult of the Saints* (Chicago, 1981), pp. 38-9.
14. Ibid., p. 9.
15. Peter Damian, *Sermo* 36 in *Corpus Christianorum*, n. 3, p. 217.
16. 1 C, nn. 30, 137.
17. Peter Damian, nn. 5-11, pp. 218-21.
18. *S. Bernardi opera*, VIII, ed. Leclercq and Rochais (Rome, 1977), pp. 15-16.
19. NV, I, pt. 1, p. 55, n. 1.
20. LM, c. 3, n. 9.
21. M. Chibnall, *The World of Orderic Vitalis* (Oxford, 1984), p. 101.
22. *The Prayers and Meditations of Saint Anselm*, trans. B. Ward (Penguin Classics; Harmondsworth, 1973), pp. 207-11.
23. 2 C. , n. 158.
24. Thomas of Eccleston, *Tractatus de adventu*, p. 47.
25. *Fratris Johannis Pecham quondam archiepiscopi Cantuariensis Tractatus tres de Paupertate*, ed C. L. Kingsford, A. G. Little and F. Tocco (BSFS, 2; Aberdeen, 1910), p. 168.
26. Augustine, *Confessiones*, lib. 9, c. 7, n. 16, in PL, 32. 770, and *Corpus Christianorum, Series Latina*, 27, ed. L. Verheijen (1981), p. 142. Cf. Ambrose, *Epistola* 22, in PL, 16. 1019-26.
27. *The Letters and Poems of Fulbert of Chartres*, ed. F. Behrends (OMT; 1976), pp. 10-11, n. 2.
28. NV, I, pt. 1, p. 137. Cf. A. Fortini, *Assisi nel medioevo* (Rome, 1940), pp. 68-9. D. Waley, *The Italian City-Republics* (London, 3rd edn., 1988), p. 102, offers some examples of how Italian cities celebrated the feast of their patron saint.
29. NV, I, pt. 1, pp. 238-40 and Fortini, *Assisi nel medioevo*, pp. 35-41, for an Italian translation of the *passio*.
30. 2 C, nn. 202, 55; *Scripta Leonis*, pp. 346-7.
31. S. J. P. Van Dijk and J. H. Walker, *The Origins of the Modern Roman Liturgy* (London, 1960), p. 117.
32. LTS, c. 6, n. 19.
33. 2 C, n. 12.
34. LM, c. 2, n. 4.
35. Cf. M. Bihl, 'De canonizatione S. Francisci' in AFH, 21 (1928), pp. 468-514.
36. NV, I, pt. 1, pp. 31-2. Cf. III, pp. 543-5, where the papal bull is transcribed.
37. Ibid., I, pt. 1, p. 32.
38. *Regesta Honorii Papae III*, ii, ed. P. Pressutti (Rome, 1895), n. 4958, p. 242; NV, I, i, p. 323.
39. NV, I, i, pp. 323-4; cf. III, p. 165. *Regesta Honorii Papae III*, ii, n. 3739, pp. 33-4; *Les registres de Grégoire IX*, ed. L. Auvray, I (Paris, 1896), nn. 2319-20, pp. 1222-5.
40. NV, III, pp. 494-6.
41. *Compilatio Assisiensis*, c. 84.
42. LTS, c. 7, n. 21.
43. Ibid., c. 3, n. 10. This testimony should also be read in the light of Bonaventure's evidence. Cf. *Opuscula Sancti Patris Francisci Assisiensis*, p. 310; LM, c. 12, n. 2.
44. P. Sabatier, *Life of St Francis of Assisi*, trans. from French L. S. Houghton (London, 1899), p. 54.
45. J. R. H. Moorman, *Saint Francis of Assisi* (London, 1950), p. 43.
46. L. Bracaloni, *Storia di San Damiano in Assisi* (Todi, 2nd edn., 1926), pp. 53-4.
47. Moorman, *Saint Francis of Assisi*, pp. 15-16.
48. L. K. Little, *Religious Poverty and the Profit Economy in Medieval Europe* (London, 1978), p. 148.
49. 1 C, nn. 30, 34; 2 C, n. 21.
50. Anon. Perug., c. 3, n. 17; LTS, c. 9, n. 35; cf. R. B. Brooke, 'Recent work on St Francis of Assisi', *Analecta Bollandiana*, 100 (1982), pp. 653-76, 657, observes that this text tends to exalt the role of the bishop of Assisi. This observation is particularly significant in Francis's early dealings with Guido.
51. LTS, c. 9, n. 35.
52. R. B. Brooke, *Early Franciscan Government: Elias to Bonaventure* (Cambridge Studies in Medieval Life and Thought; 1959), pp. 59-61.
53. Moorman, *Saint Francis of Assisi*, p. 54.
54. W. R. Thomson, 'The earliest Cardinal-Protectors of the Franciscan Order: a study in administrative history, 1210-1261', *Studies in Medieval and Renaissance History*, 9 (1972), pp. 21-80, 31.
55. J. E. Sayers, *Innocent III: Leader of Europe, 1198-1216* (London, 1994), p. 151.
56. C. Morris, *The Papal Monarchy: The Western Church from 1050 to 1250* (Oxford History of the Christian Church 1989), pp. 204, 419; M. Bihl, 'De Iohanne de S. Paulo, Cardinali episcopo Sabinensi, primo S. Francisci in Curia Romana an. 1209 fautore' in AFH, 19 (1926), pp. 282-5.
57. P. Paschini, 'Il cardinale Giovanni di San Paolo' in *Studi di Storia e Diritto in onore di Carlo Carlisse*, III (Milan, 1940), pp. 109-18.

58. 1 C, n. 23.
59. LM, c. 4, n. 4.
60. Sabatier, p. 81, holds that Guido began to rue the encouragement which he had formerly offered to Francis, whom he distrusted.
61. *Compilatio Assisiensis*, c. 54; 2 C, n. 100.
62. LSC, n. 7; cf. F. Casolini, *Nell'anno 750 della vestizione di Santa Chiara d'Assisi (1211-1961)*, Assisi, 1961.
63. A. P. Tini, 'La culla delle Damianite e Guido Vescovo', *Miscellanea Francescana*, 14 (1912), pp. 33-7, 36.
64. *Compilatio Assisiensis*, c. 56.
65. LSC, n. 10; Process, 12. n. 5; 20. n. 7.
66. Bracaloni, *Storia di San Damiano in Assisi* (Todi, 2nd edn, 1926), p. 20.
67. Tini, 'La culla', pp. 35-6.
68. Bracaloni, *Storia di San Damiano*, p. 24.
69. Fra Tommaso da Celano, *Vita di S. Chiara Vergine d'Assisi*, translated by Casolini (Assisi, 3rd edn, 1976), p. 51, n. 1, who places this joint intervention about 1220.
70. M. Carney, 'Francis and Clare. A critical examination of the sources', *Laurentianum*, 30 (1989), pp. 25-60, 43.
71. Process, 2. 12, p. 449.
72. LSC, n. 28, pp. 39-40.
73. Ibid., n. 39, pp. 54-5.
74. J. R. H. Moorman, *The Sources for the Life of S. Francis of Assisi* (University of Manchester, Historical Series, 79; 1940), p. 15, n. 2.
75. D. Knowles, *From Pachomius to Ignatius: A Study in the Constitutional History of the Religious Orders* (Oxford, 1966), p. 39.
76. *Compilatio Assisiensis*, c. 20.
77. Ibid., c. 58; *Scripta Leonis*, pp. 114-15.
78. *Opuscula Sancti Patris Francisci Assisiensis*, pp. 234, 308; 1 C, n. 74; 2 C, n. 147.
79. 2 C, n. 141; 1 C, nn. 75, 78; 1 C, n. 75.
80. 1 C, n. 62; *Compilatio Assisiensis*, c. 58; 2 C, nn. 86, 41, 50.
81. Sabatier, *Life of St Francis*, p. 331, seems to confuse the chronology, suggesting that Guido grew tired of having friars in the *vescovado* with the sick Francis. This is another manifestation of Sabatier's negative account of the bishop's role.
82. 1 C, n. 105; 2 C, nn. 218-20.
83. LM, c. 14, n. 6.
84. Benignitas, c. 19, nn. 1-9.
85. NV, III, pp. 234-7; II, pp. 367-70.
86. R. Foreville and G. Keir (eds), *The Book of St Gilbert* (OMT; 1987), pp. xc-xcvi.
87. Thomas of Celano, 'Tractatus de miraculis', n. 5, pp. 274-5. Cf. LM, c. 13, n. 8.
88. M. Goodich, 'The politics of canonisation in the thirteenth century: lay and mendicant saints' in *Saints and their Cults: Studies in Religious Sociology, Folklore and History*, ed. S. Wilson (Cambridge, 1983), pp. 169-87, 173.
89. Assidua, c. 27, n. 4. The Holy See was petitioned by the bishop and clergy, the city magistrate and the nobles and people. And it should be borne in mind that Francis's connections with Assisi were considerably stronger and of far greater duration than those of Anthony with Padua, a city in which he had lived for a very short time.
90. 1 C, nn. 124, 126.

3

Pope Innocent III

Francis and his successors as head of this fraternity promise obedience and
reverence to the lord Pope Innocent and his successors[1]

Just as Guido's contribution to Francis and the fraternity was invaluable, so
Innocent III[2] played a similar role at a universal level; without his approval and
practical assistance the nascent fraternity would have been stillborn. In Assisi
Francis had respected Guido as the vicar of San Rufino and in Rome he revered
the pope as the vicar and successor of St Peter, whose spiritual authority he
exercised. His desire to win papal approval was inextricably linked to his
perception of the bishop of Rome; this was the episcopal seat once occupied by St
Peter, the prince of apostles, and the single patriarchate in the West. The stature
of the medieval papacy, moreover, was heightened by the reforming credentials
exhibited by a series of popes following Gregory VII (1073-85) and people
became accustomed to look to Rome for reform and vigorous leadership. By the
early thirteenth century Innocent III was regularly describing himself as the vicar
of Christ, a title which signalled his universal aspirations. His promotion of
ecclesiastical reform culminated in the Fourth Lateran Council of 1215 which set
the agenda for the early preaching of the friars.

THE PAPACY AND ST FRANCIS

Francis's vocation to live in the manner of the apostles and their divine master
was firmly rooted within the Church. He fostered good relations with the local
bishop and the pope and this pivotal connection provided a context for the
fraternity's growth and development. Rome, one of the principal centres of
pilgrimage in the West, was a city of shrines, the most important of which were
the tombs of the apostles, Peter and Paul. Francis, who made many pilgrimages
to the shrine of St Peter, regarded the pope as the one who exercised the spiritual
authority of the apostles buried in the eternal city and accordingly revered him as
the vicar and successor of St Peter: the pope spoke with apostolic authority and
was the highest individual source of authority within the Church. Francis located
his incipient fraternity within the wider concerns of the universal Church and

wished to gain the approval of the prince of apostles and vicar of Jesus Christ; no higher ecclesiastical authority could be envisaged by Francis. Accordingly, it was essential that papal approbation should be achieved, especially because by the beginning of the thirteenth century popes were styling themselves as vicars of Christ. Innocent III was a man intent on the renewal of the Church and he endeavoured to raise the standards of behaviour for both clergy and laity. In Francis he found an enthusiastic collaborator, a man determined to live in imitation of Jesus Christ, renewing the apostolic life.

The tombs of the apostles

St Peter was honoured as the founder of the Church in Rome, where St Paul was imprisoned; both were executed there and their tombs became centres of pilgrimage. Early tradition regarded both martyrs as founders of the Roman Church, but Peter was revered as the first bishop of that Church. It was also the city to which many Christians were sent for execution, such as Ignatius, bishop of Antioch, about 107. Evidence for the veneration of the shrine of St Peter at the Vatican dates from the last quarter of the second century. The close bodily association with Peter was an advantage which the bishop of Rome exploited in support of his reforms. R. W. Southern explains that, for the western Church, from the seventh to the eleventh century, the existence of the tomb of St Peter was the most significant fact in Christendom. The body within the tomb, which would one day clothe the doorkeeper of heaven, was the link between the presence in heaven and in the Church on earth. It was pre-eminently through his continuous physical presence that St Peter continued to bless and to curse, to cure and to guarantee.[3] In June 716, Ceolfrith, abbot of Wearmouth, set out for Rome carrying a copy of the Vulgate as a gift from an abbot at the extreme edge of the world (*Anglorum extremis de finibus abbas*), to the body of St Peter.[4]

A strong devotion to the Roman Church, its tradition and its discipline was one of the hallmarks of the conversion of the Anglo-Saxons. Some of the leaders of the newly converted peoples went to Rome for baptism and spent their last days near the apostle's tomb in the hope that the doorkeeper of heaven would admit them at their death. In 670 Oswiu, king of the Northumbrians, was so attached to Roman and apostolic customs that he had intended to go to Rome and end his life there among the holy places, but death intervened. In 689 Caedwalla, king of the West Saxons, was more successful. He renounced his throne and went to Rome where he wished to be baptized within the threshold of the apostles; he was given the name of Peter and buried in the Petrine basilica.[5] Rome's perennial attraction to the Anglo-Saxons prompted Stephen, an English friar, in 1248 to seek the minister general's permission to reside in Rome where he visited the city's shrines and lectured to the friars.[6]

The traditional pilgrimage to the apostles' tombs, *ad limina apostolorum*, attracted people from all over Christendom and was very popular in medieval Assisi;[7] such pilgrimages feature in the early biographies of both Francis and Clare. Ortolana, Clare's mother, made a number of pilgrimages, including one to the apostles' tombs. Francis's piety reflects that of the age and of his own local church and his respect for St Peter was emphasized by Thomas of Celano, who reports the saint's dismay at the meagre offerings of pilgrims. He himself dramatically threw down a handful of coins at the tomb, showing that the apostle whom God honoured above the rest should be honoured by all in a special way. The biographer may have interpreted this concern for the saint's tomb as presaging Francis's own glorification by the Church of Rome. Francis visited Rome during the period of uncertainty which gripped him and, as he prayed at the tomb of the prince of apostles, he sought direction from the one who guards the gates of heaven. Kneeling before the tomb of the leader of the apostles, he felt that he was drawing closer to the world of the New Testament. The fisherman's life had been so dramatically changed by his meeting with the Son of God. Feeling that his own world was changing in an ever more unpredictable manner, Francis entreated the apostle to intercede for him so that he might obtain the strength and the graces necessary for a new form of life. He prayed for the courage to respond to whatever calls God would make on him and his talents. He meditated on the apostle's access to the Son of God and the new strength which had been granted to him. His conventional piety expressed itself when, having secured papal support, he went to St Peter's tomb to give thanks.[8] His visits to Rome do not seem to have been rare and it is probable that he visited St Peter's shrine on his numerous trips, when he attended to the business of the fraternity and visited friends.

Francis's biographers emphasize his traditional piety, an important focus of which was devotion to the apostles. Bonaventure reports that Francis embraced all the apostles with the greatest affection, especially Sts Peter and Paul because of their passionate love of Christ. In his reverence and love of them he used to keep a special 40-day fast in their honour. The second church which he repaired was dedicated to St Peter, although Thomas of Celano did not supply its name. Like other churches restored by Francis in the vicinity of Assisi, this was well-nigh destroyed. The symbolism in the restoration of a church dedicated to St Peter was typical of the kind of symbolism which the biographers loved to develop. This restoration accorded with the biographer's conviction that Francis had played a central role in the renewal of the universal Church and that he always had a strong devotion to the prince of the apostles.[9]

Teaching authority of the Church of Rome

From an early stage Rome was renowned as a city of the martyrs' tombs and it was one of the five ancient patriarchal sees, along with Constantinople,

Alexandria, Antioch and Jerusalem. The Church and its bishops assumed a responsibility for other parts of the western Church and intervened on a variety of questions, both doctrinal and disciplinary. At the Council of Constantinople in 381 it was decreed that Constantinople should hold the first rank after the bishop of Rome, but the Council of Chalcedon in 451 placed the two patriarchal sees on a level of parity. However, the late fifth-century *Legend of St Sylvester*, which was represented in the portico or main entrance of the Lateran basilica in the Middle Ages, claimed that Constantine recognized the unique spiritual status of the Roman see, confirming its primacy over the other four patriarchal sees.[10]

The central place claimed by Rome as the source and support of the mission to convert the Anglo-Saxons is recounted by Bede. Direction and advice were sought from Rome and, following the arrival of Augustine and the monks, Gregory the Great dispatched a fresh influx of missionaries along with sacred vessels, altar cloths, ecclesiastical ornaments, vestments, relics of the apostles and martyrs and several manuscripts. Augustine sent Laurence and Peter to inform Gregory about the progress of the mission and to seek advice and a few years later Melitus, bishop of London, went to Rome to confer with Boniface IV. In the eyes of Wilfrid, who subsequently became bishop of Ripon, Rome was the best place for the study of ecclesiastical discipline and he himself studied there. Benedict Biscop, abbot of Wearmouth, made six visits to Rome and brought back with him Abbot John to train the monks in the chant sung at St Peter's basilica.[11] The new converts looked upon Rome with gratitude for the launching of the mission and Gregory came to be regarded as the apostle of the Anglo-Saxons. G. Barraclough explains that the veneration for St Peter, so characteristic of Anglo-Saxon England, betokened a new attitude towards Rome, the Roman Church and its bishop, and missionaries from England carried it with them wherever they went.[12] Those who worked for the conversion of the Anglo-Saxons also communicated their own reverence for the Church of Rome, its bishops and their authority, its disciplinary and liturgical practices and its numerous shrines. The same reverential and deferential instincts informed the Anglo-Saxon mission to evangelize Frisia and then parts of Holland and Germany at the end of the seventh century and at the beginning of the eighth.[13] And, while Charlemagne came to the aid of the beleaguered Leo III (795–816), he, too, turned towards Rome for guidance in sacred music, bringing monks from the eternal city to his Frankish kingdom.[14]

In 731 the council that met in Rome assembled before the most holy burial place of St Peter, and this physical contact between the councils and the source of their authority was frequently recalled. Examples could be multiplied indefinitely, but what they all make clear is the fact that, from the eighth to the eleventh centuries, more emphatically than at any other time before or since, the active force in Rome was seen as St Peter himself.[15] Peter's position as the head of the apostles proved to be a very useful tool to the Gregorian reformers, who emphasized his leadership and authority within the western Church. The Fourth Lateran Council reaffirmed the unique role of the Church of Rome and its fifth canon declared that by divine disposition the Roman Church enjoyed a primacy of ordinary power over all other churches because it was the mother and mistress of all Christ's faithful. The patriarchal sees of the East were then named in order of precedence: Constantinople, Alexandria, Antioch and then Jerusalem, each maintaining its own rank. These patriarchs were required to receive the pallium from the pope, to whom they were to take an oath of fidelity and obedience.

Vicar of St Peter

The close relationship between the prince of the apostles and the bishop of Rome was mirrored in the title 'vicar of St Peter'. For instance, when Thurstan was consecrated as archbishop of York by Calixtus II at Rheims on 19 October 1119, the chronicler reported that the consecration was carried out by the pope 'as representing St Peter'.[16] So strong was the identification between St Peter and the pope that the concept of Petrine authority was extended to include papal legates. About 28 June 1078, Gregory VII wrote to the faithful of Narbonne, Gascony and Spain, urging them to accept the ministrations and judgements of the Roman legate, who was acting on behalf of St Peter and the pope; he reminded them of the earlier system of dispatching papal legates and charged them by apostolic authority to receive the legates as though the pope, or rather St Peter, were present; out of reverence for the apostolic see whose messenger he was, the faithful were instructed to obey and heed him in all things as though they saw the pope or actually heard him speaking. Gregory exhorted them to show themselves obedient in all things to God and St Peter that, by the intervention of the prince of the apostles himself, they might deserve to obtain glory and felicity both in this life and in the next.[17]

Sayers points out that by the ninth century the Lateran palace and basilica contained paintings and mosaics depicting the history of the papacy.[18] B. Kempers comments that the popes had consolidated their position as territorial rulers in central Italy since the twelfth century. They laid claim not only to a greater sacred authority than that possessed by secular rulers, but also to territorial power and the right to levy taxes, like emperors and princes. The art of the Roman basilicas confirmed the papacy's superiority over secular princes. Calixtus II (1119-24) and Innocent II (1130-43) commissioned paintings in the Lateran palace depicting the papal claims to power over the emperor and the antipopes, who were regularly pictured as being trodden underfoot by the pope seated on a far larger throne. Later popes introduced images with comparable messages into the four large basilicas and several other churches in Rome. The popes supported their theological claims by including images of St Peter receiving the keys from Christ, the symbol of his authority.[19] In a letter written in the summer of 1160 John of Salisbury confirms that the pictures in the Lateran palace depicted the overthrow of the schismatics, who became the pope's footstools.[20]

Vicar of Christ

From the beginning of the twelfth century new currents of reform, both clerical and lay, were flowing through the Church. Reforming energies filled itinerant preachers, such as Henry of Lausanne and Arnold of Brescia, who called for renewal in the Church and criticized both aspects of its traditional teaching and the shortcomings of the clergy.[21] They contrasted the lives of the apostles and the contemporary clergy, some of whose lives were stained by the pursuit of money, simony and concubinage. The apostolic community in Jerusalem had provided the norm for Christian conduct, but by the end of the twelfth century there was a new interpretation of the apostolic life and associated with this was a growing concentration on the imitation of Christ as the highest form of Christian perfection. The change of focus from the apostles to their master provided the papacy with a new image which corresponded to the increasingly global aspirations of the papacy. The new title 'vicar of Christ' reflected the Petrine dignity and his universal mission.[22]

Southern reports that after Gregory VII the papal emphasis upon St Peter diminished. The overwhelming dependence on the apostle belonged to the days when Rome had been a city of shrines and pilgrims with little power of practical direction. As this situation changed, the title 'vicar of St Peter' gradually fell out of use and was replaced by another which pointed to a higher authority and more extensive field of activity. From about the middle of the twelfth century the popes began to arrogate to themselves the title 'vicar of Christ' and to claim it for themselves alone. In the past, kings and priests had called themselves vicars of Christ; but not the pope. For him the title was too vague because he was pre-eminently the vicar of St Peter: in a world dominated by saints and relics, this title alone could express the uniqueness of the pope's position.[23] An early illustration of this change of emphasis is Bernard of Clairvaux's exhortation to Eugene III (1145–53) to imitate the saint who had showed himself to be the vicar of Christ.[24] Southern argues that the title 'vicar of Christ' supplied what was needed by all twelfth-century governments—to trace claims back to their source. The new formula showed that the popes no longer looked backwards, and were no longer primarily concerned to preserve an ancient tradition as the earthly trustees of St Peter. They were the deputies of Christ in all the fullness of his power, and by the end of the twelfth century Innocent III could deliberately sweep aside the limitations implied in the old title.[25] The powers with which Innocent felt himself to be invested were summed up in his letter to Philip II of France:

the word of God in our mouth must not be bound, but free, that we may freely warn the unruly and fulfil, whenever expedient, the command of the apostle which we regard as addressed the more directly to us as we hold a higher position in the Church, indeed the highest position of all: for others are called to a share of responsibility, but we alone have been given plenary authority … Therefore, because Jesus began both to do and to teach, … we who, however unworthily, act as his vicar on earth ought also to walk, even as he walked.

And in a letter to King John of England he asserted that Jesus Christ had set one man over all, appointing him as his vicar on earth, so that, as every knee is bowed to Jesus, of things in heaven, and things in earth, and things under the earth (Philippians 2:10), so all men should obey his vicar and strive that there may be one fold and one shepherd (John 10:16). All secular kings for the sake of God so venerate this vicar, that unless they seek to serve him devotedly, they doubt if they are reigning properly.[26]

Francis's respect for papal teaching

As a native of Assisi, Francis was familiar with the world of saints and their sphere of influence, both spiritual and material. Just as he viewed Guido as the custodian of the spiritual authority of San Rufino, so he believed that Innocent III was not only the vicar of St Peter. In addition, by the early thirteenth century the pope was perceived as the vicar of Christ. He was regarded as the highest spiritual authority within the Church and his blessing and approval were deemed essential for Francis and his fraternity. Francis's deeply rooted commitment to the Church was emphasized by Thomas of Celano, who provided a context for the saint's desire to gain papal approval for the fraternity. Francis looked to the universal Church as the place where salvation might be gained. His biographers depict him as someone wholly and entirely catholic and filled from the beginning with reverence towards the ministers and the ministry of God. Within a few years of his gaining that approval the first canon of the Fourth Lateran Council reiterated the traditional formula that there was one universal Church of the faithful, outside of which nobody at all is saved (*una vero est fidelium universalis ecclesia, extra quam nullus omnino salvatur*). This teaching was echoed in Francis's own writings, which underline the way in which he strove to locate himself and the fraternity within the heart of the Church. His reform sprang from deep catholic roots and he never tired of reminding his followers of the reverence and obedience due to the catholic and apostolic Church.[27] He taught that all the friars should be Catholics and live and speak as such. Should anyone deviate from this norm and fail to correct himself, he should be expelled from the fraternity.[28]

The new papal nomenclature was already in vogue by the time of Francis's death. Early Franciscan hagiography, with its concern to be orthodox in all matters and faithful to the Church, was firmly rooted in the new papal claims.

Innocent III and Gregory IX were described as the successors of Peter the apostle, the supreme pontiff, the vicar of Christ, the lord and father of the whole Christian people, the supreme pastor, the highest of all bishops, the leader of Christians, the lord of the world, the pastor of the Church and the anointed of the Lord.[29] Nonetheless, the popes continued to invoke the authority of St Peter, which was sometimes associated with that of St Paul. For instance, Honorius III appeals to the authority of Sts Peter and Paul as well as God in his postscript to the Rule of St Francis.[30] Francis believed that the pope held the place of Christ on earth[31] and that Honorius held the whole world in his hands.[32]

INNOCENT III AND REFORM GROUPS

The numerous challenges which faced the Church at the beginning of the thirteenth century are summarized by Lawrence. Heresy was widespread and Catharism had taken root under the patronage of the landed classes; it was organized as a counter-church with its own hierarchy. The towns of northern Italy had long been nurseries of various heretical sects against which the secular clergy could make no headway. The bourgeoisie and the swelling population of artisans offered a ready audience for freelance itinerant preachers who moved along the trade routes in increasing numbers. New and radical forms of lay piety were appearing, drawing their inspiration from a first-hand study of the New Testament, now circulating in unofficial vernacular translations. The question was whether this unruly flood of enthusiasm could be canalized and made to serve the cause of orthodoxy.[33] This list might be extended to include a certain nervousness on the part of the papacy towards groups which wished to pursue a more rigorous lifestyle within the Church. At first the omens were not good and the two major urban groups, intent on a closer observation of the Gospel, had their own teething troubles with the papacy.

First, the Waldensians had originated about 1174 with the conversion of Peter Valdès, a rich citizen of Lyon. He was resolved to undertake a ministry of poverty and preaching, giving an example within the Church. He sought advice from theologians in Rome and asked clerics to translate the Bible for him. The local bishop, however, forbade their preaching. At the Third Lateran Council in 1179, however, he appeared before Alexander III, who is said to have welcomed his view of voluntary poverty, but forbade him to preach except at the request of priests. Valdès's lack of theological instruction begot a certain degree of nervousness on the part of the hierarchy. The papal legate, Abbot Henry of Clairvaux, obtained an orthodox profession of faith from Valdès, who declared his intention to live in poverty and to obey the precepts of the Gospels as commands. Soon afterwards, however, there was further strain on his relationship with the bishops, when his followers were expelled from Lyon, apparently for unauthorized preaching. In addition, in 1184 the Council of Verona listed the 'poor men of Lyon' as heretics and condemned them for preaching without permission.[34] Valdès's scheme seems to have aroused uneasiness within the Curia, which decided against him and his followers. Secondly, the Humiliati, from Lombardy, established early communities in northern Italy and went to Rome in search of papal approbation; they, too, pursued an austere personal life, while continuing to live with their families. They fostered good relations with the local clergy and sought papal recognition in case they were accused of heresy, but they too were disappointed. Sayers explains that the stumbling block for both groups was preaching.[35]

The early fate of these groups was recounted by Burchard of Ursberg, who testified that Lucius III (1181–85) had listed the Humiliati and the Waldensians among the heretics because they had been found teaching dogmas contrary to the faith and practising superstitious observances. Their clandestine preaching, which they held most of the time in very secret haunts, aroused suspicion and hostility within the hierarchy. They regarded themselves as living the life of the apostles: they refused all ownership, even a dwelling, and they went about from city to town. The pope took them to task for certain strange practices: they cut off the upper part of their shoes and walked around almost barefooted; they wore mantles like religious, but had their hair cut exactly like the laity. The chronicler reported that the most reprehensible thing about them was that men and women travelled about together, lived together most of the time in the same house and it was reported that they sometimes shared the same bed. They claimed that all these practices were derived from the apostles.[36] This type of comment was normally reserved for the Church's opponents, such as heretics, and it is abundantly clear that this observer took a very dim view of their practices.

Both groups found much greater understanding from Innocent III, who was much more accommodating towards reforming groups within the Church. He was anxious to keep the Waldensians and the Humiliati in the fold of the Church and displayed liking and understanding for men and women of sanctity. He welcomed reformers and critics, whom he was concerned to avoid driving out of the Church. He was keen to employ peaceful persuasion, especially in winning back champions of poverty and preaching. The conciliatory policy also enabled new movements to emerge under the protection of the Church, and not in opposition to it. C. Morris believes thus Innocent restored the link between the Roman Church and the apostolic poverty movement, which his predecessors had broken.[37] Powell regards this pontificate as all the more notable because it endeavoured to address some of the difficulties which had arisen since the Third Lateran Council of 1179, including a more constructive response to the reform groups.[38] This pope gave the reform groups permission to preach, provided they did not address questions of doctrine or criticize the clergy. J. B. Freed notes that Innocent approved the statutes of repentant Humiliati and Waldensians who had submitted to Rome in exchange for a papal approbation of their distinctive lifestyle. The benefits of this policy in the heretic-ridden diocese of Milan were noted by Jacques de Vitry, who reported that by 1216 the reconciled Humiliati had become the Church's staunchest supporters.[39] By 1215 the Humiliati had some 150 houses in the neighbourhood of Milan.[40]

Burchard of Ursberg attributed the papal approval of the new mendicant orders to the Church's anxieties about the continuing success of the Humiliati and Waldensians. The mendicants clearly benefited from the more accommodating policies of Innocent towards reforming groups. B. Bolton emphasizes the vital differences between the Humiliati and the Franciscans. The former had no outstanding leader and no cardinal protector to defend them against their enemies or to vouch for their orthodoxy. They were bound by a compromise Rule, an amalgam of diverse elements. Francis's followers had the advantage of entering the Church several years later with their own Rule.[41] An awareness of the tension between the papacy and the Waldensians and Humiliati at the end of the twelfth century may have led Franciscan hagiography to emphasize the saint's respect for the successor of St Peter and vicar of Christ and his collaboration with the papal policies of reform. Francis and Dominic responded to the crises confronting the Church at the beginning of the thirteenth century and provided armies of fervent and highly gifted preachers who took the message of the Gospel into the growing cities of western Europe and defended its teaching against heretical groups, which had enjoyed success in detaching men and women from the Church. The followers of Francis and Dominic provided the papacy with a highly mobile and exemplary nucleus of faithful evangelical lieutenants.

FRANCIS'S QUEST FOR PAPAL APPROVAL

Franciscan biographers looked upon Innocent III as one of the leading popes of the Middle Ages and readily acknowledged his decisive contribution to the emergence of the fraternity. Thomas of Celano depicts him as a glorious man, greatly learned, renowned in discourse, fervent in his zeal for justice and in everything pertaining to Christianity, and Bonaventure records that he was famous for his wisdom. Salimbene's verdict of this pontificate was that the Church grew and flourished, maintaining its pre-eminence over the Roman Empire and all the kings and princes of the world.[42] Sayers comments that the simple and almost revolutionary style of Francis had the fortune to reach the ears and attention of a pope of spiritual vision, because Innocent had not lost sight of the Church's mission to evangelize.[43]

Like the early Cistercians, the friars experienced a modest level of recruitment[44] with most of their first vocations coming from Assisi and the neighbouring cities and towns of Umbria. The later growth of the fraternity was compared to the increase in the early Christians in Jerusalem (Acts 2:47; 5:14), as Franciscan hagiography established a parallel between the growth of the Church and the expansion of the fraternity. The eventual attainment of the apostolic number of twelve was, however, a moment of special significance for the first friars and prompted Francis to write for himself and his brothers simply and concisely a Rule. The first biographer carefully explains that the document was based primarily upon the Gospels and indicates that the saint's only wish was to live according to the teaching of his divine master with the approval of the pope. This portrait of the primitive Rule, which is no longer extant,[45] underlines the scriptural foundation of the fraternity and this root was decisive in the eventual approval of the friars' petition. Unlike the early Cistercian reformers in the century before his birth, Francis set out for Rome to seek approval for the fraternity which had gathered around him. By this time the papacy had become the legitimizing authority for new religious movements.[46] When the friars began their journey, they chose Bernard to lead them to the eternal city. On their arrival, however, Bernard was not mentioned as Francis moved to the centre of the stage.

Francis received by Cardinal John of St Paul

The Franciscans and the Dominicans were the beneficiaries of the Church's reappraisal of its earlier dealings with the Waldensians and Humiliati. From the outset both groups of friars were not perceived as posing a threat because their applications were supported by the warm commendations of Bishops Guido of Assisi and Fulk of Toulouse. While Thomas of Celano emphasizes the way in which the ministry of Francis and his followers had so impressed Guido, he does not pay sufficient attention to their dependence upon his strong endorsement of their ministry. For instance, it would have been very difficult for this fledgling fraternity to have moved into another diocese without his warm approval. Guido's glowing testimonial to the fraternity's impact was never more necessary than when the friars petitioned the pope to approve their community.

Guido arranged for Francis to meet Cardinal John of St Paul, who was recognized as the friend of reform within the Church; this was a decisive introduction. The *Anonymous of Perugia* notes that Guido's testimonial was so powerful that the cardinal sent out servants to invite the friars to his palace. Francis and some of the friars took part in the preliminary meetings with the cardinal, who was very impressed by these encounters. The first biographer offers a summary of the meetings between the cardinal, a prudent and discreet man, and the visionary. Francis was closely questioned by the cardinal, whose first impulse seems to have been to point him in the direction of a flourishing religious community in one of the great abbeys or churches. The cardinal urged him to consider becoming a hermit, a suggestion which was nearer Francis's heart than life in a large monastic community. Francis retorted that he did not have such a vocation and claimed to be inspired by a higher desire. He explained his conviction that he had not been called to the monastic or any other form of religious life; his was a different vocation, rooted in the literal interpretation of the Gospels, and he not only wished his friars to own no private property, but also they were to have nothing in common, a requirement unprecedented among the established religious orders. Compromise was precluded by Francis's unshakeable conviction that his was a vocation entrusted to him by God and this made him all the more adamant. The strength of his views was matched by the cardinal's knowledge of how the pope and cardinals would respond to this petition for another new religious order at a time when the climate was turning against such new foundations. While the cardinal's caution may have surprised Francis, it convinced him that the drive for papal approval was not going to be easy and that some fundamental questions would be raised by the cardinals present in the Curia. The pope and cardinals would have to be *convinced*. The cardinal reiterated his anxieties lest Francis fail to persevere and urged an easier and less demanding form of religious life, but in the end he was persuaded by the saint's constancy. He then agreed to present Francis's petition to the pope. The first biography provides a summary of the exchanges at the papal court, but reveals little of the complexity of the situation, which survives only by inference in the account of Francis's interview with the cardinal. A fuller report of the exchanges between Francis and the cardinal was contained in the *Anonymous of Perugia*. The friars had stayed with the cardinal for some time and Francis impressed him so deeply that he announced to Innocent III that he had found the most perfect man who wished to live according to the form of the Gospel and that the fraternity was capable of playing its part in the regeneration of the Church.

Francis received by Innocent III

The benign intervention of Bishop Guido and Cardinal John of St Paul paved the way for Francis to be received by the pope. This meeting brought together two extremes. Innocent III was a graduate of both Paris and Bologna, two of the most prestigious universities in the western world. Francis's education was local and he attended the school conducted by the canons of San Rufino in Assisi. While Innocent was an accomplished writer on both philosophical and sacramental matters, even Franciscan chroniclers pointed out the shortcomings in the founder's command of Latin. The pope's dwelling was a magnificent and opulent apartment at the Lateran palace. Francis, who had firmly turned his back on the pursuit of wealth and comfort, chose to find a home in a hovel outside Assisi. One of the most powerful men in the western world, who did not shrink from imposing his will upon recalcitrant kings, such as John of England, admitted a man who had spurned all power and influence in order to devote himself to the principles of the Gospel. The pope was in a position to promote reforms from the very apex of the universal Church, while Francis fostered devotion among the inhabitants of the towns and villages of Umbria. The point of convergence between the two men was a passion for the renewal of the life and vigour of the apostolic community. Innocent's reforms were enshrined in the canons of the Fourth Lateran Council and these shaped the reforms propagated by Francis and thousands of his itinerant followers in the thirteenth century. The meeting between the aristocratic pope and the son of a merchant was one of the most decisive moments in the history of the medieval Church, although neither man could have predicted the outcome of this providential meeting. The way in which the pope received Francis and his openness to the saint reflect his own pastoral instincts and his wish to encourage higher standards of Christian observance.

The first biographer reports briefly that Francis was received by the pope, who examined the petition and then gave his assent. This summary account was amplified by the *Anonymous of Perugia*. At the outset the pope rehearsed many of the suggestions put to Francis by Cardinal John of St Paul. His anxieties about the friars' wish to abandon ownership and the level of austerity which seemed to be beyond human attainment were aired. In response Francis confidently proclaimed his trust in divine providence. The pope was not intending to make his decision on the spot. Instead, his sensitivity and confidence in the power of prayer were displayed in his request that Francis should withdraw until God should reveal his wish to them. Francis was exhorted to go away and pray for further guidance on this matter. On his return he told the pope a parable about a wealthy monarch, who freely married a poor but very beautiful woman who bore him a number of children. While she was pondering how she might provide for her children, the great king appeared and assured her that her children would be fed. The poor woman symbolized poverty and confirmed Francis in his resolve to live according to this value. The explanation of this dream convinced Innocent that Francis's petition should be granted.

When Innocent had ascertained the friars' wishes, he first examined their petition and later gave his consent. A papal blessing was imparted to Francis and his brothers, who were sent out to preach penance to all. Innocent instructed them to return when God should increase their numbers and promised to entrust other responsibilities to them. Sayers reports that in 1210 the pope committed himself to nothing and gave no more than verbal encouragement to the friars because a formal Rule of life still had to be drawn up.[47] Despite moves to limit the number of new religious Rules in the Church, Innocent was content to let time test the authenticity of this small group of men intent on living in the apostolic manner and advised them to return when their numbers had increased. Powell takes the view that Innocent's promise to provide the friars with further assistance at a later date was the beginning of a process leading to the complete confirmation of the Rule and order. He adds that the confirmation of the Rule by Honorius III was an extension of the earlier approval granted by Innocent III.[48]

Later accounts of the meetings between Innocent and Francis

A fuller and more circumspect account of the chain of events leading to the approval of the fraternity was woven into Thomas of Celano's second biography, which was composed in a decade when the friars' role in the Church was being openly questioned by some priests; there was some speculation that the friars' pastoral activities might be curtailed by the first Council of Lyon in 1245. This narrative attests that, when Francis and his followers presented themselves at the papal court, Innocent replied that the request was beyond his powers. Accordingly, he exhorted Francis to pray that the divine will would be manifested to guide them. Francis agreed and gave himself to fervent prayer, exhorting his companions to do the same. Mindful of Christ's use of parables, he returned to the pope and told him about the parable of the poor but beautiful woman who had married a king. Innocent wondered at the parable proposed to him and recognized without doubt that Christ had spoken in Francis.

Additional detail was provided by Bonaventure's later account. Innocent was in the Lateran palace, walking in a hall known as the Hall of Mirrors and lost in deep thought, when Francis was announced. He knew nothing about the man from Assisi and indignantly sent him away. This contradicts Thomas of Celano's narrative of how Guido had made the crucial introduction with Cardinal John of St Paul. The following night, however, the pope had a vision in which he saw a palm tree sprouting between his feet and growing into a fine tree. As he wondered what the vision meant, the divine light made it clear to him that the palm tree was the beggar whom he had turned away the previous day. The next morning he gave his servants orders to search the city for Francis whom they found in St Anthony's hospice. Francis was then immediately brought before Innocent and unfolded his plans, imploring him to approve the Rule.

It was left to Bonaventure to recount the appearance of Francis before the pope and cardinals and he supplies a fuller treatment of the exchanges among the cardinals on the subject of Francis's petition. It is not unlikely that some, possibly many, cardinals were at first wary about the nature of Francis's petition on the basis of its rigorous level of observance and its novelty; within a few years the Fourth Lateran Council would proscribe the writing of new Rules, insisting that new institutions should model themselves on the older Rules. Some of the cardinals explained their reservations about the new vocation on the grounds of the novelty of the petition and its high level of austerity. At this juncture a telling intervention was made by John of St Paul, who had not hitherto been introduced. Caution was counselled and the cardinals were reminded that, if they were to reject this legitimate request on the grounds of novelty or austerity, they would be offending the Gospel. He added that the grounds of their objections were perilous because those who declared that a vow to live according to the perfection of the Gospel contained something new or unreasonable or too difficult to observe, were guilty of blasphemy against the Gospel. This point carried the day and the biographies single out John of St Paul as the friars' sole advocate in the meeting of the cardinals. There is no suggestion that Cardinal Ugolino was present on these occasions or intervened on the friars' behalf, though Angelo da Clareno articulates the tradition that Ugolino joined forces with John of St Paul.[49] Later sources claim that this cardinal often helped and advised Francis, praising his life and works and recommending them to the cardinals.[50] The friars were insistent that their order had sprung from the pure roots of the Gospel and that they were restoring the vigour of the Christian community.[51]

Leo and companions report that Innocent approved Francis's Rule and afterwards informed everyone at the Lateran Council, although no such report was included among the acts of the council. R. B. Brooke observes that this was the only early evidence that the Rule was confirmed by the Fourth Lateran Council. Francis, like Dominic, was under pressure to accept an existing Rule after the decree of the council which in effect forbade new Rules. This seems to be confirmed by the long gap between Innocent's first approval—which was verbal, and therefore, informal, but clearly a historical fact, because we have Francis's word for it in the *Testament*—and the formal confirmation of the *Regula bullata* in 1223.[52] Is this an indication that Francis received an assurance that the fraternity would not be affected by the thirteenth canon of the council regarding the composition of new Rules of life? Francis's dialogue with Innocent III paved the way for the later confirmation of the Rule by Honorius III. D. Knowles points out that Francis's Rule was the only new one composed between that of St Benedict and the Constitutions of St Ignatius.[53]

While the biographers record the various accounts of how the friars gained papal approval, Francis's writings supply a significant detail which was absent from the earliest biographers. He announces that Innocent III granted his request and approved the Rule for him and his friars, present and to come. Then he discloses that he and his friars bound themselves in obedience and reverence to Innocent. The Rule of 1223 opens with the friars' promise to live the Gospel in accordance with their vows of poverty, chastity and obedience before going on to profess the friars' obedience and reverence to Honorius III and his canonically elected successors.[54] At the very outset Francis bound his fraternity to the papacy with a solemn promise, which was captured by the Giotto school in the basilica of San Francesco in Assisi: the friars knelt before Innocent III who stretched forth his hand in blessing. Knowles explains that through the friars' close contact with the Curia and their cardinal protector the pope began to exercise a direct control upon the fraternity which would have been unthinkable a century earlier. The minister general was closely bound to the pope, his cardinals and the Curia. From the start the first centralized institute was based upon Rome.[55]

The last act in the friars' visit to the papal court was an event of enormous significance. Just as Innocent had authorized the Humiliati to preach penance,[56] so he commissioned the friars to preach penance to all. The *Vita prima* reports that the pope gave the friars authority to preach penance to all. More specific information is provided by the later biographies. Bonaventure testifies that Innocent tonsured the friars so that they might preach without interference. Cardinal John of St Paul's role was noted by the *Legenda trium sociorum* which records that the cardinal wished the twelve friars to be clerics. There is no indication that Francis was ordained to the diaconate on this occasion, though it cannot be ruled out. He was a deacon by the time of the general chapter of 1221, when he read the Gospel at Mass. The early tradition of why Francis remained a deacon was articulated by John Pecham, who attributes it to the saint's humility.[57] While Francis is frequently heralded as the 'lay presence' within the Church, the clerical tonsure and his ordination to the diaconate drew him into the clerical ranks and the friars' first visit to the papal court brought with it an unmistakable clerical dimension. The early biographies do not record any word of protest from the founder about this step in the direction of clericalism. The silence of the seminal biographies leaves as a matter of conjecture the question of whether Francis sought or accepted the clerical status. Was the conferral of the tonsure a papal method for binding the friars to the mission of the Church? The writings of Francis and the early biographies unite in their emphasis on the friars' responsibilities to carry forward the policies of the reforming papacy.

The bond between the papacy and the fraternity was strengthened and produced comments by both the friars and their neighbours. Salimbene, reporting that Innocent confirmed the Rule and the order, added that from that point onwards both cardinals and popes had greatly loved the friars, recognizing that they had been sent for the salvation of the world and that they were useful to the Church.[58] Matthew Paris testifies that the friars were favoured by Innocent III.[59] There may have been further meetings between Innocent and Francis, because the latter was one of the few who remained with Innocent on his death bed at Perugia on 16 July 1216. His profound reverence for the papacy was communicated to his followers and found theological expression in the friars' pro-papal ecclesiology in the 1240s and 1250s at Paris. For instance, Bonaventure places the pope at the apex of the hierarchy, arguing that the higher the degree of authority the more narrowly it is concentrated. There are many bishops, a lesser number of archbishops, very few patriarchs and one father of fathers, the pope.[60]

LATERAN IV, ECCLESIASTICAL REFORM AND FRANCIS

The Gregorian reformers had waged war on the clerical abuses of simony and concubinage and promoted their policies at the annual councils held in Rome as well as in synods in other parts of western Europe. Though the papacy was determined to impose clerical celibacy and to extirpate simony, there was some deeply entrenched resistance. One of those who encountered violent opposition was John, archbishop of Rouen. From 1074 he had led a merciless campaign against vice and for a decade he fulfilled his duties as metropolitan courageously and thoroughly, continuously striving to separate priests from their mistresses. On one occasion, when he forbade them to keep concubines, he was driven from the synod by stones.[61] Opposition to the papal measures was accompanied by a measure of indifference in some quarters. The frequency with which reforming canons were drawn up is an indication that the problems were not eradicated at a stroke. Popes dispatched legates to various countries in an attempt to ensure that their policies informed and guided the decisions of national synods. Nonetheless, as the medieval chronicles and collections of letters show, papally-inspired reforms required implementation at parochial level.

Freed states that in the twelfth century the Church had neglected the cities. The prelates, usually recruited from the ranks of the feudal aristocracy, were suspicious of the new urban culture. With the exception of the Augustinian canons, the new orders of the twelfth century located their houses in isolated spots and ignored the towns. The neglect of these new centres of population provided the wandering, evangelical preachers and heretics with an appreciative audience among the urban population.[62] Few of the parish clergy possessed the educational or theological resources necessary to preach or instruct their people. Examples of priests lacking the appropriate theological preparation for their ministry are not scarce in medieval texts and writers like Gerald of Wales happily provide abundant examples of clerical ignorance. Few of the parish clergy, in fact, had enough education to be able to offer their people sufficient doctrinal or moral instruction. This lack of instruction created a vacuum which was a cause of concern to conscientious prelates. The combined pressure of the reform movements which embraced the laity, the increasing levels of literacy and the urban concentration brought sound theological instruction to the top of the papal agenda. It was left to the friars to lead and impose their trade mark upon a revival of popular preaching throughout the western Church.

Towards the end of his life Innocent convened the Fourth Lateran Council, which was to assemble in 1215. He summoned the council and proclaimed his twin objectives of recovering the Holy Land and reforming the Church. The fact that many elements of the reforms promulgated at the council had appeared in Innocent's correspondence throughout the pontificate was noted by Morris.[63] The council has been seen as a great summary of Innocent's work, even though his death the following year meant that the implementation of these decrees fell to others.[64] Powell observes that the council which met between 11 and 30 November 1215 was the largest and most comprehensive assembly of the ecclesiastical hierarchy ever held in the Middle Ages. Its ecumenical character was established by the attendance of the primate of the Maronites and Deacon Peter, representing the Melkite archbishop of Alexandria. The Latin patriarchs of Jerusalem, Antioch and Constantinople were present with many of their suffragans. The work of the council was more than the culmination of Innocent's plans; it was the culmination of his life[65] and it was attended by 412 bishops, over 800 abbots and priors, ambassadors of the Emperor Frederick II and many others.[66] Sayers notes that the proceedings of this council were well in line with the principles on pastoral care emanating from Paris at the end of the twelfth century.[67]

Canons 1–21 on the agenda emphasized the pastoral responsibilities of bishops and priests. The decrees began with a reaffirmation of the Church's teaching, and then reproved the trinitarian teaching of Abbot Joachim of Fiore, laid down penalties for heretics, addressed the difficulties with the Greek Church, the importance of holding provincial councils on a regular basis, the prelate's responsibility to correct offences, especially those perpetrated by clerics, the need to appoint suitable preachers to assist bishops, the establishment of teachers and theologians in each diocese, the punishment of clerical incontinence, the prevention of drunkenness among the clergy, dress appropriate for clerics, due respect for churches, the safe keeping of the chrism and the reserved Eucharist and annual confession and communion. Canonical issues loomed large in many of the later decrees, though measures were enacted to combat clerical simony and avarice. The keys to Innocent's pastoral strategy were preaching, confession and the Mass and he endeavoured to create a clergy detached from material and carnal pursuits and intent on the promotion of Christian ideals. The followers of Dominic and Francis provided the papacy with an army of zealous and fervent preachers, missionaries and defenders of Christian doctrine, who carried the reforming measures of the council into virtually every city, town and parish in western Europe. Not a few of the theological formulations and themes chosen by the Lateran Council appear also in Francis's writings. Gerald of Frachet, the Dominican biographer, claimed that both Francis and Dominic were present at the Lateran Council.[68] The friars looked to the papacy for approval and from the 1220s a series of popes turned to them more and more for a variety of measures as they, along with the Dominicans, rapidly became instruments of the papal reforms. Among the many topics addressed by the council special attention was given to the reinvigoration of the priesthood, the ministry of preaching and the promotion of eucharistic piety.

Priestly office

Innocent's resolve to raise the standards of clerical behaviour and ministry pervades the numerous canons of the council. Canons 14–17 targeted various abuses and laid down appropriate remedies. Clerical continence was reaffirmed as the ideal state for those in holy orders; the incontinent were to be punished according to the canonical sanctions in proportion to the seriousness of their sins. Those who had been suspended and still presumed to celebrate the sacred liturgy were to be deprived of their benefices and further sanctions were demanded for persistent offenders and prelates who countenanced incontinence. Clerics were admonished to avoid gluttony and drunkenness and were forbidden to hunt or to fowl; accordingly, they should not have dogs or birds for fowling. Neither should they practise callings or business of a secular nature; they were barred from watching mimes, entertainers and actors and they should not play at games of dice or chance. Taverns were to be avoided except in the case of necessity when travelling. Priests should wear a suitable tonsure and devote themselves to the divine service. Regulations for clerical dress were then enacted; it was reported that some clerics and prelates were accustomed to pass half the night in unnecessary feasting, forbidden conversation and, as a result, they were accustomed to spend the following morning in bed. Others celebrated Mass barely four times a year and did not bother to attend at other times. On the few occasions when they were present at the sacred liturgy, they did not give an attentive ear to the things of God. Such clerics were required to celebrate the divine office with both zeal and devotion day and night alike.

A salient feature of Francis's writings is his profound reverence for the priestly office, a theme which also pervades the early biographies. Priests at San Damiano, the Portiuncula and San Nicola in Assisi were instrumental in the clarification of Francis's vocation, though he was also very conscious that the behaviour of some priests around Assisi fell short of their sacred office; the biographers specify some of the faults of the priests who came into contact with Francis.[69] Despite his awareness of such clerical failings, his attitude towards the priesthood was reverential. Thomas of Celano reports that in the period before his conversion Francis had been generous to poor priests, providing sacred vessels for their churches and showed due honour to the clergy. His experiences with Guido were positive and resulted in a strong reverence for bishops and priests. A profound respect for the priestly office informed his conduct, preaching and teaching and this was strengthened by the newly defined doctrine of transubstantiation.

Francis revered priests and affirmed that God had given him such faith in them on account of their dignity that, even if they were to persecute him, he would still go back to them for aid. He added that, if he were as wise as Solomon and met the poorest priests of the world, he would still refuse to preach against their will in their parishes.[70] He would often say that, if he happened to meet a saint from heaven and a priest simultaneously, he would first show honour to the priest on account of his liturgical privilege in presiding at the celebration of the Eucharist; the saint would be instructed to wait. At San Damiano he kissed the hands of the poor priest with great faith and offered him the money he had with him. He wanted great reverence shown to the hands of priests; for to these had been given divine authority over the consecrated bread and wine.[71]

He bewailed the fate of those who despised priests and he maintained that, even if priests fell into sin, no one should pass judgement on them. With his customary directness Francis reminded contemporaries that judgement on wayward priests and others was reserved to God. He taught that priests were in a privileged position because they had charge of the Body and Blood of Christ, which they received and they alone administered to others. Anyone who sinned against them committed a greater crime than if he had sinned against anyone else in the whole world. Here and elsewhere Francis expressed his reverence for priests who lived according to the form of the Roman Church.[72] His respect for priests, however, was contingent upon their obedience to the Church and his emphasis upon their sacred office prompted him to remind them of the dignity of their vocation. While on several occasions he refers to the sins of priests, his advice was that the friars should focus upon the priestly office which these men exercised rather than their personal failings. His teaching was summed up thus:

> blessed is the servant who has faith in the clergy who live uprightly according to the norms of the Roman Church. And woe to those who look down upon them; for even though they may be sinners, none the less no one is to judge them since the Lord alone reserves judgement on them to Himself. For inasmuch as their ministry is greater in that it concerns the most holy Body and Blood of our Lord Jesus Christ, which they receive and which they alone administer to others, so those who sin against them commit a greater sin than [if they sinned] against all other people of this world.[73]

A close link was thus established between respect for the clergy and the office which they discharged, although Francis readily concedes that priests may be sinners. He was determined to reverence, love and honour them as his lords and on that account he refused to consider their sins because he could see the Son of God in them and they were better than him. His reverence was rooted in the fact that in this world he could not see the Son of God with his own eyes, except for the Eucharist.[74] An immense respect for the priesthood was thus one of the major themes which pervades the collection of letters and admonitions composed by Francis. He was anxious to promote the reforms set forth by Innocent III and to ensure that the exercise of this office was not compromised by an unbalanced attitude towards people or material goods. His letter to the clergy calls upon them to implement the recent reforms of the council and to ensure that the sacred Scriptures and everything else associated with their ministry of the altar were accorded a fitting respect and reverence. In his letter to the entire order he entreats the priests in the order to exercise their sacred office, with a strong eucharistic focus, in a spiritual and dignified manner.

Eucharistic piety

One of the major themes of the papal programme, enshrined in the first canon of the council, was the promotion of eucharistic doctrine and piety. The council taught that the Body and Blood of Christ were truly contained in the sacrament of the altar and it was reaffirmed that only a priest was empowered to confect the sacrament. Canons 19–21 turned on disciplinary matters: churches were to be kept as sacred places and people's furniture could no longer be stored there; churches, altar vessels, corporals and vestments were to be kept neat and clean; the chrism and the reserved Eucharist were to be locked away in a safe place in all churches to protect them from the malevolent; those who had attained the age of discernment should individually confess all their sins to their own priest annually and reverently receive the Eucharist during Eastertide at least. Penalties for the failure to implement these reforms were laid down.

The defective dispositions towards the reception of the Eucharist in the Middle Ages can be inferred from the biographies of Francis and the letters and exhortations which he circulated. An important stage in Francis's conversion was situated in a eucharistic context by Bonaventure, who emphasizes the saint's devotional participation in the liturgy with a heart and mind receptive to the Gospel. While Francis regarded the Eucharist in sacrificial terms, he viewed it as a way of associating himself ever more deeply with his divine master and a source of strength and vitality in his efforts to live according to the norms of the Gospel. For this reason he frequently reiterated his desire that the sacrament should be celebrated with a fitting dignity and reverence and the sense of the sacred was to be recovered and extended to everything associated with the liturgy. He was presented as a model of eucharistic piety based on the reforms prosecuted by the papacy and his deep-rooted devotion was summed up by Thomas of Celano: Francis burned with a love that came from his whole being for the sacrament of the Lord's Body and he was carried away with wonder at the loving condescension and most condescending love displayed in this sacrament. He attended at least one Mass a day and he considered it wrong not to take daily advantage of this sacramental remedy. He communicated often, though this is to be interpreted in the context of the medieval Church and its practice of infrequently receiving the Eucharist. His devout reception of the Eucharist was contagious, stirring others towards a more profound and warm piety. He showed this sacrament all the devotion he could muster and it became a daily means of affirming and renewing his own consecration to God. He regarded France as a country with a strong devotion to the Eucharist and yearned to die there on account of its reverence for sacred things.[75]

In a series of letters Francis provides guidance on the dispositions needed for the beneficial celebration and reception of the Eucharist. Friars were advised to show the greatest possible reverence and honour to the Body and Blood of

Christ. A special plea was addressed to all the priests of the order that in the celebration of Mass they should be free from all earthly affection, offering with single-mindedness and reverence the true sacrifice of the Body and Blood of Jesus Christ; a holy and pure intention was to be the priest's companion in going to the altar. The Eucharist was not to be offered for any worldly gain, neither for human respect or love for any human being. With the help of God's grace, the priests' whole attention should be centred on God and their will should be fixed on pleasing him alone. The dominical words 'Do this in remembrance of me' (Luke 22:19; 1 Corinthians 11:24) were quoted and were followed by the stark warning that priests who acted otherwise associated themselves with Judas, the symbol of ingratitude and treachery. Francis taught that it was a great misery and miserable weakness that, when priests had Jesus Christ present sacramentally on the altar, they concerned themselves with anything else in the entire world. A person despises, defiles and tramples on the Lamb of God when, as the Apostle says, he does not recognize (1 Corinthians 11:29) and discern the holy bread of Christ from other foods or actions or eats it unworthily or indeed, even if he were worthy, eats it unthinkingly or without the proper dispositions. In Francis's mind there was only one legitimate reason for celebrating the Eucharist: the desire to offer praise, reverence and honour to God and to advance in love of neighbour. The faithful should communicate with a pure heart and a chaste body (*puro corde et casto corpore nostro*),[76] a term which mirrors the fourteenth canon, *puro corde et mundo corpore*. This emphasis upon purity of heart reaffirms his own perception that the sacrament was a vehicle for growth, strength and integrity. Friars were instructed that, when they had confessed their sins with due contrition, they should receive the Eucharist with great humility and reverence. In addition, they were instructed to publicize the teaching of the recent council and in every sermon they were to impress upon the people that no one could be saved without receiving the Body of Christ.[77]

Whenever the friars deemed it appropriate, they should humbly beg the clergy to revere above everything else the Body and Blood of Christ and the written words which consecrate the elements. Chalices, corporals, altar furnishings must be of precious materials. When the sacred elements were present on the altar or being carried to the sick, the people on bended knee should praise, glorify and honour God. Friars were urged to visit churches frequently[78] and, when they approached a church, even from a distance, they were taught a prayer, which Francis incorporated into his *Testament*.[79]

Francis's devotion to the Eucharist embraced everything associated with the celebration of Mass and the Church. The spirit of the Lateran Council is reflected in Francis's practice of going through the villages and churches in the neighbourhood of Assisi preaching penance and carrying a broom to sweep the churches. Distressed to find unclean churches, he directed priests to be careful and diligent in keeping clean their churches, altars, and everything connected with the celebration of the divine mysteries.[80] Van Dijk and Walker assert that the private adoration of the reserved sacrament is attested to have been spread from Umbria in the first quarter of the thirteenth century by thousands of Francis's followers, though no documentary support is provided for this claim.[81] The friars' promotion of eucharistic reverence made a deep impression on Mansuetus, a nuncio of Alexander IV. He testified that, as a boy of about 10, the friars had taught him to regard the Eucharist with special reverence and he was accustomed to fast almost throughout Lent in order to make a good communion at Easter.[82]

Preaching

The first canon of the council contained a summary of Catholic doctrine to combat the propaganda of the Cathars. The necessity of nourishing the faithful with the word of God was spelt out in the tenth canon and there was an admission that the bishops by themselves were unable to provide such sustenance single-handedly, especially in large and scattered dioceses. In the past prelates had been hindered by numerous occupations, bodily infirmities and the plague of warfare and there was a suggestion that some bishops were hampered by a lack of knowledge, an obstacle which would not be countenanced in the future. The council proposed a remedy whereby bishops were required to appoint suitable men to carry out with profit the office of preaching. Such men were to be powerful in word and deed and should visit with care the peoples entrusted to them in place of the bishops. Furthermore, bishops were required to furnish these preachers with whatever was necessary. In cathedral and conventual churches suitable men were to be appointed to assist the bishop in the office of preaching, hearing confessions and imposing penances. The importance of this measure is reflected in the punitive policies to be visited upon bishops who neglected to appoint such assistants.

It is ironical that the young Francis, one of the most gifted preachers of the Middle Ages, had probably heard few sermons in his youth. Nonetheless, the ministry of the Word had played a central part in his conversion and this gave him a heightened sense of the importance of the proclamation of the divine truth. At the end of the previous century Alan of Lille had complained about those whose preaching included jesting words or childish remarks, or the melodiousness and harmony resulting from the use of rhythm or metre; these were better fitted to delight the ear than to edify the soul. Such preaching was theatrical and full of buffoonery and in every way to be condemned.[83] The sacredness of the office of preaching emerges in the instructions which Francis gave to friars entrusted with the office of preaching:

> I also admonish and exhort these brothers that, in their preaching, their words be
> well chosen and chaste (cf. Psalms 11:7; 17:31), for the instruction and edification of

the people, speaking to them of vices and virtues, punishment and glory in a discourse that is brief, because it was in few words that the Lord preached while on earth.[84]

Francis and the friars were commissioned to preach penance and the result of their fervent preaching was that a sharper awareness of Christian responsibilities came to obtain in a region where the people had grown negligent of the Gospel. The friars were situated within the apostolic tradition as they moved from town to town.[85] Their preaching was marked by a strong respect for the ecclesiastical hierarchy and the ministers were charged to exercise vigilance about this most important office. Francis's Rules of life in 1221 and 1223 contain his instructions that the friars should not preach contrary to ecclesiastical law or without the permission of their minister, who must exercise appropriate care in the appointment of preachers; friars should be examined before they are assigned to the ministry of preaching.

The ministry of preaching was central to the mendicant ideal and both Dominic and Francis made this a central plank of their fraternities. By the second decade of the thirteenth century the friars were becoming increasingly visible in the cities and towns of western Europe. Moreover, they preached with fervour and imagination, taking the Gospel into the main streets of the urban centres and this coexisted with programmes of preaching in the countryside and in missionary territories. In an age when few priests preached, the advent of the friars caused a wave of excitement and provided instruction for those dwelling in cities and the countryside. The friars' immense contribution was widely acknowledged and bishops regarded them as providential assistants in their ministry of instructing and encouraging the laity.

Their success, however, provoked resentment among some of the secular clergy, who believed that the friars were subverting the relationship between a parish priest and his parishioners. When the secular clergy began to complain about the extent of that ministry of mendicant preaching, the friars pointed to a unique element in their Rule. Bonaventure explains that the Rule expressly imposed upon the friars the authority and office of preaching; he adds that he has not found such an explicit directive in any other Rule.[86] Similar capital was made by John Pecham, who reminds Robert Kilwardby, his Dominican opponent, that the Rule of St Augustine makes no mention of the office of preaching. In contrast the Rule of St Francis contained such a provision, which was treated in two chapters.[87] The mendicants themselves claimed that preaching had been a rarity prior to their emergence. This view was confidently espoused by Bonaventure in his polemics with the secular masters.[88] Roger Bacon complains of the ignorance of the clerics and rural priests, who understand little or nothing of the divine office they read, like brute animals;[89] reforming bishops freely acknowledged that some priests were hampered by an incomplete grasp of both the Scriptures and the Latin language with which the Liturgy was celebrated.[90] In the context of the mendicant controversy Salimbene states that the preaching office belonged to the secular clergy. If they possessed the knowledge to preach and led a good life, they could preach in their own churches and not be scorned by the people. Their evil lives and ignorance, claims the chronicler, had rendered them unworthy of the exercise of this sacred trust. In contrast the Franciscans have made the people accustomed to hearing preachers with both knowledge and good lives.[91]

FRANCISCANS AND THE RESTORATION OF THE CHURCH

One of the images employed by the early biographers was that of Francis's role as the restorer of ancient churches and this presages his contribution to the vitality of the universal Church. Thomas of Celano summarizes Francis's balanced piety towards the chapel of San Damiano. On his return from Foligno he wished to restore the ancient chapel where he met the poor priest, whose penury mirrored the dilapidated buildings. In his enthusiasm for the restoration of the chapel he offered the priest the money which he had received. At this stage his thoughts were on the restoration of the aged house of God and the money was seen as a way of accomplishing this. The offer of money was declined, but Francis was allowed to remain there and, after the dramatic rift with his father, he began the restoration of the chapel. The details bristle with symbolism and the first biographer showed himself to be aware of their potential by reporting that Francis did not try to construct the church anew, rather he restored the ancient one, building upon the foundations laid by Jesus Christ. A feature of the building process was the fact that the restored chapel became the home of the Poor Clares.[92] Mockler comments that this was an age of rebuilding and restoring and that, if Francis had been a nobleman's son, he would probably have set about repairing ruined towers.[93]

E. Peters points out that the whole episode had been thoroughly recast with very different emphasis in the *Vita secunda*,[94] a much more theological account, teeming with propaganda to underline the friars' impact on the medieval Church. During the transitional period in his life Francis was walking one day near San Damiano, which had nearly fallen to ruin and was abandoned by everyone. He was inspired to enter the chapel and prayed before the crucifix. As he did so a remarkable event occurred: the painted image of Christ crucified moved its lips and commanded him to restore the house which was falling into ruin. The biographer reveals that Francis trembled and was amazed; the mandate from the crucified Christ almost deranged him. He braced himself to obey and gave himself completely to the fulfilment of this command. The later account was stronger and refers to an unprecedented act: the message from the cross to restore the crumbling church. Francis's reaction was to take the message literally, as he did so often in this period, and he spent a couple of years restoring churches. Within this grace-laden context the biographer introduces Francis's prophecy about the rise of a community of admirable sisters and Clare, too, steps forward to play her part in the renewal of the Church in Umbria.

Having repaired San Damiano, Francis went to another place near Assisi, where he began to rebuild the dilapidated and well-nigh destroyed church. The biographers note that the three chapels were old, ruined and abandoned, though Mass was celebrated in them, perhaps on an occasional basis. They present the saint as a man whose energies were devoted to restoring the Church which was falling into decay. The symbolism of Francis restoring churches dedicated to Sts Damian, Peter and the Blessed Virgin was ripe for the biographers. The first church, dedicated to a martyr of the early Church, reflects his strong devotion to the martyrs of Assisi and his own unfulfilled ambition to win the martyr's crown. The second church, in honour of the prince of the apostles, expresses his reverence for the first bishop of Rome and his successor, the vicar of Christ, and the third, devoted to the Mother of God, took Francis to the mystery of the Incarnation. The restoration of the three chapels near Assisi charts Francis's own pilgrimage from the theme of martyrdom, through devotion to the see of Peter and his own desire to promote reform from the bosom of the Church, to a fuller understanding of the way in which the redemption of the human race was launched.

Francis's task in rebuilding ruined churches was initially a local matter, but his contribution to the restoration of the universal Church became much more explicit in the papal dream about the Lateran basilica, the cathedral church of Rome and principal church in the West. Medieval chroniclers enthused about the impact made by the early friars, who were seen to be reviving the life of the apostolic Church. The friars, too, eventually came to see themselves in this light and shaped their rhetoric accordingly. They proclaimed their conviction that their ministry was renewing the Church and this belief makes an early appearance in the account of the events leading to Francis's canonization: Gregory IX delighted in the fact that the Church was renewed by the miracles being performed at Francis's tomb.[95]

Events surrounding Francis's petition for the papal approbation of the fraternity included the celebrated dream. In his sleep Innocent III had seen the Lateran basilica about to fall to ruin, when a certain religious, small and despised, supported it by putting his own back under it lest it fall. The pope remarked that surely this man, by his works and by the teaching of Christ, would give support to the Church, and for this reason he also recalled a certain vision he had a few days earlier, which, he affirmed under the guidance of the Holy Spirit, would be fulfilled in this man. He believed that this figure would support the Church by his works and the teaching of Christ and for this reason he acceded to Francis's petition; the phenomenal success of the friars' preaching programme confirmed the interpretation given to the papal dream. At the time of the composition of the *Vita secunda* the friars cherished warm memories of the benevolent intervention by Innocent, whom Celano depicts as having a special love for Francis. The biographer leaves the reader in no doubt that the man in Innocent's dream was Francis. Sayers adds that the scene of Francis propping up the Lateran basilica was depicted in mosaic in the church of Santa Maria in Aracoeli in Rome and was associated with Nicholas IV, the first Franciscan pope (1288-92). In a long mosaic inscription in the Lateran Nicholas explicitly connected his restoration of that basilica with Innocent III's dream of Francis sustaining the Church.[96] J. Gardner argues that this propaganda suited both the papacy and the Franciscans.[97]

While Franciscan hagiography and art laid claim to Innocent's dream about the Lateran, the Dominicans associated their founder with the figure supporting the basilica. An early illustration of this is the work of Nicola Pisano and his assistants in San Domenico at Bologna on the occasion of the second translation of the founder on 5 June 1267.[98] This rests upon the *Legenda* by Constantine of Orvieto who identifies Dominic in the pope's dream.[99] S. Tugwell explains that some manuscripts of the chronicle of Gerald of Frachet claim that the source of the Dominican version of the story was Cardinal Rainerio Capocci, who would probably have been in a position to know anything that was being said about Innocent's dreams in 1215. It is possible that in the 1240s Capocci was telling a story about the pope's dream; as a supporter of both orders of friars the cardinal may have felt that the dream was being fulfilled in either or both of them.[100]

If this story was in circulation in the late 1220s, it is difficult to imagine why it was not inserted into the *Vita prima*. It did not make its first appearance in Franciscan hagiography until the second half of the 1240s. The Dominican interest in this dream appears about the same time, because the *Vita secunda* and the *Legenda* by Constantine of Orvieto were both written in 1246-48 in response to appeals for miracle stories about the two founders in the Franciscan general chapter of 1244 and the Dominican chapter of 1245. The spur behind the mendicant claims to the dream of Innocent III may have been the friars' increasingly troubled relations with the secular clergy. Supported by Cardinal Capocci, the friars may have turned this dream to their advantage in the propaganda war about their particular relationship with the papacy. This was a powerful piece of propaganda for the friars, who had to deal with a growing chorus of criticism from both prelates and parish priests at a time when there were some bishops who sought to curb the pastoral privileges of the mendicant orders. This explanation draws support from the succession of privileges and permissions granted to the mendicants by Innocent III, Honorius III and Gregory IX especially because those privileges stirred up resentment among the secular clergy.

Peters states that from the eleventh century onwards the building and restoration of churches were primarily the work of prelates. Such enterprises were often deemed the most the important activities of some prelates. The desire to take a higher profile in terms of building schools and churches was one of the major factors in the growing Catholic population of England in the first half of the twentieth century. The twelfth century was perhaps the greatest age of church restoration that Europe had ever witnessed and nowhere was this work more dramatically evident than in Rome itself. From the end of the Investiture Conflict with the Concordat of Worms and the First Lateran Council in 1123, popes and cardinals enlarged, rebuilt, restored and remodelled a large number of Roman churches. Despite some criticism, prelates continued to build and dedicate churches and symbolic theologians continued to expound upon the spiritual significance of their work.[101] It was in the interests of Francis's followers to identify him as the figure from the dreams of the pope, symbolizing the saint's association with one of the most reforming popes of the Middle Ages and his part in the renewal of the Church at all levels.

CONCLUSION

Francis's ideas about the ecclesiastical authority were traditional: the bishop of Assisi was the custodian of the spiritual authority of San Rufino and this outlook was extended to the papacy. In addition, by the early thirteenth century the pope was perceived as the successor of St Peter and the vicar of Christ. For Francis there was no comparable power within the Church; no other authority would have had such legitimacy in his eyes. The combined influence and wisdom of Guido and John of St Paul ensured that the friars' petition received a fair hearing in the Roman Curia, saving Francis and his followers from the fate which had earlier befallen the Waldensians and Humiliati. The friars found in Innocent III a pope who was more positive than some of his immediate predecessors about the vitality which reform groups might bring to the Church. Though the friars were few when Francis sought papal approval and remained a relatively small group at the time of Innocent's death, the pope seems to have regarded them as potential allies in the promotion of ecclesiastical renewal. Sayers judges that Innocent's greatest contribution was to recognize the opportunity that the friars offered within the authoritative framework and in this there seems to have been a certain amount of personal action on his part.[102] The friars, too, regarded this pope with gratitude and annually commemorated his anniversary on 16 July.[103] John Pecham reminded the friars that they, above all others, should pay special respect to the pope.[104] The development of the fraternity was watched with close interest at the papal court. Jordan of Giano describes the presence of a cardinal and several bishops at the general chapter of 1221.

From the middle of the eleventh century the papacy had been the instrument of reform, calling for renewal at all levels within the Church. No longer would clerical concubinage and simony be tolerated and attempts were made to carry these reforms into every part of the western Church by papal legates at provincial councils. Nonetheless, opposition was deeply rooted and the papal policies could be frustrated at local level. The friars' zeal for the proclamation of the Gospel, their highly acclaimed ministry of preaching, their rejection of material possessions in imitation of Jesus Christ and their itinerant lifestyle recommended them to Innocent III. They spread quickly throughout the western world and this made them ideal instruments of papal reforms. They were capable of remedying one of the weaknesses of the papal policy, whereby an effective opposition could be mounted locally.

The friars carried the spirit of reform into almost all large centres of population and contemporaries recognized them as stalwart and valued supporters of the papacy.[105] The friars' preaching focused on the reforms emanating from Innocent III, culminating in the decrees of the Fourth Lateran Council. There is a verbal correspondence between the words of decrees and some of Francis's own writings. Friars were particularly conspicuous in their respect for the priesthood, the promotion of devotion to the Eucharist and their ministry of preaching. They made an enormous impact upon the life of the Church and in the 1220s and 1230s there were many prelates and monastic chroniclers who praised the sterling work which they were carrying out. Their patrons and friends encouraged them to think that they had been sent to renew the Church in its last hour and the dream of Innocent III was exploited by both Franciscan and Dominican hagiographers in the 1240s to symbolize their zealous ministry at the heart of the Church. The way in which they accomplished these reforms was by a literal interpretation of the Gospel and an imitation of their divine master, who had nowhere to lay his head. Their emphasis on evangelical poverty revived the prophetical spirit and impressed their con- temporaries immensely, as the next chapter demonstrates.

Notes

1. *Opuscula Sancti Patris Francisci Assisiensis*, p. 242.
2. In addition to the texts cited in this chapter the reader is advised to consult the variety of papers in J. M. Powell (ed.), *Innocent III: Vicar of Christ or Lord of the World?* (Washington, DC, 2nd edn, 1994).
3. R. W. Southern, *Western Society and the Church in the Middle Ages* (London, 1970), p. 94.
4. Bede, *Historiam Ecclesiasticam, gentis Anglorum, Historiam Abbatum, Epistolam ad Ecgberctum una cum Historia Abbatum auctore anonymo*, I, ed. C. Plummer (Oxford, 1896), p. 402.
5. Bede, *Ecclesiastical History of the English People*, ed. B. Colgrave and R. A. B. Mynors (OMT; 1969), pp. 348-9, 470-1, 516-17.
6. Salimbene de Adam, *Cronica*, ed. G. Scalia (Scrittori d'Italia, 232-3; Bari, 1966), pp. 431, 459.
7. NV, II, pp. 221-4, 343. Other places of pilgrimage favoured by the people of Assisi were Mount Gargano, Venice and the Holy Land.
8. 2 C, n. 8; 1 C, n. 34.
9. LM, c. 9, n. 3.
10. J. E. Sayers, *Innocent III: Leader of Europe, 1198-1216* (London, 1994), pp. 11-12.
11. Bede, *Ecclesiastical History*, pp. 78-9, 104-5, 296-7, 388-9.
12. G. Barraclough, *The Medieval Papacy* (London, 1968), p. 48.
13. Bede, *Ecclesiastical History*, pp. 484-5.
14. *Einhard and Notker the Stammerer: Two Lives of Charlemagne*, trans. L. Thorpe (London, 1969), pp. 103-4.
15. Southern, *Western Society*, pp. 94-6.

16. Hugh the Chanter, *The History of the Church of York 1066-1127*, ed. and trans. C. Johnson, revised by M. Brett, C. N. L. Brooke and M. Winterbottom (OMT; 1990), pp. 118-21.

17. *The Epistolae Vagantes of Pope Gregory VII*, ed. H. E. J. Cowdrey (OMT; 1972), pp. 56-9.

18. Sayers, *Innocent III*, pp. 10-11.

19. B. Kempers, *Painting, Power and Patronage: The Rise of the Professional Artist in the Italian Renaissance*, trans. from Dutch by B. Jackson (London, 1992), pp. 23-4.

20. *The Letters of John of Salisbury (1153-1161)*, I, ed. W. J. Millor and H. E. Butler, revised by C. N. L. Brooke (NMT; 1953), and reprinted (OMT; 1986), pp. 207-8.

21. R. B. Brooke, *The Coming of the Friars* (Historical Problems, Studies and Documents, 24; London, 1975), offers a good introduction to the century and the movements of reform.

22. Cf. M. Maccarrone, *Vicarius Christi: storia del titolo papale* (Rome, 1952).

23. Southern, *Western Society*, pp. 104-5.

24. *S. Bernardi opera*, III, pp. 424, 465-6. Sayers, *Innocent III*, pp. 15-16, believes that the title 'vicar of Christ' probably originated with Bernard and this particular treatise. She adds that Innocent III was the first pope to proclaim publicly that he was the vicar of Christ and that afterwards it became commonplace in the official correspondence of the Curia.

25. Southern, *Western Society*, p. 105.

26. *Selected Letters of Pope Innocent III concerning England (1198-1216)*, ed. C. R. Cheney and W. H. Semple (NMT; 1953), pp. 56-7, 177.

27. 2 C, n. 8; *Opuscula Sancti Patris Francisci Assisiensis*, p. 290.

28. Ibid., pp. 119, 242, 275-6.

29. LM, c. 3, n. 9; Julian of Speyer, 'Vita Sancti Francisci' in AF, 10, pp. 344-5, where the term is mentioned thrice; 2 C, n. 16; 1 C, nn. 34, 121.

30. *Opuscula Sancti Patris Francisci Assisiensis*, pp. 237-8.

31. *S. Bonaventurae opera omnia*, V, p. 149.

32. 2 C, n. 25.

33. C. H. Lawrence, *Medieval Monasticism* (London, 1989), p. 241.

34. C. Morris, *The Papal Monarchy* (Oxford History of the Christian Church; 1989), p. 348, n. 19, comments that the Verona decree is badly worded and may not be intended to condemn the poor men of Lyon nor is it certain that preaching was the issue.

35. Sayers, *Innocent III*, pp. 143-4.

36. *Buchardi Praepositi Urspergensis Chronicon* (MGH SS; 2nd edn, 1916), pp. 107-8.

37. Morris, *The Papal Monarchy*, p. 450.

38. J. M. Powell (ed.), *Innocent III: Vicar of Christ or Lord of the World?* (Washington, 1994), pp. 5-6. He argues that Lucius III's condemnation of the Waldensians should be regarded as a lack of policy.

39. J. B. Freed, *The Friars and German Society in the Thirteenth Century* (Cambridge, MA, 1977), pp. 9-10.

40. Morris, *The Papal Monarchy*, p. 444.

41. B. Bolton, 'Innocent III and the Humiliati' in Powell (ed.), *Innocent III: Vicar of Christ or Lord of the World?*, pp. 114-20, 119.

42. 1 C, n. 33; LM, c. 3, n. 9; Salimbene, *Cronica*, p. 43. Nonetheless, he makes some critical remarks about Innocent.

43. Sayers, *Innocent III*, p. 127.

44. Lawrence, *Medieval Monasticism*, pp. 174-6, shows that the Cistercian reform initially made a slow start. At first the monastery at Cîteaux, known as the new monastery, was housed in wooden huts, built by the monks themselves. The life was austere and the site was damp and unhealthy. No new postulants came to fill the thinning ranks, and the experiment seemed doomed to extinction when, in April 1112, the young Bernard of Fontaine knocked on the gate and sought admission. The son of a landed Burgundian family, he brought with him a troop of 30 young men, including several of his brothers, whom he had persuaded to take the habit. Following this infusion of new blood, there was a rapid expansion. New colonies were founded at La Ferté in 1113 and at Pontigny in 1114 and in 1115 Bernard was sent to establish a community at Clairvaux.

45. J. R. H. Moorman, *Saint Francis of Assisi* (London, 1950), pp. 50-4, offers his own reconstruction of the contents of this lost document.

46. Cf. J. A. Watt, *The Theory of Papal Monarchy in the Thirteenth Century: The Contribution of the Canonists* (London, 1965), p. 84.

47. Sayers, *Innocent III*, p. 151.

48. J. M. Powell, 'The papacy and the early Franciscans', *Franciscan Studies*, 36 (1976), pp. 254-5.

49. E.g., Angelo da Clareno, *Rendiconti della Reale Accademia dei Lincei, Classe di Scienza morali, storiche e filologiche*, serie 5a, XVII (Rome, 1908), pp. 21-2.

50. LTS, c. 15, n. 61.

51.   *S. Bonaventurae opera omnia*, VIII (Florence, 1898), p. 393. John Pecham affirms that the friars' Rule was not a form of novelty, *nova res*.
52.   *Compilatio Assisiensis*, c. 101; *Scripta Leonis*, pp. 204-5, n. 3.
53.   D. Knowles, *From Pachomius to Ignatius* (Oxford, 1966), p. 46.
54.   *Opuscula Sancti Patris Francisci Assisiensis*, pp. 242, 226-7.
55.   Knowles, *Pachomius to Ignatius*, pp. 39, 47.
56.   Sayers, *Innocent III*, pp. 44-5, reports that Innocent III declared himself prepared to accept the desire of the sects to preach, provided that they did not discuss doctrine and that the position of the clergy was not attacked.
57.   *S. Bonaventurae opera omnia*, VIII, p. 426.
58.   Salimbene, *Cronica*, p. 421.
59.   *Historia Anglorum*, II, ed. F. Madden (RS 44, ii; London, 1866), pp. 109-10.
60.   *S. Bonaventurae opera omnia*, V (Florence, 1891), p. 278.
61.   Orderic Vitalis, *The Ecclesiastical History*, II, ed. Chibnall (OMT; 1969), pp. 200-1.
62.   Freed, *Friars and German Society*, pp. 9-10.
63.   Morris, *Papal Monarchy*, p. 433.
64.   N. P. Tanner (ed.), *Decrees of the Ecumenical Councils*, I (London, 1990), p. 227.
65.   J. M. Powell, 'Innocent III and the Crusade' in *Innocent III: Vicar of Christ or Lord of the World?*, pp. 121-34, 128-9.
66.   A. Gransden (ed.), *The Chronicle of Bury St Edmunds 1212-1301* (NMT; London, 1964), pp. 2-3.
67.   Sayers, *Innocent III*, pp. 20-1.
68.   Gerald of Frachet, 'Vitae fratrum', I, n. 4, in MOPH, 1, ed. B. M. Reichert (Rome, 1897), pp. 9-11.
69.   1 C, n. 46.
70.   2 C, n. 8; 1 C, n. 62; *Opuscula Sancti Patris Francisci Assisiensis*, p. 308.
71.   1 C, n. 9; 2 C, n. 201.
72.   *Opuscula Sancti Patris Francisci Assisiensis*, p. 80.
73.   R. J. Armstrong and I. C. Brady, *Francis and Clare: The Complete Works* (Classics of Western Spirituality; New York, 1982), p. 35.
74.   *Opuscula Sancti Patris Francisci Assisiensis*, pp. 308-9.
75.   2 C, n. 201.
76.   *Opuscula Sancti Patris Francisci Assisiensis*, pp. 117, 118, 140-2, 144.
77.   Ibid., p. 103.
78.   Ibid., pp. 102-3, 119-20.
79.   Ibid., p. 308; 1 C, n. 45.
80.   *Compilatio Assisiensis*, c. 60.
81.   S. J. P. Van Dijk and J. H. Walker, *The Myth of the Aumbry* (London, 1957), p. 69.
82.   Thomas of Eccleston, *Tractatus de adventu fratrum minorum in Angliam*, ed. A. G. Little (Manchester, 1951), p. 96.
83.   *Summa de arte praedicandi*, c. 1, in PL, 210. 111-14.
84.   Armstrong and Brady, *Francis and Clare*, p. 143.
85.   1 C, nn. 33-37.
86.   Bonaventure, 'Epistola de tribus quaestionibus ad magistrum innominatum', p. 214.
87.   *Fratris Johannis Pecham quondam archiepiscopi Cantuariensis Tractatus tres de Paupertate*, ed. C. L. Kingsford, A. G. Little and F. Tocco (BSFS, 2; Aberdeen, 1910), p. 127.
88.   *S. Bonaventurae opera omnia*, VIII, pp. 318-19.
89.   Roger Bacon, *Opera quaedam hactenus inedita*, v. 1, ed. J. S. Brewer (RS 15; London, 1859), p. 413.
90.   S. Gieben, 'Robert Grosseteste on preaching, with the edition of the sermon "Ex rerum initiatarum" on redemption', *Collectanea Franciscana*, 37 (1967), pp. 100-41, 112; *Roberti Grosseteste episcopi quondam Lincolniensis Epistolae*, ed. H. R. Luard (RS 25; London, 1861), pp. 154-5, 164.
91.   Salimbene, *Cronica*, p. 596.
92.   1 C, nn. 9, 18.
93.   A. Mockler, *Francis of Assisi* (Oxford, 1976), p. 94.
94.   E. Peters, 'Restoring the Church and restoring churches: event and image in Franciscan biography', *Franziskanische Studien*, 68 (1986), pp. 213-36, 215.
95.   1 C, n. 121.
96.   Sayers, *Innocent III*, p. 126, who points out that this church served as the headquarters of the fraternity.
97.   J. Gardner, 'Patterns of papal patronage circa 1260-circa 1300' in *The Religious Roles of the Papacy: Ideals and Realities, 1150-1300* (Pontifical Institute of Mediaeval Studies, Papers in Mediaeval Studies, 8), ed. C. Ryan (Toronto, 1989), pp. 439-56, 442-4, 449.

98.   Ibid., p. 449.

99.   Constantine of Orvieto, 'Legenda Sancti Dominici', n. 21, in MOPH, 16, pp. 301-2.

100. S. Tugwell, 'Notes on the life of St Dominic', *Archivum Fratrum Praedicatorum*, 65 (1995), pp. 5-169. I would like to record my gratitude to Dr Tugwell for his generous response to my enquiries and for a copy of the proofs of this article.

101. Peters, 'Restoring the Church', pp. 225-6.

102. Sayers, *Innocent III*, p. 163.

103. M. Bihl, 'Statuta generalia Ordinis edita in Capitulis generalibus celebratis Narbonae an. 1260', XII, viii, p. 316.

104. *S. Bonaventurae opera omnia*, VIII, p. 396.

105. Matthew Paris, *Chronica majora*, IV, ed. Luard (RS 57, iv; London, 1877), p. 256. For an introduction to some of the areas in which the papacy deployed the friars consult J. R. H. Moorman, *A History of the Franciscan Order from its Origins to the Year 1517* (Oxford, 1968), pp. 295-304.

4

❧❧❧❧❧❧❧❧❧❧❧❧

Lady Poverty

Francis said that poverty was the foundation of the whole order[1]

Francis's vocation achieved a clear form only two years after his appearance before Bishop Guido. During this transitional phase he had already developed a strong sense of detachment from the values which governed the market place. His views on contemporary monasticism are not recorded, though he did receive kindness and help from the monastery of San Benedetto on Monte Subasio. The impoverished of the medieval cities are accorded a telling role in the evolution of his vocation, which then found a biblical basis in the instructions to the apostles and the advice to the rich young man. When he heard how Jesus Christ had sent out his apostles to preach, he suddenly realized that God was calling him to do the same and thereafter he dressed and lived as an apostle. The opening of the Gospels at random gave further direction and pointed to the poverty experienced by Jesus Christ, his mother and the apostles. From that point Francis regarded himself as pledged to evangelical poverty, which he characterized as Lady Poverty, in whose service he spent the remaining eighteen years of his life. His earlier experience of commerce, which brought benefits to some and poverty to others, was confirmed by what he heard in the Gospels. The Scriptures provided him with a remedy as he entered more deeply into the mystery of the Incarnation and came to see evangelical poverty as an eschatological value: we bring nothing into the world and take nothing when we leave it.

POVERTY AND THE CONVERSION EXPERIENCES

Francis's biographers imply that the movement towards a new vocation began while he was in chains and exploit the theme of his imprisonment as a symbol of his earlier lifestyle. There is little documentary evidence for Francis's early years and the civil war provides a convenient starting point, opening a phase in which the biographical material increases and leads towards the conflict with his father. The *Vita secunda* concedes that there was a gradual clarification of his vocation and this seems to have lasted for more than two years. While the biographers may be correct in taking the Perugian captivity as a beginning, the formation of a vocation and the beginning of an unsettled period in life are mysterious events; not even close friends are able to pinpoint the moment of the process of change. It is equally feasible that the seeds of a vocation were beginning to sprout in an earlier, less well chronicled, period.

The saints' care for the poor was awarded a prominent role in the hagiographical tradition and it comes as no surprise that this element was stressed by Franciscan biographers, who were very careful to show that their saint was always solicitous for the poor and come forward with example after example of his Christian charity. Francis was a saint renowned for his care for the poor, whose ranks he was to join voluntarily as a friar. The *Legenda trium Sociorum* testifies that, while he remained in his father's house, he displayed a generosity of mind and spirit and this was a factor in the leadership which he had exercised among the youth of Assisi. He was resolved to give alms to anyone who begged from him in God's name[2]; it was, however, a failure to act in accordance with a compassionate and generous spirit that served as one of the pivotal events in the process of conversion. The biographers carefully point out that Francis was a most courteous man, who acted out of character when approached by a pauper. Asked for alms one day, he upbraided a poor man and immediately regretted his selfishness. His earlier resolution had been broken and he began to reproach himself for withholding what was asked of him in God's name. The *Anonymous of Perugia* locates this incident when Francis was selling cloth in his father's shop. Distracted by commercial preoccupations, he refused to give alms. Later he deplored his own conduct and sought out the pauper, thrusting alms into his hands.[3]

This episode demonstrates that the pursuit of commercial prosperity can be conducted in such a single-minded manner that the plight of others receives insufficient attention. Despite his good resolutions, Francis was so immersed in his commercial activities that his thoughts were focused primarily on his own business and the drive for profit to the detriment of those less privileged. He recognized that a preoccupation with his family's commercial prosperity had dulled his awareness of the needs of those who did not share in the new commercial prosperity of the cities. The event was an early betrayal of the good resolutions which he had formed and this is identified as one of the important events in the process leading to his conversion because it illustrated the way in which involvement in material pursuits is capable of blinding some to the needs of others. In a flash of insight Francis realized what he had done and took steps to ensure that the same error was never repeated. Whatever the thoughts that passed through his mind, the encounter left an indelible mark upon him and, in effect, it signalled the beginning of his withdrawal from his commercial activities. Thomas of Celano depicts a predisposition on the part of Francis to respect and assist the poor whenever this was possible. In this sense Francis's conversion stands as an enhancement of the virtues that were present earlier.

The biographer comments that on his release from prison Francis became more attentive to the needy and was determined not to turn his face away from any poor person begging for the love of God. The failure to respond generously to the pauper in the shop had unnerved him and indicated that a greater vigilance was required in order to implement his noble resolve. Armed with these renewed resolutions, his generosity soon met another test. One day he met a poverty-stricken knight, whom Thomas of Celano describes as poor and well nigh naked. On this occasion Francis, instructed by his earlier failure, was more prepared for a generous response. In a symbolic and flamboyant gesture he gave the knight his own costly garments. This incident was exploited by Thomas of Celano, who compared Francis with the classic biography of St Martin of Tours. In triumphalistic tone he reports that Francis first gave his garments before the rest of his things; St Martin first gave up the rest of his things and then finally his garments. Both lived poor and feeble in this world and entered heaven rich. The latter, a knight, but poor, cut his garment in two to clothe a poor man; the former, not a knight, but rich, clothed a poor knight with his whole garment. Both, having fulfilled the command of Jesus Christ, merited to be visited by him in a vision; one was praised for his perfection, the other was graciously invited to fulfil what was yet lacking.[4] The impoverished knight was probably one of the nobles whose castles had been ruined in the civil war and the overthrow of the feudal system. Hitherto he and his ilk had been regarded as opponents in the recent internecine strife in Assisi. Instead of seeing an adversary, Francis discerned suffering humanity, regardless of social and political considerations. This incident reveals a change in Francis, who was learning to rise above the feelings which had guided him in the civil war and was beginning to adopt a more global perspective, viewing the world not through partisan eyes and the assumptions of his former colleagues and neighbours. Compassion for a suffering member of society had taken hold of him and he was beginning to give more thought to the dictates of the Gospel and the alleviation of suffering wherever he found it. At this stage he may have started to ponder the parable of judgement and the responsibility to clothe the naked (Matthew 25:31–46).

Francis's pilgrimage to Rome was used by Thomas of Celano to indicate the direction which the saint's future would take. At the basilica of St Peter he swapped his fine garments for those of a pauper and joyfully took his place among the numerous poor in the vestibule of the basilica. Was this the fulfilment of a plan conceived in Assisi? Why did he don the beggar's clothes? Certainly it was a fortunate pauper who surrendered his own mean garb for the fine clothes of the merchant's son. Did he regard this as an act of reparation for his shabby treatment of the beggar in the shop? Did he want to learn the embarrassment of the poor who were at the mercy of the small change disbursed by pilgrims at the shrine? He was badly shaken by his earlier dealings with the pauper whom he had initially spurned; his failure to act with compassion and generosity had dented his self-confidence. The episode had shaken his self-assurance and he regarded himself as an agent in perpetuating destitution. J. Le Goff reports that Francis not only mixed with outcasts, but wanted to become one of them.[5]

Considering himself one of the poor, he ate eagerly with them. At this juncture the *Vita secunda* hailed Francis as the chief lover of the poor, but this judgement was premature. It is not improbable that he began to give more thought to the plight of the poor and their dependence upon others; this reliance on the generosity of others symbolized the sinner's limited room for manoeuvre and the need of the divine condescension. He, too, was beginning to realize that the set of presuppositions which had guided him so far were incapable of bringing him contentment and tranquillity. Francis's capacity to enter into the joys and sufferings of others became a salient feature of the various accounts of his life. His visit to the shrine of St Peter supplied the ideal opportunity to associate himself with the lot of the paupers and there he began to enter into the experience of the beggars, though its duration was short. This experience probably deepened his own instinct of generosity to the poor on his return to Assisi and foreshadowed his begging as a friar, a practice which was rooted in the experience of the Son of God and his mother.[6] The priest at San Damiano was poor and this was one of the reasons why Francis decided to dwell there in contrast to the comfort of his parental home in the city.

The poor were central to the account of Francis's conversion and care for them was presented as one of the criteria for perfect discipleship. The dependence which he discerned in his meeting with the poor man in his father's shop, the impoverished knight and the experience of living as a beggar, albeit for a single day, at the apostle's shrine, all pointed to his new vocation in which he embraced evangelical poverty in imitation of his poor master. His meditation on the conditions of the poor led him to consider how to spend the remainder of his life in a more just manner with particular care for the impoverished. He joined the ranks of the poor and alleviated their needs wherever possible[7] and the biographies provide several instances of his distress when he found anyone poorer than himself. Among the early miracles attributed to Francis are those in favour of beggars.[8] He continued to make use of money, however tempting it was for the biographers to label him as already the lover of the poor. For instance, he pressed money into the hands of the leper whom he met at a pivotal stage in his own conversion and then went to the leprosarium where he gave money to each leper. After hearing the message from the crucifix at San Damiano he gave the priest some money for the purchase of a lamp and oil to be lit before the same image. The events surrounding Bernard of Quintavalle's conversion confirm that Francis had once bought some stones from Sylvester, a secular priest in Assisi.[9]

WEALTH AND DIVISIONS IN SOCIETY

Francis was very much a man of Assisi and was steeped in his city's history, traditions and customs. In the closing years of the twelfth century he is thought to have taken part in the sack of the Rocca Maggiore and then fought in the civil war. Many wars have cultural and economic dimensions, as did Assisi's civil war whose consequences intrude into the biographies of the saint. The casualties of that civil war form part of the landscape for Francis's radical change of life and the impoverished make many appearances in early Franciscan hagiography. During his period of imprisonment Francis had time to reflect upon the abuse of power and money which had brought so much suffering and division upon the city of his birth. The war had brought distress, destruction and death to many in Assisi. The period of imprisonment gave Francis time to reflect upon the causes of violence and the divisions within society and form some new resolutions. The emergence of Assisi from this period of turmoil provided the context and the spur to adjust his own lifestyle, making him a promoter of peace and social harmony.

Francis became aware of the powerful role allotted to money, which was capable of introducing and sustaining divisions within families, sometimes leading to bloodshed. As the son of a successful merchant he was ideally placed to meditate upon the controlling power of money, especially at a time when the bustling markets offered undreamed of wealth and security. He became painfully aware that money was capable of first arousing and then stimulating the less attractive side of the personality. His own experience demonstrated that the pursuit of commercial profit could blind him to the needs of others, as his encounter with the pauper underlined. His withdrawal from the commercial world of his father exposed the limitations of this enterprise and eventually he concluded that the merchants' world did not satisfy his aspirations. In spite of such reflections, the ambition to become a knight, nonetheless, remained a more attractive alternative and only when this failed did he begin to undergo a series of experiences which eventually led him among the less prosperous members of society.

A recurring theme of Thomas of Celano's second biography is the reformed Francis's sympathy for the poor whom he encountered both at home and on his travels in different parts of Italy. His conflict with his father reminded him very clearly that an undue attachment to money was capable of undermining and eroding even family ties. During this transitional phase he was horrified by the power of material possessions and the accumulation of wealth, which perpetuated such deep divisions within society. He had no remedy of his own to hand and his only response was to turn his back on the family business and spend a growing amount of time outside the city. When he eventually turned to the Gospel for direction, he found that the views which he had already reached were confirmed and, more importantly, that a remedy was being proposed. Evangelical poverty offered him a way of emancipating himself from the disorders at work within society. The fact that Jesus Christ had chosen to live in poverty had important ramifications for Francis and his disciples. Reflecting upon the life of the Son of God and his disciples, Francis began to regard money as something extrinsic to humanity and therefore something to be used with an appropriate caution. Lawrence observes that more than in the countryside great disparities of wealth and poverty were made conspicuous by the crowded conditions of medieval town life. Meditation on the Gospel and the spectacle of luxury in the midst of destitution led Francis to reject the values of the new urban aristocracy.[10]

A purer set of ideals than those which he had encountered in commerce was provided by the Gospels. However, the sight of priests overly concerned with the accumulation of material benefits filled him with a sense of disappointment. Nonetheless, this did not discourage him from returning to the source of Christian teaching, the Bible. One of the problems which had so energized the reformers from the middle of the eleventh century was the desire to remove the deeply rooted scourge of simony and to combat avarice among clerics. This purification of the clerical ranks was designed to revitalize the Church's mission of spreading the Gospel and ensure that ecclesiastical offices were the means of sanctification rather than the accumulation of wealth. The *acta* of medieval councils and numerous medieval chronicles contain abundant examples of bishops, abbots and priests whose witness to the truth was compromised by Simon Magus, the father of simony (Acts 8:9-24). Those who thirsted for a more authentic form of Christian witness treated the scourge of simony as a grotesque perversion of any office within the Church. The persistence of this vice encouraged the reforming instincts of Bonaventure, who towards 1260 laments the number of priests who seek profit, the satisfaction of their own ambition and the accumulation of riches. They further their own pleasure, wealth and glory and their ambition induces them to grab rather than obtain ecclesiastical dignities by means of much litigation and simony. He concluded that they had deviated from the ideals of their sacred office and had succumbed to the devil's prompting.[11]

A few years before Francis abandoned the market place, Gerald of Wales had fulminated against the venal disposition which some priests brought to their celebration of the Eucharist, a sacrament instituted to foster fraternal love and compassion. In this he anticipates by a few years some of the emphases of Francis's own teaching on the Eucharist. Gerald complained that in France priests' avarice was such that they had begun the practice of multiplying Gospels for the sake of money. The practice had been condemned by the synods of bishops in France, and he predicted that the abuse would soon be outlawed in England. Soldiers and lay people with a special liking for certain Gospels were accustomed to make offerings for them as well as for Masses. Gerald overheard a soldier making facetious comments about avarice among priests and commenting that some years earlier there had been only one Gospel for each Mass; he observed that there were now three or four. He tearfully lamented the practice whereby some priests celebrate the Mass of the Faithful ten times or more, calling down curses on someone in the hope that before the tenth day, or shortly afterwards, the individual may die. A simple remedy was proposed: that there be fewer churches and fewer altars in them, that there be fewer and more select priests ordained and more careful selection of those to be ordained.[12]

In the twelfth and early thirteenth century there were some reformers who found themselves first at odds with the Church and then outside it. Such zealots adopted a simple lifestyle which was based upon the Scriptures. In the attempts to curb the spread of various heresies some preachers were convinced that ecclesiastical trappings and wealth impeded their ministry. The changing climate and the way in which wealth was seen as a potential hindrance to the Church's preaching mission were instrumental in the birth of the Dominicans. Innocent III had recently sent twelve Cistercian abbots and a papal legate to preach against the Albigensians. They were holding a council at Montpellier with the prelates of the region to discuss how they might discharge their responsibility, when Diego, bishop of Osma, and Dominic passed through the city in 1203. Diego noticed that the Albigensians were enticing people into their party by their arguing and preaching and by a feigned example of holiness. The Albigensians' simplicity was contrasted with the missionaries' enormous supply of provisions, horses and clothing, and accordingly the missionaries were exhorted to reconsider their strategy. Diego argued that the Albigensians would not be converted through preaching alone, whereas they would be swayed more by example. Heretical propaganda was given increased credence by their example of evangelical austerity and asceticism. Diego urged the prelates to follow his example and directed his companions to return to Osma with his horses and goods and all the various kinds of provisions that he had brought with him. One of those who stayed behind was Dominic. Inspired by Diego's example, they agreed to adopt a similar policy themselves and sent back to their monasteries everything they had brought with them, except the books required for the divine office, study and debate. When the Albigensians saw this, they launched a counter-offensive of more insistent preaching.[13] The rise of the mendicant movement with its army of attractive preachers was soon channelled into the Church's operation against heretics.

THE MONASTIC WORLD AND FRANCIS

Monasticism was part of the fabric of the medieval world and from time to time monks make fleeting appearances in the earliest biographies of Francis. Accounts of Francis's visits to monasteries and his dealings with individual monks and officials of the monastery are few. He was, nonetheless, drawn to the eremetical life and this proved to be an enduring attraction. He stayed at a monastery near Gubbio on more than one occasion, though his first visit was less than happy and the biographer seems to delight in recounting a sequel which placed the monastery in a poor light. The monastery of San Benedetto on Monte Subasio gave him the use of the chapel of the Portiuncula and monks appeared as witnesses to Francis's sanctity and miracles. There was no hint that monasticism played any significant part in his conversion, though it would not be in the interests of Franciscan hagiographers to imply that their saint had once toyed with the prospect of a monastic vocation, especially when they were so intent on showing the superiority of their new form of religious life over the monastic model. Silence does not necessarily mean that Francis was not drawn by certain aspects of monasticism, particularly because the eremetical tradition remained an attraction throughout his years as a friar.

During the transitional phase in Francis's life there was, however, one significant and precise reference to monasticism and this was located shortly after his decision to leave home. He withdrew from Assisi and for several days he stayed at a monastery where he worked as a scullion; he wore a ragged shirt and was satisfied to be filled only with broth. Thomas of Celano indicates that the saint was not received with sympathy and that, when all pity was withdrawn from him, he could not get even an old garment. The visit ended abruptly and unhappily and he was given short shrift. The biographer adds that, once Francis's fame had begun to spread, the prior of the monastery recalled the poor treatment meted out to him and apologized, seeking pardon on behalf of himself and his monks.[14] The monastery has been identified as San Verecundo, a Benedictine community at Vallingegno, about six miles south of Gubbio. The reference is tantalizingly brief and it is difficult to ascertain whether Francis was taking temporary refuge there or whether he had gone there to share in the monks' life for some days or weeks. There was no attempt to explain the unhappy ending to this visit and the biographers refer only to a lack of compassion shown to Francis, who did not even receive a garment. Is the latter a euphemism for his failure to be clothed in the monastic habit, even though the first biographer was careful to point out that Francis obtained a small tunic from a friend at Gubbio? There is no suggestion that he was in need of a garment when he arrived at the monastery. The evidence must not be overburdened, but it is so specific and turns on the question of clothing. Is this a clue that Francis's mind was running along more conventional lines in the earliest days of his vocation or does it point to the fact that a different form of religious clothing would be used by Francis?

Following his appearance before the bishop, Francis turned his back on the world of trade, which he had found to be potentially divisive and increasingly distasteful. Two years were spent in toiling over the restoration of three ruined churches. In this prolonged search for his own particular vocation his mind must have turned to the monastic world, with its rhetoric about an exalted vocation, on more than one occasion. It is very difficult to imagine that, throughout this lengthy period in which he worked manually, he did not give a second thought to this traditional mode of the consecrated life, especially in view of his own prolonged periods of retreat and contemplation; about this time he was living as a hermit. A growing awareness of social divisions had left him disillusioned with the world of commerce and he was turning increasingly towards God in search of an alternative vocation, whose precise form was not yet revealed to him.

There is no indication that he was beginning to think of models of religious life and all thought of how best he might live the apostolic life still lay in the future. At this stage there is no hint that he took a critical view of contemporary monasticism. It is, however, unlikely that he spent two years repairing ruined churches without giving serious consideration to a monastic vocation, which offered a way of life regulated by the world of the New Testament. The gradual clarification of his vocation came only later in the form of his literal response to the Gospel. Did Francis regard the monasteries as too well rooted in the economic landscape to be places of resort for young men with high ideals? Or was it the case that the ordered routine of the monastic life did not appeal to him at that stage? There is no reliable evidence that Francis was critical of the monastic life. The lack of clear evidence gives rise to conjecture. The simpler answer remains as viable: Francis, who had little idea of where his own future lay, went to the monastery to seek casual labour for a few days while he considered his next step.

After the failure of his plans to go Apulia, Francis began to withdraw from society for a while and to frequent lonely places, though on occasion he was accompanied by a friend whom Thomas of Celano did not name; they frequently went to a remote grotto where they discussed Francis's growing disenchantment with society. Francis used to enter the grotto for prayer and reflection.[15] Lawrence refers to Francis's early struggles when he renounced the family home and the lifestyle of his class and suggests that they indicate that his mind was captivated by the eremetical ideal, which reasserted itself in his later years. In the first stage of his spiritual saga he lived as a hermit in caves and ruinous churches.[16] The basis of his appearance before the episcopal tribunal was his new status as a man who had passed under ecclesiastical jurisdiction. During the same period he seems to have acquired the status of a hermit and dressed as one when he completed the restoration of the churches of San Damiano and San Pietro. He wore a leather girdle around his waist and shoes on his feet and carried a staff in his hands. There are several indications that he was uncertain about which course to take and this confirms that his vocation was not settled at a particular moment; the evidence implies that there was a gradual process of evolution, culminating in the Gospel which he heard at the Portiuncula. After the rift with his father he lived as a hermit and the attraction of that life remained with him until death.

The medieval Church looked back to the life of the apostolic community at Jerusalem, as it is briefly described in the Acts of the Apostles (Acts 2:41-45 and 4:35). The apostolic community, regarded as the halcyon days of the Church, became the norm by which all reform movements were measured. These texts had long been invoked by apologists for the cenobitical life of monks, and they believed that the essence of the apostolic life entailed an ascetical community based upon renunciation of marriage and personal property and organized for corporate prayer. Monastic writers maintained a close relationship between the origins of the Church and their own communities. Bernard of Clairvaux argued that the monastic order was the first order in the Church and that the latter developed from the former. He proclaimed that on all the earth there was nothing more angelic, nothing closer to the heavenly Jerusalem, our mother, because of the beauty of its chastity and fervour of its love. The apostles were its moderators, and its members were those whom Paul often calls the saints. It was their practice to keep nothing as private property, for, as it is written, distribution was made to each as he had need.[17] A century later these monastic presuppositions no longer attracted widespread acceptance and new forms of religious life, also based on the apostolic community and the imitation of their divine master, gained currency.

By the twelfth century the Benedictine abbeys, Lawrence notes, were deeply implicated in the economic and political fabric of society as landlords, territorial rulers, holders of military fiefs and patrons of churches. In a memorable phrase he adds that is not easy to view one's landlord as a paradigm of sanctity, especially when he raises the rent. Like the reformed monasticism, this reappraisal of the Christian life was modelled on the primitive Church. The cult of voluntary poverty and the ideas about the apostolic life had found expression in the various new forms of religious life in the course of the twelfth century. Individual ascetics like Norbert of Xanten and Robert of Abrissel combined mendicancy with the role of the itinerant preacher. But their vision of the apostolic life, the *vita apostolica*, was a personal one which they did not succeed in communicating to the institutions which they founded.[18] The older image focused upon the picture of a settled community in Jerusalem where resources were pooled and the needs of the poor were supplied. The currents of renewal at the end of the twelfth century were taking a different course which concentrated on the needs of popular piety. Obedience to the Gospel was no longer viewed as demanding a retreat from society and the goodness of the created order. The optimism of the period called for a spirituality aimed at the aspirations of people dwelling in the towns and cities. There was a growing awareness that Christians should be engaged with the secular world which should be sanctified by their witness. Reformers became interested in other passages from the Scriptures, some of which narrated the itinerant ministry of Jesus Christ and the apostles.

The discrepancy between the image of the apostolic and the medieval Church was pointed out by R. B. Brooke, who observes that Jesus Christ and the apostles were frequently represented as bearded and barefoot in the art of the twelfth century: in manuscript illuminations, in stained-glass windows, in the sculpted figures of tympana and capitals. This image was historical in concept, but contemporary churchmen were not depicted in this guise.[19] Such scriptural images, reinforced by Christian art, placed in sharp relief the image of the itinerant teacher and his followers. Apostolic imagery was contrasted with the security and wealth amassed by some of the monasteries. The monastic communities of St Augustine's and the cathedral priory of Christ Church dominated the skyline of medieval Canterbury and their estates stretched forth into the Kent countryside. Their sheer size and economic power conjured up images of stability, power and wealth and these were not the values articulated in the New Testament. Bishops, too, were made responsible for large tracts of land and were entrusted with political responsibilities which sometimes took them outside their cathedral cities and dioceses. The involvement of abbots and bishops in secular activities detracted from the exercise of their spiritual offices and effectively compromised both their prophetical role and pastoral impact.

In the later decades of the twelfth century new and radical forms of lay piety began to appear and drew their inspiration from a study of the New Testament. The Scriptures provided them with a broader understanding of the apostolic life than that projected by monastic rhetoric. The apostles were presented as itinerant preachers and this change of focus meant that the apostolic life was no longer perceived solely in terms of monastic stability. Attention was given to the missionary labours of the apostles and the hardship and privations endured on their travels. This dimension was strengthened by a greater concentration upon the earthly life of Jesus Christ. The initiative was moving from monastic stability to a community of men and women who strove to imitate the life of Jesus Christ. The mission entrusted to the apostles, proclaimed in the Gospel at the Portiuncula, marked the beginning of Francis's mission as an itinerant preacher. His new role in life was perceived as the continuation of the apostles' ministry, but within a relatively short time this vision moved to a focus on the imitation of his divine master. His own letters and exhortations reflect the growing concentration on the imitation of Christ, particularly his writings on poverty. Indeed, these also draw attention to the poverty chosen by the mother of God. Thomas of Celano, too, considers Francis's most perfect imitation of Jesus Christ and only then does he add that the saint had followed the life and footsteps of the apostles.[20] Francis's understanding of his vocation reflects the new spirit in the Church and it was rooted in passages from the Gospel.

GOSPEL TEXTS AND POVERTY

The voice from the crucifix at San Damiano instructed Francis to restore the church and this was interpreted in a literal manner. Thus for two years Francis, acting on the literal message, spent his energies on the restoration of churches. The change in his life occurred within a scriptural context and he is a saint whose whole life was modelled on the words of the Scriptures, for which he developed an immense reverence. The word of God offered him the direction for which he had thirsted and completed the process of guidance for him and his small band of followers. For that reason, he held the Scriptures in the greatest honour. Although his followers were exhorted to show the utmost reverence towards the Eucharist, they received similar instructions about the devout care of the word of God.

Just as Francis acted on the literal instructions of the crucified Christ at San Damiano, so the literal understanding of the Scriptures was a salient feature in the process of change which ensued in his life. Throughout the following twenty years he was determined to model his life on the Scriptures. At the Portiuncula he resolved to put into effect the advice which had been issued to the disciples and the type of vocation entrusted to him by God was shaped by the threefold opening of the Gospel at San Nicola; towards the end of his life, when he strove to identify himself ever more fully with his master, there was another threefold opening of the Gospel at La Verna before he received the stigmata. Scriptural quotations form the basis of his primitive Rule and litter his small collection of writings. In short, his whole life was rooted in what he heard proclaimed in the Scriptures and this aspect was exploited to the full by biographers such as Thomas of Celano and Bonaventure. The former locates the Mass at the Portiuncula in the context of his Marian piety and the birth of the fraternity. The latter draws a parallel between the Marian role in the Incarnation and the direction and clarification of Francis's vocation. The evolution of the fraternity was shaped by a series of scriptural quotations, which Francis interpreted literally and so enabled the friars to recover a long-forgotten concentration on the poverty experienced by Jesus Christ, his mother and disciples.

Mass at the Portiuncula

After he had restored two churches Francis turned his attention to the ancient and deserted church of Santa Maria degli Angeli at the Portiuncula. As a hermit he made his home at the church which would become so important to him as friar. One day he attended Mass in the small chapel, where he heard how the disciples had been sent out to preach the Gospel. He grasped something of the text's significance, but after Mass he asked the priest to explain the text more fully. He was told that the disciples should not possess gold or silver or money; nor carry along the way scrip, wallet, or bread, or a staff; they should not have shoes or two tunics; but they should preach the kingdom of God and penance. The priest can hardly have been aware of the impact which that brief exposition of the Gospel would have upon the history of Assisi and the universal Church.

In a flash Francis saw that the priest was mapping out the programme which he must follow and with a new clarity he recognized the personal call to continue the apostles' mission. This was undoubtedly a familiar passage which he had heard countless times: yet on this one occasion he was especially receptive and the text provided him with the hitherto elusive key to his future. The words of the Gospel struck him with a new power and vitality. A. Jessopp comments that the dominical words to the apostles seemed to Francis to be written in letters of flame; they haunted him waking and sleeping.[21] Moorman reflects that it sometimes happens that when we read or hear some quite familiar passage suddenly a phrase seems to stand out from all the rest as if written in letters of gold and solely for our benefit. To the awe-struck Francis these words were a personal message; they were the answer to all his prayers for guidance and he saw clearly what Jesus Christ was calling him to do. All the strange experiences of the last few years had been but a preparation for this moment.[22] The words were addressed to him and he learned that his divine master was issuing the same instructions to him. He, too, must continue the apostolic mission in the first decade of the thirteenth century. No more did he doubt his mission. Thenceforth he abandoned himself to providence without any thought or anxiety wherever it would take him. His only ambition was to obey the sacred texts and his confidence in God's word was unshakeable. He was ready to listen and follow and this capacity to place himself at God's disposal was a paradigm of his vocation.

Lawrence comments that the same model of the apostolic life in the Gospel passage heard at the Portiuncula had inspired other lay movements like the Humiliati and the Waldensians. They, too, had embraced a life of poverty and devoted themselves to preaching, like many other freelance evangelists of the time. But Francis went further in his insistence on poverty.[23] With overflowing joy he immediately began to implement what he had heard and he obeyed the divine voice in the Scriptures down to the tiniest detail. It was not enough for him to fix the text indelibly in his memory: it was necessary to dress and preach as an apostle. His girdle, shoes and staff were cast aside at once. A tunic was designed with a resemblance to the cross and a small cord was tied around his waist. His poor and mean tunic was in stark contrast to the fine garments which he had formerly worn. The scene was summarized by the first biographer, who declared that Francis was not a deaf hearer of the Gospel and endeavoured to carry it out to the letter.

This conviction terminated his life as a hermit and ruled out the more conventional form of religious life in the monasteries because he must be free to live and travel as an apostle. The passage from the Gospel pointed to a new vocation which required him to imitate the apostles' lifestyle and this entailed a life of itinerancy. From now on Francis was to model his life on the apostles. Moorman comments that there was inaugurated at that quiet Mass an experiment in Christian living so fascinating and so courageous that it has held the world's admiration across the centuries.[24] Francis's literal response to the words of the Gospel reflected his desire to accept the divine guidance and to fulfil this, even down to points of detail regarding dress. He did not seek to interpret and apply what he had heard. Glosses on the Bible had resulted in his earlier difficulties and his failure to treat lepers in an appropriate manner. From now on he was resolved to let the Scriptures regulate his dealings with everyone.

The Gospel which Francis heard supplied him with a larger framework to understand the instructions which he had received at San Damiano. The mandate to proclaim the Gospel to all in the manner of the apostles gave him a crucial context for the earlier directive to restore the Church. Now he realized that the earlier directive should be understood in a more general sense and that the dilapidated church symbolized a more wide-ranging task of restoration: the universal Church was to be renewed through the proclamation of the Scriptures; the challenge to continue the apostolic mission was perennial. His days of restoring churches were at end and the cloud of uncertainty had been unexpectedly dispersed. A clearer future beckoned him, one in which he felt a personal responsibility for the proclamation of the Gospel.

The threefold opening of the Gospels

In the period following Mass at the Portiuncula Francis adopted an apostolic lifestyle that gradually began to attract respect and admiration. The biographers cease to speak of the abuse which had been heaped upon him in the streets of Assisi in the prelude to the conflict with his father. The *Vita prima* indicates that his first recruit was a simple and pious man of Assisi and that he was followed by Bernard of Quintavalle. The account of the latter's conversion is full, offering a welcome insight into Francis's new reliance on the guidance supplied by the Scriptures. Attracted by Francis's conduct and ideas, Bernard wanted to know more about the ideals which inspired him and invited him to his house. After an evening filled with discussion of Francis's vision, Bernard observed that his guest slept little and passed most of the night in prayer. His earlier perception was confirmed and he concluded that Francis was a man of God. He was so impressed by the saint that he took the decision to abandon his numerous possessions and to become his pupil.

At first Bernard spoke in a veiled way, asking Francis what would be the best way of disposing of goods which had been entrusted to him by a lord. Francis's advice was that they should be restored to that lord from whom they had been received. All reservations were cast aside as Bernard revealed the state of his own mind: his intention was to return his material goods to God from whom they had come. In addition, it was his intention to join Francis. It is regrettable that the biographers pass over in silence the subsequent dialogue between the two men. Questions about their future life were raised and settled. It was agreed that the following morning they would go to the church of San Nicola in the main piazza in search of divine direction. The Gospels had indicated to Francis that he should continue the apostolic mission and now guidance was sought on how he and his new companion would live.

Hitherto Francis had been guided by the advice dispensed to the apostles and he had no plans for the next stage, but Bernard's decision was about to change the lifestyle which Francis had adopted so recently. From that point Francis was no longer dealing solely with a *personal* vocation to live as an apostle and itinerant preacher. He was required to assume the role of spiritual leader and this was a decisive moment. Now he had to think about how he might live with disciples, however few they were to be. From the outset he does not seem to have considered the prospect of being joined by any one else and Bernard's declaration of interest confirms that he had not devised a plan for dealing with such inquiries. The biographers do not suggest that Francis had given much thought to the question of whether he would be joined by disciples and he may initially have been taken aback by Bernard's request. This was a decision of enormous significance for both Bernard and Francis and for the history of religious life in the western Church. The reading of the Gospel at the Portiuncula filled Francis with a new-found dependence upon the Scriptures and, when approached by Bernard, his instinct was to turn to the sacred texts once more. The next morning the two men made the short journey to the church of San Nicola, where after prayer they opened the book of the Gospel, proposing to follow whatever instruction should first appear. They were so sure of God's providence and guidance that they were prepared to base their lives together on whatever directives the Gospel gave. This, too, was a decisive moment in the birth of the fraternity, which was shaped by the passages which opened before Francis and Bernard; the *Anonymous of Perugia* adds that Peter, the first recruit, accompanied Francis and Bernard on this quest.

The first text contained the advice given to the rich young man to sell his goods and donate the proceeds to the poor (Matthew 19:21); the second dealt with the advice addressed to the apostles who were to take nothing for their journey (Luke 9:3); and the third concerned the carrying of the cross (Luke 9:23;

Matthew 16:24). The first passage instructed Francis and Bernard that the path to perfection lay in the renunciation of material goods for the benefit of the economically marginalized and then the following of Jesus Christ. The advice to the rich young man answered the question posed by Bernard's parable. What was more important for Francis was the dominical focus on the conditions for discipleship. After Mass at the Portiuncula he had been considering the way in which he might live in imitation of the apostles. The figure of the rich young man broadened the focus to a reflection on voluntary poverty and Francis came to the decision that he must go beyond the traditional model of the common ownership of the apostolic community to the life of Christ as an itinerant preacher who had nowhere to lay his head (Matthew 8:20); this already constituted an advance on the advice which he had gleaned from the Gospel at the Portiuncula. The second passage reinforced these instructions. The first and second messages merged in the theme of poverty and the third dealt with the way in which the disciple follows his master with the cross. The three passages from the Gospel were so arranged that there was an implied progression: material goods have to be discarded in order to follow Jesus Christ, the itinerant teacher, and then the disciple has to unite himself with the Crucified. The life of poverty thus paves the way for a more complete identification with the Crucified. Leo and companions report that poverty and weakness were the marks which Christ bore in his body for the salvation of the human race.[25] This seems to imply that the friars' imitation of their divine master in this manner was perceived in terms of continuing his salvific ministry.

The renunciation of material goods

Francis testifies that, after consulting the Scriptures, Bernard began his religious life in the most perfect manner by observing the Gospel to the letter and distributing his goods to the poor. This was regarded as the fulfilment of the dominical advice to the rich young man.[26] An event of that sort could not be concealed in the small city of Assisi and amidst all the excitement and gossip it evoked images of the apostolic Church in Jerusalem. It also played some part in drawing at least two more men to the fraternity. One of the witnesses to this public act of renunciation was Sylvester, a secular priest of Assisi. Thomas of Celano contrasts Bernard's liberality with the avarice of the priest, who had once sold Francis some stones for the restoration of a church, possibly San Damiano. This scene stirred the poison of avarice within him so that he took the opportunity of complaining that he had not received a good price for the stones which he had sold him. In a typically flamboyant gesture Francis filled Sylvester's hands with money without checking the amount. This encounter was a seminal experience for the priest's own vocation as a friar. The *Life of Brother Giles* is another witness to Bernard's renunciation because some of Giles's kinsmen and others informed him that Bernard had sold all his goods in conformity with the instructions contained in the Gospel. On the saint's example and advice, Giles distributed everything in his presence to the numerous poor people gathered in the piazza of San Giorgio. He, too, was admitted to the company of Francis, Bernard and Peter.[27]

The early biographies do not contain an account of Francis's renunciation of his goods in order to follow the Son of God. His journey to the fair in Foligno, however, was presented in terms of his renunciation of all material things, because it is the point from which Francis began to detach himself from a love of money and to serve God. This reference to Francis selling all that he owned may be one way of showing that there was a solemn renunciation. The narrative in the *Vita prima* is imprecise and does not suggest that Francis wished to surrender his goods entirely at this point, particularly because the clarification of his vocation came only later. The point which the biographer may have been wishing to make at this stage was that Francis was becoming increasingly discontented with money and was beginning to feel that the teachings of the Gospel could give him a much greater form of enrichment and contentment.

The threefold opening of the Gospel also had perennial implications for the history of the fraternity which clustered around Francis, because it formed the basis of the friars' vocation. The opening words of Francis's Rule of 1221 state that the friars were required to live in obedience, chastity and without anything of their own and to walk in the footsteps of Jesus Christ. Religious were required to live in obedience and chastity, but the provision that the friars should live without anything, personal or communal, was a new element in the history of the approved religious orders. After the opening sentence concerning the vows of religion, Francis expands the theme of voluntary poverty and the advice tendered to the rich young man was quoted along with the injunction to take up the cross. Two of the three passages seen by Francis and Bernard were incorporated into the first chapter of this Rule.[28] The imagery of renunciation of material possessions also informs the events at the episcopal tribunal, when Francis returned everything to his father and then formally embarked upon a life in obedience to the Gospel.

Within a short time others were admitted to the fraternity. Bernard's implementation of the advice to the rich young man became the first of many public acts of renunciation to mark the beginning of the Franciscan vocation. Hugh of Digne characterizes the friars as men who had espoused extreme poverty, the visible insignia of the fraternity. This virtue arose from a spontaneous renunciation of material things on account of God.[29] Aspirants to the order were instructed that they should act in accordance with the teaching of Matthew 19:21.[30] They were admonished by Francis that they should give a notice of dismissal to society by offering first their outward possessions to God and then themselves inwardly. Only those who had given away all their goods and retained absolutely nothing were admitted to the order, both on account of the Gospel and in order that no scandal would arise over any treasures kept back.[31] Bonaventure strengthens the formula by adding that it was revealed to the saint that anyone entering the order should begin by fulfilling the precept of the Gospel. A basic requirement of those entering the order was that they should satisfy certain texts from the Gospels. This text sets the conditions of admission to the fraternity, which seeks to base itself on the Gospel.

In obedience to the Gospel and in order to avoid scandal, such as might arise if a friar retained his property, Francis never received any one into the order unless he had renounced everything and kept nothing for himself. When a man asked to be received into the order in the Marches of Ancona, he was told that, if he wanted to join Christ's poor, he must give what he had to the poor in the world. At that the candidate went off, but he gave his belongings to his relatives instead of the poor. When he came back and told the saint what he had done, he was bitterly reproached and dismissed as Brother Fly. Francis told him that he had failed to leave his home and family and that his attempts to begin religious life had enriched his relations and cheated the poor. The aspirant was sent away because he was unworthy of Christ's poor and had begun his religious life by yielding to an earthly attachment; a worthless foundation for a spiritual building had been laid. He immediately returned to his family and demanded his property; he had refused to give it to the poor and so he quickly abandoned the idea of embracing the religious life.[32]

Francis's new perception of the religious life

Monasticism did not offer Francis the opportunity to embrace a life of itinerant preaching in imitation of Christ and the apostles. It promised a life of stability and security, which failed to meet his aspirations because he had already spurned the security and the material comforts of his father's house. He had no interest in swapping one form of security for another, even though monasticism would have satisfied some of his spiritual yearnings such as a community of prayer. Despite Francis's interest in aspects of the monastic world as an alternative to the greed which he discerned in the new cities, his own conception of religious life differed sharply from that of the monks and a new concept of the *vita apostolica* carried him in a very different direction. His vocation was shaped by a passage from the Gospel which forced him to locate his apostolate in the midst of society, even though he had rejected its values. The mendicant orders represented a new departure, a radical breakaway, from the prevalent monastic traditions. Francis's perception of poverty was both personal and communal. His vision of the religious life discarded endowments and other sources of revenue and sprang from a firm confidence in divine providence. Where monastic communities required a solid endowment in terms of land and income, the friars were content to beg for alms in cases of necessity. Another important departure from the monastic model was the substitution of the itinerant life of preaching for the stable life of contemplative prayer.

By the time that Francis was introduced to Cardinal John of St Paul, he had no doubt that his future lay in the literal following of the Gospel, wherever it might take him. He was so adamant in his literal obedience to the Gospel that he was able to fend off the various attempts to persuade him to adopt a monastic Rule. The power of this conviction enabled him to resist pressure from the cardinal to become a monk or hermit. Thomas of Celano shows that this advice was resisted by Francis, who was drawn to another form of religious life by a higher desire. His fervour and insistence eventually carried the day with the cardinals and the worries expressed by members of the papal court about the austerity of Francis's plans were countered by his declaration that he wished only to follow the Gospel. On their way back to the valley of Spoleto the friars discussed whether they should dwell among men or go to solitary places. After prayer Francis came to understand that he was sent to win souls for God,[33] though doubts returned to haunt him in later years; on that occasion he consulted Clare and Sylvester. The traditional monastic Rules were in tension with Francis's ideal of an itinerant apostle and for that reason he set his face against all the pressure to adopt a monastic life.

A triumphalistic tone informs the miracles associated with monasteries, as if to imply that the leadership in religious life had passed from the cloister to the friary, from the countryside to the city. The monastery of San Verecundo near Gubbio had been the scene of Francis's humiliation and in the account of the miracles it provided the venue for a display of Francis's prophetical powers.[34] In the months preceding his death Francis was offered hospitality more than once at this monastery and there he received a gracious welcome from the abbot and monks, who venerated him.[35] The Benedictine abbot of St Justin in the diocese of Perugia was another witness to the extraordinary power of Francis's interces- sion.[36] Nonetheless, aspects of the monastic life were found in the life of the early fraternity, especially in the large network of hermitages and the domestic organization of the larger friaries in the cities along conventual lines.

POVERTY EMBRACED

As a hermit Francis had been living in simple surroundings at the churches which he repaired, even after hearing the decisive passage from the Gospel. When Giles decided to join Francis, they met near the leper hospital.[37] The arrival of a small knot of followers raised the question of where they should make their home and it was decided that the enlarged group would travel along the plain to the abandoned hovel named Rivo Torto, a short distance from Assisi. Thomas of Celano, with hagiographical exaggeration, waxes eloquently about the discomfort of the place: 'in that shelter the despiser of great and beautiful homes lived'. This seems to reveal more about the state of the biographer's mind than the outlook of the first friars. The early reports of Francis's conversion seem to contain a suspicion of urban mores and values. Instead, there was a much more constructive spirit and the early vocations were rooted in the firm conviction that the quest for evangelical perfection required friars to devote themselves primarily to the Gospel. There is no indication that Francis ever scorned those who lived in fine homes, and the second chapter of his Rule contains an admonition for the friars not to condemn or look down on those who enjoy soft or colourful clothes and enjoy luxuries in food and drink; instead, they should indulge in self-criticism. Francis himself was received into the homes of rich friends and associates from time to time and developed enriching friendships with some people who were not afflicted by poverty. The phrase is manifestly a case of hagiographical excess, which even parts company with the founder's instructions! The shelter, Thomas of Celano continues, was sufficient to protect the friars from the rains. The small band of friars lived and worked in that place where they lacked everything. Often they went without bread and were content with turnips which they managed to beg on the plain of Assisi. Conditions in the hovel were so cramped that they could hardly sit down or rest in it. The biographer proudly relates that no word of complaint escaped the lips of the friars, who endured their life of poverty with serenity and patience. Francis was very exacting in relation to himself and disciplined his body. He instructed the friars in the principles of their vocation: vices were to be mortified and the senses were to be informed by the teaching of the Gospel.

The friars embarked upon a life of simplicity and poverty. Their names were written on the beams of their dwelling by Francis so that, if each one wished to pray or rest, he would know his place and that the cramped conditions might not disturb the silence of the mind. This hovel remained the friars' home for some time until it was claimed by a man who led in his ass. Francis divined the intentions of a bellicose character, who seemed to be suggesting that the friars were likely to expand. The charge that the friars were thinking of enlarging their meagre premises must have stung Francis, who did not wish to lay claim to anything in this world. This brought him face to face with the harsh realities in life and the emotional attachment to places associated with happy memories. Nonetheless, Francis, who had abandoned a comfortable home in Assisi, was not about to compromise his principles. Despite the fact that Rivo Torto had been the friars' home, he decided not to contest the man's claim. Instead he immediately moved his friars from the site and settled them at the Portiuncula. This event was treated by Francis's first biographer as an illustration of his firm resolution to reject ownership.[38]

Thomas of Celano reports that the friars went from Rivo Torto to the Portiuncula, though this does not rule out the possibility that they spent a short time in temporary shelter. While a precise chronology is difficult to reconstruct, Leo and companions situate the gift of the chapel at the Portiuncula in the terms of the friars' liturgical needs. It is not clear whether the friars were living on land adjacent to the chapel at the time of their request to the Benedictines on Monte Subasio or whether it was made in the aftermath of their retreat from Rivo Torto. When the number of friars began to increase, it was felt that a church was required and Francis consulted the local ecclesiastical authorities. Unsuccessful approaches were made to the bishop of Assisi and the canons of San Rufino. The same request was considered by the abbot of San Benedetto, who agreed to place it before the monks. Traditional language was used by Leo and companions in referring to the abbot's piety and the will of God in determining the outcome of this petition. The monks' decision was that the church of the Portiuncula, the poorest in the neighbourhood of Assisi, was placed at the friars' disposal. The abbot expressed his wish that, should the fraternity expand, the chapel would be the centre of the order. Francis was overjoyed at the donation of the site and willingly agreed to the abbot's wishes. Dedicated to the mother of God, the chapel was nicknamed as the 'little portion', prefiguring that in the future it would be the mother house and head of the fraternity. Although the abbot and his monks had freely conceded the church to the friars without any reversionary right or annual rent, Francis sent a small wicker basket full of little fish to the monks annually in token of humility and poverty. Each year the friars carried fish to the monastery and in return received a jar full of oil. This arrangement ensured that the friars did not have the power to sell or alienate the property in any way.[39]

The move to the Portiuncula was a momentous one. The friars' first home, where they had dwelled for a couple of years, was abandoned because someone else had staked a claim to it. Francis's abhorrence of ownership produced a predictable reaction in the form of his withdrawal in the belief that his commitment to follow the poor and itinerant Christ demanded it. By moving to a church which belonged to the Benedictines he accepted a more secure arrangement. His own determination to spurn ownership ensured that the chapel remained in the ownership of the monastery. While Francis's companions do not specify whether the chapel came with a small amount of land, the friars entered into an agreement that was legally binding in the sense that only the monks could oblige them to leave. Another stranger with an ass would have been powerless to evict the friars from this site. The gift of the Portiuncula opened the door to the principle which Gregory IX would invoke in *Quo elongati* on 28 September 1230 that the friars might have the use of things while ownership belonged to others.

The *Vita secunda* summarizes the founder's commitment to a life of poverty: Francis considered the wealth of men as mere trifles, he was ambitious for higher things, longing for poverty with all his heart; poverty was regarded as the route to perfection. No one was so desirous of gold as he was desirous of poverty and he guarded that treasure with great care. The sight of anything contrary to poverty among the friars filled him with dismay. The friars were directed to make poor wooden dwellings, reflecting their vocation to humility. They were frequently reminded that their divine master had endured poverty and had nowhere to lay his head; Matthew 8:20 served as a proof-text for the poverty to which the friars aspired. Francis did not want the friars to live in any place unless there was a specific patron in whom ownership was vested. He always wanted the laws of strangers to be observed by the friars: they should be gathered together under the roof of another. His complete abhorrence of ownership was demonstrated at Sarteano when he overheard a friar referring to the founder's cell. He then intervened and announced his dismay at any hint of ownership, refusing to enter that cell again. This represents a retreat from the earlier practice of chalking the friars' names on the beams at Rivo Torto. This was justified by his belief that in the desert Jesus Christ did not establish a house or a cell for himself; instead, he lived beneath the rock of the mountain. He proclaimed that the friars could do without ownership according to the form prescribed, although they needed the use of houses.[40] Although Francis was determined to take the Gospel literally, the biographer indicates that the process of interpretation was under way.

IMITATION OF THE POOR CHRIST AND NUPTIAL IMAGERY

The Gospel speaks of the hardship and poverty experienced by Jesus Christ and this shaped Francis's lifestyle. Initially he had been merely content to imitate his divine master, but his lengthy reflections on the Gospel led him to the conclusion that the choice had both practical and theological ramifications. He recalled that, though Jesus Christ was rich beyond everything else (2 Corinthians 8:9), together with his mother he chose a life of poverty. One of the responsibilities which Francis entrusted to the cardinal protector was to ensure that the friars observed the poverty and humility of Jesus Christ. The friars were required to acquire nothing, neither house nor place nor anything; they were to pass through the world as strangers and pilgrims. They were instructed that they should not develop an undue attachment to material things. The model of the pilgrim admonished them to ensure that their progress was not encumbered by an enslavement to material goods. Thus material things should be used with an appropriate air of detachment, rather than pursued for their own sake. Having renounced their material possessions in accordance with the Gospel, the friars should confidently seek alms, when they had no other means of support. They should seek alms and should not be embarrassed by this, because Jesus Christ did not feel such shame. He was poor and a guest and lived off alms, along with his mother and disciples. When people refuse alms, the friars should give thanks and not be ashamed, for they will earn merit before God. On his death bed Francis affirmed that he had worked with his own hands and he exhorted his followers to shun idleness and engage in work which caused no scandal. When they received no recompense for their labour, they were to turn to God's table and beg alms from door to door.[41]

The friars' fortunes in begging for alms probably varied a great deal from place to place and according to circumstances. On their triumphant return from Rome, armed with the approval of Innocent III, they begged for alms near Orte and got little.[42] The friars in Coimbra begged for alms at the Augustinian house of which Anthony of Padua was a member. This practice made the Franciscans visibly different from the older orders of monks and canons. In an expanding order it became all the more imperative to preserve the friars' distinctive character. While the *Vita secunda* applies Francis's teaching to various aspects of the friars' life, the practice of begging for alms became a central feature of the fraternity and the tone of some of the views placed in the founder's mouth suggests that some friars were beginning to question this practice, which they found very embarrassing.[43] The mendicants' critics accused Francis and Dominic of the novelty of having introduced the practice of mendicancy.[44] These claims were firmly rejected and Bonaventure, who situated the friars within the main strand of the history of religious life, argued that Francis's mendicancy was confirmed by miracles. He added that other saints, such as Dominic, Alexius, Benedict and the ranks of apostles and prophets, had begged for alms as well.[45]

Moorman believes that, while poverty was the most characteristic thing about the friars, it is doubtful whether Francis would have regarded it as the most important virtue.[46] His judgement is sustained by an examination of the *Vita prima*, which treats poverty as one of a number of virtues. Evangelical poverty became synonymous with the Franciscans as chroniclers commented on what they viewed as a new dimension in the medieval Church. The friars, even when their critics were on the increase, emphasized this distinctive element, which separated them from the orders with possessions. A passage from a friars' sermon collection, written in the fourteenth century, dwells upon the wonder of Francis's new order, pointing out that it was a new thing to found so great a religious order upon poverty, that is, upon nothing. When Benedict founded his order of monks, he acquired great revenues and possessions. Similarly, Augustine founded his order of regular canons. The preacher attributed the continuing vigour and influence of the friars to Christ, who placed the foundation and rules it through his own self.[47] J. V. Fleming, however, notes that, while there is inevitably much in medieval Franciscan literature that is not unique or even markedly distinctive, poverty is the Franciscan theme *par excellence*, but that it was not monopolized by the Franciscans.[48] It is regrettable that later in the thirteenth century poverty was exalted at the expense of fraternal charity, as the embittered disputes within the fraternity confirm.

The theme of poverty, however, has deep patristic roots. For example, Leo the Great celebrates the virtue, commenting that gentleness goes with poverty and pride more commonly with riches. A blessed poverty is not beguiled by a longing for earthly goods and does not seek increase of the world's riches, but desires to be enriched with heavenly blessings. Next to Christ, the apostles were foremost in exemplifying this noble poverty, leaving all their possessions at once at the call of their heavenly master. Dividing their goods and possessions, they were enriched with eternal blessings through their generous poverty. They rejoiced in having nothing from this world and possessing all things with Jesus Christ. Leo asks what could be richer than the apostles' poverty?[49] This passage makes it abundantly clear that Francis was not making a new discovery, even though he can have had little familiarity with the sermons of Leo the Great. Instead, it was another case of his *recovering* from the Gospel a theme which had been aired by some of the Fathers of the Church. Moreover, neither was Francis alone in his feminization of the virtue of poverty. About 390 John Chrysostom contrasted poverty and covetousness and rooted the former virtue in the Old Testament, believing that it resembled a beautiful, fair and well-favoured woman. He expatiated at length on the beauty of this woman and affirmed that the eye of poverty was mild, calm, looking kindly on all, meek, gentle, hating no one and shunning no one.[50] There can be no question of Francis having a familiarity with the homilies of this celebrated preacher at a time when few theologians in the West knew the Greek texts. R. B. Brooke and C. N. L. Brooke detect a romantic quality in Francis's elevation of poverty to a holy virtue, in the concept of Lady Poverty; but it was no false romance he wove around her, because he and his followers knew only too well the harsh and hideous face of actual want.[51]

Towards the beginning of the transitional phase of Francis's life people wondered whether he had fallen in love. He replied by saying that he would take a more noble and more beautiful spouse than his friends had ever seen. She would surpass all others in beauty and excel them in wisdom.[52] At this stage he probably had a very vague idea of his future, as the unfolding of the drama indicates. This perception of Lady Poverty was inspired by the Gospels, but was supplemented by the world of romantic literature and chivalry. Above the high altar in the lower church of San Francesco in Assisi there is a portrait of the marriage between the saint and Lady Poverty. The friars' fidelity to the vow of poverty was seen as a vital ingredient for the vitality and prosperity of the order. Francis taught that, so long as the friars remained faithful to Lady Poverty, the world would be attentive to them because they brought it the message of salvation. A further reminiscence of the saint's teaching was that a contract had been drawn up between the world and the fraternity: friars were required to give good example and in return the world was to provide for their needs. Should the friars break faith and neglect to give good example, the world would withdraw its support in a just censure. Some of the friars—and Thomas of Celano seems to have been one of them—perceived dangers in the spectacular level of recruitment in the various provinces. What some regarded as a sign of divine favour, others regarded with some misgivings, especially because the increased number of friars called for a greater organization and formality. Thus the founder was credited with an unease which many of the friars must have felt at the spectacular growth of the fraternity, particularly because such expansion might jeopardize the observance of poverty. Francis was reported to have wished that the world would rarely see the friars and be filled with wonder at the smallness of their number.[53] At the end of his life he rejoiced that he had kept faith with Lady Poverty. For he had done all things out of zeal for poverty, so that he would not have even a habit that was his own, but, as it were, one lent to him by another.

Francis's decision to follow the poor Christ gave him a different perspective on the values of the market place. In comparison with the wealth available through communion with Jesus Christ, society was deemed to offer him little. Thomas of Celano employs biblical imagery to present poverty in the highest terms, echoing St Paul's encomium of charity; Francis was ambitious for the higher gifts (1 Corinthians 12:31–13:13), which were identified in terms of poverty. His commitment to the life of evangelical poverty assumes nuptial forms and imagery. The biographer then proceeds to describe the saint's fidelity to this beautiful image. He gathered her to himself with chaste embraces and he strove to be constantly faithful to her. He was greatly offended by anything that appeared contrary to poverty among the friars. Throughout his religious life he was rich in having only one tunic, and this revealed the source of his riches. He rejoiced to exchange a perishable treasure for the hundredfold and taught his followers that such was the route to perfection and the pledge and earnest of eternal riches (Matthew 19:29). His decision to leave his parents' home was cast in matrimonial imagery (Genesis 2:24; Matthew 19:5–6; Mark 10:7) as he espoused himself to Lady Poverty. He left his parents and put aside everything so that he might cling to her the more closely as his spouse and that they might be two in one spirit.[54]

MEDIEVAL PERCEPTION OF FRANCIS AND HIS FRATERNITY

The friars' impact upon their contemporaries may be gauged from the observations of prominent prelates and chroniclers. Francis's presence generated excitement and admiration wherever he went and he was hailed as one of the most perfect followers of Christ, a belief which Franciscan propaganda was not slow to turn to its own advantage; this claim found expression in hagiography, art and polemics. Friars were seen to be reviving the fervour and exemplary behaviour which medieval ecclesiastics associated with the primitive Church, even though their inspiration led them to focus on apostolic poverty. The widespread admiration for the saint was such that Matthew Paris described him in exalted terms as a man who had followed Christ in the most perfect manner (*perfectissime*) and walked in the apostles' footsteps.[55] Francis's heroic witness to his divine master had caught the popular imagination and breathed a new vitality into the life of the medieval Church.

Chroniclers of the period convey something of the excitement generated by this saint and his followers. Jacques de Vitry, the bishop of Acre, was an important witness to the birth of the fraternity. In 1216 he reported that, amidst the corruption of the age, he had received consolation from the great number of men and women who had renounced their possessions and left the world for the love of Christ. The friars were held in high esteem by the pope and the cardinals. Totally detached from temporal things, their one passion was to snatch endangered souls from the vanities of the world and to prevail upon them to follow the Gospel more perfectly. They had already achieved important successes and made numerous conquests. Their lives were based on the pattern of the primitive Church and daily they went into cities and villages, giving themselves over to the active life of the apostolate; at night they returned to their hermitages or withdrew into solitude for the contemplative life. The bishop was convinced that these friars were sent to save a large number of souls and that their example put to shame contemporary prelates, who were like dumb dogs who did not even have the strength to bark.[56]

Just as patristic figures had spoken of the poverty of Jesus Christ, so observers believed that the friars were restoring an element long forgotten in the western Church. Jacques de Vitry comments that the friars were reviving the way of life of the early Church and that their Rule was not new; rather it was the revival of an old one. It resembled a sick person who has been cured. God had raised up new athletes in the face of the dangers of Antichrist and they were more humble than contemporary religious in their habit, poverty and contempt of the world. With great solicitude they strove to reproduce in themselves the religion, poverty and humility of the primitive Church. Trait for trait they mirrored the life of the apostles. They gave up everything that they owned, renounced themselves, took up their cross and naked followed the naked Christ. The bishop elaborates upon the evangelical form of religious life chosen by the friars, evoking biblical imagery: these poor men of Jesus Christ travelled with neither purse, haversack, bread nor money; they had no gold or silver and wore no sandals; they had no right to own anything. Their lifestyle differed from that of the traditional orders with their revenues and estates because they had neither monasteries, churches, fields, vineyards, animals, houses nor property, and no place to rest their head. Their clothing distinguished them from the monks and canons because they had nothing to do with furs and linen; they used only woollen tunics with a capuche. They had neither capes, mantles, cowls nor other garments.[57]

Matthew Paris testifies that the friars, favoured by Innocent III, speedily spread throughout the world, dwelling in cities and towns. They possessed nothing, living according to the Gospels. Their bare feet and their mean clothing testified to their humility. Clad in their grey habit and with a cord around their waist, on

Sundays and holidays they went out to preach in parish churches and other places where the people assembled. Mindful of the Gospel, they ate and drank what was put before them.[58] In 1239 Robert Grosseteste, bishop of Lincoln, informed Gregory IX about the friars' wide-ranging impact upon England. They illuminated the whole country with the bright light of their preaching and teaching. Their most holy conversation gave a powerful impetus to contempt of the world, voluntary poverty and humility, even among those in high places. Their preaching and conduct promoted full obedience to prelates and the pope, abstinence in the midst of plenty and in short they fostered all the virtues. People devoutly and humbly listened to the friars' sermons, confessed their sins and received guidance for their lives. Their good example spurred both the secular and regular clergy to greater devotion.[59]

The friars' bare feet distinguished them from clerics and fellow religious and symbolized their poverty. Francis was disposed to take the word of God at face value, even though he developed a deepening understanding of the sacred text. Roger of Wendover recorded Francis's death, recalling his poverty and how he cast aside his shoes; his followers imitated this poverty and went barefoot about their ministry.[60] Burchard of Ursberg observed that the friars travelled barefoot throughout the year. Matthew Paris refers to the friars with their bare feet (*nudis pedibus*).[61] One of the earliest images of the Franciscans in England was found in the margin of his *Chronica majora*, under the year 1227, illustrating the bare feet and simple habit of the friars which so impressed their contemporaries.[62] This practice was cherished by the friars, who were inclined to draw attention to one of the ways in which they differed visibly from their fellow religious. Some examples were cited by Thomas of Eccleston. The friars travelled great distances to the schools each day in their bare feet, even in bitter cold and deep mud. After an ordination they returned to Canterbury barefoot in the snow, which lay so deep that it daunted all who saw it. Agnellus of Pisa was taken ill with dysentery at Oxford on account of the cold and exhaustion which he experienced when he was working to restore peace between Henry III and his marshal in the Marches of Wales. Albert of Pisa, who had served as minister provincial in different provinces before becoming the minister general (1239-40), underlined the importance of this practice by affirming that it was one of the three features of the friars' witness to poverty which exalted the fraternity.[63] From the beginning of the fraternity it was the friars' practice to go barefoot.[64] In the 1270s John Pecham boasted that the friars' feet were their witness to their having turned their backs on society and that no winter had ever prevented the barefoot friars from making long journeys among the Tartars, Greeks and Saracens. Hot soil made going barefoot in summer as great a sacrifice as it is in winter.[65] Dante speaks of Francis's first companions, Bernard, Giles and Sylvester, going barefoot in pursuit of the bridegroom, the poor Christ.

While the *Vita prima* treats poverty as one of a number of the virtues which adorned Francis, the *Vita secunda* treats the vow of poverty and its interpretation in a more extensive manner. The second biography affirms that Francis looked upon poverty as especially dear to the Son of God, although it was spurned throughout the world. In order to espouse poverty he not only left his father and mother, he put aside everything that he might cling to her the more closely as his spouse. He looked upon poverty as especially dear to the Son of God, though it was rejected by contemporaries. He saw this as the road to perfection.[66] Dante attests that Francis was joined to Lady Poverty, who had been bereft of her first husband, despised and obscure 1100 years and more, remaining without a suitor until he came.[67]

Franciscan apologists regarded their founder's poverty as a providential antidote to a twofold problem afflicting both society and the Church: the greed of the new urban centres and clerical avarice, which had long exercised the minds of ardent reformers. One such exponent was Bonaventure, who maintained that mendicant preaching was divinely ordained to combat the vice of avarice; this claim was located in the context of the history of the Church. In his defence of the friars' mendicancy a historical model was invoked: in the early Church God provided men powerful in miracles and signs such as the apostles and their disciples who destroyed idolatry and the idols' portents. In the intermediate period God introduced men who were steeped in the Scriptures and were powerful in expounding them and they eradicated heresy. In the medieval period God provided men who voluntarily embraced mendicancy and poverty in material possessions and they routed avarice. The friars had a divinely commissioned role in the history of the Church and were an antidote to the materialism which had infected so many of the clergy. In view of this conviction Bonaventure was very anxious to defend what had come to be regarded as the order's special heritage. He maintained that poverty was the foundation of evangelical perfection and its complement, which had flourished in the beginning of the Church. It was all the more congruent in the final age of the Church, especially because it had flourished in the early Church.[68] A similarly eschatological perception of Francis's poverty was taken by John Pecham. The saint, discerning the danger and sacrileges of affluence, chose the apostolic model in the last era (*istis novissimis temporibus*) of the world to combat avarice, even in ecclesiastical circles.[69] His teaching and example chided contemporary clerics who were too attached to material things. The clerics who panted after revenues were castigated by the saint's example. When they were repaid in the revenue of torments, they would discover the extent of Francis's riches.[70]

CONCLUSION

At the end of the twelfth century and the beginning of the thirteenth the proliferation of cities in western Europe brought new opportunities for international trade and commercial prosperity. Wealth was unevenly distributed and the poor, who lived on the fringes of urban life, were mentioned more than once in the biographies of Francis. A series of incidents helped to clarify Francis's future and some of these involved the marginalized members of society: the pauper in his father's shop, the impoverished knight and his experience with the poor at the shrine of St Peter. His own sense of disenchantment led him from his father's house to the margins of the city, where he awaited fuller direction as he devoted himself to the restoration of old churches. When he heard the Gospel being read at the Portiuncula, his life was changed spectacularly and the Scriptures became the source of direction and correction. Henceforth, he was an evangelist living in imitation of his divine master and his experience of life was confirmed by the Gospel, which then offered him a remedy for the greed which divided society.

Francis's youth coincided with the emergence of a new understanding of the apostolic life. The monasteries were part of the cultural and economic landscape of the western Church and represented a tried and tested form of religious life, which had existed for almost a thousand years. Aspects of monasticism appealed to the young Francis, who spent some time at a monastery near Gubbio. For the remainder of his life he was drawn to the eremetical life. The growing urban focus questioned the long-held belief that the settled monastic life was the most perfect way of living the Gospel. The rhetoric of evangelical perfection was being transferred from a venerable model to one that was brand new. One expression of this reconsideration of the model of the apostolic life was the heightened awareness that such a life entailed engagement with society and this brought to the fore the image of the itinerant life of Jesus Christ and his disciples. Francis's conversion was rooted in the resolve to follow the apostolic pattern, which he suddenly realized at the Portiuncula. Initially he adopted the desire to live as the apostles had done, but within a short time the focus had switched to the person of Jesus Christ. The scriptural passages which fell before his eyes at San Nicola drew him towards a complete self-identification with his divine master. These emphasized the fact that the Son of God had no permanent home, that his itinerant ministry entailed hardship and that the renunciation of material goods was one route to perfection. Francis came to the conclusion that his divine master had lived without possessions and his mother and disciples had shared similar hardship. Moreover, the summit of perfection had been identified as selling goods and giving the proceeds to the poor and then following Jesus Christ. As he reflected continually on this mystery Francis came to regard poverty as a fundamental virtue which liberated him to follow more closely the life of his divine teacher.

The ecclesiastical reformers of the Middle Ages devoted their efforts to promoting a priesthood which was not tainted by the vices of simony and avarice. These two vices had deep roots, as the conciliar canons and provincial statutes attest. Critics within the Church lampooned the shortcomings of the clergy and their efforts to acquire material benefits; even the monastic orders did not escape criticism. Reform movements within the Church endorsed the simple lifestyle which they identified with Jesus Christ and the apostles. The ideals of Francis injected a breath of fresh air into the Church and were welcomed by many. His reform was to provide a remedy for the greed afflicting society and the careerism that stained the lives of clergymen intent on the accumulation of wealth and the attainment of high office. His voluntary poverty was praised by contemporaries who regarded him as reviving a significant dimension of the life of the apostolic Church. While many contemporaries asserted that the friars were introducing a new element into the life of the medieval Church, it is more accurate to say that Francis *recovered* part of the earlier tradition. Some of the Fathers had considered the values of poverty and described it in exalted terms. Similarly, Francis was not the first saint to glorify evangelical poverty in the form of Lady Poverty. His genius was to draw attention to an aspect of his divine teacher's lifestyle and to make that a principal part of his own programme of personal renewal. What he recovered enriched the medieval Church immensely. He preached a healthy and necessary detachment in the use of material things, which must always be informed by the teaching of the Gospel. While people crave ownership and thirst for security, Francis was concerned that such drives were capable of creating and sustaining barriers between people and obscuring the treasure imparted by the teaching of Jesus Christ, who entered the poverty of the human race in order to enrich it with virtues and talents. The preservation of such insights into evangelical poverty stood at the centre of Francis's relationship with another reforming prelate, Cardinal Ugolino.

Notes

1. LM, c. 7, nn. 1-2.
2. LTS, n. 9.
3. 1 C, n. 17; Anon. Perug., c. 1, n. 4b.
4. 2 C, n. 5.
5. J. Le Goff, *Medieval Civilisation 400-1500*, translated by J. Barrow from *La civilisation de l'Occident médiéval* (Oxford, 1988), p. 317.
6. 2 C, nn. 5, 8.
7. *Scripta Leonis*, pp. 322-3, where Francis directed Giles to give his cloak to an impoverished woman.
8. 1 C, nn. 128, 135, 147.
9. 2 C, nn. 9, 11, 15, 109.
10. C. H. Lawrence, *Medieval Monasticism* (London, 2nd edn, 1989), p. 248.
11. *S. Bonaventurae opera omnia*, VIII (Florence, 1898), p. 104.
12. *Giraldi Cambrensis opera*, II, ed. Brewer (RS 21, ii; London, 1862), pp. 126-38.
13. Jordan of Saxony, 'Libellus de principiis Ordinis Praedicatorum' in MOPH, ed. M. H. Laurent, 16 (Rome, 1935), nn. 19-22, pp. 35-7.
14. 1 C, n. 16.
15. Ibid., n. 6.
16. Lawrence, *Medieval Monasticism*, p. 246.
17. *S. Bernardi opera*, III, ed. J. Leclercq and H. M. Rochais (Rome, 1963), p. 101. It was common practice in the Middle Ages to speak of organized monastic life as a continuation of the apostolic community described in the Acts of the Apostles.

18. C. H. Lawrence, *The Friars* (Medieval World; London, 1994), p. 15; Lawrence, *Medieval Monasticism*, p. 239.
19. R. B. Brooke, *The Coming of the Friars* (Historical Problems, Studies and Documents; London, 1975), p. 40.
20. 1 C, n. 88.
21. A. Jessopp, *The Coming of the Friars and Other Historic Essays* (London, 1889), pp. 13, 15.
22. J. R. H. Moorman, *Saint Francis of Assisi* (London, 1950), p. 19.
23. Lawrence, *Medieval Monasticism*, p. 246.
24. Moorman, *Saint Francis of Assisi*, pp. 23-4.
25. *Compilatio Assisiensis*, c. 114.
26. *Opuscula Sancti Patris Francisci Assisiensis*, pp. 319-20; 1 C, n. 24.
27. 2 C, nn. 15, 109; *Scripta Leonis*, pp. 318-21.
28. *Opuscula Sancti Patris Francisci Assisiensis*, pp. 242-3.
29. 'De finibus paupertatis auctore Hugone de Digna, O.F.M.', ed. C. Florovsky, in AFH., 5 (1912), pp. 277-90, 281, 283.
30. *Opuscula Sancti Patris Francisci Assisiensis*, pp. 227-8.
31. 2 C, n. 80.
32. LM, c. 7, n. 3.
33. 1 C, n. 35.
34. *Scripta Leonis*, pp. 300-3. He was being entertained for the night at the monastery, when a newly born lamb was killed by a sow. Francis cursed the sow, which died three days later. The monks later informed the friars of this.
35. *Fonti Francescane* (Padua, 3rd edn, 1980), nn. 2249-51, pp. 1930-1, reports that near this monastery Francis had assembled the first 300 friars for a chapter; the abbot and his monks provided the friars with food and lodging. Towards the end of his life Francis, weak and exhausted through his penances, travelled by donkey towards the monastery and disregarded warnings about wolves in the vicinity.
36. 2 C, n. 101, which offers a fuller account than that contained in the *Compilatio Assisiensis*, c. 76. When the abbot met the saint on the road, he discussed the welfare of his soul with him. As he was leaving, he humbly asked Francis to pray for him. Addressing the prelate in respectful manner as 'my lord', Francis willingly promised to pray for him. While he prayed for him, the abbot suddenly felt in his soul an unusual warmth and sweetness, the like of which he had never experienced, so much so that he seemed to be completely carried out of himself in ecstasy. He paused for a moment and when he came to himself, he recognized the power of Francis's prayers. Thereafter he always burned with a greater love for the order and related the happening to many as a miracle.
37. *Scripta Leonis*, pp. 318-21.
38. 1 C, nn. 42-44.
39. *Compilatio Assisiensis*, c. 56.
40. 2 C, nn. 55, 56, 59.
41. *Opuscula Sancti Patris Francisci Assisiensis*, pp. 115-16, 173, 231-2, 237, 258, 311, 318.
42. 1 C, n. 34.
43. 2 C, nn. 71-74.
44. *S. Bonaventurae opera omnia*, V (Florence, 1891), p. 136.
45. Ibid., pp. 138-9, 141-2.
46. Moorman, *Saint Francis of Assisi*, p. 25.
47. B. Smalley, 'The Gospels in the Paris Schools in the late 12th and early 13th centuries', *Franciscan Studies*, 40 (1980), pp. 298-369, 365.
48. J. V. Fleming, *An Introduction to the Franciscan Literature of the Middle Ages* (Chicago, 1977), p. 12.
49. Leo the Great, *Sermon on the Beatitudes*, 95. 2-3, PL, 54, 461-2.
50. John Chrysostom, *The Gospel of Saint Matthew*, homily 90, n. 4, in PG, 58, 791-2.
51. C. N. L. Brooke and R. B. Brooke, *Popular Religion in the Middle Ages* (London, 1984), p. 128.
52. 1 C, n. 7.
53. 2 C, n. 70.
54. Ibid., n. 55.
55. Matthew Paris, *Chronica majora*, III, ed. Luard (RS 57, iii; London, 1876), p. 119.
56. *Lettres de Jacques de Vitry*, ed. R. B. C. Huygens (Leiden, 1960), pp. 75-6.
57. Jacques de Vitry, 'Histoire de l'Orient', c. 32, in G. Golubovich, *Biblioteca Bio-Bibliografica...*, I (Florence, 1906), pp. 8-10.
58. Matthew Paris, *Historia Anglorum*, II, ed. F. Madden (RS 44, ii; London, 1866), pp. 109-10.
59. Robert Grosseteste, *Epistolae*, p. 180.

60. Roger of Wendover, *Flores historiarum*, II, ed. H. G. Hewlett (RS 84, ii; London, 1887), pp. 328-9.
61. Matthew Paris, *Historia Anglorum*, II, p. 109.
62. A. G. Little, 'Brother William of England, companion of St Francis, and some Franciscan drawings in the Matthew Paris manuscripts', *Collectanea Franciscana*, 1 (BSFS, 5), ed. A. G. Little et al. (Aberdeen, 1914), pp. 1-8.
63. Thomas of Eccleston, *Tractatus de adventu fratrum minorum in Angliam*, ed. A. G. Little (Manchester, 1951), pp. 27, 12, 76, 82.
64. M. Bihl, 'Statuta generalia Ordinis edita in Capitulis generalibus celebratis Narbonae an. 1260', II, viii, p. 43.
65. John Pecham, *Tractatus tres de Paupertate*, ed. C. L. Kingsford, A. G. Little and F. Tocco (BSFS, 2; Aberdeen, 1910), pp. 112, 129.
66. 2 C, n. 55.
67. Dante, *Paradiso*, XI, 64-66, pp. 164-5.
68. *S. Bonaventurae opera omnia*, V, pp. 147-8.
69. Ibid., pp. 400, 421.
70. 2 C, n. 84.

5

Ugolino, cardinal protector and then Pope Gregory IX

The friars in Assisi hailed Gregory IX as the man whom the saint chose as a father[1]

Cardinal Ugolino dei Conti di Segni was related to Innocent III and had studied canon law at both Bologna and Paris before being promoted as a cardinal deacon of St Eustace's in 1198. A prominent member of the sacred college, he had become cardinal bishop of Ostia by May 1206. He was also a unique figure in the constitutional development and expansion of the mendicant movement, enjoying close relations with both Francis and Dominic. His first appearance in the early biographies of Francis was during his stint as papal legate in Tuscany and other provinces. At Francis's request, he was appointed as cardinal protector of the fraternity and his position at the papal court enabled him to defend the friars from their critics and to ensure that the Rule was safely confirmed by Honorius III. His influence on the fraternity did not cease with the death of Francis. On 19 March 1227 he was elected pope with the name of Gregory IX. He supervised the process of Francis's canonization and presided over the ceremonies in Assisi on 16 July 1228. On the following day he laid the foundation stone of the basilica to be built to the honour of the new saint. He bestowed various pastoral privileges on the friars, whom he employed increasingly as agents of papal policies. He was the first pope to provide an authoritative interpretation of Francis's Rule in *Quo elongati*, which came to be regarded as a moderate and sensible document. The two men, whose interests found a different focus, were undoubtedly united in a strong and warm friendship, which also had an enigmatic quality. The one was the senior cardinal bishop and the other was a simple man intent on a life of evangelical poverty. Their communications reflect the tension between the institutional Church and its prophetical voice.

THE GROWTH OF THE FRATERNITY

It was not uncommon for new religious movements to experience slow recruitment in their early years. The spectacular expansion of the Cistercian reform in the early twelfth century was in marked contrast to the trickle of vocations to Cîteaux in the 1090s.[2] The Franciscans had a similar beginning and for a couple of years Francis lived as a hermit intent on the restoration of dilapidated churches. The first friars were men of Assisi and, as their witness started to attract wider attention, they were joined by men from other parts of Umbria. Recruitment remained slow even after the initial papal approbation of the fraternity. After his abortive attempts to preach to the Muslims and earn martyrdom about 1212, Francis returned to Ancona and resumed his ministry as an itinerant preacher. One result of this campaign of preaching in various centres was that several good and suitable men, clerics and lay, were drawn to the fraternity. About three years later Francis's second attempt to reach Syria proved equally unsuccessful, with illness forcing him to turn back from Spain. Not long after, he had returned to the Portiuncula, where he received some educated and noble men into the order. Recruitment was often linked to Francis's magnetic personality and the power of his sermons. For instance, after a sermon at Ascoli, where people trampled upon one another in their eagerness to see and hear him, he received some thirty men, clerics and lay, into the fraternity.[3]

This increase in the friars' ranks created new possibilities and enabled their founder to look further afield. From the vantage point of 1228 Thomas of Celano recalls Francis's prophecy that a vast multitude of men would come to take the habit: the roads would be filled with their great numbers coming together from almost every nation: Frenchmen, Spaniards, Germans and Englishmen.[4] However, most of the recruits in this period seem to have come from the ranks of the laymen and by 1220 there was already a dearth of priests among the friars in northern Italy.[5] By the end of the decade the order had its first minister general in holy orders, Albert of Pisa, and the fraternity was confidently moving in the direction of clericalization. The general chapter of 1217 sent friars to France, Germany, Hungary, Spain and the other provinces of Italy. Jordan of Giano testifies to the early history of these missions and their teething troubles.

When the fraternity was small Francis made the necessary decisions in his own charismatic manner. The moment of expansion, the sign that the friars were beginning to make their mark in the contemporary Church, ironically issued in a painful process of growth, frustration and learning for both the founder and the fraternity. The increase in the friars' ranks exposed some of Francis's weaknesses as the leader of a growing army of zealous and increasingly accomplished men. The friars who were sent to France had little idea of the conditions that awaited them there and the divisions within Christendom. When asked whether they were Albigensians, they answered that they did not know who the Albigensians were and they themselves were taken for heretics. When, however, the bishop and masters of the University of Paris examined their Rule, they consulted Honorius III, who vouched for their orthodoxy; this is an early indication that the friars were accustomed to carry copies of their Rule. The combination of local episcopal assistance and papal assurances combined to salvage this mission.

A similarly inadequate preparation, coupled with a linguistic naivety, jeopardized the early missions to Germany and Hungary. A large band of friars set out for Germany without taking the precaution of learning the language. Their early experience was that an affirmative response to questions brought them numerous benefits, especially hospitality. They tended to rely on the word and, when asked whether they were heretics who had travelled to Germany to sow heresy, they replied affirmatively. On this occasion the result was not nearly so pleasant. Their treatment was such that they abandoned the mission and returned to Italy, where Germany gained the reputation as a province in which martyrdom might be gained without much difficulty. The friars sent to Hungary travelled there by sea in the company of a bishop from that country. As they walked through the fields, they were derided, and shepherds set their dogs upon them and kept striking them with their staves, the point, however, being turned away. When they discussed the reasons for such inhospitable treatment, they wondered whether the local populace wanted to steal all their clothes. One of the friars told Jordan of Giano that he had lost his trousers fifteen times in this way. Afflicted with other insults too, these friars returned to Italy.[6]

Reflecting on such disastrous missions, Ugolino, now playing an active role in the life of the fraternity, prevailed upon Francis to ensure that friars should not be treated as heretics. The cardinal used his influence at the papal court to obtain from Honorius III on 11 June 1219 a letter which attested the friars' orthodoxy. A second wave of missionaries to Germany in the 1220s led to a much happier foundation. The benefits of a thorough preparation were visible in the mission to England. A band of nine friars landed in Kent on 10 September 1224, some years after the missions to France, Germany and Hungary. This mission bears all the marks of much more careful preparation, with a clear plan of expansion and development. Three of the nine friars in the original party were English and they made first for Canterbury, the archiepiscopal seat, and from there moved to London, the capital city. Within seven weeks of their arrival in the country they had established themselves in the university city of Oxford and about a year later they had settled in Cambridge, where there was a young university. An explosion in terms of recruitment enabled them to found communities in the major cities and towns before 1230. The development of the province suggests that the friars had learned from their earlier experiences and there was a marked contrast between the initial reports filed by Jordan of Giano on France, Germany and Hungary and Thomas of Eccleston on England. This more successful strategy coincided with a period when Francis was beginning to step back from the leadership of the fraternity and the influence of Cardinal Ugolino was on the increase.

Francis had been forced to abandon his dream of becoming a celebrated knight and with it surrendered the initiative to divine providence. His own vocation became clearer once he had cast aside his old plans and ambitions and he was happy to continue in that vein. He became convinced that he should repose complete trust in the promises enshrined in the Gospels. The Scriptures had provided him with direction for his new life as an itinerant evangelist. When Bernard of Quintavalle asked him for guidance, he did not offer a carefully crafted plan. Instead, his response was simple and direct: he led him to the church of San Nicola and had the book of the Gospels opened thrice at random. Nor was this the last time that he had the book of the Gospels opened in search of further guidance and he was not unhappy with the notion of asking others to pray that his future work might be revealed. This was not an abdication of responsibility. It was, rather, a profession of faith in God who would direct his future course. This absolute dependence on providence helped to make Francis one of the most attractive saints.

Jordan of Giano's testimony underlines the shortcomings of this lack of preparation and failure to learn the languages necessary to work in other countries. Many commentators claim that Francis was less at home in planning strategy for the fraternity. Lawrence concludes that thanks either to the more practical, if worldlier, intelligence of Elias or the more prudent guidance of Ugolino, the shortcomings in Francis's plans were remedied; Francis, unlike Dominic, lacked organizational skills.[7] R. B. Brooke regards Francis as more of an idealist than a realist, believing that he was not gifted as a legislator.[8] More recently she and C. N. L. Brooke remarked that the fraternity grew in an untidy and shapeless way.[9] Similarly, Francis's radical decision to embark upon a life of evangelical poverty went hand in hand with his wishes that provision should be made for the sick, that the friars should have breviaries for the Divine Office and that the reserved sacrament should be kept in the most precious receptacles. While his trust in divine providence was such that he did not take the necessary steps for the launching of his missions, he was acutely aware of his own limitations and freely acknowledged his need of assistance in certain situations. He knew when he needed guidance and turned to a small group of friends, including Guido, Clare and Ugolino; the cardinal bishop provided him with a great deal of practical and canonical help. This accounts for his early dealings with Guido who was content to make practical suggestions and then leave Francis to take the decisions regarding the fraternity. Guido's concerns, however, were local, while Ugolino, immersed in the life of the Roman Curia, had a more global perspective and was anxious to bring the mendicant movement into the heart of the Church and to make good use of the many enormously gifted men who had taken the Franciscan and Dominican habit. For this reason his interventions were the more telling as he tried to protect the friars' constitutional position at the Curia.

THE MEETING IN FLORENCE

While Ugolino may have met Francis at the Fourth Lateran Council, he was definitely in touch with Dominic by this time and in the autumn of 1215 he began a series of conversations regarding the business of the fraternity. Following the death of Innocent III, he assured Dominic that the confirmation of the order of Preachers would be forthcoming and he was one of the 18 cardinals who signed the consistorial privilege of 22 December 1216, confirming the order. Dominic also visited the cardinal at the Curia in 1218, at the end of 1219 and at the beginning of 1221.[10] Dominicans believed that Ugolino had known their founder intimately and had loved him warmly. When he heard of Dominic's death, the cardinal hastened to the priory in Bologna and presided at his funeral.[11] This broader mendicant context should be considered in any evaluation of the cardinal's place in the gestation of the Franciscan fraternity, especially in matters of legislation.

One tradition records that on the death of Cardinal John of St Paul the pope appointed Ugolino as cardinal protector.[12] While John of St Paul appears at the head of the list of cardinal protectors, later historians explained his role in terms of the office which was first filled by Ugolino, one of Innocent III's most trusted advisers among the cardinals.[13] Gregory IX was revered as a man greatly conspicuous for his virtue and holiness. The biographers' intention was to narrate the wondrous witness and teaching of the saint and the manifestations of his holiness in miracles. Questions of chronology or constitutional history were not high on their agenda. The context of the first known meeting between Francis and Ugolino was the general chapter of 1217 when it was decided to establish communities in France, Germany, Hungary, Spain and some new provinces in Italy. Scholars have long been exercised by the antecedents to the momentous first meeting between the two men. The meeting took place in Florence at a critical moment in the evolution of the fraternity and served as a preamble for Ugolino's appointment as cardinal protector.

At long last Francis sensed that he was about to fulfil his cherished ambition of going to France; the fraternity was still small and potentially vulnerable. Even though Thomas of Celano implies that the cardinal had already assumed some responsibility for the fraternity, he is reported to have asked Francis about the purpose of his visit to Florence. The biographer implies that the cardinal was making the saint's acquaintance and learning something about his outlook on the world; perhaps Honorius III had briefed the cardinal about Francis. It is not known whether Ugolino was at the court of Innocent III when Francis arrived there in search of papal approbation. Another occasion on which they may have met was the Fourth Lateran Council. Francis's first biographer emphasizes that the cardinal combined his lofty ecclesiastical office with his search for sanctity and indicates that a mutually beneficial bond grew between the two men: the cardinal sought the saint's prayers and offered him his protection in everything. Ugolino was familiar with the business of the fledgling fraternity and had already assumed some responsibility for it. His influence was such that he prevailed upon Francis not to continue his journey to France and to devote himself to the care of the friars in Italy. The report of the interview closed with the observation that Francis was overjoyed to see that the prince of the Church was so well disposed towards the friars and was happy to receive his advice. He fell at Ugolino's feet and entrusted himself and the friars to him. By the time of their first recorded meeting the cardinal emerged as a figure aware of opposition to the nascent fraternity and anxious to use his influence on its behalf, even though its constitutional status in the life of the Church was not yet settled.

A fuller account, complete with more circumstantial detail regarding the general chapter of 1217, was provided by the saint's early companions. Francis felt the call to go to France, a country whose people were catholics renowned for their deep devotion to the Eucharist. In due course he set out and at Florence met Ugolino, whose legatine responsibilities included Spoleto, Lombardy and the Marches of Treviso as well as Tuscany. The cardinal, however, forbade him to go to France on the grounds that some members of the Curia and others were hostile to the interests of the friars. He and a group of cardinals, favourable to the fraternity, were anxious to protect and help it provided Francis did not withdraw from Italy. This text provides invaluable information on the reactions to the fraternity within the Roman Curia. A group of cardinals may have been anxious to make the friars accept an older Rule, especially after the decision of the Fourth Lateran Council not to approve any new Rules. Talk of such danger did not deflect the saint from articulating his own missionary ambition, protesting that he wished to accompany the friars on their journey to France and that he should not send friars to face dangers which he himself would avoid. He must have been briefed by the cardinal about the type of arguments which were being turned against the friars. Was he unaware that powerful figures at the papal court entertained serious reservations about his fraternity? Already he was in need of the type of assistance which Ugolino supplied, particularly in areas where his own personal influence was minimal.

Ugolino upbraided him by asking him why he had sent the friars to face hunger and so many other tribulations. He may have heard reports about Francis's need of assistance in organizing missions to lands where the threat of heresy was strong. Did the cardinal predict some of the difficulties in which the friars would find themselves in France? At least he did not intervene to cancel the mission. Francis then expatiated on his vision of the friars and their contribution to the Church: they had been selected and sent out by God for the profit and salvation of souls throughout the world and their mission included the lands of the infidels. His companions report that the cardinal wondered at these words and acknowledged that the truth had been spoken. Ugolino did insist, nonetheless, that it was necessary for Francis to stay in Italy and his authority was such that it overruled Francis's own wishes and his desire to lead the friars by example. Francis capitulated and sent Pacifico and others, while he returned to Spoleto. The dark clouds to which the cardinal referred were sufficiently menacing for Francis to cut short his journey and to return to Umbria. Francis's biographers say no more about the hostility which some cardinals were showing to the new fraternity; the combination of the cardinal's influence and Francis's continued presence in Italy may have frustrated those efforts. Equally, the wily cardinal may have been the one responsible for the silence which seems to have enveloped the friars' critics in this period. From the 1220s Ugolino was regarded as the friars' defender.

This passage raises some of the larger questions about the communication between the two men. Ugolino was a prince of the Church who had been drawn into the reforming currents of the mendicant movement and he regarded the friars as invaluable allies in the cause of reform. The image projected by the saint's companions was that the cardinal, who was undoubtedly favourable to Francis and his order, did not unfailingly discern and comprehend the spirit which animated the fraternity. Images of the cardinal bowing to the saint's teaching are not uncommon. Thomas of Celano's account, with the cardinal cast in the stronger role, seems the more realistic version and mirrors Francis's respectful dealings with the hierarchy. C. T. Maier treats this meeting as a milestone in the history of the order and thinks that Ugolino prevailed on Francis to remain in Italy, probably because he foresaw that the planned expansion would place an enormous strain on the inner fabric of the fraternity, particularly over the question of leadership.[14] This meeting was momentous because the cardinal made so strong an impression on Francis. When the office of cardinal protector was conceived, a petition was addressed to the pope. By that time Francis had in mind only one candidate for that influential office.

APPOINTMENT OF A CARDINAL PROTECTOR

The friars' close dependence upon the papal Curia was due in the first instance to Francis's initiative. Papal recognition of the fraternity enabled the friars to grow into a great movement. Francis's resolve to remain at the heart of the Church's reforming programme was expressed in the petition for a cardinal protector in the last chapter of the Rule:

> I command the ministers through obedience to petition the Lord Pope for one of the cardinals of the holy Roman Church, who would be the governor, protector, and corrector of this fraternity, so that, always submissive and prostrate at the feet of the same holy Church, and steadfast in the Catholic faith, we may observe the poverty and the humility and the holy Gospel of our Lord Jesus Christ which we have firmly promised.[15]

The cardinal's responsibility was to keep the friars faithful to their vows and in the bosom of the universal Church to which they should always be subject. This provision, absent from the earlier draft of the Rule in 1221, may represent an attempt to bind the friars into closer communication with the hierarchy and the cardinal into closer communion with the friars. Lawrence treats the official status of the cardinal protector as an innovation made in response to Francis's petition and for a long time it had no counterpart in other religious orders.[16]

Ugolino's relationship with the friars was formalized when Honorius III appointed him as cardinal protector at the request of Francis, who was undoubtedly distressed to find that the government of the order was becoming increasingly onerous and troublesome. Events following his visit to the East confirmed that the leadership of a fraternity which was expanding to the Holy Land, France, Spain, Germany and Hungary was beginning to make greater demands on him; the community was evolving rapidly. In the early days he had been its animator and seems to have taken all the decisions about its life and development; the early recruits were probably admitted to the fraternity on his approval. His personal involvement at the heart of the order and the policies which he had followed in earlier days no longer served a rapidly expanding fraternity.

The first few years after the Fourth Lateran Council saw the beginnings of a remarkable expansion and the missions dispatched by the general chapter in 1217 led to the formation of new provinces, some of which Francis did not visit. In addition, he could no longer personally admit new members. It was one of the ironies of history that the growth of the order meant the founder's influence diminished because the number of friars being admitted in various provinces meant that he could not hope to know these friars in person. Decision-making had to be shared and policies formulated. While accounts of debate at the early general chapters are not abundant, it is difficult to imagine that this forum suited Francis; there are several instances of his imposing his will upon the friars. The transition from being a small fraternity, whose activities were at first local in Umbria, to an international order, with provinces in different parts of Christendom, meant that Francis was required to look for help in order to preserve his vision of the community. The two biographies by Thomas of Celano explain the background to Ugolino's appointment in 1220 and these accounts were supplemented by Jordan of Giano's fuller record of the events of 1219–20.

Vita prima

A short description of Ugolino's appointment was supplied within the context of Francis's friendship with him. Francis had chosen Ugolino with the consent and will of Honorius III as the father and lord of the friars because voluntary poverty was very pleasing to him and holy simplicity was held in great reverence by him.

Ugolino's virtues were displayed when he conformed himself to the friars' ways, particularly on his visits to friaries. In his desire for sanctity he displayed simplicity and poverty and often laid aside his princely robes to don the friars' mean garb; he went around barefoot like the friars, asking terms of peace. Francis predicted that the cardinal would be elected pope,[17] although Ugolino's position and influence within the Roman Curia were so strong that his ultimate election as pope can have caused few surprises.

Ugolino was keen to promote the order and establish it throughout Christendom, even in remote places. Did he have the foresight to see that the geographical dissemination of the fraternity would provide a remedy for an earlier weakness in the promotion of reform? By encouraging the friars to settle in different parts of Christendom he was ensuring that the voice of reform would be heard in every city, large town and village. The biographer acknowledges that the friars benefited from the cardinal's reputation. Even though the diffusion of the Franciscan ideal was already under way when the men first met, the cardinal encouraged the friars to spread throughout the Christian world. His circle of contacts and influence undoubtedly eased the friars' path in some places, such as France, where the mission was rescued by the local ecclesiastic and the Roman court. The cardinal's hand was undoubtedly behind the better organization which distinguished the friars' missions in the early 1220s. The biographer states somewhat tersely that, when the friars were beginning to spread, earning renown and stretching forth their sacred branches to the limits of the world, Francis asked Honorius III to appoint Ugolino as cardinal protector. The pope granted Francis's petition and made over his own authority over the friars to the cardinal. The office was accepted reverently and devoutly by the cardinal who solicitously cared for the friars. His ministrations were likened to those of the faithful and prudent servant (Matthew 24:45). Francis submitted himself to the cardinal in all things and revered him with a wonderful and respectful affection.

The narrative was very conventional and respectful of the hierarchy, probably reflecting the fact that Gregory IX was the reigning pope when the text was completed. The claim that Francis submitted himself in all things to Ugolino calls for some qualification because other biographies mention his role as a teacher and expounder of Scripture; on occasion the cardinal appears among his pupils and does not always grasp the expositions of Scripture and the friars' vocation in the Church. The biographer goes on to state expressly that Francis, at the inspiration of the Holy Spirit, would refresh the cardinal with his words. In such meetings Francis raised the spirits of the cardinal, who was so deeply immersed in ecclesiastical politics. On occasion he wrote to the cardinal about the business of the order, though regrettably these letters are no longer extant. Such correspondence between the saint and the cardinal would have illuminated aspects of the fraternity's early history and the quest for an approved Rule, which was granted only late in Francis's life. Ugolino, who watched with interest the way in which the Dominicans and Franciscans were spreading throughout western Europe, sensed that the mendicant ideal could be just as contagious in the early thirteenth century as the Cistercian reform had been in the previous century. It is quite conceivable that the cardinal had given more thought to the advantages of an expanding fraternity than the founder. As a reforming cardinal he foresaw the benefits which the followers of the *poverello* would bring to the Church, although this expansion produced tensions within the fraternity.

Vita secunda

Thomas of Celano's second biography locates Ugolino's appointment within the context of Francis's concerns for the future of the fraternity and a visit which he made to the papal court where he delivered a homily. As the order was increasing in numbers and provinces Francis began to give more thought to the preservation and unity of the community. This biography contains a stronger hint of the forces which were ranged against the friars; these were described as raging savagely against the friars. Thomas of Celano contrasts the men grown old in evil with the youthfulness and vitality of the nascent fraternity. Moreover, the saint was depicted as foreseeing that some of the friars would act contrary to peace and unity. While he was considering these matters, he had a vision in his sleep. He saw a little black hen, much like a tame dove, with innumerable chicks pressing close to her, but they could not all get under her wings. Awaking from sleep, he interpreted the dream for himself and saw that the hen represented himself and the chicks denoted the friars whose number had multiplied. The founder's strength did not permit him to defend them from the disturbances. His acceptance of this vision and its interpretation provides an acknowledgement that the growth within the order produced pressures with which he could not deal adequately. Informed by this vision, Francis decided to commend his friars to the Roman Curia, where he hoped to find a defence against the fraternity's detractors, whose complaints were not specified by the early biographers. This alliance was regarded as a condition of the friars spreading everywhere and working for the salvation of souls and as creating a bond between the papacy and the friars. The biographer speaks of this commendation in terms of the friars' relationship with the cardinal protector, who would keep the friars in peace and strike those who attacked them. This decision to seek help was another instance of the saint coming face to face with his own limitations and dependence upon ecclesiastical authority. The move also mirrors his profound faith in the papacy, which would protect his fledgling community from its critics.

After a homily at the papal court Francis put before Honorius III a plan which would ensure that he had access to the papal court through a cardinal specially designated to protect the friars' interests. He commented that access to the pope, who held the whole world in his hands and was involved in crucial decisions, was limited. He asked that Ugolino be assigned as his pope (*pro papa*). The creation of the new office would enable the friars to have recourse to the cardinal and to obtain whatever was needed and to receive his protection and guidance whenever they were necessary. This petition was accepted by the pope who, as requested, appointed Ugolino. The cardinal accepted the flock entrusted to his care and became its diligent guardian, its shepherd and its foster child. These events were sketched in brief by Thomas of Celano, who presents them in a matter-of-fact way. Francis's request undoubtedly issued in a lengthy process of consultation, involving Honorius III, Ugolino and Francis; the members of the Roman Curia were engaged in the deliberative process, especially because the petition was creating a new office among the cardinals. Full discussion was required to fix the parameters of the new office. For example, the pope would have wished to circumscribe the powers of the cardinal protector to ensure that there was due consultation on all major decisions. The biographer explains that the friars' subjection to the papacy earned the latter's special love and care. The shape of this part of the biography leaves us with the strong impression that Francis had come to the realization that he could not deal with the friars and their critics alone and that external help from the papal court was necessary for the defence and prosperity of the friars.

Jordan of Giano

The fullest circumstantial treatment of the institution of the office of cardinal protector is provided by the celebrated chronicler Jordan of Giano, who links it with the confusion and disorder which followed Francis's departure for the East, revealing the power and charisma of his personality. When Francis realized his long-held wish to go to the Holy Land, he appointed two vicars, Matthew of Narni and Gregory of Naples. Matthew was in residence at the Portiuncula and Gregory was entrusted with the roving commission of encouraging the friars throughout Italy. The first Rule required the friars to fast on Wednesday and Friday and, with the permission of Francis, on Monday and Saturday. The vicars set alarm bells ringing when they proceeded to hold a chapter with some of the senior friars in Italy and decided to add to the founder's Rule. These events raised what was to become a perennial question in the life of the friars: the source of ultimate authority within the community and how that was to be applied to new circumstances.

The addition to the saint's teaching caused indignation in some quarters and an incensed lay brother set off for the East without permission, carrying a copy of the constitutions across the sea to Francis. He informed the saint that the vicars had added constitutions to the Rule and were disturbing the order throughout Italy; he also imparted the bad news that factions were rising among the friars. The constitutions were examined and this disturbing news brought an abrupt end to Francis's sojourn in the East. He immediately withdrew from the Holy Land to deal with the troubled state of the fraternity. On his return to Italy he expressed his alarm at the growing indifference towards the ownership of property and easy living by removing his vicars and taking up a personal command once more. Moreover, Brother Philip, a zealot in visiting the Poor Clares in opposition to the will of Francis, had obtained apostolic letters to protect the Poor Clares and excommunicate those who disturbed them. The vacuum in leadership and uncertainty about the authority of the vicars were exacerbated by persistent rumours that Francis was dead; it was thought that he had been killed or drowned. These caused considerable disturbance within the order. In addition, the fraternity was also threatened by schism because John Conpella, after he had gathered together a large crowd of lepers, withdrew with the intention of founding a new order. He wrote a Rule and presented himself with his followers before the Holy See to have it confirmed.

On his return Francis had been accompanied by Elias, Peter Catanii and Caesar, the minister in Syria. He betook himself to Honorius III, petitioning him to appoint a cardinal to deal with the problems of the order, asking that the bishop of Ostia be appointed. He explained to the pope the causes of his distress. The pope immediately revoked the letters of Brother Philip, and Brother John was sent away from the Curia with his followers in shame. Francis reformed the order according to his own statutes. The chronicler then goes on to state that Francis commissioned Caesar of Speyer to provide the scriptural passages for the Rule. Perhaps the sequence of events during Francis's absence in the East convinced him of the urgency of having his Rule ratified.[18] Knowles asserts that it was only in 1219 that the papacy responded to the lack of leadership during Francis's absence in the East, moved in and applied to the friars some of the most elementary of the canonical rules governing all religious institutions, such as the year's novitiate, formal profession of vows and the local control of individuals.[19]

CARDINAL AND FRANCIS

Thomas of Celano waxed eloquently on the confidence which Francis reposed in Ugolino, remarking that the saint clung to the cardinal as a son to his father and as an only son to his mother, sleeping and resting securely upon the bosom of his kindness. Ugolino held the place and did the work of a shepherd, but he left the title to Francis. Francis provided what was necessary, but the cardinal kindly carried it into effect. The biographer acts as a spokesman for the early Franciscan tradition when he blessed the day that Francis joined forces with the cardinal. Ugolino's respectful attitude towards Francis mirrored his reverence for all those promoting the renewal of the Church. Was Thomas of Celano also thinking of the cardinal's close links with the Dominicans? In a hagiographical flourish he testifies that at their first meeting Ugolino received Francis with humble devotion, as he did with all those who professed holy religion, particularly those who loved the noble insignia of poverty and simplicity. He venerated Francis with special affection and was afire with love for him; whatever Francis did pleased him and he was deeply affected even by the mere sight of him. Ugolino testified that he was never so greatly disturbed or upset but that, upon seeing Francis or talking with him, every mental cloud would be dispersed and serenity return, melancholy would be put to flight and joy breathed on him from above.[20] Such meetings must have been a source of comfort and solace to the cardinal in the midst of his ecclesiastical and political activities.

The friars' heroic witness to poverty made a deep impression on Ugolino, whose sense of wonder was aroused when he attended a general chapter at the Portiuncula. Together with a large group of knights, clerics and monks, he entered the friary and visited the dormitory. When he observed that the friars were accustomed to sleep on the ground with nothing beneath them but a little straw, no pillows and a few coverlets, which were in a poor condition, he wept bitterly. He then went on to contrast the friars' poverty with his own relatively opulent lifestyle as a prince of the Church. He also observed that the friars did not have a table and that they ate on the ground. This confession of admiration for the friars moved his hearers to tears and they departed greatly edified.[21]

Ugolino was responsible for arranging at least one sermon which Francis preached at the papal court. As usual, the biographer's account favours the saint, claiming that he greatly longed to preach before Honorius III and the cardinals. Francis, intent on preaching, was contrasted with the patron, who was anxious lest his client should fail to impress the members of the Curia. The whole episode made Ugolino very nervous, especially in a climate where certain cardinals were opposed to the fraternity and may have been inclined to look disdainfully at the pauper from Umbria. Hagiographical conventions depicted Ugolino as confident of the divine mercy. He was filled with both fear and joy, admiring the fervour of the holy man, but conscious of his simple purity. His more direct involvement was suggested by the observation that he introduced Francis to the cardinals. Ecclesiastical etiquette was observed whereby Francis sought the cardinals' blessing to commence his sermon. Like an evangelist, he began to speak fearlessly.

The biographer demonstrates that the cardinal's fears were unfounded and that Francis not only spoke with great fervour of spirit, but was unable to contain his joy. As he preached with such warmth and fervour, he moved his feet as though he were dancing; a puritanical strain prompted the biographer to quash any smear that Francis was acting in a libidinous manner. Francis danced as one burning with the fire of divine love, not provoking laughter, but drawing forth tears of grief. Many of the cardinals were pierced to the heart in admiration of divine grace and of such great constancy in man.[22] It was to the biographer's credit that he felt sufficiently at ease to describe the reigning pope as being kept in suspense by fear and praying with all his strength that Francis's simplicity would not be ridiculed and despised. Ugolino was well aware of the difference between Francis's stirring sermons and the more formal style of preaching in vogue at the papal court. Stephen of Bourbon testifies that one of the more eminent bishops present, undoubtedly Ugolino, was afraid that Francis would embarrass himself and invited him to his house, offering him a polished sermon which he might commit to memory for such a significant occasion. At the crucial moment Francis, who had spent a great deal of time in memorizing the sermon, was unable to recall the text. He then decided to put his trust in God, opened a Psalter and embarked upon a sermon on the duties of prelates.[23] Thomas of Celano describes another sermon in the presence of the pope and cardinals. Francis preached with ready and fervent foresight, speaking without restraint whatever the Spirit suggested.[24]

FRANCIS INSTRUCTS UGOLINO

A saint was presented as a prophetical figure who imitated Christ in a most exemplary manner. One dimension of his charism was his capacity to expound the Gospel to people of all ranks, including bishops, the teachers in the Church; in such situations the normal ecclesiastical order was not necessarily observed because the saints instructed popes and prelates. Thus, despite Francis's lack of formal education, his biographers dwell upon the advice which he dispensed to people of all ranks. This, of course, is an illustration of the saint's capacity to instruct contemporaries on the fuller implications of the Gospel. Ugolino was firmly placed in the pupil's seat from time to time and he was shown to have been initially foxed by the saint's teaching. There are echoes of the Gospels in the biographers' claim that, like the apostles, Ugolino was slow to grasp the full impact of his teaching. In addition, he showed himself to be unsure about the evangelical principles which animated Francis and the character of the community which assembled around him. On at least two occasions Francis was depicted as instructing Ugolino. While the cardinal played a decisive role in the life of the nascent fraternity, biographers after 1241 seem to have no scruples about showing how Francis instructed him in certain situations. Though the cardinal had generously provided the saint with certain qualities and administrative expertise, Francis played the role of the prophet and the teacher. The two accounts underline the prelate's respect for the saint, whose explanation he accepts, making no attempt to impose his will.

When Francis travelled around Italy and preached in different cities, he often received hospitality at a time when the fraternity was small and did not have friaries in many cities. On these occasions he insisted on begging for alms before meals and sometimes he was accompanied by his host. On a visit to the home of Ugolino he did the same, though there is some indication that, on this occasion, the begging was carried out furtively on account of his host's dignity as a senior cardinal. Francis's companions focus primarily upon his role as a teacher, recounting vividly the changes of mood undergone by his host. When Francis had gathered sufficient alms, he returned to the cardinal's home after the meal had begun; no doubt the cardinal, who had invited some knights for the occasion, had grown weary of waiting for the saint, who on this occasion does not seem to have been governed by a sense of punctuality. When he entered his host's dining room, Francis deposited the alms, in the form of food, on the table and took a seat beside his host; not for the first time the cardinal struggled to understand the guest whose conduct was an embarrassment. Nonetheless, the presence of his other guests served as a restraint.

Having eaten a little, Francis took out his alms and sent a little to the knights and chaplains at table; these were received with gratitude. The chroniclers record a change of mind on the part of Ugolino who rejoiced at his guests' devotion. After the meal the cardinal took Francis aside, embraced him and addressed a gentle word of reproach. Francis responded that his conduct had, in fact, brought great honour to his host and that his vocation required him to become a model and example for all. Moreover, his behaviour was designed to encourage the friars to overcome all shame in asking for alms because Christ, the lord of all, became the servant of all. He who was rich and glorious in his majesty stooped to fallen humanity. Thus Francis considered the bread of alms as holy bread sanctified by the praise and love of God. The account closes with a statement that Francis's teaching edified the cardinal who encouraged him to do what seemed best because God was with him. The saint acts as an effective teacher, challenging the cardinal to a more rigorous observance of the Gospel. The cardinal's understanding of the Gospel was being diluted by a concern to observe the niceties of social conventions. Thomas of Celano's second life, which was mindful of criticisms about the friars, summarizes the material emanating from Leo and companions and offers an account of the dinner which acknowledges the prelate's dignity.[25] Ugolino was reminded that Francis's primary responsibility was to pay honour and reverence to God and then to his servants.

The meeting between Ugolino, Dominic and Francis in the cardinal's house at Rome places two factors in bold relief. First, it exemplifies the way in which the friars were perceived as reviving the halcyon days of the Christian community, the apostolic Church, the criterion by which reforms were gauged. Secondly, it reflects the thoughts and intentions of the reformers within the college of cardinals, who wished to make good use of the friars' talents in every part of the Church. Nonetheless, Francis's first biographers treat this as a temptation to deviate from the fraternity's ministry of humble service within the Church. Ugolino reminded the two saints that in the early Church the pastors were poor and men of charity, implying that many bishops in the early thirteenth century were greedy. He wished to revive the golden age of the early Church with its exemplary bishops and to revitalize the hierarchy. This encounter was skilfully orchestrated by the cardinal in order to broach the vexed question of friars becoming bishops. He regarded the friars as men whose learning and example surpassed that of the secular clergy. Nonetheless, the cardinal does not seem to have been optimistic about his hope of persuading Dominic and Francis and, for this reason, he drew upon an argument from history. His appeal was based on the model of the apostolic Church and it was addressed to two saints who were determined to restore apostolic excellence. In addition, he added that both the Dominicans and Franciscans excelled other clerics by their learning and example. The suggestion was cloaked in its most attractive form. Dominic's terse reply noted that his followers had already been called to a high station in the Church. This response was of minimal interest to the Franciscan biographers, anxious to offer an orthodox interpretation of Francis's wishes.

Francis's biographers use the saint's response to the cardinal's suggestion as an opportunity to reaffirm the friars' vocation. Francis emphasized that his followers were not called to take their place among the more powerful and influential, the *maiores*. The friars' role was to be lesser brethren, who eschew high office and walk in the footsteps of the humble Christ. They would bear fruit only by remaining in their lowly station. The episode highlights the tensions between the demands of the Church and the charism of religious orders. Francis was adamant that, if the friars were to be of use to the Church, they must not be promoted to bishoprics, lest they succumb to pride and arrogance. Leo and companions report that Ugolino was edified. Thomas of Celano concludes with Francis's petition that his friars should not be consecrated as bishops, neglecting to register the cardinal's response.[26] This meeting must have been situated between 1215 and the summer of 1221, at a time when the two orders were beginning to expand more spectacularly, although at the earlier date the Franciscans' ranks were not teeming with candidates for bishoprics. The cardinal's somewhat tentative suggestion would have applied more to the later 1230s and the 1240s than twenty years earlier. Thomson points out that in the fourteen years of his pontificate Ugolino, now Gregory IX, seems to have recognized only one Franciscan bishop, Agnellus, bishop of Fez, in Morocco about 1226. Leo was appointed archbishop of Milan on 15 June 1241 by Gregory of Montelongo, the papal legate. The friar, who had served as minister provincial in Milan and Lombardy, was not consecrated until 13 April 1245.[27] Thus, the question explored by the saint's biographers in the middle of the 1240s had its own urgency and, while Thomas of Celano was completing his second biography, in late 1247 negotiations were taking place leading to the appointment of Eudes Rigaud, the third master of the Franciscan school in Paris, to the archbishopric of Rouen. Gregory appointed some 31 Dominicans who were made bishops. Matters changed under following popes and Alexander IV (1254-61) appointed more than 40 Franciscan bishops. By 1288 there were several Franciscan bishops, archbishops, some cardinals and even a Franciscan pope, Nicholas IV.

INTERVENTIONS BY UGOLINO

Ugolino had a deep-rooted admiration and love for Francis and respectfully listened to his expositions of the Gospel. In addition, the austerity of the friars' practices impressed him, leading him to reconsider his own lifestyle. However much the biographers emphasized Francis's role as a teacher, it is an indisputable fact that the cardinal made a number of telling interventions in the life of the saint and his fraternity. Sometimes he told Francis what to do and the command met with compliance or obedience. Moreover, the cardinal's work as the friars' defender cannot be underestimated, because their critics were well positioned to inflict much harm upon the vulnerable fraternity. His intervention at Bologna defused the situation and enabled the friars to remain in their new surroundings and his care for the ailing Francis sprang from a desire to prolong his life for the benefit of the Church.

The hagiographical tradition's exaltation of the saint complicates the attempt to evaluate the influence exercised by the cardinal. One of Ugolino's major contributions, however, was to ensure the survival, development and growth of the fraternity throughout Christendom. Thomas of Celano, identifying the friars as the agents of God's work, bewailed the fact that many were plotting to destroy the new order that had been planted; many were trying to choke off this new 'chosen vineyard' that the Lord had planted in the world. They were trying to steal and consume the first and purest fruits of the fraternity. Such critics were routed by Ugolino, who was a river of eloquence, a wall of the Church, a champion of truth and a lover of the humble. God had given the cardinal a learned tongue with which he confounded adversaries of the truth and refuted the enemies of the cross. These comments confirm that by 1228 at least there were influential parties opposed to the fraternity. There had been opposition from a group of cardinals as early as 1217 and by the middle of the 1220s other prelates were beginning to protest about the friars' pastoral ministry;[28] many were plotting to destroy the new order.[29] After his election to the papacy Gregory always resisted the friars' foes until his death.[30] Certain cardinals known to have been favourable towards the Franciscans were listed by Thomson. From these indications, both general and specific, there also seems to have been a substantial amount of support for the friars at the very top of the hierarchy. The idea that a strong nucleus of opposition to the order worked to counteract the reforms inaugurated by Innocent may not be totally untrue.[31]

On his return to Italy in 1220 Francis was determined to recall the friars from certain unwelcome innovations and reaffirmed the principles which animated the fraternity. All talk of the friars owning property was anathema to him. He had travelled from Verona to the outskirts of Bologna, when he was approached by a friar disaffected by the recent changes. It was claimed that the friars in Bologna were talking about their new friary in terms of ownership and this filled Francis with dismay. The ideas of the market place, which he had long ago renounced, were now pursuing Francis in his religious vocation and threatening to subvert the life of the fraternity. Because no compromise was acceptable to him, he gave vent to his disgust and decided to bypass the university city. However, he was not prepared to pass by in silence and messengers were dispatched to the friary. The friars were ordered to evacuate the building with haste and not even the sick were permitted to remain. One of those ejected from the friary acted as Thomas of Celano's informant.

News of the rumpus had reached Ugolino, who hurried to the friary and halted the evacuation of the building. This was the earliest reference to the cardinal protector claiming a property which was then placed at the friars' disposal. Thomas of Celano narrates this event as the third of four chapters on the poverty of the friaries. The first chapter enunciates the principle of poverty and the second deals with a house built by the commune of Assisi for a general chapter. Francis's abhorrence of the theme of ownership by the friars was expressed there and in the account of the friary at Bologna. Ugolino's intervention in the university city saved the situation and provides an early example of Francis's willingness to accept the principle of 'use' rather than 'ownership'. The biographer concludes with the comment that the friars were not permitted to return to the house until the cardinal had publicly proclaimed his ownership of the property. Francis was content to allow the friars to dwell there on condition that the premises were owned by the cardinal.[32]

Thomas of Celano provides a summary of this important chapter, leaving many questions unanswered, and then hurries on to another application of the saint's defence of his ideal. It is clear, for instance, that Francis did not know that the property was owned by the cardinal. Was the cardinal also the owner of other properties which were placed at the friars' disposal? It is not clear whether the cardinal happened to be in Bologna at that time. Did Francis approach him in his exasperation? Or did the friars alert him to the founder's strong reaction? Francis's acceptance of the cardinal's ownership of this property drove a wedge between the use and ownership of things, a device that was enlisted frequently throughout the rest of the century. Within a decade Ugolino would invoke this distinction in *Quo elongati*. Whatever the circumstances, this appears to have been of the first time that Ugolino stepped in to preserve unity and harmony on the questions which were capable of dividing the fraternity. The event also gave Ugolino pause for thought, reminding him that the saint abhorred all suggestion of ownership.

The same combination of Francis's absolute determination to resist ownership and his willingness to accept the use of a building was exemplified by the house constructed for the friars attending a chapter in Assisi. At the approach of a general chapter the people of Assisi, seeking to give a tangible sign of their affection for the friars, supplied material assistance. They held a meeting, observing that the number of friars was increasing and that they would have nothing for their chapter but a poor little cottage thatched with straw. They were unable to consult the absent Francis and within a few days they built a large stone house with limed walls. On his return he was both dismayed and astonished, believing that the friars had built this extravagant house, in a place where the level of religious observance should be at its highest. His first instinct was to demolish this insult to Lady Poverty and, before the end of the chapter, he clambered on to the roof, inviting friars to join him. They began to hurl the wooden tiles to the ground, wishing to destroy the house. Some knights of Assisi and others, who were there representing the city commune to guard the house, intervened to protest that the house belonged to the commune, commanding the friars to desist. The biographers do not state whether Francis or the friars attempted to make good what they had removed. The people of Assisi decreed that their *podestà* should be responsible for having the house roofed and repaired when necessary. Martin of Barton adds that there were 5,000 friars present at this chapter and that his own brother had been marshal of the chapter and had been obliged to protect the building on behalf of the citizens.[33]

Towards the end of his life Francis was dogged by failing health; his eyes were in need of treatment and both Ugolino and the much maligned Elias prevailed upon him to take medical advice; many doctors attempted to alleviate his pain with their medicines; but no remedy was found. Francis went to Rieti to consult a doctor and there he met Ugolino, who sought a cure because he regarded Francis as a holy and just man, one very necessary and useful to the Church. He admonished Francis to take care of himself and not to discard what was necessary in his infirmity. Francis humbly listened and acted more cautiously thereafter and with less fear regarding things necessary for his cure. But because the disease had already increased so much, for any remedy at all there was required the most skilful advice and the harshest treatment. Francis's head was cauterized in several places, his veins opened, plasters put on and eye-salves applied; but he made no progress and seemed only to get constantly worse. Ugolino's injunction to Francis that he should take better care of his health and so discharge his duties to the friars is reminiscent of the exhortation made in Florence, when Francis was advised to return home and oversee the direction of the fraternity.[34]

APPROVAL OF THE RULE

One of the greatest debts of gratitude which the fraternity owed Ugolino was for his part in the confirmation of the Rule by Honorius III. The crises which arose during Francis's time in the East, coupled with a deterioration in his health, convinced the cardinal that a written Rule confirmed by the successor of St Peter and the vicar of Christ was becoming all the more urgent in order to safeguard the fraternity in the years after his death. The circle of friars at Greccio furnish a vivid account of the tensions in the period when the Rule was being composed and finalized. They firmly placed the ministers in the role of striving to temper Francis's rigour and occasionally they associated the cardinal with the ministers' efforts. This perception of the ministers' role, however, calls for some qualifications because the saint's old companions regarded the Rule, which they believed to be inspired by the Holy Spirit, as a sacrosanct expression of the friars' contribution to the Church. They show little awareness of the delicacy of the fraternity's constitutional position, especially in view of the thirteenth canon of the Fourth Lateran Council forbidding the composition of new Rules of life for religious fraternities.

Those who greatly admire Francis concede that some measures dear to him were rooted more in the ideal than the practical. For example, the Rule of 1221 entailed the expulsion of friars guilty of sexual misconduct. However much Francis saw this as an expression of the reforming spirit of the Fourth Lateran Council, its constitutional application was fraught with difficulty. This measure would have required a skilfully crafted statement balancing the friars' canonical profession with justice and the sound reputation of the fraternity as a religious order within the Church. A disagreement between the founder and the ministers turned on the question of ensuring a proper respect for the reserved Eucharist. Francis wanted the Rule to incorporate the directive that the friars should concern themselves lovingly in this matter. Furthermore, the friars should admonish and preach to the clergy, exhorting them to preserve the reserved sacrament in a suitable and good place. Should the clergy fail to do this, he wanted the friars themselves to ensure that this was done. At one time he wished to send some friars through all the provinces with pyxes so that wherever they might find the sacrament reserved in an inappropriate place, they might house it honourably in these. In addition, his reverence for the Eucharist made him want to insert into his Rule that, wherever the friars might find the sacred words carelessly kept or lying scattered about the place, they were to gather them up and put them back, honouring God in the words which he had spoken. Once again the ministers prevailed upon Francis to omit this prescription from the Rule, though he did insert such advice into his *Testament* and some of his letters and exhortations.[35] The inclusion of such a directive, however laudable, would have been the cause of endless and additional friction with the secular clergy. It is to the ministers' credit that such passages were omitted from the final text of the Rule. Perhaps on this occasion they recruited Ugolino to use his influence with Francis. The Rule of 1221, which was not tendered to the pope for confirmation, was much longer than that approved by Honorius III. Ugolino's role as cardinal protector gave him unique insights into the framing of the Rule of 1223, though the sources are generally reticent. While Francis might insist upon the divine source of the Rule, the cardinal had the responsibility of steering it through the Roman Curia and gaining the approval of the pope. In *Quo elongati* the pope, now Gregory IX, acknowledged his own influence on the composition of the Rule.

Debates about the content of the Rule enflamed passions and caused some polarization, which increasingly infected Franciscan hagiography from the 1240s. Leo and companions presented the conflict between the founder and the ministers in the early 1220s. They report that Francis's attempts to raise standards of observance were opposed by the ministers, who pressed for a less exacting interpretation of the Rule. As the saint's vicar Elias was asked by several ministers provincial to tell Francis that they were unwilling to be bound by the new Rule which was being written. Their anxieties were communicated by Elias. As Francis turned his face towards heaven, the voice of Jesus Christ was heard affirming that the Rule was his work rather than Francis's and that it should be obeyed to the letter (*sine glossa*). This became the favourite refrain of the champions of the stricter view. On another occasion, when Francis showed his text to the ministers, they deemed it to be severe and insupportable, saying that they did not know what would happen in the order after his death. For his part he did not struggle with them, because he dreaded giving offence himself or through the friars. He reluctantly complied with their wishes, excusing himself before God. He appeased his conscience by implementing in his own life what he had received from God. The companions were with Francis when he wrote the Rule and imply that illness sapped his capacity to argue with the ministers about its contents and for that reason his *Testament* laid down guidelines about the poverty of houses.[36] Friction between Francis and the ministers on the question of what should be included in the Rule was at its height in the period following his return from the East. In the context of discussions about whether a minister might retain some valuable books the companions claim that the ministers had sought to delete from the Rule the injunction that the friars should take nothing on their way.[37]

The lengthy interval between the initial papal approval of the Rule by Innocent III and its confirmation by Honorius III undoubtedly generated unease and insecurity, especially as the founder's health was deteriorating in the early 1220s. The situation was ripe for speculation of all sorts. During the general chapter of the mats, attended by some 5,000 friars, an old question about the Franciscan identity reappeared. Debate about the Rule was so wide-ranging about 1220 that some friars were urging that the fraternity should adopt one of the traditional Rules. Advocates of this solution to the community's canonical standing seem to have been led by the better educated friars, though the details of their vision for the fraternity have not survived. Some friars pointed to the success being enjoyed by the Dominicans, who had embraced the Rule of St Augustine, which they adapted according to their own constitutions. They may have recommended that the Franciscan fraternity should take the same course involving an accommodation with an earlier Rule. Advocates of that view enlisted the services of Ugolino to persuade Francis to listen to their recommendations and be guided by them. They were particularly interested in the prescriptions contained in the older monastic rules of life.

Francis patiently listened to this advice and then took the cardinal by the hand into the midst of the friars, categorically refusing to follow another Rule. He expostulated that God had shown him the way of humility and simplicity and indicated the course which he should take. No further consideration was given to the suggestion that Francis might choose to follow the Rules of Augustine, Bernard and Benedict. Francis remained as adamant as he had done in Rome more than a decade earlier when he vigorously rejected the advice that he should became a monk or adopt one of the more traditional Rules. Not for the first time the companions of Francis show Ugolino as one who bowed before the ideals and wisdom of the saint.[38] While they give a triumphant account of the saint's dealings with the cardinal protector, Francis did not have an entirely free hand in drawing up the Rule and he was required to produce a text which would win the approval of the pope and cardinals. The association of the cardinal with the ministers on this occasion was a departure from the earlier biographies, which had lionized the cardinal.

A less strident account of the approval of the Rule was given by Bonaventure, whose own attitude to the text was very reverential; the scriptural context requires no further comment. He reports that Francis decided to shorten the Rule which he wanted to have confirmed, because it had become too long by the addition of numerous texts from the Gospel. Then he was led by the Holy Spirit into the mountains with two companions, where he fasted on bread and water; and there he dictated the Rule as the Holy Spirit inspired him in prayer. When he came down from the mountain, he gave the Rule to the vicar of the order, who claimed a few days later that he had accidentally mislaid it. He went into solitude once more and rewrote the Rule just as before, as if he heard the words from God's own lips.[39]

GREGORY IX AND THE FRANCISCANS

As soon as Ugolino was appointed as cardinal protector he began to use his influence in the papal Curia and beyond to protect the friars and to further their apostolate, securing various privileges and permissions for them. Following his election to the papacy, with the name of Gregory IX, his friendship with and admiration for the friars continued and he drew upon their talents in support of various dimensions of the papal policies. Within a few years of his election he produced the first papal interpretation of the Rule which he had helped Francis to draw up.

In the period following Francis's death the former cardinal protector enjoyed an enhanced authority in the fraternity and in both *Mira circa nos*, issued on 19 July 1228, and *Quo elongati* he underlined his long familiarity with the saint. He confidently declared that he himself had fully understood the saint's intention in drawing up the Rule and in securing its confirmation.[40] His claim was recognized among the friars. Bonaventure depicts Gregory as a man learned in civil and canon law and zealous for the order and evangelical perfection.[41] Both Thomas of Eccleston and John Pecham emphasized Gregory's close contact with the saint. Augustine of Nottingham informed the friars at London that he had been present when the pope preached in the saint's church in Assisi. As he moved to the pulpit the friars sang 'this is the man whom the saint chose as his father'; the pope smiled in pleasure.[42] Pecham affirmed that Gregory had resolved various doubts about the Rule because he had unique insights into the founder's wishes (*intentio beati Francisci*), a term which reformers would frequently invoke later in the thirteenth century.[43] The pope spoke as an unimpeachable authority against which there could be no appeal. However, these assumptions were given a particularly strong Franciscan dimension because the pope claimed a long-standing association with Francis.

Crisis in the order

The death of Francis removed the source of unity and authority among the friars and this cannot have been a surprise to those who had witnessed the confusion following his departure for the Holy Land in 1219. His personality had been magnetic enough to hold together the two main strands among the friars, who seem not to have learned the lesson taught them a decade earlier. The reminiscences of his early companions identify the ministers as those who thwarted the founder's wishes regarding the Rule and this conviction gave them little sympathy for the policies pursued by the ministers. They voiced concern about the evolution of the fraternity and they barely stifled their criticism about the diluted standards of poverty and the retreat from the life of the hermitage in favour of an urban focus. This literature showed little support for the growth of large communities and the development of studies. Those who favoured a more progressive policy, which put the friars at the service of the Church, realized that the preservation and institutionalization of Francis's vision entailed some accommodation with poverty; the ministers were aware that some adjustment was necessary to deal with the demands of a rapidly growing fraternity. The simplicity of the early days, when friars were few, could not be reproduced in large communities, where provision had to be made for the sick and the aged, as well as for students and preachers whose apostolate was reaping great benefits for the Church. Moreover, the fraternity was at the cross-roads and the central question was: what role did the friars see themselves as playing in the Church of the late 1220s and 1230s?

These questions were given a sharper focus by the last *Testament* drawn up on Francis's death bed. There he stated quite unequivocally that the friars should not regard the document as another Rule. He explained that he was laying out principles for a more catholic observance of the Rule. He added, however, that the ministers were bound not to add to or subtract from his words and that they should always hold the document along with the Rule. The dictation of the *Testament* was intended to offer an insight into the dying founder's will for his fraternity. Such disciples would have welcomed his teaching on respect for priests, the reserved sacrament, manual labour and the poverty of churches and friaries. An unforeseen consequence was that the document fomented a twin-track approach to Franciscan observance in the form of loyalty to the Rule and the *Testament*.

Francis's early companions saw the *Testament* as a rallying standard and some of them clothed the text with a juridical character, even though the saint had expressly denied that it should be regarded as another Rule. The emerging rigorist tradition placed considerable weight upon the text. The death of the founder created a vacuum of authority within the fraternity, even though he had stepped aside from the administration of the community; he was still regarded as the highest authority and approached for a ruling on new developments by the more conscientious friars. The period between October 1226 and May 1230 was turbulent for the friars, who struggled to come to terms with the saint's death. The general chapter of 1227 was probably too close to the saint's death for any major problems to have been brought to the meeting. Prior to the general chapter of 1230 points of doubt and uncertainty may have been sent in by the friars or may have arisen as a result of extensive canvassing of opinion within the provinces by the ministers. By the spring of 1230 it was acknowledged that these matters should not be settled locally and hence they were forwarded to the general chapter for an authoritative ruling. This instinct contained the seed of the later notion that the general chapter was the highest form of authority within the fraternity.

The 1230 general chapter was one of the most unruly on record in the order's brief history and the controversy turned on the unseemly struggle for the office of minister general. The disturbances were chronicled by Thomas of Eccleston, who drew his information from friars in England. John Parenti, minister general (1227–32), was deprived of office by the supporters of Elias, who had packed the chapter with supporters determined to elect him in defiance of the wishes of the ministers provincial. They carried him on their shoulders from his cell to the door of the chapter house and, breaking it down, intended to place him on the minister general's seat. When John Parenti saw what was happening, he stripped off his habit before the whole chapter. At length the intruders, after creating a great commotion, felt ashamed, although they still refused to listen to Anthony of Padua or any of the ministers provincial. Five novices, who had been soldiers, were present at the chapter and wept at such a disturbance. They prophesied that this would ultimately prove a blessing to the fraternity on the grounds that no order could tolerate such indiscipline. Order was restored and the troublemakers were banished to separate provinces to do penance; Elias retired to a hermitage, where he grew his beard and hair in a show of penitence, which ultimately resulted in his rehabilitation at the general chapter of 1232.

First papal interpretation of the Rule, Quo elongati

The general chapter of 1230 discussed the vexed questions from the Rule, but they failed to reach a conclusion. It was decided that the way out of the impasse was to seek a definitive interpretation from the pope. A delegation consisting of Anthony of Padua, Gerard of Rusinol, papal penitentiary, Haymo of Faversham, Leo, who later became archbishop of Milan, Gerard of Modena and Peter of Brescia was dispatched to Rome; the growing influence of the clerical party within the order was expressed in the composition of the delegation. The clandestine translation of Francis's relics from San Giorgio to the new basilica, coupled with the unruly behaviour of the supporters of Elias, did not cast the general chapter of 1230 in a very impressive light. One school of thought among the friars was that the central administration of the order was in too much turmoil and this was a further reason for the approach to the pope, whom the friars revered as the highest authority within the Church. In addition, it was known that in his moments of perplexity and difficulty Francis had turned to the pope or cardinal protector for guidance and assistance.

A pressing question was the type of authority vested in the *Testament*, which contained Francis's last appeal to the friars, whom he wished to establish in poverty, simplicity and humility. However admirable the document was, other friars carefully distinguished between the papal bull confirming the Rule and the exhortation of the dying saint. Moorman comments that Gregory's task was no enviable one. On the one hand, he had the extremists who would hear of no departure from the strictest poverty, and who were content that the order should continue as a band of homeless evangelists. On the other hand, he had those who frankly hoped that the order would develop along Benedictine or Dominican lines with the establishment of large convents and the growth of scholarship. Between the extremists were probably the majority of the friars, who realized that some change was inevitable, but who yet cherished the hope that the order would preserve its distinctive characteristics and remain the chief bodyguard to Lady Poverty.[44] Moorman fails to cite any medieval texts in support of this contentious interpretation.

After receiving the delegation of friars, the pope worked quickly, though it is not known whether he consulted many friars in drafting *Quo elongati*, issued on 28 September 1230. The circumstances of the letter were rehearsed and Gregory disclosed that the delegation from the recent general chapter had informed him that there were some dubious, obscure and difficult passages in the Rule. The nub of the problem, as Gregory declared, was that Francis neither wanted his Rule to be interpreted nor privileges to be sought from the pope. Gregory's pretext for proceeding to offer guidance on the interpretation of the Rule was his own long-standing friendship with the saint, whom he had assisted in the composition of the Rule and gaining papal approval for it. His first step was to address the vexed question of the status to be accorded to the *Testament*, which was recognized as a laudable expression of the saint's objectives. Gregory acknowledged that the document could occasion scruples and was resolved to remove these and any attendant spiritual dangers. He went on to declare that the document did not bind the friars and that the saint had proceeded without the friars' consent; Gregory ruled that Francis's successors could not be bound in such a matter.

Gregory then proceeded to address the question of money, property in common, reserved sins, the office of preaching, the admission and dismissal of friars, the custodians, the general chapter and access to monasteries of the Poor Clares. Noting that some friars maintained that moveable things should pertain to the whole order in common, the pope reaffirmed that the friars were unable to have any property. The friars were, however, given the use of objects, such as books and other moveable things according to the licence of the ministers general or provincial. The principle that the friars might use, rather than own, items had been accepted by Francis about a decade earlier in the dispute about the ownership of the friary in Bologna. This declaration paved the way for the development of studies within the fraternity on condition that ownership was vested with others. Even though the Rule forbade friars to accept coins or money, a representative might receive money in their name and even purchase whatever items were needed by the friars. Those instructed in the study of theology were to be exempted from the examination of candidates for the office of preaching by the minister general or the ministers provincial at the time of the general chapter. In such cases these friars may be licensed to preach unless the minister general decrees otherwise. R. B. Brooke maintains that the papal bull may be cited as evidence of the speed with which the Franciscans developed into a student order. Gregory declared that theologians might preach without special permission from the minister general.[45]

There is little extant evidence that the friars in the 1230s and 1240s took exception to the provisions of *Quo elongati*, although Clare of Assisi regarded it as weakening her own Franciscan identity. While Leo and companions emphasized the saint's teaching authority in the *Testament*,[46] the papal document was perceived as outlining a moderate degree of observance and Thomas of Celano's second biography mirrors the papal concern that pride of place be given to the Rule. The authority which the papal ruling enjoyed among the friars was reflected in the decision of the general chapter in Genoa to waive the permissions granted by *Ordinem vestrum*, promulgated by Innocent IV on 14 November 1245, where these exceeded the terms of *Quo elongati*. The perception that the Franciscans had accepted a compromise regarding the Rule featured in their polemics with the Dominicans later in the thirteenth century. The latter taunted their mendicant rivals with the allegation that they followed the Rule of Gregory IX rather than that of their founder.[47] Writing from a very different vantage point and with the benefit of hindsight, Moorman judged that *Quo elongati* did more than anything else to shape the future policy of the order and to lead it away from the strict and unflinching renunciation which Francis had enjoined, towards a manner of living much nearer the practice of the monastic orders.[48] This verdict reflects much of Moorman's own view that compromise was already in the air and that the former cardinal protector was instrumental in leading the friars away from their primitive observance.

Gregory's testimony to the stigmata

A sermon preached by Gregory in Assisi on the feast of St Francis pointed to the saint's closeness to his divine master, the stigmata, and the customs associated with that feast. He announced that two heretical leaders, converted at Venice, had been sent to him with letters from the cardinal legates. These letters related that one night at the same hour both these men had seen Jesus Christ sitting in judgement, accompanied by the apostles and all the religious in the world. Nowhere, however, had they seen Francis or the friars, although one of the legates had been preaching about him and had described him as even greater than St John the Evangelist because he had received the stigmata, that is, the five wounds inflicted on the body of the crucified Christ. But they saw Jesus Christ leaning on the breast of the Evangelist and the Evangelist on the breast of our Lord. The heretics, who saw this as confirmation that the legate had spoken blasphemously, were scandalized and denounced the sermon. But when the Son of God opened the wound in his side with his own hand, Francis was clearly revealed within his breast. He then closed the wound, and enclosed Francis within his heart. The following day the two men described their dream and publicly confessed their error to the cardinals, who sent them to the pope, through whom they were formally reconciled to the Church. After Gregory's sermon two young soldiers approached him and he laid a garland of flowers on the head of each one. From this incident arose the practice that all who intended to become soldiers received their arms at this festival.[49]

Gregory also informed the friars that, before the canonization, he had entertained doubts about the stigmata. One night, as he himself used to relate with tears, Francis appeared to him in a dream. His face seemed a little hard and he reproached him for his doubts. Then he raised his right arm and showed him the wound and told him to get a glass and catch the blood which was streaming from his side. The pope got the glass in the vision and it seemed to fill up to the brim with blood. After that he was so devoted to the stigmata and so eager in his conviction that he could never allow anyone to call these wonderful signs into doubt by attacking them in their pride, and he corrected such people severely.[50] Gregory became a stout champion of this miracle and issued three documents between 31 March and 5 April 1237, *Usque ad terminos, Non minus dolentes* and *Confessor Domini,* affirming the truth of the stigmata.

Gregory's influence

Ugolino's respect and admiration for Francis were beyond doubt and his devotion to the saint moved him to compose the hymn *Proles de celo prodiit*, the response *De paupertatis horreo* and the prose *Caput draconis ultimum.*[51] Thomas of Celano saw him as the saint's friend, guide and protector and the early biographers and chroniclers lauded his promotion of the friars and his defence of their work. Salimbene regarded him as a pope with a great love for the fraternity.[52] Leo and companions contributed a number of anecdotes about the relations between Francis and the cardinal, with the former emerging as the sagacious saint intent on instructing a somewhat worldly-minded cardinal; the senior cardinal bishop and future pope did not always fully comprehend the saint's teaching. The series of reminiscences does not necessarily imply a criticism of the cardinal, because medieval hagiography emphasized the didactic role played by the saint. Thomas of Celano's report of these exchanges was softened and seems to have been composed in order to disarm the fraternity's growing band of critics.

While Ugolino was sometimes presented as an ally of the ministers in their attempts to thwart the founder's wishes in the materials emanating from Leo and companions, the saint acknowledged his need for advice and canonical guidance; this made it all the more necessary for him to draw upon the support of patrons like Guido and Ugolino. The failure of the first missions to Germany and Hungary underlined the absence of an organizing principle and the success of the later missions to Germany and England was based on the principle of organization, a great deal of which was supplied by Ugolino. One of the most important tasks successfully completed by the cardinal was the papal confirmation of the Rule. He had to ensure that the document was agreeable to both the founder and the Roman Curia. Moorman's contentious view that Ugolino was the ally of Elias in modifying Francis's ideals[53] springs from an overly romantic view of the saint's ideals. That view does, however, place the spotlight on the tensions between the inspiration of the founders of religious orders and the institution which approves them.

The biographies do not focus upon Gregory's later dealings with the friars, though the *Vita secunda* contains hints of criticism levelled at those friars who became papal chaplains and offers little encouragement to any friar desirous of promotion to the episcopate. As pope he continued the policies of his predecessors who had deployed the friars in combating heresy in northern Italy and southern France. By the end of the 1220s the friars were growing into a large army of zealous preachers and Gregory wished to channel their talents for the benefit of the Church. The friars' theological and linguistic skills were deployed in the attempts to promote reconciliation with the Eastern Christians. In 1233–34 Gregory appointed Haymo of Faversham and Ralph of Rheims and two Dominicans to enter into dialogue with theologians from the East and in the following forty years friars were employed by the popes to foster unity between East and West. A much more contentious role played by the friars was in seeking funds for the Crusade, and in this the pope seems to confirm the hints given by Leo and companions that he had not fully grasped the saint's concept of the Franciscan vocation. From 1234 the mendicant orders promoted the Crusades and participated in the dubious practice of receiving the Crusading vows from all manner of people, including the sick and the aged, and then dispensing them on payment of a fee. Thomas of Eccleston and Jordan of Giano passed over these incidents in silence and did not mention the embarrassment which such practices brought on the friars; their energies were focused more on internal struggles. Monastic chroniclers were less reticent and seized such opportunities to heap blame upon the friars.[54]

CONCLUSION

Ugolino provided Francis with a great deal of ecclesiastical and canonical assistance. There is a less immediate answer to the question of how fully he understood the saint and endeavoured to safeguard his vision of the fraternity. While a bond of trust and affection developed between the two men, their objectives were not the same: the one was a curial figure who promoted the welfare of the Church and recognized that the friars were immensely powerful allies to be pressed into service on a broad variety of fronts; the other was a prophetical spirit intent on a more profound understanding of the Gospel with a burning desire to communicate this to his contemporaries and an unquenchable thirst for self-identification with Jesus Christ. The tension between an international institution and the saint's search for harmony with the Creator and all his creatures was communicated to the fraternity. Thus by the 1220s the friars were being pulled towards clericalization with the appointment of preachers and the emergence of schools to prepare friars for the ministry of itinerant preachers. The early biographers and chroniclers of the order drew attention to Ugolino's benign interventions in the life of the order in a positive manner. R. B. Brooke points out that the criticisms which modern writers have levelled against the protector are based on a realization of dangers and tendencies in his policy that were hardly, if at all, apparent at the time. Ugolino's relations with the friars were kindly and well-intentioned.[55]

Gregory was close to Francis, showed some sensitivity for his struggles and ideals, and was eager to promote his cause in the life of the Church. He was a central figure in ensuring the survival of the fraternity by defending it against its vociferous and powerful critics. However much he claimed friendship with Francis, he saw the friars as a dedicated group of reformers within the Church and drew upon their talents in a variety of areas. As the papacy faced demands on many fronts the temptation to draft friars into inappropriate activities was ever present and his use of the friars to collect funds for the Crusades was not consistent with their vocation; such policies would no doubt have earned Gregory another lecture from his canonized friend. At his death on 22 August 1241 Gregory was mourned as the friend, father and benefactor of the order.[56] Le Goff remarks that Francis was caught between his own ideal and his passionate attachment to the Church and to orthodoxy.[57] That combination was preserved through the friars' studies, which prepared them for the ministry of preaching and hearing confessions after the example of St Anthony of Padua.

Notes

1. Thomas of Eccleston, *Tractatus de adventu fratrum minorum in Angliam*, ed. A. G. Little (Manchester, 1951), pp. 89–90. For a full study of the relationship between Francis and Ugolino see A. Callebaut, 'Autour de la rencontre à Florence de S. François et du Cardinal Hugolin (en été 1217)' in AFH, 19 (1926), pp. 530–58, 541; R. B. Brooke, *Early Franciscan Government* (Cambridge Studies in Medieval Life and Thought; 1959), pp. 56–122, especially the first pages of the chapter; and E. Pasztor, 'San Francesco e il cardinale Ugolino nella "questione francescana"', *Collectanea Franciscana*, 46 (1976), pp. 209–39.
2. Orderic Vitalis, *The Ecclesiastical History*, IV, ed. Chibnall (OMT; 1973), pp. 324–5, writes about 36 years after the foundation of Cîteaux. In that time such a great multitude of men had flocked to the monastery that 65 abbeys had been founded from there.
3. 1 C, nn. 55–57, 62.
4. Ibid., n. 27.
5. Raymundina, pp. 49, 226–7; cf. *S. Bonaventurae opera omnia*, VIII, p. 426, where John Pecham suggests that this was a more widespread shortage.
6. *Chronica Fratris Jordani*, nn. 3–6, pp. 3–7; cf. R. W. Emery, *The Friars in Medieval France* (New York, 1962); Freed explains the context of the early missions to Germany.
7. C. H. Lawrence, *The Friars* (The Medieval World; London, 1994), pp. 43–4, 81.
8. Brooke, *Early Franciscan Government*, pp. 86, 106.
9. C. N. L. Brooke and R. B. Brooke, *Popular Religion in the Middle Ages* (London, 1984), p. 128.
10. M.-H. Vicaire, *Histoire de Saint Dominique: au coeur de l'Église* (Paris, 1957), pp. 20, 63, 103.
11. Jordan of Saxony, 'Libellus de principiis Ordinis Praedicatorum' in MOPH, 16 (Rome, 1935), ed. M. H. Laurent, n. 96, p. 71.
12. LTS, c. 15, n. 61.
13. J. E. Sayers, *Innocent III* (London, 1994), p. 109.
14. C. T. Maier, *Preaching the Crusades: Mendicant Friars and the Cross in the Thirteenth Century* (Cambridge Studies in Medieval Life; 1994), p. 21.

15. R. J. Armstrong and I. C. Brady, *Francis and Clare* (The Classics of Western Spirituality; New York, 1982), p. 145.
16. Lawrence, *The Friars*, p. 182.
17. Salimbene, *Cronica* (Bari, 1966), pp. 727-8, boasted that all the cardinals who were the governors, protectors and correctors of the friars afterwards ascended the chair of St Peter, as did Gregory IX, Alexander IV and Nicholas III. He believed that this occurred through divine grace and the help of St Francis, though their own good lives were not an obstacle.
18. *Chronica Fratris Jordani*, nn. 11-15, pp. 9-15.
19. D. Knowles, *From Pachomius to Ignatius* (Oxford, 1966), p. 45.
20. 1 C, nn. 73-75, 101.
21. *Compilatio Assisiensis*, c. 74.
22. 1 C, n. 73.
23. L. de la Marche, *Anecdotes historiques* (Paris, 1877), p. 264.
24. 2 C, n. 25.
25. *Compilatio Assisiensis*, c. 97; 2 C, n. 73.
26. *Compilatio Assisiensis*, c. 49; 2 C, n. 148.
27. W. R. Thomson, *Friars in the Cathedral: The First Franciscan Bishops 1226-1261* (Pontifical Institute of Mediaeval Studies, Studies and Texts, 33; Toronto, 1975), pp. 11-12, 93-101.
28. 1 C, nn. 74, 99.
29. 2 C, n. 157.
30. Ibid., n. 63.
31. W. R. Thomson, 'The earliest cardinal-protectors of the Franciscan Order: a study in administrative history, 1210-1261', *Studies in Medieval and Renaissance History*, 9 (1972), pp. 21-80, at pp. 36-7.
32. 2 C, n. 58.
33. *Compilatio Assisiensis*, c. 56; Eccleston, *Tractatus*, p. 32.
34. *Compilatio Assisiensis*, c. 83; 1 C, nn. 99, 101.
35. *Compilatio Assisiensis*, c. 108.
36. Ibid., cc. 17, 101, 106.
37. Ibid., c. 102.
38. Ibid., c. 18.
39. LM, c. 4, n. 11.
40. R. J. Armstrong, 'Pope Gregory IX's view of Saint Francis of Assisi', *Analecta Tertii ordinis regularis Sancti Francisci*, 21 (1989), pp. 261-89, 266, n. 8; H. Grudundmann, 'Die Bulle "Quo elongati" Papst Gregors IX' in AFH, 54 (1961), pp. 20-1.
41. Bonaventure, 'Epistola de tribus quaestionibus ad magistrum innominatum', p. 213.
42. Eccleston, *Tractatus*, pp. 89-90.
43. John Pecham, *Tractatus tres de Paupertate*, p. 140.
44. J. R. H. Moorman, *The Sources for the Life of S. Francis of Assisi* (University of Manchester, Historical Series, 79; 1940), pp. 84-5.
45. Brooke, *Early Franciscan Government*, pp. 128-9.
46. 'Declaratio fratris Ubertini de Casali' in ALKG, III, pp. 168-9. About August 1311 Ubertino claimed that in the province of the Marches and in many others it was decreed, under obedience, that the *Testamentum* should be removed from all the friars and burned. They burned a copy of the text above the head of Friar N. de Rocanato. The ministers were anxious to annul the writings of St Francis dealing with his intentions concerning the observance of the Rule.
47. John Pecham, *Tractatus tres de Paupertate*, p. 140.
48. Moorman, *The Sources for the Life of S. Francis of Assisi*, p. 84.
49. Eccleston, *Tractatus*, pp. 89-91. This sermon may have been preached in 1235.
50. LM, miracula, I, n. 2. Cf. O. Schmucki, *The Stigmata of St Francis of Assisi*, trans. C. F. Connors (Franciscan Institute Publications, History Series, 6; New York, 1991); C. Frugoni, *Francesco e l'invenzione delle stimmate: Una storia per parole e immagini fino a Bonaventura e Giotto* (Turin, 1993).
51. Salimbene, *Cronica*, pp. 554, 657-8. He adds that at the prayers of the friars this pope secured the elevation of Rainaldo dei Conti di Segni to the cardinalate.
52. Salimbene, *Cronica*, pp. 578-9; M. Bihl, 'Statuta generalia Ordinis edita in Capitulis generalibus celebratis Narbonae an. 1260', XII, viii, p. 316: the friars were required to celebrate the anniversary of this pope on 23 August, even though his death occurred on 22 August.
53. J. R. H. Moorman, *The Grey Friars in Cambridge 1225-1538* (Cambridge, 1952), p. 4.
54. Cf. W. R. Thomson, 'The image of the mendicants in the chronicles of Matthew Paris' in AFH, 70 (1977), pp. 3-34.

55. Brooke, *Early Franciscan Government*, pp. 70-2.
56. Salimbene, *Cronica*, pp. 251-2. Cf. Eccleston, *Tractatus*, p. 95, who states that friars were also present at the death of Honorius III.
57. J. Le Goff, *Medieval Civilisation 400-1500*, trans. J. Barrow (Oxford, 1988), p. 87.

6

ᕙᕗᕙᕗᕙᕗᕙᕗᕙᕗᕙᕗᕙᕗᕙᕗ

St Anthony of Padua and the development of theological study

The virtue of humility, accompanied by the gift of knowledge, was manifest in Anthony[1]

Anthony of Padua, the first mendicant master of theology to be canonized, was one of the most famous preachers in the fraternity in the 1220s. His profile among the friars was so high that John Pecham portrayed him as the second foundation stone of the fraternity.[2] Born about 1195, Anthony joined the Augustinian canons in Lisbon and then moved to Santa Cruz in Coimbra. Shortly afterwards the remains of the five martyrs of the new order were carried from Morocco to Coimbra and interred in Santa Cruz. In search of martyrdom Anthony joined the new fraternity in 1220 and was subsequently sent on a mission to Morocco. At the general chapter of 1221 he was appointed to a hermitage in northern Italy. There were at least two direct communications between the two saints: first, the founder's miraculous appearance, when Anthony was preaching during a provincial chapter at Arles, and secondly, his letter to Anthony inaugurating the study of theology within friaries. Anthony, the first lector in the order, was faithful to the conditions laid down in that letter and treated theological study as a condition for an effective ministry of preaching. He worked to combat heretical groups in northern Italy and southern France and later served as custos in Limoges and minister provincial in northern Italy. He died on 13 June 1231. His speedy canonization on 30 May 1232 affirmed that study and piety remained as compatible as they had been in the patristic era and provided a model for those engaged in theological study.

ANTHONY'S EARLY LIFE

Anthony was a native of the distant kingdom of Portugal.[3] In the eyes of his biographers Lisbon was a very remote city on the edge of the Muslim world[4] which had recently rejoined the Christian fold. Responding to the proclamation of the second Crusade, men from England, Normandy, the Low Countries and the Rhineland arrived in Oporto on 16 June 1147. They travelled south, following the coastline, and on 28 June began their siege of Lisbon.[5] Peter, bishop of Oporto, preached an impassioned crusading sermon to a fleet-load of English, Dutch and other Crusaders who had landed in Portugal on their way to the Holy Land. After a prolonged battle the Crusaders finally took the city from the Moors on 24 October and attributed their success to divine intervention. King Afonso of Portugal, an astute ruler, more than once persuaded Crusaders whose fleets put into Portugal to defer their expeditions to the Holy Land until they had first helped him to oust the infidel—the same in Lisbon as in Jerusalem— from his kingdom. The practice of diverting Crusaders from their initial and main objective became such a hindrance to the conduct of the Crusades that more than one pope had to send stern letters to the early Portuguese kings. Cupidity and the waning of first fervour made Lisbon a popular wintering place in the twelfth and thirteenth centuries.[6]

Anthony's parents, Martin di Afonsi, a soldier, and Maria,[7] possessed a house to the west of the cathedral and at baptism they gave him the name of Ferdinand, which was changed to Anthony when he became a friar. There is conflicting testimony about their social status. An Infante of Portugal, who had known Anthony as a young religious at Coimbra, testified that he was the son of ordinary parents. Rolandino, notary of Padua during Anthony's brief stay there, records that he was born of noble and powerful parents.[8] Anthony's fears that his transfer to the friars might be impeded by his parents tend to corroborate the second view. Later biographers, perhaps echoing the biographies of Francis and Clare, paint a picture of a more conventional piety for Anthony, who was compassionate, liberal towards the poor and a frequent visitor to Lisbon's churches and monasteries.[9]

Lisbon's cathedral was dedicated to the Blessed Virgin Mary; and, thanks to the gift of King Afonso, since 1173 it had been the resting place of the relics of St Vincent. Located in the middle of the medieval part of the city, it lies at the foot of the Castelo de São Jorge, which overlooks the entire city and harbour, and which from the days of the Romans, Goths, and Moors, had served as the fortress and guardian of the town. The church is one of the typical medieval buildings of the old city, going back to the year 1147. Tradition relates that King Afonso the Conqueror began its construction on the spot occupied earlier by a great Moorish mosque.[10] The presence of the martyr's tomb in the cathedral was noted by Anthony's first biographer, who collected materials in Lisbon. The shrine of a hero and martyr from the early Church may have had a powerful effect upon Anthony's later consciousness, especially in an era when the cult of martyrdom was prevalent; the martyrs of Assisi were a similar spur to the young Francis and Clare.

Cathedral schools were to be established in every diocese towards the end of the twelfth century, in accordance with the eighteenth canon of the Third Lateran Council in 1179. Concern was expressed lest education be denied to the poor and it was decreed that in every cathedral church a master was to be provided with a benefice so that he might teach clerics and poor scholars. In other churches and monasteries the same provision was to be made. The needs of the master were to be provided in order that the way of knowledge might be opened to those keen to learn. This ruling was confirmed by the eleventh decree of the Fourth Lateran Council in 1215, which observed that the previous decree had been implemented in very few dioceses. It stipulated that in all churches with sufficient resources a suitable master, elected by the cathedral chapter, should teach grammar and other branches of study, as far as was possible, to the clerics of those and other churches. The metropolitan was obliged to provide a theologian to teach Scripture to priests and others, and especially to instruct them in matters recognized as pertaining to the care of souls. Anthony's early education was entrusted to the cathedral clergy. In its strict sense the term 'sacred letters' denotes the Bible and in a broader sense Christian doctrine.[11] The *Dialogus* records that Anthony followed 'liberal studies' at the cathedral and this is translated as liberal arts,[12] the traditional preparation for higher studies. This education equipped him with the appropriate form of training for higher theological studies as a Canon Regular, though the curriculum of his studies remains unknown.

AN AUGUSTINIAN CANON AT LISBON AND THEN COIMBRA (C. 1210-20)

Anthony spent almost half of his life as a religious with the Augustinian canons in Portugal. Lawrence notes that such monasteries began to appear about the middle of the eleventh century and were composed of groups of clergy who had renounced private property and chosen a fully communal life, observing a monastic timetable and sharing a common refectory and dormitory. Early privileges and charters of endowment in favour of houses of canons refer to them as living in community according to the 'apostolic life'. Houses of canons were often given to parish churches by lay proprietors as part of their endowment and occasionally the canons performed pastoral duties themselves. But the cure of souls was not invariably regarded as a concomitant of the apostolic life in the twelfth century; many still regarded personal poverty and community living as the authentic hallmarks of apostolicity.[13]

The ancient priory or monastery of São Vicente de Fora, which perished in an earthquake in 1755, was founded by King Afonso I soon after the conquest of Lisbon and made subject to the monastery in the capital city of Coimbra. As a royal foundation it was richly endowed, but this material advantage was to be weighed against the intrusive influence of patrons. As a result the monastery was drawn into the crown's quarrels with the Church, especially after 1211 when Afonso II, eldest son of King Sancho and persistent enemy of the bishop of

Oporto, ascended the throne.[14] The monastery was noted for its fervour and virtue[15] and this may have caught the admiration of Anthony at a crucial stage in his development. Anthony may have regarded the canons as men who were recapturing the apostolic life and providing some spiritual assistance in the towns. Admitted to the monastic community at Lisbon about 1210, his time there was marred and cut short by the intrusion of the political turbulence which gripped the country. His former friends from the city persisted in visiting him and seeking his opinion on political issues. These visits were regarded as a distraction by the young canon who sought peace and tranquillity. This prompted him to leave his home town, though one obstacle to this decision was the vow which bound him to the priory of São Vicente de Fora. But when his superiors learned of his determination, they reluctantly agreed to let him transfer to the monastery of the order in Coimbra, the city in which the king lived in his great fortress palace. Situated about 100 miles north of Lisbon on a hill along the Mondego river, it was the seat of a bishop, while the archbishop resided at Braga. Since 1131 the Augustinians had their principal convent in this city.[16]

Theological formation

Anthony's theological education began in the monastery of São Vicente de Fora and developed at Santa Cruz. The surviving lists of manuscripts from the two monasteries confirm that both libraries had amassed impressive collections of biblical and patristic materials. A list of books at the monastery in Lisbon in the middle of the thirteenth century reveals something of the theological resources available to Anthony: Augustine, Gregory the Great, Isidore of Seville, the *Vitae patrum*, glosses on the Psalter, the Pauline letters, some canonical texts, collections of homilies and some of the classics of monastic spirituality. The monastery at Coimbra benefited from the royal largesse which enabled it to compete with the famous Augustinian monasteries of France, with which it had been in continuous contact since its foundation. This comparatively rich collection of manuscripts included the standard patristic authors: Augustine, Jerome, Ambrose, Gregory the Great, Bede, Isidore of Seville. The library also contained copies of the secular works necessary for any course of studies, which in the Middle Ages remained faithful to the scholastic programme of the Roman Empire, including works of history, poetry and science.[17] Both libraries provided the basic materials for an industrious student, acquainting him with the riches of the biblical and patristic tradition, laying the foundation for his ministry of preaching and teaching as a friar.

After 1212 Anthony continued his preparation for ordination in the flourishing Augustinian school at Coimbra.[18] The most notable scholars at the latter in the second decade of the thirteenth century were Dom João, the master, who had studied theology in Paris; Dom Raimundo, a man of letters and well versed in medical sciences; Dom Pires, whose field of knowledge included grammar, logic and medicine and who also had great gifts as a preacher. To Dom Pires, who was prior in 1228, the University of Coimbra owed its early existence because he made himself responsible for the salaries of the rector, professors, officials and servants, meeting the expenses from the revenues of Santa Cruz.[19]

A thorough study of the Scriptures formed the basis of Anthony's theology, and by exploring the literal sense and then the spiritual sense, he endeavoured to attain a deeper understanding of the truths of Christianity and their application to life.[20] His studies gave him a mastery of the sacred text and his first biographer reports with approval that the saint meditated on it day and night; his close study paid attention to its historical and allegorical meanings.[21] He familiarized himself with the controversies and heresies of his day, acquiring a strong and unshakeable grounding in matters of faith. His study of the Scriptures was complemented by a detailed knowledge of the Fathers of the Church. Whatever he read in Scripture and the Fathers was impressed so deeply upon his memory that later in his priestly activity he drew on such knowledge at will. Borrowing a phrase from Athanasius's *Life of St Antony the Abbot*, the author of the *Assidua* claimed that Anthony's memory served him as a library. These patient years of biblical studies in Coimbra were the foundation stone of his outstanding knowledge of the Bible, which stood him in such good stead in his preaching and disputations as a friar. This prodigious mastery of the Bible so impressed Gregory IX that he called him the 'ark of the covenant'.[22] While some monastic authors were disturbed by the methods of theological study prevalent in the cathedral schools of the twelfth century, concern about an undue curiosity in this discipline persisted into the thirteenth century and moved eminent Franciscan theologians, such as Jean de la Rochelle and Bonaventure, the second and fifth masters in the Franciscan school at Paris, to admonish students to avoid an unhealthy curiosity. Anthony's first biographer, perhaps reflecting caution about the role of studies within the fraternity, testifies that the saint was guided by a healthy curiosity. The time and dedication which he brought to his long years of study at Coimbra, coupled with his growth in maturity and integrity, laid the foundations for his decisive role in the evolution of theological study among the friars.[23]

Anthony's sermons drew materials from the traditional group of the western Fathers and some medieval authorities. The more traditional aspect of his theological formation was represented by citations from several treatises of Augustine and Gregory the Great. These were followed by Jerome, Isidore and Bede and there were occasional citations from Ambrose, Fulgentius and Rabanus Maurus. Abundant use was made of the two principal biblical aids, the *Glossa Interlinearis* and the *Glossa Ordinaria*. Medieval authorities were represented by Bernard of Clairvaux, Peter Lombard and Innocent III and there was also some knowledge of the eastern Fathers who reached Anthony in translation. A further indication of his contacts with the new theological resources was his close friendship with Thomas Gallus, who was engaged in the task of translating and commenting on the writings of Dionysius the Areopagite. B. Smalley, who believes that Anthony had already attained the rank of master in Coimbra, judges that his use of the Scriptures was both traditional and original and that no time-saving device would explain the facility of biblical quotation which so impressed contemporaries. His use of the writings of Gregory the Great seems to rest upon a first-hand examination of his treatises rather than the *florilegia*, the collections of excerpts from the Fathers. He accepted and used the tools offered by the University of Paris at the end of the twelfth century and the beginning of the thirteenth century, supplementing them with his own wider reading of the Bible; some apocryphal materials were studied and made their way into his collection of homilies. In short, Anthony made the whole Bible his own.[24] While he studied the Bible in a context which reflects the schools of the twelfth-century monastic and cathedral schools, he was in touch with some currents flowing from the University of Paris, where the *Sentences* of Peter Lombard came to serve as a textbook for the masters' lectures.

Franciscans in Coimbra

The recent increase in the friars' numbers enabled them to expand to different countries; they launched their mission to Spain and Portugal in 1217. Queen Urraca became their friend and gave them a small church at Coimbra, while Sancia, the sister of her consort, did the same at Alenquer, north of Lisbon.[25] Anthony's first biographer contrasts the friars' lack of formal education with their admirable capacity to make the Scriptures incarnate in their daily activities. These new religious were also marked by their practice of seeking alms, a policy which led them to the monastery of Santa Cruz[26] and into direct contact with a man who would be revered as one of the most important saints in the Franciscans' cosmos. Their presence in the royal city had generated a certain amount of interest in a new style of religious life. Anthony had the opportunity of learning about the fraternity on the friars' visits to the monastery and to compare their level of observance with that obtaining in his own fragmented community. The divisions within his own community made him more painfully aware of the compromise that was liable to arise from an unhealthy dependence upon benefactors and royal patronage. These reflections heightened his growing interest in the new form of religious life which the followers of Francis of Assisi had brought to Coimbra. The very contrast between the impressive lives of the simple friars and the sad state of affairs obtaining in his priory stirred Anthony to consider whether he should make a new beginning. Although the biographers pass no comment, it is highly probable that Anthony now regarded the friars as the complete embodiment of the apostolic life. Within a short time it was clear that the initiative was passing from the older orders of monks and canons to the friars. The friars showed him that there was a viable form of religious life without endowments, patrons and benefactors and their missionary zeal took them throughout the known world. Anthony's thoughts on the nature of religious life were given a new urgency by the arrival of friars who were heading for Morocco. Anthony may have met these friars, who would play such a decisive role in his own future.

Protomartyrs of the Franciscan order

Within a decade of obtaining the approval of Innocent III, the friars won their first martyrs and news of the martyrdom of five friars created a stir in Coimbra and gave a new and unexpected direction to the life of the young canon. Francis's perception of the apostolic life was global and his Rule made provision for missionaries, offering instruction for the friars. Those who were inspired to carry the flame of the Gospel to non-Christian territories needed the permission of the ministers provincial, who were to exercise discretion.[27] The friars' missionary endeavours are as old as the fraternity, with Francis leading by example. Some of the later biographies locate the protomartyrs of the order within a broader context of the friars' missionary drive, reporting that many friars, aflame with the desire for martyrdom, went to non-Christian territories.[28] At the general chapter of 1219 Francis, hearing that Christians were being greatly persecuted in Morocco, chose six friars to send there: Vitale, Berardo, Pietro, Adiuto, Accursio and Ottone. We know nothing about them but their names.

There is an early tradition that the friars passed through Coimbra en route to Morocco and that thence they travelled to Seville, which was then in Muslim hands.[29] The missionaries reached Spain where the leader, Vitale, fell ill and had to leave his companions. In spite of numerous difficulties, the others reached Morocco where they were benevolently received by Don Pedro, the Infante of Portugal, who had been placed by the Sultan, Abu-Yâqub, now the Miramolino, at the head of his army. But the Miramolino, going through the streets one day, happened to hear one of the friars inveighing against Islam, and immediately ordered their expulsion. However, they managed to return and resumed their preaching. They were taken into custody, tortured and then executed on 16 January 1220.

Don Pedro, the Lord Infante, published throughout all the provinces of Spain that he had been miraculously freed by the merits of the martyred friars.[30] Soon news of the martyrdom reached Portugal. When the Infante himself escorted the relics first to Seville and thence to Castile and Léon, triumphant processions accompanied his party of horsemen from town to town. He dared not enter Portugal, being now more than ever, in his capacity of mercenary general for the Miramolino, in the bad graces of his brother the king. He went instead no further than Astorga, where the greatest of the many miracles that had marked the progress of the martyrs' remains took place; from Astorga he sent the caskets on to Coimbra. Queen Urraca went on foot accompanied by her court and all the clergy and citizens of Coimbra to meet the knights of Léon to whom Don Pedro had entrusted the relics. The remains were received with great honours at the priory. The canons were led by Dom João Cesar at the solemn return of the friars' relics. One of the canons, Dom João Roberto, who had gone into exile with Don Pedro, gave them a vivid account of the martyrdom.[31]

Anthony's first biographer presents his response to the arrival of the martyrs' relics in Coimbra as the catalyst in his vocation. There was no hint that he had already been impressed by the friars' lifestyle, but the author may have felt that the impact of the martyrdom, a fact of which the friars might be justifiably proud, weighed heavier with Anthony than the attraction and integrity of the friars' lives. Only afterwards does he describe the presence of the friars in Coimbra. Did Anthony feel that the surest way of earning martyrdom was by joining an order which was currently pouring men into missionary work in Muslim territories? There may well have been other reasons which brought him to the fraternity, though his criticism of the behaviour of some religious may denote a level of disenchantment arising from his own experience. It is undeniable that there were other aspects of the Franciscan vocation which appealed to his reforming instincts. The *Dialogus* and the *Benignitas* situate the arrival of the martyrs' relics within Anthony's regular meditation on the Bible and prayer, conceiving the desire to become a friar and to be martyred.[32] The quest for martyrdom, accentuated by the rhetoric of the Crusades and its literature, influenced medieval piety profoundly. The excitement generated by news of fresh martyrdoms recalled the world of St Vincent, the martyr buried in Lisbon. Anthony pondered the prospect of martyrdom and this led him among the missionaries dispatched to Morocco.[33]

FRIAR ANTHONY

Not long after the transfer of the relics Anthony made overtures to the friars, disclosing that he would willingly take their habit in the quest for martyrdom. An undertaking was sought that the friars would promise to send him overseas, perhaps to Morocco, in search of the martyr's crown. In an age where martyrdom was perceived as the closest form of the imitation of Jesus Christ the biographers placed the focus on Anthony's desire to shed his blood in missionary territory. Anthony may have regarded the fraternity, whose members he had so admired, as the best opportunity of gaining this end. The friars, however, were delighted by the prospect of such a fine recruit from the monastery and acted speedily. Anthony, too, did not delay and approached the abbot for permission to transfer to the friars. The biographers give a brief account of the decision to release Anthony. Because he was probably both a priest and a master by this stage it is probable that his petition caused a great deal of disappointment to the canons, who had invested so much in his religious and theological formation. They conceded defeat, however, in this matter and allowed Anthony to leave with good grace, although it is probable that the canons did not release such an able young man without offering some opposition. In accordance with their agreement, the friars returned early in the morning and clothed Anthony in the habit of their order. There is no mention of Anthony having to spend a year in the novitiate, though some process of instruction was necessary and took place, and this supports the view that he joined the fraternity before 22 September 1220, when Honorius III laid down the requirement of a novitiate. V. Gamboso maintains that Anthony was preparing for the priesthood and that he was probably ordained in this period at Coimbra, an interpretation which is corroborated by an early thirteenth-century manuscript of the first biography.[34]

By the autumn both the minister and the guardian deemed Anthony sufficiently grounded in the principles of the Franciscan school to allow him to set off for Morocco with his burning desire for martyrdom.[35] The early biographies make little mention of his time in Morocco and this was clearly a part of the biography which was not well researched or supported by reminiscences of the saint's companions. Anthony fell ill there and was obliged to curtail his stay, reluctantly accepting the end of his ambition of martyrdom. Plans were made for him to return to his native Portugal, but as a strong westerly gale which drove his ship far to the east of her course died down, he found himself on the coast of the Sicilian shore. This is not unlike the story of Francis's vocation, with illness being used to thwart a preconceived idea of what the future should bring.

The friars in Sicily notified Anthony about the impending general chapter to be held at Pentecost at the Portiuncula in Assisi and he decided to accompany them; at that time all friars, both professed and novices, were invited to attend the chapter.[36] The general chapter of 1221 gave Francis, now back from the East, the opportunity to reimpose his influence upon the fraternity. When the business of the chapter was concluded, the ministers provincial appointed the friars of their own jurisdiction. It is not known whether the minister from Portugal was present at the chapter and whether any steps were taken for Anthony to return to his native province; neither does the question of a return to Sicily seem to have been mentioned. Thus the man who would become one of the most popular saints, with a reputation for finding items which had been lost, had to endure the embarrassment of being left unnoticed and without an appointment at the end of the chapter. Eventually he took the initiative and requested Gratian, the minister in Romagna, to allow him to go with him. Gratian agreed to take him to Romagna. A more constitutionally circumspect account appears in the *Dialogus* which reports that the approval of the minister general was given before Anthony left the chapter.[37]

While the mendicant movement was normally perceived as an urban phenomenon, life in the hermitages was flourishing, as the biographies of Francis demonstrate. Within a year of having taken the Franciscan habit in search of martyrdom, Anthony found himself dwelling in the hermitage of Monte Paolo. This was a far cry from the Islamic cities in which he had dreamed of preaching Christ at the cost of his own life. His first biographer provides a glimpse of the rhythm of life in the hermitages. One of the friars built himself a cell in a grotto congenial for prayer. When Anthony saw it and realized how suitable it was, he went to ask the friar to give him the use of that cell. After taking part in the morning prayers of the community he was accustomed to retire to the cell, taking with him some bread and a small container of water. In this way he spent the whole day alone in prayer and reflection, forcing the body to serve the spirit; but he always returned on time for the friars' meetings. Often, when the bell rang, he would prepare to return to the friars, but, because his body was tired out by sleeplessness and weakened by abstinence, he would walk uncertainly, waver and fall. Sometimes his asceticism was such that, unless he had been held up by the friars, he would not have been able to walk back to the hermitage.[38] He limited himself to the allowance of bread.

The biographer looks ahead to Anthony's qualities as a teacher by reporting that during his period in the hermitage he was tireless in his pursuit of humility, seeking the removal of all trace of presumption.[39] His studies at Coimbra and his prayers and meditations at Monte Paolo were a crucial period of preparation for his apostolate of preaching and teaching. Prolonged study and prayer became the bases for those who were entrusted with the offices of preaching and teaching, providing a twofold foundation for the friars' success in the thirteenth century. Although Anthony is hailed as a popular preacher, his time at Monte Paolo was treasured and he never lost his love of the life of prolonged prayer and asceticism. In the last months of his life he returned to the hermitage as a place of refreshment and peace. At the end of his Lenten sermons in 1231 he withdrew to Camposanpiero, a solitary place, hoping to find peaceful seclusion there. The hermitage was owned by a nobleman named Tiso. Not far from the friars' dwelling Tiso had a thick forest, where Anthony was drawn to a tall nut tree, where he had a cell made for him; the tree offered suitable solitude and the kind of rest conducive to contemplation. Cells were also made for two of Anthony's companions, Luke Belludi and Roger. Some preferential treatment for the saint is indicated by the biographer's comment that greater care was lavished on the higher cell for the saint's use; conversely, cells for his companions received less care and attention. There Anthony led a solitary life and dedicated himself to contemplation.[40]

THE MINISTRY OF PREACHING

Anthony's life in the hermitage suddenly ended in a manner teeming with implications for him and the fraternity which he had so recently joined; this event led to the beginning of his ministry as an itinerant preacher and his related ministry of teaching. This is all the more remarkable because Anthony had been invited to preach only after several friars had declined the invitation. The occasion of this sermon was a journey to Forli, where some friars were to be ordained. When the mendicants from various friaries had assembled, the local minister began to ask the Dominicans to deliver a homily. When they excused themselves on the grounds that they would have no time to prepare, the minister extended the invitation to several friars and met with a similar response. The biographers create the impression that Anthony was the last friar to be approached and report that the guardian believed him to be a simple friar without any claims to learning, although he had heard him use Latin on occasion. The guardian's expectations of Anthony were modest and he did not believe that he knew anything of the Scriptures.[41]

Anthony's homily astonished his confrères as he proceeded to expound numerous topics with both prudence and clarity. The unexpected depth and mystical content of his sermon took the friars by surprise. He was not only competent, but also showed signs of being an unusually gifted communicator.[42] His combination of humility and the gift of knowledge earned him the friars' respect. This was a momentous day both for him and the fraternity as his remarkable abilities became plain for all to see. The biographers do not mention whether he had delivered sermons at Coimbra as an Augustinian. Neither do they claim that this was his first sermon, although they imply that he had not preached to the friars. The local and provincial authorities in the order speedily came to the conclusion that such skills were sorely needed for the Church's mission of preaching the Gospel in northern Italy, where heresy was making inroads. Anthony's transfer to the apostolate of preaching perhaps indicates that the friars did not have an abundance of preachers; in the 1220s there were still comparatively few priests in the fraternity. The minister provincial duly licensed Anthony to preach and his biographers depict him as a preacher in the apostolic mould (Matthew 9:35), moving from place to place and, in his zeal for souls, denying himself.[43]

Anthony's style of preaching was contrasted with that of some of the ostentatious preachers of the period in search of money or banquets. Having received the office of preaching from the minister provincial, he embarked upon an itinerant ministry in imitation of his divine master, travelling through cities and castles, villages and plains preaching before people. Displays of erudition and all blandishments were absent from the colourful and incisive sermons by which he endeavoured to draw people back to a more rigorous observance of the

Gospel. Instead, Anthony's long years of study and reflection on the Bible were an invaluable ally in his preaching. Examples of biblical teaching filled his mind and enabled him to illustrate the teaching of the Gospel in a homely and engaging manner. His reputation as an unusually gifted preacher was acknowledged by Thomas of Celano's first biography. His mind had been opened to understand the Scriptures and expound the words of the Gospels. His preaching was marked by its fervour and devotion and his homily to the friars on the topic 'Jesus of Nazareth, king of the Jews' (John 19:19) was the occasion of a miraculous appearance of Francis during a provincial chapter at Arles about 1224.[44] His experience confirmed the advice which he dispensed to preachers, whom he characterized as voices of joy. He urged that preachers should proclaim their joyful message not only for the just in the midst of the Church but also for those at the extreme edges of the world, that is those who did not subscribe to the commandments.[45]

Towards the end of his life Anthony passed on to the friars the fruits of his experience as a preacher and compiled collections of model sermons for Sundays and feast days. His sermons for the Sundays of the liturgical year were composed at Padua at the friars' instigation. On arrival there he decided to study throughout the winter and, at the request of Rainaldo, the bishop of Ostia and the future Alexander IV, he devoted his energies to the writing of sermons for the feasts of the saints in the yearly liturgical cycle.[46] Smalley points out that the sermons for Sundays and saints days are not transcripts of homilies preached by the saint, though he may have used his drafts of such sermons on various occasions. They offer reflections on the Gospel for Sundays and feast days, the latter incomplete, throughout the liturgical year. They serve as a comprehensive framework for a manual for preachers, confessors and penitents. Such aids multiplied from the early thirteenth century, taking the form of skeleton sermons, notes and collections of examples.

A compendious, portable type of book was needed, because a friar would carry his own luggage and travel light. Nonetheless, it would have been feasible to copy one sermon on a few leaves of parchment and sheets of this kind would have provided a friar with a wide range of themes. Each would contain matter for a number of sermons for the same Sunday or feast day, an advantage when the friar had to preach often on the same occasion. A copy of one sermon would equip its possessor with matter for sermons on many questions, with abundant supporting texts to aid his memory. Whatever immediately practical purpose they might serve, Anthony intended the whole to give a theoretical background to preaching and pastoral care. He concentrates almost exclusively on the excellence of preaching, on the preacher's call to repentance and on its hoped-for sequel – contrition, confession to a priest, satisfaction and perseverance. The vices which make repentance necessary were defined and painted in ugly colours.[47] For instance, there are two principal parts in the sermons for the first

Sunday after Christmas. The first focuses on poverty, the misery of the rich, humility, the damnation of the proud and the exaltation of the humble, the useful sadness of penitents, obedience and a homily to religious and priests. The second part explores pride and humility of heart, ruin, the resurrection of the soul from sins, those intoxicated by temporal matters, the twofold birth of the Blessed Virgin and the passion of her Son, the significance of the four seasons of the year, the annunciation or nativity and a moral sermon on penance. Anthony was among the first of the friars to compile collections of materials for the benefit of the friars' itinerant ministry.

MEASURES TO COMBAT THE SPREAD OF HERESY

The popular iconography of Anthony – holding a lily or the child Jesus on his arm – conjures up a serenity which was in stark contrast to the conditions in which he worked throughout the 1220s. One dimension of his preaching was his apostolate in areas where there was a twofold sense of alienation from the Church: first, because little pastoral provision had been made for the people of the emerging cities of the early thirteenth century and second because there was a perception that the bishops and priests, ensnared by secular interests and responsibilities as well as their own personal limitations, were failing to meet the aspirations of those who thirsted for a more authentic form of Christian living. L. Paolini explains that Catharism took root and spread throughout medieval Italy as a popular religious movement on account of an itinerant missionary activity. From the last quarter of the twelfth century onwards the presence of notable personalities within its communities favoured a penchant for controversy and doctrinal discussion. Cathars became famed for their skills in argument, however much their Catholic opponents derided the folly and illogical nature of their beliefs.[48]

One of the reasons for the success of Dominic's mission in Toulouse was the twin approach of a lifestyle which reflected the aspirations of evangelical perfection and a rigorously intellectual exposition of the Church's teaching. These were equally necessary in northern Italy, where the friars were engaged in measures to stem the tide of defections from the Church. In Umbria, where the orthodox teaching was not under much threat, Francis and his followers began by preaching penance and they later received permission to address more doctrinal matters; primarily they sought to preach by good example and to follow up their apostolate with words of admonition. Clasen explains that in northern Italy circumstances were markedly different and preachers were required to enter into disputation with heretics or preach to people infected by false doctrine.[49] The friars' approach to debate with heretics was informed by the realization that they were about to enter into debate and disputation with men who had been thoroughly grounded in the Scriptures and were eloquent on the subject of the faults or failings of the clergy.

There was a large community of Cathars, or Patarines as they were known locally, in the region of Romagna, in northern Italy. They had become hostile to the Church's teaching on a variety of questions and enjoyed a great deal of support in the region. St Aldebrand, provost of the cathedral of Rimini (1222–28), and then bishop of Fossombrone, was a witness to the conditions which prevailed in the former city. For instance, he felt compelled to maintain the Church's claim to its own property and goods, some of which had been confiscated by the local authority.[50] Finding many people who had left the Church for the Patarines, Anthony invited them to his sermons. His labours in Rimini, where there were numerous heretics, attracted the biographers' attention. His first biographer reports that Anthony's powerful words and salutary doctrine so rooted themselves in the hearts of his listeners that they returned to the Church. The impact of his sermons and disputations was such that he won over Bononillo, who had been a Patarine for 30 years.[51] While the hagiographers emphasize Anthony's impact upon the Patarine community, a cautionary note is struck by Gamboso, who believes that his hard-won successes were limited, because the number of converts was always small, and smaller still was the number of those who persevered in their conversion.[52] Studies of medieval heresy frequently mention Anthony's labours in northern Italy and southern France, but they do not present him as a man who significantly eroded support for heretical groups in those areas.

In both regions Anthony was engaged in disputation with well-trained and highly articulate exponents of various heretical ideas. A glimpse into the circumstances in which he and other friars worked is provided by Jordan of Saxony's description of Dominic's disputations with Albigensians:

> frequent debates were held, at Pamiers, Lavaur, Montréal and Fanjeaux. Judges were appointed to pronounce on the outcome of these debates, and, on the days fixed for them, rulers and knights and women and the ordinary people assembled, all wanting to listen to the arguments over the faith. On one occasion a famous debate was held at Fanjeaux, for which a large crowd of believers and unbelievers was assembled ...[53]

Tugwell explains that these debates sometimes lasted as long as a fortnight.[54] There is a similar context to Anthony's debate about the Eucharist with a heretic near Toulouse; as the debate intensified the onlookers were called to silence. This ministry of recalling people from heresy was also a feature of Anthony's later life; heretics also feature in the miracle stories compiled by his biographers. The *Benignitas* describes his public disputations in Rimini, Toulouse and Milan, earning him the title of 'hammer of the heretics';[55] in a more ecumenical climate such nomenclature occasions some unease and embarrassment. There was a direct link between the realization that a thorough preparation was necessary for the apostolates of preaching in the urban centres and disputing with heretics and the origin of theological study among the Franciscans.

References to heretics in the biographies by Thomas of Celano were few and brief. For instance, the *Vita prima* enumerates the fruit of Francis's preaching, one of which was that the wickedness of heresy was confounded; heretics were depicted as furtively slipping away from the places where the saint preached.[56] While it is not disputed that Francis encountered heresy, it was rarely mentioned. He and Anthony were products of very different parts of Christendom and their ministries did not have the same focus. In Umbria the emphasis was on simple exhortation, but in northern Italy the accent was switched to apologetics. Preachers had to be able to explain and defend the Church's doctrine, as the early Dominican experience around Toulouse confirms. Anthony's ministry in areas where heresy had made inroads was a very significant element in his apostolate.

The disturbing level of support which heretical groups were winning at the end of the twelfth century challenged the Church to provide theologically articulate bishops and priests capable of presenting the Gospel in an authentic and attractive manner. Bernard of Clairvaux derided the teaching of the Cathars at Toulouse by claiming that it was plausible only to peasant girls and imbeciles, the only adherents of that sect known to him. He emphasized that their leaders had not made any contribution to knowledge, but only reiterated the trite sayings well-aired by heretics of old; many other persuasive arguments were adduced by lying and hypocritical spirits to deceive the dull-witted and foolish people.[57] The abbot of Clairvaux's judgement was echoed by Anthony who, reflecting the language of Gregory the Great, compared heretics to the jackals who suckle their young (Lamentations 4:3); jackals had a human face, but an animal's tail. In order to deceive the more easily they project a human face and employ their blandishments; thus the heretics suckle their young when they nurture their treacherous followers in their own falsehood. Anthony claims that the recruits made by heretics were more properly called sucklings, and not sons, because they had known nothing else. They were like rustics, shoemakers and tailors, who did nothing more than bark against the Church and blaspheme its members.[58] Both men laboured in a context where the Church was under threat and their propaganda about heretical illiteracy is not supported by contemporary studies of that subject. For instance, P. Biller observes that it became a topos of Catholic propaganda to portray Cathars as both illiterate and fox-like in nature.[59]

The Fourth Lateran Council viewed theological study as an indispensable form of preparation for the propagation of the Gospel and renewed the call for the establishment of schools in each episcopal and monastic centre. The

Church's losses in the late twelfth century made the need for theologically literate priests all the more urgent. The friars' central involvement in the council's programme of renewal meant that the question of studies could not be bypassed, however uncongenial it was to Francis. Their work in the urban centres and in combating heresy called upon them to be theologically adept, articulate and resourceful in their explanation of Christian doctrine. At the end of the twelfth century the University of Paris was playing a major role in promoting higher standards of pastoral care. The council linked theological studies with an efficient pastoral ministry, insisting that those appointed to preach should be properly instructed.

Moreover, because the friars were being pitted against skilful disputants who were steeped in the Scriptures, it was becoming all the more imperative for them to receive the theological preparation necessary for their apostolate. From the end of the twelfth century heretical groups, including the Cathars, had their own schools in different parts of Italy; in the first half of the thirteenth century some Italian Cathars were sent to the University of Paris.[60] The success of their propaganda, based on solid preparation, and the Dominican participation in the schools in the early 1220s must have been instrumental in moving Francis to reconsider the question of studies in the context of the needs of an embattled Church. In addition, Ugolino's influence may have convinced Francis that some theological study was required, especially in a climate where some well-placed critics were opposed to the nascent community.

The founder's decision to approve the initiation of theological lectures was probably taken with some reluctance and worry about its repercussions for the friars' fidelity to his vision. He may have foreseen the potential conflict between the demands of study and the evangelical poverty; the materials for study were very expensive and the homes of medieval paupers were not lined with manuscripts. The matter manifestly exercised Francis's mind a great deal on his return from the East and, once he had bowed to the arguments in favour of study, he insisted that it should not distract friars from the pursuit of virtue. In his anxiety he was fortunate enough to have a future saint, Anthony, to pilot this new development. His letter to Anthony laid down the conditions for the friars' study of theology and influenced generations of students and masters:

> it pleases me that you teach sacred theology to the brothers, on condition that you 'do not extinguish the study of prayer and devotion' as the Rule declares.[61]

Anthony, whose sermons criticized bishops and priests who lacked the knowledge required for their ministry, saw no dichotomy between an appropriate theological training and virtue. His familiarity with the history of the Church taught him that many of the saints, especially in the patristic era, had been both prelates and theologians. A central feature of his apostolate was the presentation of sound doctrine and the rebuttal of the heresy, which he found in the urban centres of northern Italy and southern France. His effectiveness in expounding the Scriptures and defending the Church brought him to the attention of Francis, who in late 1223 or early 1224 invited him to instruct the friars in theology. Anthony then devoted his energies to the ministries of preaching, hearing confessions and teaching. A burning desire to communicate the values of the Gospel was at the root of all his studies and teaching; he displayed no interest in theology as a science detached from the Church's programme of evangelization. Moreover, he was determined to preserve the terms of Francis's mandate that study should not extinguish the spirit of prayer. He was revered as the first Franciscan lector and his early canonization ensured that careful attention was given to the appropriate manner of studying theology.

THE ORIGIN OF FRANCISCAN SCHOOLS

Francis's explicit teaching on studies was relatively brief, although commentators sometimes attribute to him an unbending opposition to study. This question has been vigorously debated from his death until the present day. Learning was addressed in chapter 10 of the Rule and his seventh admonition: in the first the friars were instructed not to be anxious about the acquisition of learning and in the second the dangers of study were stressed, because some acquired knowledge in order to be deemed wise, while others treated it as the path to a lucrative career. Francis should not be regarded as a lone voice raised against the dangers of studies in the cathedral schools and the new universities. Similar warnings were issued by some who had been groomed in the schools, such as John of Salisbury, who had spent many years in the French schools. In January 1165 he wrote to the exiled Thomas Becket, archbishop of Canterbury, reflecting that both canon and civil law had their value, but not in the present crisis. His advice was that the time was not ripe for such displays, which aroused idle curiosity rather than devotion. He asked Becket whether anyone arose contrite from a study of canon law and mused that scholarship sometimes swells learning into a tumour, but never or scarcely inflames devotion. The archbishop was exhorted to reflect upon the Psalms and the moral writings of Gregory the Great.[62]

Scholars groomed in the new universities urged the preservation of a balanced attitude towards theological studies. While Robert Grosseteste admonished the friars in England not to imitate religious who walked in darkness and emphasized the need for theological study, he vigorously maintained that such activity should be subordinate to the Church's pastoral ministry. Attention was drawn to the dangers confronting the learned and fears were expressed for those men who neglect to learn the art of preaching; many learned clerics preferred to be admired or to enrich themselves in the more lucrative sciences.[63] Anthony was among those who deplored the scholars' pursuit of the lucrative sciences, bemoaning the fact that legal studies were preferred to theology on the basis of finance.[64] Jean de la Rochelle complained that many scholars succumb to pride. Thus, however much more modern biographers might claim that Francis was opposed to the study of theology by the friars, it is inescapably true that he both accepted the necessity of theological study and initiated the establishment of its first school at Bologna.

While many educated men were joining the friars' ranks, Anthony was the first to teach theology in a friary. The traditions that he was the first lector and that the first school was at the university city of Bologna were recorded by the *Benignitas*, which describes the condition of that school more in terms of the later 1270s than the 1220s.[65] After serving as lector at Bologna the saint taught at Montpellier and Toulouse, where he joined the movement to stem the advances of Albigensianism, which enjoyed much popular support in an area where many felt alienated from the Church. Towards the end of his life he returned to northern Italy and settled at Padua, where his energies were devoted to preaching, teaching and hearing confessions,[66] the three major dimensions of his apostolate.

The very close bond between the ministry of preaching and theological studies was clear to contemporaries. The friars' theological studies were rooted in the apostolate, as Thomas of Eccleston made clear: when Robert Grosseteste was lecturing at the friary in Oxford, the friars quickly made very good progress both in dealing with questions and in their preaching on difficult moral problems.[67] At an early stage the friars began to take a close interest in scholastic centres, which provided them with opportunities for both preaching and recruitment. Within six weeks of landing in England the friars had reached Oxford, and the following year they established a community at Cambridge. In the 1220s and 1230s this instinct was supported by a group of prelates who were well disposed to the fraternity. Gratien de Paris observes that some prelates, including Jacques de Vitry, bishop of Acre and later cardinal bishop of Frascati, Robert Grosseteste at Oxford and then Lincoln, William d'Auvergne, a master at Paris and then bishop of that city, and Eudes de Châteauroux, chancellor of the University of Paris and then bishop of Frascati, encouraged them to follow the example of the Dominicans by embracing theological study.[68] This external encouragement to study was matched by the policies pursued by the leaders of the order at a crucial stage in its evolution. The one benefit which Salimbene attributed to Elias as minister general (1232-39) was the promotion of theological studies within the order.[69] Angelo da Clareno protested that Crescentius da Iesi, minister general (1244-47), multiplied the schools, especially in Italy, and introduced secular studies.[70] It was the strong conviction of John of Parma, minister general (1247-57), that the future prosperity of the order rested on the two walls of learning and conduct.[71]

The system of theological study in friaries, too, had its origins in Francis's letter to Anthony and at least from the later 1220s the ministers general were involved in ensuring a supply of lectors for the expanding network of Franciscan schools. The friars were accustomed make a formal approach to the minister general to provide them with a suitably trained lector. As early as 1228 the office of lector was deemed to be so central to the friars' apostolate that, when John Parenti, the minister general, heard that the friars in Magdeburg had no one to teach theology, he prevailed upon Simon, an English friar, to resign as minister provincial of Saxony and begin to teach. On Simon's death two years later the same minister general appointed the celebrated Bartholomew, another English friar, who had been lecturing on the Bible at Paris.[72] In the 1230s Philip of Wales and Adam of York were sent from England to lecture in Lyon by Elias. John of Parma sent Ralph of Corbridge, who was still a novice, from Paris to Oxford, and Stephen, an English friar, to lecture at Genoa and Rome.[73] Special attention was paid to the network of schools and the moral qualities of both the lector and the student in the earliest extant general constitutions of the order at Narbonne in 1260.

ANTHONY, PATRON OF FRANCISCAN SCHOOLS

Anthony's studies as an Augustinian canon had given him a sound working knowledge of the Bible and the Fathers of the Church. This preparation equipped him for his apostolates of preaching, disputing and then teaching as a friar whose studies had a solidly based pastoral context. He was a figure of immense psychological importance for the friars engaged in theology because of his combination of the virtue of humility with the gift of knowledge. He had revived the patristic combination of holiness of life with theological insights and was hailed as a Paul-like figure, a preacher, teacher and doctor[74] and his canonization pronounced the compatibility of learning and piety in unambiguous terms. D. Monti wonders whether the reason for his speedy canonization was Gregory IX's desire to hold up to both the order and the Church a new model of holiness in meeting contemporary pastoral needs.[75] The evidence suggests that Anthony became the patron of the friars' schools in the universities of Paris, Oxford and Cambridge, the three *studia generalia* in the fourteenth century, and his feast was marked by a sermon. At Paris lectures in the faculty of theology were suspended on 13 June,[76] when a sermon on the saint was preached in the friars' church, as the university's fourteenth-century calendar confirms.[77] Roger Marston, the sixteenth master at Oxford, presents Anthony as the patron of that school.[78] Three homilies on the saint are extant and were probably preached by Jean de la Rochelle on 13 June in the church at Paris between 1235 and 1244. There are also some indications that Anthony was the patron of the Franciscan school at Cambridge.[79]

The three sermons by Jean de la Rochelle were undoubtedly preached on

Anthony's feast, and treat the saint under the headings of preacher, confessor and doctor. The occasion provided Jean with an opportunity to praise the saint and to outline the qualities of friars called to exercise the office of lector. Anthony was hailed as the greatest preacher, *predicator maximus*, whose purity of conscience and devotion commended him and equipped him for the grace of preaching.[80] He was fervent in his desire for martyrdom[81] and his innocence of life gave him the authority to argue against those entangled in vices.[82] His example castigated those whose sermons contained fables or indulged in curiosities, which were more concerned with subtle arguments than things useful for their audience. He counselled those ensnared by their flaws, and his example rebuked those who wished to preach to the converted or the religious, who are in a state of grace, rather than addressing themselves to sinners abandoned in the darkness of fault.[83]

Anticipating a central theme from Franciscan literature and art, Jean not only draws parallels between the lives of Jesus Christ and Anthony, but also locates the qualities of the master in the Gospel. The nobility of the theologian's office was mirrored in the teaching that the master in the schools should model his conduct and instruction upon the divine example and in this the theologian echoes the words of Francis's *Testament* regarding the respect owed to theologians. The doctor should read and teach sacred Scripture (2 Timothy 3:16) and should teach, argue, correct and instruct. Virtues should be announced, faults corrected and punishments heralded. Thus the teacher should argue against vices, correct errors perpetrated and offer instruction concerning rewards and punishments.[84] In this context Jean saw no real disparity between the work of the doctor and the preacher because he viewed them as complementary elements in the proclamation of the Gospel. The close ties between the apostolates of teaching and preaching were underlined and the one was seen to depend upon the other. Theological endeavour was situated within a pastoral context by Jean, who wished to preserve and enrich the study of theology among the friars, who were called to the pursuit of holiness. The emphasis upon life and doctrine was at the heart of the early Franciscan school, where knowledge or doctrine was deemed to be inseparable from personal qualities.

Anthony was styled as an assiduous cultivator of humility, which safeguards friars from arrogance, and his knowledge was revealed by divine disposition.[85] Jean implies that in his earliest days in the fraternity Anthony concealed his theological studies under a cloak of simplicity, preferring to be deemed unlearned. What had been reported as a matter of fact in the *Assidua* had acquired a more didactic character in the hands of the Parisian master. Anthony's humility became a source of inspiration and instruction for friars, who were forbidden to exert external pressure leading to their appointment as lector. Jean again reveals his fundamentalism by returning to Jesus Christ at every question; in the divine master there was knowledge which was accompanied by humility. A series of texts from the Gospels touching on the humility displayed by the Redeemer was produced: Jesus Christ was presented as the model for the teaching friar. Anthony, his messenger, possessed perfection in knowledge and humility, a combination necessary in order to instruct people in the virtues. In the Son of God are hidden all the treasures of wisdom and knowledge (Colossians 2:3); the spirit of wisdom and under-standing filled him (Isaiah 11:2). Although many were inflated by knowledge and were taking pride in their studies, Anthony clothed himself in the perfection of humility allied to knowledge. The saint's example showed that a deeper understanding of the Scriptures rested securely on the foundations of virtue and that pride arising from studies vitiated this work. Jean refers to the many who take the highway to pride; this is a further confirmation that Francis's anxieties about learning expressed in the seventh admonition reflected some contemporary concerns.[86]

FRANCISCAN PERCEPTION OF THEOLOGY

When Bernard of Clairvaux preached to a large group of clerics at Paris in 1139 or 1140, three of them were moved by compunction and joined him. Geoffrey of Auxerre reports that these recruits were converted from vain studies to the worship of true wisdom.[87] Bernard had admonished both the masters and students of Paris to flee the Babylon in which they lived, assuring them that the forest would teach them more than books and that the woods and the rocks would teach them more than any master. Similar warnings were given by Peter of Celle about the deceptive, ravenous and sophistic Paris. He contrasted the schools with the Cistercian monastery, the school of Christ.[88] Such urgent admonitions reflected the monastic rhetoric that the quest for salvation required men to retreat from the schools in search of sanctification and salvation. In contrast, the mendicant movement brought the pursuit of wisdom, holiness and perfection back into the heart of society and the schools, established for theological study, were not exceptions. Franciscan theologians treated the school as another arena of activity where sanctification might be gained by those clothed in the appropriate dispositions and saw no chasm between sanctity and study. The traditional dangers were not underestimated and Franciscan theologians were just as worried about an unbridled curiosity as the Cistercian reformers of the twelfth century.

The principle of development in the Church and the order persuaded Bonaventure that a properly balanced study of theology was not an illegitimate growth in the fraternity. The Church had begun with simple fishermen and was enriched later with the most illustrious and learned doctors. The fraternity, likewise, had a divine beginning. Its origin and growth were accomplished by God, and scholars had been drawn to the company of simple men in some numbers. In several places Bonaventure appealed to the evolution of the Church and the role played by the Fathers in warding off the menace of error and heresy. The analogy with the Church's history enabled him to accept the evolution of the order. The order's beginnings were humble, but it was speedily transformed into an internationally recognized community, whose efforts on behalf of the Church brought them much acclaim. In this context the admission of the wealthy and influential theologian Alexander of Hales was a further indication of the role of theological study in the pursuit of virtue and wisdom. The profession of this eminent scholar was interpreted as a fulfilment of the Gospel by Bonaventure in his exposition of the founder's Rule.[89]

The conditions for a balanced study of theology, personified by Anthony in the 1220s, were mapped out by both Francis's biographers and the early constitutions of the fraternity. For instance, Bonaventure's *Legenda maior* applied the founder's teaching to the conditions of the 1260s. Francis insisted that the friars should not study merely in order to have something to say. They should study in order to practise what they have learned and then encourage others to do the same. The purpose and focus of their endeavour were summarized in the words placed on Francis's lips:

> 'I want my friars', he said, 'to be disciples of the Gospel and to progress in knowledge of the truth in such a way as to increase in pure simplicity without separating the simplicity of the dove from the wisdom of the serpent which our eminent Teacher joined together in a statement from his own blessed lips.' [90]

Bonaventure modelled his advice on the condition which Francis laid down in his letter to Anthony. He strove to be faithful to it and attributed to the founder the teaching that the friars should study theology, on condition that they did not neglect prayer, after the example of Jesus Christ; he adds that the Son of God prayed more than he studied.[91] Thus study was pronounced licit, on condition that it was based upon the example of the Son of God and was consistent with the spirit of Francis's seventh admonition. Bonaventure contrasted the study of the sciences leading to lucrative careers with the friars' studies, which were focused on an advance in charity and humility in the search for eternal life.[92] The early Franciscan school regarded theological study as a quasi-spiritual activity whose purpose was deeper union between the theologian and his Creator. This was made more explicit in the connection between sanctity and the capacity to grasp the significance of some more difficult passages of Scripture.

E. Gilson explains that in the Middle Ages it was received doctrine that the act of humility whereby a holy man renounced learning gained him remarkable insights into the Scriptures.[93] This was articulated by Thomas Gallus where he exemplifies this principle in the life of Anthony:

> often love can enter where mere natural knowledge is excluded. We read of some holy bishops that they were but poorly versed in the natural sciences, and yet they

had the gift of readily understanding mystical theology. Having left all natural knowledge behind, their purified souls ascended as it were to the very heavens, even to the most blessed Trinity. This very thing I myself, as a close friend, have been able to observe in the holy Brother Anthony of the Friars Minor. Though he was not well read in the natural sciences, he had a pure spirit and a burning heart and was a man on fire for God. All this enabled him easily to understand all the riches and depths of mystical theology with all his heart. Therefore I may apply to him the words which Sacred Scripture says of John the Baptist: 'he was a lamp, burning and shining. Because his heart was burning with love for God, he was a shining example also to men.'[94]

While this principle applies to Anthony, there was no indication that he turned his back on learning. A contemporary expression of the same belief occurred when Francis expounded a vexed passage of Scripture for a Dominican theologian and an unnamed cardinal. The Dominican exclaimed that the theologians' learning crawls on its belly along the ground, while Francis's theology, based on purity of life and contemplation, soars like an eagle.[95]

THE DEBATE ABOUT STUDIES

Moorman observes that within fifty years of Francis's death the friars had become the most learned body of men in the world, adding that the development was entirely opposed to the original wishes of the saint. In spite of many appeals, Francis remained adamant in his refusal to permit the friars to possess books or to allow themselves to get enticed into the academic world. His brethren were called to be neither brilliant preachers nor able controversialists, but simple evangelists preaching their Gospel more by the quality of their lives than by the eloquence of their words. Many of the leading friars were dismayed at this view, but nothing could shake Francis's convictions.[96] These comments by a distinguished Franciscan historian attract much support, though some modifications are required. The Dominicans would be entitled to challenge the claim that the Franciscans had become the most learned order, especially because they seem to have followed the trail of Dominic's sons into the study of theology.

As already explained, Francis himself stood at the beginning of the scholastic movement with his invitation to Anthony and the Rule envisaged the use of breviaries. The debate about books in the thirteenth century seemed to turn more on *use* than *possession*, which was rigorously resisted in the incipient constitutions of the order. Efforts were made to ensure that manuscripts were distributed by the ministers and did not become the property of friars, though by the end of the thirteenth century friars had the use of certain manuscripts throughout their lives. In the middle of the thirteenth century and later there are references to the friars lacking the parchment for their texts. While Leo and companions claimed that the founder regarded books as a betrayal of Lady Poverty, some supporters of study, commenting on the Rule in the 1250s and 1310, pointed to traditions which showed how books might be used by the friars in accordance with the founder's wishes.[97] The earliest complaints focused on the costs incurred by theological schools, the more abstract form of theological study, which seemed to be detached from the apostolate, and the arrogance displayed by some friars.

By the 1230s there is some evidence that the friars were not only beginning to feel more confident about their intellectual abilities, but were flexing their academic muscles and starting to look disdainfully at other religious. There were also some excesses which provoked the wrath of monastic chroniclers. In their dispute with the Cistercians regarding an attempted foundation at Scarborough in 1240, the Franciscans poured scorn on the learning of the monastic orders. The monastic chronicler pointed out that the friars condemned the authentic orders, founded by Sts Benedict and Augustine, and acted shamefully towards them. They considered the Cistercians to be ignorant and simple and almost laymen or peasants.[98] A few years later, in 1249, the Cistercians, following the example of the Benedictines, obtained papal permission to build a school at Paris and in other educational centres, lest they be held in contempt by the Franciscans and Dominicans.[99] The Franciscans' early sense of inferiority in relation to the Dominicans, who made a number of disparaging remarks about their simplicity, forms the context for an acerbic riposte attributed to the saintly Hugh de Digne about 1248. He proclaimed that the Dominicans would no longer depict his confrères as a bunch of ignorant men.[100]

Advocates of studies within the order were among those who voiced their misgivings about the tendency to distance theological study from the immediate needs of the apostolate. On a visit to Oxford Agnellus of Pisa, who had built the school there and engaged Robert Grosseteste as lector, was dismayed to find the friars disputing the question of whether God existed, *Utrum sit Deus*. His response was to send money for the friars to purchase some decretals instead of discussing frivolous questions.[101] A parallel question appears in Robert Grosseteste's *Tabula*, which contains a heading whether God exists, *An deus sit*; this question may have been used in the early lectures to the friars at Oxford.[102] John of Parma, an experienced lecturer on the *Sentences* at Bologna, Naples and Paris, expressed his own reservations about the curriculum and complained that the friars had raised the wall of learning beyond the heavens and heavenly things by posing the question *An Deus sit*;[103] Eccleston may have recalled the question from his own student days at Oxford. By the time that Thomas of Celano was composing his second biography the friars had a large and carefully graded system of schools. Nonetheless, this text contains a chastened tone which explains that scriptural studies did not displease Francis,[104] though their limitations and dangers were carefully set out.

The development of schools and the privileges and exemptions accorded to lectors increased the mounting unease felt by some friars from the middle of the thirteenth century. The leading school in the fraternity came in for some bitter remarks and this indignation was articulated by Giles of Assisi's lament that Paris had destroyed Assisi.[105] Jacopone da Todi (*c.* 1230-1306) treated the theologians' excesses in terms of a violation of the Rule and fulminated that not a shred of the spirit of the Rule was left, as the university city demolished the Umbrian city of the founder stone by stone. The theologians had led the order down a crooked path. The distinctions made within the community were abhorred by the poet, who complained that the honoured masters of theology enjoyed special treatment in the wing of the friary reserved for honoured guests and had a special menu. In the chapters these friars kept passing new rules which they were generally the first to break. Fraternal love was absent from these masters who, like young mules, watched and waited for the right moment to kick the others in the chest. They could not brook disagreement and exiled their opponents. They were overly familiar with women and, despite their lowly origins, they behaved as if they were of royal blood.[106] Ubertino da Casale (*c.* 1249 - 1329-41), who had spent nine years at Paris, complained that masters and lectors from Paris were dominant in the order and enjoyed numerous exemptions from the common life.[107] These champions of reform regarded the schools as a betrayal of the founder's ideals. Nonetheless, the schools continued to play a central role in the life of the fraternity in the fourteenth century.

CONCLUSION

Anthony's theological formation had taken place in Lisbon and Coimbra, where the foundations were carefully laid for his success as a popular preacher, confuter of heretics and teacher of theology. In appointing Anthony to teach at Padua in late 1223 or early 1224 Francis was participating in a wider movement which had been promoted at the Fourth Lateran Council: ecclesiastical reformers were convinced that sound instruction was essential for the office of preaching. The Cathars and other heretics had their own schools to instruct their followers. At an early stage the Dominicans, too, formed their own schools to prepare friars for the apostolate. An appreciation of the benefits of these schools may have finally tipped the balance in favour of schools of theology for the Franciscans, who were to be instructed in the Bible and the teaching of the Church. The friars' success as itinerant preachers was built upon their sound knowledge of the Bible and their capacity to present its teaching in a cogent and persuasive manner.

Virtue and knowledge of the Scriptures with the teaching of the Church were united in the person of Anthony. Smalley judges that Anthony fulfilled Francis's demands that study should not extinguish the spirit of prayer. His sermons for Sundays and feast days kept alive the spirit of prayer and devotion, calling for repentance and amendment of life.[108] Anthony was canonized within a year of his death, showing that the combination of virtue and learning was compatible. Jean de la Rochelle and Bonaventure expatiated upon the vices of an undisciplined curiosity, arrogance and presumption. Such defective approaches to the Scriptures were to be spurned by students of theology, who were required to study theology in a constructive and prayerful context.

In the 1220s and 1230s theological study among the friars proceeded along with the general expansion of the order. The early Franciscan chroniclers showed little sign of unease and do not seem to have regarded study as a betrayal of the founder's ideal. The arguments that studies were an essential preparation for the apostolate of preaching seem to have gained wide acceptance. Thus, while Thomas of Eccleston reports John of Parma's concern lest the study of theology should be detached from the apostolate, he nonetheless takes pride in the English friars' reputation for learning. Moreover, his account of the opposition to Elias features friars such as Richard Rufus of Cornwall and Haymo of Faversham, alumni of the schools of Paris. In the troubled period of Elias's term as minister general the moral leadership was exercised by Alexander of Hales and Jean de la Rochelle. R. B. Brooke comments that it was not the Zelanti who led the campaign to depose Elias as minister general; it was the learned, an intellectual élite.[109] Adam Marsh, the first Franciscan lector at Oxford, was a member of the English province's commission, which pressed for a rigorous interpretation of the Rule about 1242. At the same time four masters at Paris were selected to produce a commentary on aspects of the Rule on behalf of the French province. In his later years a master like Alexander of Hales had abandoned security and wealth to throw in his lot with the penniless friars and was unlikely to compromise such a radical and admirable decision by promoting laxity among the friars. While Bernard of Clairvaux, echoing the traditional rhetoric, had challenged clerics to abandon the schools of Paris for the school of Jesus Christ in Cistercian monasteries, Thomas of Celano spoke of those friars educated in the school of virtue, and Franciscan masters regarded theology as a discipline to be pursued in conjunction with the virtues. Anthony was the first mendicant theologian to be canonized and stands at the beginning of an epoch dominated by friar theologians, Sts Albert the Great, Bonaventure, Thomas Aquinas and Blessed John Duns Scotus. The spirit of the new movement, drawing inspiration from the example of Anthony, was encapsulated by Bonaventure's belief that the friars should study theology in order to become good and be saved.[110]

1. Assidua, c. 8, n. 9. Anthony received the name of Ferdinand at baptism, taking the name of Anthony when he became a Franciscan. For purposes of convenience I shall use Anthony also for the period prior to his becoming a friar. The papers presented at a conference in Padua between 29 May and 1 June 1995 and published in *Il Santo*, 36 (1996), contain stimulating studies on the saint.
2. John Pecham, *Tractatus tres de paupertate*, p. 170.
3. Benignitas, c. 2, n. 1.
4. Assidua, c. 2, n. 1.
5. L. and J. Riley-Smith, *The Crusades: Idea and Reality 1095-1274* (Documents of Medieval History, 4; London, 1981), pp. 18, 161. Cf. C. W. David (ed.), *De expugnatione Lyxbonensi* (New York, 1936).
6. M. Purcell, *St Anthony and his Times* (Dublin, 1960), p. 9.
7. Benignitas, c. 2, n. 1.
8. Purcell, *St Anthony* p. 18, nn. 5-6; Dialogus, c. 3, n. 4.
9. Benignitas, c. 2, nn. 2-3.
10. S. Clasen, *St Anthony, Doctor of the Church*, trans. from German by I. Brady (Chicago, 1973), pp. 5-6.
11. Assidua, c. 2, nn. 3, 5.
12. Dialogus, c. 3, n. 6.
13. C. H. Lawrence, *Medieval Monasticism* (London, 2nd edn, 1989), pp. 163-7.
14. Clasen, *St Anthony*, p. 7.
15. Purcell, *St Anthony*, p. 35.
16. V. Gamboso, *St Anthony of Padua: His Life and His Teaching*, trans. from Italian H. Partridge, rev. by L. Poloniato (Padua, 1991), p. 24, states that the monastery was founded in 1134.
17. F. da Gama Caeiro, 'Fonti portoghesi della formazione culturale di sant'Antonio' in A.Poppi (ed.), *Le fonti e la teologia dei sermoni Antoniani* (Padua, 1982), pp. 145-69; A. Figueredo Frias, 'Lettura ermeneutica di sant'Antonio di Padova', *Il Santo*, 35 (1995), pp. 279-458.
18. Clasen, *St Anthony*, p. 8.
19. Purcell, *St Anthony*, pp. 42-3.
20. Clasen, *St Anthony*, p. 8.
21. Assidua, c. 4, nn. 3-4, Dialogus, c. 3, n. 9.
22. Assidua, cc. 4, 8, 10.
23. Ibid., c. 4, nn. 5-6.
24. B. Smalley, 'The use of Scripture in St Anthony's "Sermones"' in Poppi (ed.), *Le fonti e la teologia dei sermoni Antoniani*, pp. 285-97, 285-9.
25. Clasen, *St Anthony*, pp. 11-12.
26. Assidua, c. 5, nn. 3, 4.
27. *Opuscula Sancti Patris Francisci Assisiensis*, p. 237.
28. Rigaldina, c. 4, n. 1.
29. 'Chronica XXIV generalium ordinis minorum' in AF III (Quaracchi, Florence, 1897), pp. 15-19.
30. Assidua, c. 5, n. 1.
31. Purcell, *St Anthony*, pp. 55-6.
32. Dialogus, c. 3, nn. 9-12; Benignitas, c. 3, n. 1.
33. Assidua, c. 5, n. 2.
34. Gamboso, *St Anthony of Padua*, p. 25.
35. Dialogus, c. 3, n. 14.
36. *Chronica Fratris Jordani*, n. 16, pp. 16-17.
37. Assidua, cc. 6, 7; Dialogus, c. 5, n. 2.
38. Assidua, c. 7, nn. 5-11.
39. Dialogus, c. 5, nn. 3, 4.
40. Assidua, c. 15, nn. 2-8.
41. Ibid., c. 8, n. 5.
42. Dialogus, c. 5, n. 5.
43. Assidua, c. 8, nn. 1-9; c. 9, nn. 1-4.
44. 1 C, c. 48.
45. Anthony of Padua, *Sermones Dominicales et Festivi*, I, ed. B. Costa, L. Frasson and I. Luisetto (Padua, 1979), p. 341.
46. Assidua, c. 11, nn. 3, 4.
47. Smalley, 'The use of Scripture', pp. 285-7.
48. L. Paolini, 'Italian Catharism and written culture' in P. Biller and A. Hudson (eds), *Heresy and*

Literacy, 1000-1530 (Cambridge Studies in Medieval Literature, 23; 1994), pp. 83-103, 84, 86, 90.

49.   Clasen, *St Anthony*, pp. 23-4.

50.   Gamboso, *St Anthony of Padua*, pp. 60-1.

51.   Assidua, c. 9, nn. 4-6.

52.   Gamboso, *St Anthony of Padua*, p. 61.

53.   Jordan of Saxony, *On the Beginnings of the Order of Preachers*, trans. S. Tugwell (Dominican Sources, new editions in English; Dublin, 1982), p. 7.

54.   S. Tugwell, *Saint Dominic* (Strasbourg, 1995), p. 11.

55.   Benignitas, c. 16, nn. 1-19; cf. M. d'Alatri, 'Antonio, martello degli eretici?', *Il Santo*, 5 (1965), pp. 123-30.

56.   1 C, n. 62.

57.   *S. Bernardi opera*, II, ed. J. Leclercq, C. H. Talbot and H. M. Rochais (Rome, 1958), pp. 172-88.

58.   Anthony of Padua, *Sermones Dominicales et Festivi*, p. 71.

59.   P. Biller, 'Heresy and literacy: earlier history of the theme' in Biller and Hudson (eds), *Heresy and Literacy, 1000-1530*, pp. 1-18, 3-5.

60.   Paolini, 'Italian Catharism and written culture', pp. 96-7.

61.   R. J. Armstrong and I. C. Brady, *Francis and Clare* (Classics of Western Spirituality; New York, 1982), p. 79.

62.   *The Letters of John of Salisbury*, II: *The Later Letters (1163-1180)*, ed. W. J. Millor and C. N. L. Brooke, (OMT; 1979), pp. 32-5.

63.   Thomas of Eccleston, *Tractatus de adventu*, p. 91; S. Gieben, 'Robert Grosseteste on preaching, with the edition of the sermon "Ex rerum initiatarum" on redemption', *Collectanea Franciscana*, 37 (1967), pp. 107-8 and 'Robert Grosseteste and the evolution of the Franciscan Order' in *Robert Grosseteste: New Perspectives on His Thought and Scholarship*, ed. J. McEvoy (Instrumenta Patristica, XXVII; Turnhout, Brepols, 1995), pp. 215-32.

64.   Anthony of Padua, *Sermones Dominicales et Festivi*, II, pp. 18-19.

65.   Benignitas, c. 13, n. 2.

66.   Assidua, c. 11, n. 7.

67.   Thomas of Eccleston, *Tractatus de adventu*, p. 48.

68.   Gratien de Paris, *Histoire de la fondation et de l'évolution de l'ordre des frères mineurs au xiiie siècle* (Rome, 1926), reprinted with an updated bibliography by M. d'Alatri and S. Gieben (Bibiotheca seraphico-Capuccina cura instituti historici ord.Fr.Min.Capuccinorum, 29; Rome, 1982), p. 127; E. Longpré, 'Guillaume d'Auvergne et l'école franciscaine de Paris', *France Franciscaine*, 10 (1922), pp. 5-45.

69.   Salimbene, *Cronica*, p. 147.

70.   Angelo da Clareno, 'Historia de septem tribulationibus' in ALKG, II, pp. 256-7.

71.   Eccleston, *Tractatus de adventu*, p. 74.

72.   *Chronica Fratris Jordani*, nn. 54, 58-60, pp. 47-54; Salimbene, *Cronica*, p. 134.

73.   Eccleston, *Tractatus*, pp. 49-50; Salimbene, *Cronica*, pp. 430-1, 455, 458-9.

74.   Benignitas, c. 22, n. 8.

75.   D. V. Monti, *Works of St Bonaventure* (New York, 1994), p. 17, n. 44.

76.   H. Denifle (ed.), *Chartularium Universitatis Parisiensis*, II (Paris, 1891), n. 1192, p. 712; I. Brady, 'The authenticity of two sermons of St Bonaventure', *Franciscan Studies*, 28 (1968), pp. 4-26, 13.

77.   S. Gibson (ed.), *Statuta Antiqua Universitatis Oxoniensis* (Oxford, 1931), p. 7.

78.   Roger Marston, *Quodlibeta quatuor ad fidem codicum nunc primum edita*, ed. G. F. Etzkorn and I. Brady (BFSMA, 26; Florence, 1968), pp. 30*, 57*, 61*.

79.   *Documents relating to the University and Colleges of Cambridge* (1852), I, n. 173, p. 400. The text does not mention Anthony expressly, but confuses him with Peter the Martyr who is described as a Franciscan whose feast occurs on 13 June. Cf. M. Robson, 'Saint Anthony of Padua in medieval Cambridge', *Il Santo*, 34 (1994), pp. 341-8.

80.   K. F. Lynch, 'Three sermons on The Doctor Evangelicus, by John de la Rochelle', *Franciscan Studies*, 23 (1963), pp. 213-37, 220, 227.

81.   Ibid., p. 224, where Jean de la Rochelle portrays Anthony as a martyr and, employing the words of Sulpicius Severus, states that, even if the sword of the persecutor did not touch him, he did not lose the palm of martyrdom.

82.   Ibid., p. 231.

83.   Ibid., pp. 222-3.

84.   Ibid., p. 231. Note the way in which this resembles the advice dispensed by Francis. Anthony of Padua, *Dominica I post Pentecosten*, I, p. 391, states that in order to be effective a preacher should wield a sling with two thongs: that of 'knowledge' and that of a 'good life'. His deeds must correspond to his words

and his lifestyle to his preaching. Thus armed, a preacher can then go forth against the Philistine and successfully overcome him.

85. Dialogus, c. 5, nn. 5, 7.
86. Lynch, 'Three sermons', pp. 220-1, 226, 231-2.
87. Geoffrey of Auxerre, *S. Bernardi vita prima*, IV. 11. 10, PL, 183. 327.
88. L. K. Little, *Religious Poverty and the Profit Economy in Medieval Europe* (London, 1978), pp. 92-3.
89. Bonaventure, 'Epistola de tribus quaestionibus ad magistrum innominatum', pp. 216-17.
90. Bonaventure, *The Soul's Journey into God; the Tree of Life; the Life of St Francis*, trans. by E. Cousins (The Classics of Western Spirituality; New York, 1978), p. 281.
91. LM, c. 11, n. 1.
92. *S. Bonaventurae opera omnia*, V, p. 142.
93. E. Gilson, *La philosophie de saint Bonaventure* (Études de philosophie médiévale, 4; Paris, 1943), p. 41, n. 2.
94. Thomas Gallus, *De ecclesiastica hierarchia*, III, 5, from cod. lat. 695 of the Nationalbibliothek, Vienna, c. 135r., cited by da Gama Caeiro, 'Fonti portoghesi', p. 147; Clasen, *St Anthony*, pp. 31-2.
95. 2 C, nn. 103-4.
96. J. R. H. Moorman, *Saint Francis of Assisi* (London, 1950), p. 29.
97. E.g., Bonaventure's 'Epistola de tribus quaestionibus ad magistrum innominatum', p. 216; A. Chiappini, 'Communitatis Responsio "Religiosi Viri" ad Rotulum Fr. Ubertino de Casali' in AFH, 7 (1914), pp. 654-75, and 8 (1915), pp. 56-80, 67.
98. Matthew Paris, *Chronica majora*, IV (RS 57, v; London, 1880), pp. 279-80.
99. Ibid., p. 79.
100. Salimbene, *Cronica*, p. 364.
101. Bartholomew of Pisa, 'De conformitate vitae Beati Francisci ad vitam Domini Iesu' in AF, IV (Quaracchi, Florence, 1906), p. 331.
102. P. W. Rosemann (ed.) in *Opera Roberti Grosseteste Lincolniensis*, ed. J. McEvoy (Corpus Christianorum, continuatio mediaevalis, 130; Steenbrugge, 1995), pp. 235-320, 265.
103. Eccleston, *Tractatus*, p. 74.
104. 2 C, n. 195.
105. *Dicta Beati Aegidii Assisiensis* (BFAMA, 3; Quaracchi, Florence, 1905), p. 91.
106. Jacopone da Todi, *The Lauds*, trans. S. and E. Hughes (The Classics of Western Spirituality; London, 1982), pp. 123-4. 2 C, n. 163, reveals that one of the earlier manifestations of distinctions between the friars was for the office of preaching. The biographer attributed to the founder the teaching that preachers should not be hindered by other duties. This may have paved the way for exemptions later extended to lectors.
107. Ubertino da Casale, 'Incipiunt articuli accepti de regula, contra quos sepe transgressiones fiunt' in ALKG, III, pp. 118, 73.
108. B. Smalley, 'The use of Scripture' in Poppi (ed.), *Le fonti e la teologia dei sermoni Antoniani*, p. 296.
109. R. B. Brooke, *Early Franciscan Government* (Cambridge Studies in Medieval Life and Thought; 1959), pp. 161, 181.
110. *S. Bonaventurae opera omnia*, V, p. 206.

7

※※※※※※※※※※※※※※※※

St Clare, the faithful custodian of Francis's ideals

Clare, who was the first little plant of the order of sisters, … and emulator of St
Francis in preserving always the poverty of the Son of God[1]

While Francis eventually developed a friendship with Guido and Ugolino, the
one person with whom he shared his ideals until the end of his life was Clare.
Their vocations were running along parallel lines for some time before their first
meeting. While she repeatedly voiced her conviction that she had been converted
by the preaching and example of Francis, the pupil rapidly became an equal of
her master, who came to depend on her in his later years. From the early 1220s
she was one of his main supports at a time when he was dogged by illness and
plagued by the growing divisions in his fraternity. That dependence did not end
with his death on 3 October 1226 and from that point until her own death, on 11
August 1253, she heroically fought for and valiantly protected his ideals.
Although a succession of popes provided the friars with interpretations of vexed
aspects of the Rule and various dispensations, Clare clung tenaciously to her
friend's vision. She resisted attempts by popes to temper her poverty and earned
the respect of the papal court. Eventually Innocent IV (1243–54) confirmed her
Rule, the first to be written for women in the Middle Ages. The admiration with
which the Roman Curia regarded her was expressed when the same pope
wanted to canonize her on the day of her funeral. Sabatier maintains that in
general it was at San Damiano that Francis was most perfectly himself[2] and it has
been suggested that without Clare we cannot properly understand Francis.[3]
While Francis was a highly acclaimed itinerant preacher, Clare's life of evangelical
poverty, contemplation and asceticism reflects more accurately his own thirst for
fuller communion with his Creator and his fellow creatures.

CLARE'S FAMILY

While Francis was the son of a prosperous merchant, Clare was born into the
nobility. Her father was a knight, as were her relatives on both sides;[4] there were
seven knights in her family. Sister Pacifica de Guelfuccio of Assisi, who had been
Clare's neighbour and distant relative, lived on the piazza di San Rufino and

testified that Clare was born of noble stock. Pietro de Damiano of Assisi, who had lived near Clare's house, added that her father, Favarone, was a noble, great and powerful in the city;[5] Sister Pacifica stated that she had never seen Favarone, who had died perhaps in Clare's infancy. Ioanni de Ventura of Assisi, who had been a watchman in Clare's house, gave evidence that her parental home was one of the largest in the city and that great sums of money were spent there.[6] Their house was at the left of the old Ugonian cathedral of San Rufino, the Parlascio side. It was a tall and proud palazzo, built on the same wall of boulders that supports the church.

In Assisi the custom of making pilgrimages to holy places was well established with records identifying Rome, Mount Gargano, Venice and the Holy Land as shrines visited.[7] To this list might be added the pilgrimage to St James, which recurs in the Franciscan literature. After the Crusaders' recapture of Jerusalem in 1099 the Holy Land became more accessible.[8] Some women of Assisi went to Palestine and among them was Ortolana, the mother of Clare. Her companion on the journey was Pacifica, the young daughter of Guelfuccio di Bernardo, her relative and neighbour. The pilgrims who went to the Holy Land travelled by way of Egypt. They reached Damietta by galley and from there went on, through Sinai and Gaza, to Jerusalem. Certainly the devout pilgrims from Assisi also took this route. Pacifica reported that she had accompanied Ortolana on pilgrimages to the Holy Land, Rome and Sant'Angelo.[9] Ortolana visited St Michael the archangel on pilgrimage.[10]

The social differences between Francis and Clare were made clear by the civil war which gripped Assisi. Clare was a young child in an aristocratic family when the people of the commune took the law into their hands and attacked castles. One of her special friends was Philippa, the young daughter of Leonardo di Gislerio, the castellan of Sasso Rosso, the political exile and sworn enemy of the commune. As the war flared up, members of the aristocracy were given asylum in Perugia. Clare's family received hospitality from her uncle Monaldo, who had taken citizenship, according to the terms imposed on the knights who had committed themselves to fight against Assisi. In Perugia she again found Philippa, and she lived in the house of a girl who would become one of her first companions at San Damiano with the name of Benvenuta.[11] She listened to the bitter talk of the partisans, still stirred up over the battle of Collestrada, and saw throngs of prisoners, humiliated and derided. The tradition that she visited the prisoners of war in Perugia and there met Francis appears in the later histories.

MANIFESTATIONS OF A VOCATION AND FRANCIS'S IMPACT

Clare's qualities and virtues were known to many who regarded her as an adolescent of outstanding goodness.[12] From infancy she bore a compassionate attitude[13] and the poor had a particular claim upon her affections.[14] She used to send them her own food; Lady Bona, daughter of Guelfuccio of Assisi, confirmed that many times she had carried Clare's gifts to them; the same testimony was given by Ioanni de Ventura.[15] An early point of contact, albeit indirect, between Clare and Francis was her gift of money for those who were restoring the chapel at the Portiuncula; Bona was the messenger on this occasion.[16] This gift sheds some light on Francis's restoration of churches and indicates that some local enthusiasm and collaboration were generated for these projects.

While the virtues attributed to the young Clare expressed the piety in the Middle Ages, she was not merely indulging in a somewhat remote and cerebral devotion which stipulated that those blessed with resources should come to the aid of the needy. However conventional the roots to her piety were, she developed a heightened sense of compassion for the impoverished members of society. In a society which was recovering from the ravages of civil war there were numerous calls upon her compassion and generosity. Her growing wish was to associate herself as fully as possible with those in need. It was not sufficient to give her superfluous and unwanted food and clothing to the paupers around Assisi in order to silence a scrupulous conscience. These gifts became symbols for her own desire to lay aside the advantages of social rank with its privileges and wealth as she, like Francis, was increasingly drawn to the ranks of the poor. The financial security and relative comfort of her own surroundings enabled her to alleviate some of the distress and need in the city, but in the longer term she decided that it was no longer satisfactory to provide help from a safe distance.

Such an early interest in the plight of the needy and poor may have led Clare to consider a religious vocation. In the locality there were several monasteries for women and some or one of these may have appealed to her at some stage in her religious development. At a time when the focus of the apostolic life was being switched from the older monastic centres to newer forms of religious life Clare may have felt that life in an established monastery would have cut her off from the desire to meet the needs of the poor, whose ranks she wished to join, and did not associate her closely enough with the poverty experienced by the Son of God. Life in a wealthy monastery may have seemed like exchanging one form of security for another. Moreover, the Gospel texts proclaimed the poverty experienced by Jesus Christ and that became her ideal before which everything else was swept aside.

At the time that Clare was considering these matters Assisi was filled with talk about the remarkable change which had occurred in the life of Francis, a former leader of the young men of the city. The radical transformation in his behaviour had precipitated a crisis in his dealings with his family and had resulted in scenes enacted before Guido at the *vescovado*. In such a small city news of these events cannot have failed to reach Clare's ears. She must have followed his activities with interest and sympathy as he struggled to find the final form of his own vocation. Reports of his restoration of ancient churches around Assisi were known to her and she may even have seen him looking for stones and oil for his work at San Damiano; she provided food for those restoring the Portiuncula. The taunts of 'madman', when Francis entered the piazza, undoubtedly reached her sympathetic ears. When did she become aware of his prediction about the women whose virtues would one day make San Damiano famous? Was this before she left her parental home? The intervening two or three years transformed the situation as Francis slowly discerned his vocation. After hearing the decisive text from the Gospel being read at the Portiuncula Francis's life changed dramatically and he strove to live and preach as an apostle.

With a sense of wonder and awe she observed the growth of the nascent fraternity, which was providing so many examples of evangelical perfection. Francis's efficacious preaching made him and his ideas all the more fascinating. Once the fraternity began to grow beyond two or three it became clear that an extraordinary change was being wrought through Francis. She regarded him as the divinely ordained minister of a renewal which was being achieved in the Church. These reflections sharpened her interest in Francis's insights into the Gospel. His indefatigable pursuit of poverty led her to examine her own attachment to material possessions in the light of the new reforming currents in the Church, which were sustained by a prolonged meditation on the New Testament. His conduct was winning him new respect and admiration in the city and beyond. Within a short time some recruits were attracted and news of the solemn acts of renunciation by Bernard of Quintavalle and Giles in the principal squares in Assisi passed to Clare's ears. Such scenes recalled the events narrated in the Acts of the Apostles and caused much comment and consternation in the city. In her very own city Clare observed the evolution of what became one of the most significant developments in the history of religious life in the western Church. The new fraternity was consciously modelling itself on the life of the apostles and their divine master. This was a new model of religious life which was quite detached from the life of the monks and canons and within a short time it gained the approval of the pope, who in turn authorized the friars to preach. This permission meant that the churches of Assisi were thrown open to them.

After his conversion experience at the Portiuncula, Francis began to preach penance to all with great fervour of spirit and joy of mind, edifying his hearers with his simple words and his greatness of heart. The *Vita prima* gives a brief account of the power and directness of his preaching. His words were like a burning fire, penetrating the inmost reaches of the heart, and they filled the minds of all the hearers with admiration. Moreover, he seemed a completely changed man and became more visible in the city, where he began to speak in moving terms about the Gospel; soon the first recruits arrived. He first began to preach at San Giorgio where as a child he had learned to read and where he was for a time buried amid great honour. His biographers situate his ministry of preaching in the apostolic mould and his itinerant ministry in the cities, towns and villages of Umbria was ready-made for comparisons with the apostles. In an atmosphere of uncertainty and suspicion he preached peace and applied his teaching to all those who came to hear him. His ambitions to become a famous knight had been discarded and had been clothed in a new Christian significance of which he had never dreamed: he became the bravest knight of Christ. He was an animated preacher who spoke directly and fearlessly and his preaching enjoyed a wide success. In flamboyant terms Thomas of Celano states that men ran, and women ran too, clerics hurried and religious hastened that they might see and hear the holy man of God who seemed to all to be a man of another world. Francis was perceived as the divine instrument for the renewal of the Church in Umbria.[17]

The remarkable events which were happening around Francis filled Clare with a sense of wonder and she discerned the hand of God in the ministry being conducted by the small fraternity. All this heightened her interest in hearing him preach in the city's churches and she looked forward to these sermons, especially those preached in the cathedral. These homilies gave her a fuller understanding of the reforms which impelled him. His preaching was not colourless and insipid, because he was accustomed to spend the previous night in intense prayer. When Francis preached at San Rufino, he was accustomed to spend the night in prayer in a shelter in the garden belonging to the canons. Such intensive preparations for the ministry of the Word must have singled Francis out from the other local clerics, whose preparations lacked such a firm grounding in prayer and reflection. In an age when there were comparatively few sermons preached Francis's fervent message must have stood out like a beacon pointing the way to closer communion with Creator and creature. These sermons in the cathedral must have fascinated the adolescent Clare, whose own spiritual aspirations were in a state of evolution. Her biographer emphasizes her enjoyment on listening to sermons.[18]

CLARE'S CONVERSION

While Clare was giving more and more of her thoughts to the novel form of religious life initiated by Francis and his first followers, her family pursued other plans for her. Their wish to arrange a suitable marriage caused her a great deal of anxiety and she felt that time was not on her side, particularly because she was seeking the clarification of her future. The talk of marriage may have focused her mind much more clearly on what she wanted to do in order to satisfy her spiritual yearnings. All talk of marriage was parried, although she hinted that she would enter into marriage at a later date,[19] a fact which was ripe for exploitation by her biographers, who interpreted this as a reference to her future espousal of the religious life. Pietro de Damiano from Assisi attested that Clare's mother, father and relatives wanted her to marry someone great and powerful, in accordance with her noble family. Aged 17 or 18, Clare could not be convinced, because her heart was elsewhere.[20] Lord Ranieri de Bernardo of Assisi was not only her unsuccessful suitor, but also a witness at the process of canonization. He confirmed that many of her family begged her to accept his hand, but his overtures and proposals were firmly rejected. By this stage she had obviously made up her mind that her future was to be a religious. She not only refused the offer of his hand, but also proceeded to encourage Ranieri to turn his back on the values of society.[21] Did she exhort him to become a friar? Her determination to avoid a grand and advantageous marriage serves as one of the earliest demonstrations of her resolve to withdraw from her family and to live in the poverty experienced by Jesus Christ and his mother. Throughout the remaining years of her life this unshakeable determination expressed itself again and again in resisting any measures intended to detach her from her ideals.

Rufino was one of Francis's first followers and accompanied him to La Verna where he witnessed the stigmata. He was Clare's cousin[22] and may have been instrumental in arranging an introduction between the two future saints, though there is no indication that he took part in the series of secret meetings. While Francis was beginning to enjoy some fame, he heard the good reports about Clare's qualities and wished to see her. The desire to meet was mutual and Clare had numerous questions to put to Francis. Had Rufino informed Francis about her ideals, asceticism and compassion for the poor? Such a meeting would have been deemed inappropriate for a variety of reasons in that society and opposition from her family was anticipated. Hence there was a clandestine character to their prolonged discussions, which were carefully orchestrated to avoid any suspicion on the part of Clare's family.[23] Their arrangements were so successful that Clare's flight from home came as a bolt from the blue. Her sister Beatrice, who later joined her at San Damiano, testified that after Francis had heard the fame of Clare's holiness, he went many times to preach to her.[24]

Clare's companion on many of these exploratory discussions was Bona. In these meetings several subjects were explored and it is a disappointment that the various witnesses in the process of canonization generally confined themselves to a single observation: that Francis encouraged Clare to turn her back on society and to embrace the life of evangelical poverty. Among the topics under discussion were Francis's understanding of the Gospel and its implications for him and the small band of friars. The conduct of the Son of God and the apostles was examined at length as well as Francis's deepening insights into the reasons why his divine master chose a life of poverty. His understanding of the apostolic life and the imitation of Christ must have been explored at length because it formed the very basis of the fraternity. His confidence in divine providence and his reliance on the literal understanding of the sacred Scriptures, which had so revolutionized his life, were explained at length. The conversations included the nature of the religious vocation and its relationship with society; the centrality of evangelical poverty as a means of personal emancipation and enrichment as well as an antidote to the greed which was manifestly creating divisions in society; and the purity of the evangelical ideal which required a return to the norms of the first Christian communities with an appropriate sense of detachment from material goods. And finally the discussion turned to Clare's act of renunciation and the form of the commitment which she would make to serve God in accordance with the teaching of the Gospel. Bona adds the detail that Philip, who had accompanied Francis, joined him in urging Clare to unite herself to her Saviour.[25] Sister Frances Teresa comments that the direction offered by Francis confirmed what was already in Clare's heart.[26]

The full discussion of the spiritual matters was complemented by more practical issues which required a decision in principle. Arrangements had to be made for Clare's departure from home and her profession. There was the question of how she would take her leave of Assisi, whose gates were locked after curfew. Agreement was reached on the date of her departure from home, but this must have been conditional upon episcopal consent and licence. Approaches had to be made to Guido for the appropriate authorization for the ceremony of initiation and to the monastery of San Paolo in Bastia for temporary hospitality. Plans were made for Clare's nocturnal journey from the city to the woods where she was to be met by a group of friars, who would escort her to the chapel where she would make her commitment to live in the manner of the apostles and their divine master.

Clare decided to act on the advice of the man whom she regarded as a divine channel. She accepted him as her mentor after God, as her guide on the pilgrimage through life; and the *Vita prima* proclaims that she was converted to God through the counsel of Francis.[27] Like Bernard of Quintavalle and Giles, she was required to renounce her goods and distribute them to the poor. Her first biographer discloses that she sold the paternal inheritance that would have come to her, keeping nothing of its worth for herself.[28] Sister Beatrice testified that Clare sold her entire inheritance and part of that belonging to herself and gave it to the poor. Because Clare was the oldest daughter and had no brothers it might have been easier for her to have access to her patrimony. The sources are not specific on the precise point at which this was done. It is not clear whether she divested herself of her goods before joining the community. If so, this had to be accomplished in a way which did not arouse any suspicion. Pietro de Damiano commented that she sold her inheritance and gave it to the poor.[29]

As Palm Sunday approached, Clare discussed with Francis the details of her conversion and what form it should take. He instructed her that on the highly symbolic feast day she should take part in the celebration of the liturgy in the usual way and on that night she should leave her parental home. This plan was implemented and on the appointed day Clare, radiant with festive splendour, entered the cathedral, where the patron saint was buried. She knew that she was entering the cathedral for the last time; there she had been baptized and received the Eucharist for the first time and listened to Francis's stirring sermons, which had led her to this moment of decision. As the ceremonies progressed she became absorbed in the movement of the liturgy. In the customary way members of her family and her neighbours advanced slowly towards the altar to receive the newly blessed palms but she remained in her place. For such a pious young woman not to join the queue for the palms would have set tongues wagging in the small city. Within minutes an even more remarkable event occurred: Guido, the vicar of San Rufino, watched her closely and noticed that she had not come forward. He then descended the steps and walked to her place, putting the palm in her hands.[30] Here was a gesture rippling with symbolism and historians have long interpreted this unexpected action as an indication of some communication between the bishop and the two saints.

The daughter of Bernardo da Suppo of Assisi was staying in the Favarone household on the night of Clare's departure; later she joined the community at San Damiano and took the name of Christina. When the household retired that night, Clare seized her opportunity and made her way to the door. She feared that her escape would be impeded and so did not leave the house through the usual exit. She left by the 'door of the dead', which had been barricaded with heavy wooden beams and an iron bar so that it could not be opened even by a large number of men. Aided by divine grace, she removed the obstacles and opened the door. On the following morning, when many people saw that door opened, they were astonished at how a young girl left the house in such a manner.[31]

Clare hurried to Santa Maria degli Angeli, leaving behind her home with its material and emotional security, her former lifestyle and her city. The friars were awaiting her arrival and went out to receive her with torches. At the small chapel, which was Francis's spiritual home, plans were made for her ceremony of initiation. Her hair was shorn by the hands of the friars and she swapped her fine clothes for the mean garment of poverty. These two actions signalled her break with the past and her commitment to espouse the values of the Gospel according to the insights of Francis. This pledge served as the equivalent to the scene enacted before the bishop when Francis solemnly renounced his desire to continue in the world of commerce. The Marian dedication of the Portiuncula chapel and Mary's role in the gestation of both communities of friars and sisters were emphasized by Clare's first biographer.[32] Her decision to throw in her lot with this new form of religious inspiration was rich in symbolism. The protracted and clandestine exploratory talks with Francis had come to an end and she had taken her decision.

The celebration of Palm Sunday was an ideal day for Clare to abandon her home and embrace a life of poverty. The sacred liturgy marks the beginning of

Holy Week with the triumphal entry of the Messiah into Jerusalem and then leads into the celebration of the week, with its prolonged meditation on the means of the redemption of the human race. Thus a note of rejoicing stands at the beginning of the week leading up to the drama of the cross and resurrection. As Jesus Christ entered Jerusalem to the acclaim of the crowds, so Clare donned her fine garments for the last time and cast her eyes around the cathedral, reflecting on her short life, which was now about to take a fundamental change. Her sense of joy in pledging herself to God was tinged with the sorrow of parting from her mother and sisters, whom she loved so dearly. The fact that she was to be joined by her mother and two sisters at San Damiano indicates the strength of the family bonds. Nonetheless, as she accompanied her mother and sisters to the cathedral for the last time, Clare cannot have foreseen that the family would be reunited in this unexpected and unusual manner at San Damiano. The act of the bishop in presenting her with the palm symbolized that her new life would not be without its moments of suffering, pain and frustration. Her desire for martyrdom grew stronger in her later years and perhaps the reception of the palm symbolized that she would identify herself with her divine master. Just as the Son of God had laid aside the more triumphal trappings of his ministry in the last days of his life, so Clare left her own home and embraced a life of asceticism, penance and contemplation. Her decision was a more hazardous one than that of Bernard, Giles and the other recruits. While they were joining the beginnings of a community, Clare had no such assurance of like-minded company among women and there was no guarantee that recruits would follow. This was an act of immense faith and trust in God's promises, a manifestation of her absolute confidence in divine providence. She overcame the barriers which blocked the door of the dead and this display of remarkable strength and determination symbolized the persistence which marked her lifelong battle to remain at the heart of the Franciscan fraternity, where she would defend the ideals of her mentor and friend. This palm may be seen as a foretaste of the lifelong struggle which she waged to protect the purity of Francis's ideals.

TEMPORARY REFUGE AND FAMILY OPPOSITION

Clare made her way from the sleeping city of Assisi and hurried to the tiny chapel of the Portiuncula, where Francis's religious life had its definitive beginning. There she received the insignia of holy penance from her mentor, but amidst the euphoria surrounding the admission of such a noble recruit there were remaining questions of some urgency about how she might live; she was embarking upon an entirely new path. She was not taking a vow which would admit her to a noble and financially secure monastery, where she might live in a style befitting her aristocratic background. How would she live? Like Francis, she had exchanged security, with all its benefits and numerous privileges, for a life of uncertainty, inspired and sustained only by a profound trust in the divine promises. The very ceremony was an act of absolute faith in the divine providence proclaimed by the Gospel. After the ceremony Francis immediately led her to the monastery of San Paolo, where she would remain until a more permanent home might be found for her. His plans were no more than provisional, because he was seeking temporary monastic refuge for a young woman newly consecrated to the religious life.

The monastery of San Paolo delle Ancelle di Dio, more commonly known as delle Abbadesse, was famous throughout the region for its wealth, influence and noble status. Papal bulls enumerated its estates: the fields on both sides of the Chiagio beyond the pool of water, and beyond the Ripa road; the men and lands of the *castello* of Isola Romano; houses, cottages and gardens in Assisi in the *contrade* of Santo Stefano, Sant'Andrea and San Pietro; olive orchards below the walls; vineyards in Mosciole, Fiano and Compagna; the rights on the chapels of San Giovanni in Campiglione, San Bartolomeo del Chiagio and Santa Lucia, the chapel of Sant'Andrea della Valle outside the city of Foligno, with all its possessions. A bull of Innocent III, dated 5 May 1201, addressed to the abbess and sisters, confirmed that the monastery followed the Rule of St Benedict and enumerated their special privileges. No one could impose tithes or exactions on them; the bishop of Assisi was forbidden to put their chapel under interdict and, even then, they had the right to celebrate the divine offices with doors closed, without songs or sound of bells; they were able to receive free women from secular life who had been converted to their Rule and they were empowered to reject every objection or claim made in opposition to their entrance; there were severe prohibitions against anyone molesting them. Those who did so and persevered in their offences would, after the third warning, incur interdict and divine anathema.

The advent of Clare puzzled some of the more traditional members of this community, who were schooled in the conviction that their own form of religious observance was the summit of perfection; they were accustomed to draw financial support from the monastery's estates and lands. Like the nuns, Clare was driven by the desire for deeper communion with her Creator, but her vision of the apostolic life differed sharply. The properties and privileges listed by Innocent III constituted an obstacle for Clare, who sought to liberate herself from what she had come regard as a constraint, something which effectively partitioned society between those who had possessions and those who lacked them. Her perception of the religious life was based upon a rejection of such security and an identification with her divine master, who was not among the holders of property. Material comforts and financial security had been part of her life for the better part of two decades and she was determined to leave these behind in her search for a form of life which corresponded more closely to the Gospels. The older form of religious life had no appeal to Clare, who was eager to cast herself upon providence, taking no thought for tomorrow. Indeed, she would spend the next forty years resisting those who attempted to temper the rigour of her poverty.

Clare's family might have reluctantly permitted her to join a well-established and celebrated Benedictine monastery in the locality. But they could not countenance her decision to align herself with Francis and his small band of followers, whose own future was absolutely insecure in material terms. When it became known that she had slipped from the house at the dead of night to join the company of the friars, her relations were incensed. Their anger may have been intensified on account of delicate matrimonial negotiations for Clare's hand. Did they suspect that she had eloped with someone unsuitable? How did they discover her whereabouts? Had she entered a monastery? Had her relatives made a systematic search of the city and its environs for her? Someone may have seen her slipping through the night to the Portiuncula or accompanying Francis to Bastia. Whatever the precise source of information on Clare, the intelligence was very accurate and so her vocation to the consecrated life was not a complete surprise.

Clare's family hastened to the monastery determined to persuade her to put the regrettable episode behind her and to return to her home on the piazza di San Rufino. Their attempt to take her home again, like a recalcitrant schoolgirl, betrayed a serious misunderstanding of her strength of character. She was not a woman who was likely to admit her mistake and meekly return home. This young woman of immense courage would face up to greater dangers in the years ahead, when she would resist the marauding armies of Vitale d'Aversa and the efforts of popes from Honorius III to Innocent IV, who wished to grant her security and possessions. The scene was set for a confrontation which would demonstrate her steady nerve and iron will. She was shown into the presence of members of her family, who felt that her folly had dishonoured both herself and her family. First, persuasion and blandishments were tried and then promises were made, but they achieved nothing. Her family had tried to prevail upon her to give up such a worthless vocation that was unbecoming to her class and unprecedented in her family. In their frustration they had recourse to more violent methods and attempted to drag her from the chapel. Despite the rights and privileges of the monastery, there is no hint that the nuns tried to intervene. Instead, Clare was left alone to face the violence of her family. She responded in a defiant manner, clinging to the altar cloths. She displayed her resolve to embark upon a new form of life by lifting her veil to reveal a shorn head. She was absolutely adamant that she would in no way be torn from her desire to devote herself primarily to the evangelical life.[33] This fearless show of determination foreshadowed her unshakeable resolve to live in accordance with her own insights into the Gospel. There may also have been an element of expediency in her relations' retreat because the bull of Innocent III recognized the broad rights of asylum at the monastery and forbade the use of violence under the pain of excommunication.[34]

The contest which took place at the monastery hastened the moment of Clare's departure. Did the abbess, fearful of any repeated appeal by Clare's family, oblige her to leave? After only a few days Francis, along with Bernard and Philip, removed her to the church of Sant'Angelo in Panzo, where her mind was not completely at peace.[35] Beatrice, Clare's sister, testified that she stayed there for a little time.[36] After some days Clare realized that she had not gained very much by changing from the monastery by the river to the community on the side of the mountain. The community's litigation with Bishop Guido would have seemed the antithesis of the evangelical path which Francis mapped out for his followers. These nuns quarrelled with the chapter of the cathedral and with the bishop over the jurisdiction of the church, about the olive groves of Salcaiano and the pastures of Mount Subasio. The very air was heavy with a dull prosperity, and in it there was no room for mystic rushes of renunciation.[37] Such conflict would have seemed repugnant to Clare, who nurtured ideals which sprang from the pure root of the Gospel rather than the search for material security.

Clare soon began to miss her sister Catherine, with whom she had enjoyed a special rapport in their family home. She now prayed especially that she might join her in the search for union with God after the inspiration of Francis. A line of communication was opened between Clare and her sister in the family home; friars were undoubtedly among the intermediaries through whom arrangements were made for Catherine to follow Clare, who had left home only sixteen days earlier. Her relations can hardly have had time to lick their wounds after failing to detach Clare from her resolve to become a religious before they faced a second crisis. Clare and Catherine had hardly spent much time together in their common resolve to walk in the footprints of their divine master before the repetition of the ugly scene which had been enacted some days earlier at Bastia. Twelve men hastened up the mountain to Sant'Angelo. When their blandishments had been unsuccessful, they turned to violence and tried to drag Catherine away by force. In her plight she appealed to Clare who prayed that her sister should be given constancy of mind. In a miracle which resembled the attempts to carry the sarcophagus of San Rufino to the old cathedral of Santa Maria Maggiore, the twelve men were unable to move Catherine from the spot. After this display of aggression Clare implored her uncle and his companions to desist and leave Catherine to her care. Afterwards Catherine committed herself perpetually to the service of the Son of God. Francis, who had probably heard of the violence, went to the monastery where he cut off her hair as a symbol of her new vocation.[38]

M. Bartoli believes that at the end of the tussle Catherine received the tonsure at the hands of Francis and that it was probably then that she was given the name of Agnes by which she is better known. Perhaps it was due to these vicissitudes that Francis was drawn to take a more direct interest in the struggles of Clare and her sister,[39] although the events of his own conversion were relatively fresh. Nonetheless, Clare and Agnes undoubtedly regarded him as a prophetical figure through whom wondrous things were being achieved for the Church in Umbria. Now that Clare was no longer alone in her desire to pursue the perfection of the Gospel the prospect of a small community became the more viable and there must have been discussions on this point between Francis and Clare. Guido, too, was drawn into the discussions, from the moment that he presented Clare with the blessed palm in the cathedral and was publicly involved in the formation of a community of women pledged to live the Gospel according to the insights and instruction of Francis. This new religious community in his diocese attracted his interest and sympathy and, as in the early religious life of Francis, there would be instances when he would intervene.

SAN DAMIANO AND THE VOCATIONS OF FRANCIS AND CLARE

Conversations between Francis, Clare and Guido led to the decision to settle Clare and Agnes at San Damiano. The first biographer of Clare provides a brief report that on the advice of Francis the two sisters moved to San Damiano where the order of Poor Ladies was begun. There is no further mention of the priest who had lived at San Damiano; he may have died in the intervening years or withdrawn in order to make way for the sisters' arrival. Guido had placed the church at the sisters' disposal and the community was soon augmented by women from Assisi and Umbria. The documentary sources for this period of Clare's life are frustratingly sparse, though it is clear that Francis played a central role in the early formation of the community, schooling these aristocratic women in the poverty which he had discerned in the Gospels.

Clare consistently proclaimed that she had been converted through the preaching and example of Francis, who was a guiding influence from his first sermons in San Giorgio and San Rufino until the end of his life. He had persuaded her to follow Jesus Christ in the most literal manner and was central to the arrangements for her departure from home. He had clothed her as a religious at the Portiuncula and found temporary refuge for her in the two religious communities. The process was repeated in Agnes's profession and then Francis once again entered into discussion with Guido to obtain the use of San Damiano for Clare and Agnes. The sisters were Francis's vocations and in the earliest days he seems to have spent a great deal of time at San Damiano as he gradually instructed them in the ways of poverty and asceticism. His early guidance took shape in the Rule of life which he composed for the sisters. This primitive Rule for the sisters may have resembled the first Rule which he had drawn up for presentation to Innocent III. Clare promised obedience to Francis and never deviated from that promise, even when she was confronted by compromise and danger. For example, in the aftermath of the Fourth Lateran

Council, with its ban on the composition of new Rules for religious, Francis overruled Clare's natural disinclination for the office of abbess and obliged her to accept the office, even though she had previously declined it. Sister Pacifica testified that, at the prayers and insistence of Francis, who almost forced her, Clare accepted the direction and government of the sisters.[40]

Clare reveals that, when Francis realized that the sisters at San Damiano delighted in poverty, hard work, trial, shame or contempt of the world, he wrote a form of life for them and promised them his loving care and solicitude. Throughout his life he and the friars had fulfilled that promise. Her Rule incorporated Francis's exhortation that the sisters should never deviate from the poverty which they had promised:

> shortly before his death he [Francis] once more wrote his last will for us that we – or those, as well, who would come after us – would never turn aside from the holy poverty we had embraced. He said: 'I, little brother Francis, wish to follow the life and poverty of our most high Lord Jesus Christ and of His holy mother and to persevere in this until the end; and I ask and counsel you, my ladies, to live always in this most holy life and in poverty. And keep most careful watch that you never depart from this by reason of the teaching and advice of anyone.'[41]

The sisters' determination to live in an evangelical manner made a strong impression on Francis, whose respect for them grew.

Clare had been accustomed to take no food on three days in the week, that is, Monday, Wednesday and Friday. It is not surprising that such rigour, observed over a long period of time, reduced her to weakness, consumed her strength and weakened the vigour of her body. The sisters bewailed her failing health. Francis and Guido ordered Clare to discontinue the deadly fast of three days, insisting that she should let no day pass without taking at least an ounce and a half of bread. Agnes, the daughter of Oportulo de Bernardo of Assisi, gave evidence that before she had joined the community about 1220 she had heard that Clare had been accustomed to make her bed of twigs. However, this level of asceticism began to take its toll on her health and accordingly it, too, was banned by Francis, who obliged her to use a bed of straw.[42]

San Damiano is a place sacred to the memory of both Francis and Clare, who recognized the beginning of their own vocations in that rustic chapel which had fallen into disrepair. Francis's biographers leave us in no doubt that it was a place of immense psychological importance to him as he took his first unsteady steps in the service of his new master. He returned from Foligno intent on restoring the ancient chapel and was obliged to acknowledge his own frailty and fear. The would-be soldier and knight was reduced to hiding from his father for the period of one month. This weakness and cowardice, which he bitterly lamented, convinced him that he could no longer rely solely upon his own efforts. He had to confront his own limitations and compensate by relying more on God's strength and grace. Following his appearance before the episcopal tribunal,

Francis returned to San Damiano and gave himself to the restoration of the ancient chapel. Slowly he set about the task of rebuilding, perhaps to the amazement of the priest who celebrated Mass there. On some occasions he begged for stones in Assisi and on others he purchased them; there is some indication that he stirred up some enthusiasm in Assisi for the restoration. His deep sacramental sense found expression in the oil which he provided to burn continually before the image of the crucified Christ, who had directed him to restore the neglected church. The divine mandate for him to rebuild the church ensured that the tiny chapel had a permanent place in his affections.

The later biography's inclusion of the saint's prediction that San Damiano would one day be graced by women dedicated to the pursuit of Christian perfection placed the beginnings of his vocation within the context of a wider process of renewal of the Church in Umbria. J. Dalarun treats the prophecy as an episode of primary importance in the evaluation of Francis's relations with the Poor Ladies and raises the question of whether the saint had envisaged the foundation of the sisters' community.[43] Clare was convinced that the sisters' religious life sprang from the same root as the ideals which animated Francis and she carefully recorded the latter's prediction about the emergence of the sorority during the rebuilding of San Damiano.[44] His prophecy lent a divine dimension to the growth of the sisters' community and persuaded them that they, too, were playing their part in the restoration of the wider Church, a claim made on the sisters' behalf by Clare's first biographer. He attached a particular significance to her making San Damiano her home and the fact that Francis had laboured to restore that church, had offered money for that purpose to the priest there and had heard the voice from the cross directing him to rebuild the church.

San Damiano was situated close to the ancient chapel of San Feliciano who had laboured to plant the seed of the Gospel in the third century. Local tradition puts the beginnings of Christianity in Assisi close to San Damiano. Francis and Clare were groomed on the accounts of the heroism of the martyrs of Assisi and Umbria and these may have been instrumental in promoting the highest ideals of Christian witness. Were they conscious that their reforms represented a flowering of the faith which had been preached by the aged bishop, Feliciano? The biographers of Francis and Clare regarded them as divine instruments for the renewal of the Church in Umbria and then throughout western Europe. The flowering of their vocation and their friendship was closely connected with the wayside chapel of San Damiano. While the biographers varied in their treatment of the sacred bond which united the two saints, Francis and Clare saw their lives as intertwined in some mysterious way, which they themselves may not have fully understood. A partnership was born between them on the basis of their common commitment to the literal understanding of the Gospel. Mutual respect and admiration bound them together into one of the most famous and fruitful friendships in the history of the Church. This was a partnership of equals, who regarded each other as channels of divine inspiration and grace. In moments of stress and anxiety they turned to each other for support. Francis's prophecy that San Damiano would become famous on account of the sisters' heroic witness to the Gospel may be seen in terms of the immediate future. The settlement of the expanding sorority would have satisfied the conditions of his prophecy. That prediction might, however, be viewed in the longer term and again it was amply fulfilled by the towering role which Clare played after the death of Francis in 1226. Although the friars were unable to resolve their ideological disputes and there was some evidence that relaxations were not unwelcome, the sacred flame had passed to Clare and Francis's early followers turned to her as a sign of hope. The admiration and reverence with which Francis's biographers speak of the constancy and strength of the sorority offer some support for the view that the increasingly divided order was being inspired and sustained by the community at San Damiano, which stimulated renewal among both women and men in Umbria. Thus Clare and the sisters were perceived as the agents for the rebuilding of the Church, fulfilling the messages about the renewal of the Church granted to Francis as he prayed at San Damiano and to Innocent III in his dream at the Lateran palace.

FRANCIS'S RELIANCE ON CLARE

The friendship which bound Clare and Francis together passed through different stages during its two decades. It began with her interest in the remarkable change in his life and the events which were taking place around him in Assisi. She was profoundly touched by the stirring words of a most powerful preacher, who was unmistakably a prophetical figure. Her first biographer points out that Francis had heard of Clare's qualities and wished to meet her. When she settled at San Damiano, her virtues and uncompromising witness to evangelical poverty deeply impressed him. Just as he had initially been indebted to Guido and Ugolino, who became his friends, so Clare quickly became Francis's equal. The friendship between them was based on equality with moments in which each of them displayed a particular strength or leadership. Francis respected her ability to lead the community and deferred to her judgement on certain matters. Moreover, he came to depend upon her more and more in the period following his return from the East, when his health began to fail and there were growing divisions within the community. While the biographers were circumspect about direct contact between the two saints, Clare remained the one person who had shared Francis's ideals and the one on whom he increasingly relied in his later years.

While some of the most influential theologians of the thirteenth century assigned a weaker role to women, Francis had no doubt about Clare's holiness and her position as a channel of grace: she was unmistakably his equal, his partner in the reinvigoration of the Church. This sacred bond was fruitful for both Francis and Clare. One occasion, and there may have been more of this kind, on which he turned to her for advice and prayers was well documented. While he was being tortured by uncertainty about whether he should be a hermit or an evangelist he asked for the prayers of two contemplatives. One of those whose prayerful intercession he enlisted was Clare. She and the sisters were invited to pray and ascertain what God wanted him to do with his life; he had also sought the prayers of Sylvester, who was living on the mountain above Assisi. Bonaventure regarded Clare and Sylvester as channels of the Holy Spirit; they both advised Francis that his vocation was to go out and preach as a herald.[45] The fact that she mediated the divine will to him assured her of a place of prominence and undoubtedly augmented his reverence for her. A further manifestation of his admiration and reverence towards her was his decision to associate her with the ministry of healing. He sent her a friar who was afflicted with madness. At Francis's command she made the sign of the cross over Stephen, and permitted him to sleep for a while in the place where she was accustomed to pray. Refreshed by a little sleep, he got up healed and returned to Francis.[46] By this stage the pupil was well on the way to equality with her mentor.

Towards the end of his life Francis was nursed at San Damiano for a relatively long period. His companions report that two years before his death, when he was very ill, especially from his eye illness, a little cell made of rushes was constructed for him; this lean-to was attached to one side of the 'monastery. The minister general, seeing that he was so afflicted by his eye illness, ordered him to seek a cure for his eyes. Francis lay there for 50 days in the winter and could no longer see by day or by night, but always remained in the house and in the little cell in darkness. A permanent pain in his eyes deprived him of his rest day and night and this exacerbated his other infirmities. There were mice both in the house and in his cell and these ran backwards and forwards and over him, robbing him of sleep and interrupting his prayers. There is some evidence that he succumbed to self-pity, perhaps depression, until an inner voice directed him to triumph over his sufferings and to rejoice. His joy and creativity returned. Even though his eyesight was deteriorating, he saw the world and all its beauty with a new clarity and appreciation. This reinvigorated spirit led him to produce one of the most famous pieces of poetry, the *Canticle of Brother Sun*, which celebrates the bounty of creation and was employed to break the deadlock between the bishop and the *podestà*, whose daughter was a member of the community at San Damiano.

Sister Frances Teresa, who notes that almost any friary would have been more comfortable than the mice-infested hut at San Damiano, believes that he went there to be near Clare.[47] In this period Francis was entering into a more contemplative phase and was liberated from the constraints of the ministry of leadership. This prolonged visit was an unexpected bonus for both Francis and Clare and gave them a precious opportunity for daily contact, and ample time to reflect upon their developing understanding of the theological dimensions of voluntary poverty in imitation of their divine master and to consider how best their common ideal might be preserved and transmitted to their disciples. By this stage the fraternity had expanded at a remarkable rate and the sorority was beginning to spread throughout Italy and beyond, albeit at a slower pace. During those days he composed some words of consolation with an accompanying tune for the Poor Ladies. This brief exhortation, written in the vernacular, may be quoted in full:

> Listen, poor little ones called by the Lord,
> who have come together from many parts and provinces:
> Live always in truth,
> that you may die in obedience.
> Do not look at the life outside,
> for that of the Spirit is better.
> I beg you through great love,
> to use with discretion
> the alms which the Lord gives you.
> Those who are weighed down by sickness
> and the others who are wearied because of them,
> all of you: bear it in peace.
> For you will sell this fatigue at a very high price
> and each one [of you] will be crowned queen
> in heaven with the Virgin Mary.[48]

A further reason for writing the song was to console the sisters, who were very grieved at his illness. Because his illness prevented Francis from visiting or comforting them he wanted these words passed on to them by his companions. His thoughts passed to the sisters at San Damiano, expressing his appreciation and support for their place in the Franciscan family. He encouraged them to be of one mind and live together in charity because they had been converted to Jesus Christ by his example and preaching when the friars were as yet few. Their conversion and way of life not only ennobled and edified the order of friars, whose little plant they were, but also God's universal Church. As Francis knew, from the beginning of their conversion they had led and were still leading a very hard and poor life, both by choice and by necessity. Therefore, he entreated them, as the Lord had gathered them together from many parts into one congregation dedicated to holy charity, holy poverty and holy obedience, always to live and die in these virtues: in particular they should provide for their bodies wisely, with cheerfulness and thankfulness, out of the alms that God gave them, and most of all see that those who were well should be patient in the labours they bore for their sick sisters, and the sick patient in their sickness and in the unavoidable suffering they had to bear.[49]

Francis's companions provide a rather refreshing account of the last exchanges between the two saints. The hagiographical circumspection, so conspicuous in the *Vita secunda,* was entirely absent from their recollections and they spoke with a natural simplicity about the bond between the two saints. They were not afraid to report the emotion with which Clare prepared to face the death of her friend. She was inconsolable at the prospect of not meeting Francis, her mentor, her comforter in soul and body. She had sent a friar to the Portiuncula in order to convey her distress to the dying Francis, who loved Clare and the sisters with a paternal affection on account of their holy lives. He wrote her his blessing in a letter to comfort her and absolved her from all failings, if she had any, in obeying his commands and wishes and the commands and wishes of the Son of God. In order to console her and the sisters he prophesied that they would see him shortly after his death.[50] Did Clare and the sisters nurture the hope of seeing him alive? Or was his message interpreted as a reference to the funeral procession?

The friars remembered Francis's message to Clare and arranged for his body to be borne to Assisi via San Damiano. The funeral cortège wound its way up the hill from the Portiuncula and Francis's corpse was placed in the sisters' church. The little window through which the sisters were accustomed to communicate was opened. When the lid of the coffin was opened, Clare and the sisters sighed and sorrowfully and tearfully looked upon the body of their mentor. They hailed him as the father of the poor, the lover of poverty, and kissed his hands.[51] The sisters' sense of bereavement was no doubt exacerbated by an awareness that their special guide and protector had passed from their midst. Francis had provided the community with its inspiration to serve Jesus Christ in poverty and simplicity. The problems which had occurred during his absence in the East had been addressed. The sisters were conscious that without Francis's inspirational leadership they would have to face many dangers and sensed a renewal of the attempts to detach them from his community; perhaps their Franciscan identity would be placed under further strain. The struggles of the last seven years reminded them of Francis's influence with Cardinal Ugolino and other ecclesiastics.

CLARE IN THOMAS OF CELANO'S BIOGRAPHIES

Thomas of Celano voices the friars' immense admiration and reverence for Clare and the sisters. The *Vita prima* was both poetic and fulsome in its commendation of the witness given by Clare and the sisters. The *Vita secunda* gives a restrained report of Clare's qualities and Francis's dealings with the community; the biographer seems to be more concerned to ensure that the friars kept distant relations with the sisters. While the earlier biography pays tribute to the sisters, the second one is suffused with a caution which the founder would neither have recognized nor approved. The uncertainty surrounding the sisters' constitutional future in the 1240s was partially responsible for the more restrained account of the friars' contact with the sisters. Despite the fact that the biographer seems to be expounding the friars' Rule, he emphasizes Francis's promise of continual assistance for the sisters, whom he recognized as an integral part of the Franciscan community.

The Vita prima

In the context of Francis's conversion the first biographer chronicles the restoration of San Damiano, the first work undertaken by the saint after he had left home. Clare's conversion was presented as the fruit of his own penitence and the symbolism of the sisters settling on the site of a key event in Francis's own vocation was not lost on the first biographer. This sacred place in Franciscan history was associated with ecclesiastical renewal on a grand scale through the arrival of the sisters and the speedy rise of a new community. The biographer then proceeds to enumerate the qualities of the sisters and Dalarun finds traces of this encomium in the bull of Clare's canonization.[52] Both Francis and Clare were determined to base their lives upon the teaching of the Son of God and the grace and strength which he made available. The glowing account of Clare was all the more remarkable because it was written a quarter of a century before her death and at a time when Gregory IX was anxiously trying to persuade her to dilute the rigour of her community's attachment to poverty. Saluted as the foundation of the spiritual edifice, the cloistered Clare exercised a far-reaching apostolate because she lived to the advantage of many and as an example to a countless multitude. A series of contrasts emphasized her virtues: she was of noble parentage, but she was more noble by grace; she was a virgin in the body, but most chaste in the mind; a youth in age, but mature in spirit; steadfast in purpose and most ardent in her desire for divine love; endowed with wisdom and excelling in humility. The sisters' virtues were then listed, though the biographer concedes that his limited understanding does not permit him to offer an adequate description of these qualities. The biographer speaks enthusiastically about the virtues of the enclosed sisters. Despite his undoubted respect for the sisters, he does not pay much attention to the marks of the new movement which Francis and Clare had inaugurated. From the vantage point of 1228 or 1229 the biographer took a benign view of the constitutions which Ugolino had prepared for them, though it would not have been easy for him to criticize the reigning pope who had commissioned the biography. This litany of Clare's praises closes with the prayer that this work of God may continue and attain a holy end.[53]

The biographer's commendation of the sisters' virtues does not single out their poverty, which was perceived as a distinctive aspect of their lives and one which visibly distinguished them from contemporary monasticism. In the life of Francis, famed for his voluntary poverty, it is remarkable that the biographer did not linger to offer a fuller report of the poverty prevailing at San Damiano. While he spends much more time on the question of poverty in the later biography, he treats it as one of the numerous virtues with which Francis was clothed. This may have been because an attempt was being made to show that Francis and Clare were adorned with a variety of gifts, of which poverty was merely one. On the other hand, it may signify that by this stage the friars were celebrated for various reasons and were not known primarily on account of their restoration of apostolic poverty. The tribute to the sisters was presented in brief and the impression was given that the biographer was eager to demonstrate the sisters' credentials as religious. The virtues enumerated in the *Vita prima* reflect monasticism in general more than a Franciscan adaptation and Dalarun detects vestiges of a monastic outlook in some of the advice dispensed by Thomas of Celano.[54]

The Vita secunda

The establishment of a celibate clergy was one of the major objectives of medieval reformers, though throughout the thirteenth century they met some deeply entrenched resistance. Because the decrees of the Fourth Lateran Council set the agenda for the friars' programme, it was incumbent upon them to behave in an exemplary manner and this concern shapes the *Vita secunda*'s treatment of Francis's relations with Clare and the sisters. While the praise heaped upon the sisters in the *Vita prima* caused some blushes and embarrassment at San Damiano, the later biography puzzled them because it gave such a cautious and circumspect version of Francis's dealings with the community which he had inspired and nurtured. This account owed more to the biographer's anxieties lest the friars be too closely associated with the sisters than to the conduct of a magnetic personality who had brought the Gospel to life for countless people. The biographer wished to provide guidance to friars in the 1240s and to ensure that any whiff of suspicion and scandal was avoided.

Thomas of Celano reflects that it would be unfitting to pass over the memory of the spiritual edifice which Francis founded at San Damiano under the guidance of the Holy Spirit after he had repaired the building. The Holy Spirit had prophesied that the Church should be renewed by the sisters. Virgins had gathered there from various parts of the world and professed the greatest perfection, adorning themselves with every virtue. This passage confirms that the biographer believed that the Church was being renewed not only by the friars, but also by the contemplative apostolate of the sisters. The image chosen by the biographer leads him to exaggerate the universal impact of the sisters, many of whom were drawn from Umbria. Francis gave the sisters his affection in the Holy Spirit by caring for them, though he gradually withdrew from them. This withdrawal was explained as something which was feasible when Francis had recognized the sisters' devoted service of Jesus Christ, promising his help and advice as well as that of his friars.

The friars' speculation about the reason for Francis's infrequent visits to San Damiano was a topic of some concern in the 1240s and the question was being raised about the provision of the care which he had promised them. These issues intrude into the second biography, which firmly rejected the suggestion that the saint lacked affection or respect for the sisters. The biographer carefully laid out the saint's guidelines for the appointment of friars to assist the sisters: such friars should be unwilling and most reluctant to take on this charge and they should be spiritual men, proved by a worthy and long religious life. Those who presumed to make unauthorized visits to monasteries of Poor Clares were severely punished. In a strongly apologetic note the biographer asserts that throughout his life Francis remained true to his promise to provide for the sisters and reiterated it on his death bed. Thus, the biographer nails his colours to the mast on this controversial question and champions the sisters' cause in attributing to the founder the conviction that a single spirit had taken both the friars and the sisters from society to serve Jesus Christ. Francis's visits to San Damiano were very useful, but they were forced upon him and rare, as the biographer explains. Such was his will for the friars, whom he wished to serve the sisters in their devotion to their divine master. The same cautious and circumspect spirit governs the report of one of the most dramatic sermons delivered by Francis within the context of his reluctance to visit San Damiano and preach to the community.[55]

Accounts of Francis's communications with the Poor Clares must be assessed within the context of the hagiographical caution about relations between men and women.[56] Francis's 'reported behaviour' mirrors the admiration which Hugh of Avalon, bishop of Lincoln (1186-1200), expressed for St Ancelin, his Carthusian confrère and bishop of Bellay, who never deliberately gazed on any women, with the exception of a woman who needed spiritual direction. He refused to observe the features of women and explained that no one should allow himself to be ensnared by beauty.[57] Without any hint of embarrassment the biographer announces that Francis was aware of the dangers of dealings with women for anything other than spiritual matters. He would stand with his face cast down, addressing only virtuous and holy women in wonderful but brief words. He spoke in a loud voice to women so that he could be heard by all and once told a companion that he only recognized the faces of two women, whom Angelo da Clareno identified as his mother and Clare.[58] Escaping from the 'official summary' of Francis's dealings with woman in general and the Poor Clares in particular, it is safe to believe that the saint dealt as easily with women as with men and that there was a more natural communication between him and Clare than the biographers dare suggest.

There are two additional considerations which influence the account of Francis's visits to San Damiano. First, the friars' access to the monasteries of Poor

Clares was already limited by chapter 11 of the Rule and *Quo elongati*; these injunctions were followed by legislation enacted by the general chapters. Secondly, by the late 1230s there was evidence that the Franciscan family was under strain and some friars wished to be freed from any obligation towards the sisters. Bartoli observes that men's orders were often very reluctant to assume the spiritual care of the sisters who followed the same inspiration. At the start of the thirteenth century the Cistercians and Premonstratensians and later the friars, including the Dominicans, all tried ways of avoiding this burden.[59] Lawrence reports that for a time both the Dominican and Franciscan sisters came close to being cast off by the friars.[60] On 17 August 1251, at a time when the tide was beginning to turn in Clare's favour, Innocent IV instructed the bishops of England not to allow the sisters to establish any new foundations in the country without the leave of the minister provincial.[61]

CLARE AND THE ROMAN CURIA

While Francis obtained the initial approval of Innocent III at an early date, Clare entered into a titanic struggle which would last until the penultimate day of her life, when she finally received the copy of the Rule approved by Innocent IV. In this she found herself pitted against a series of popes, who had serious reservations about the sisters' lack of endowment and income. Accordingly, they applied a great deal of pressure and attempted to dilute her observance of the ideal of poverty. The popes from Honorius III to Innocent IV were united in their respect and affection for Clare; Gregory IX and Innocent IV visited her at San Damiano. Innocent's admiration for her was such that he urged that the normal process of canonization should be waived so that he might canonize her on the day of her funeral. Thwarted by some members of his entourage, he opened the process for her canonization within nine weeks of her death. In their concern for Clare these popes were distinctly uneasy about her desire to live without an assured guarantee of material support. In spite of their immense respect, Clare endured a long and lonely struggle to preserve the ideals of her friend at a time when the friars were taking their place in the landscape of the medieval Church and, in some instances, achieving some accommodation with poverty in order to pursue their apostolate.

The privilege of poverty and Franciscan identity

Clare petitioned Innocent III to grant her permission to live in the poverty of which she read in the Gospels and asked that the community at San Damiano should be known by the title of poverty. The unusual nature of this application was noted by the pope, who claimed that it was unprecedented in the history of the Apostolic See. This request must have caused some consternation in the papal chancery, where the scribes were more accustomed to copying out charters and privileges which safeguarded the ancient rights and possessions of churches and monasteries. This unique petition was granted by Innocent at an unknown date between the conclusion of the Council in 1215 and his death on 16 July 1216. He authorized the Poor Ladies to live as a community without property, something that was entirely new and unheard of for a monastic foundation. He observed that the sisters had renounced the desire for temporal things in order to dedicate themselves to God alone. Having followed the advice given to the rich young man, they had renounced their material possessions in order to identify themselves with Jesus Christ. Moreover, their voluntary poverty did not frighten them because they had abandoned themselves to the Lord's care, in accordance with the Gospel. The pope granted Clare's request that no one should legitimately compel them to accept possessions. His respect for Clare was such that he himself wrote the first draft of the privilege.[62]

Ugolino, both as cardinal and as pope, had a deep respect and reverence for the Franciscan vocation in its various forms. His visits to the monasteries of the Poor Clares brought him rest and an opportunity to appreciate the cloistered life. He spent the Easter of 1220 at San Damiano and one of his letters refers to his discussions with Clare about the Eucharist.[63] Frequently, when some new difficulties arose, he enlisted and received Clare's assistance.[64] As pope he visited the Poor Clare monastery near Spoleto, where the sisters' witness to contemplation and the highest poverty moved him and the cardinals to tears.[65] He began to take a strong interest in the business of the order when Francis was in the East and set about providing a more stable form of living for the sisters in accordance with the directives of the recent Lateran Council. In 1219 he drew up his constitutions, which the *Vita prima* described as glorious;[66] it is doubtful whether Clare shared the biographer's enthusiasm for the constitutions, which were based on the Rule of St Benedict. The two central dimensions were absent: first, the pursuit of Gospel poverty inspired by Francis; and secondly, dependence upon the friars. Ugolino was aware of how difficult it was for the sisters to live the type of poverty which they proposed; for it demanded a total dependence upon the generosity and dedication of others for their well-being. And he regarded that as an insecure foundation for a religious community of women. Bartoli maintains that the constitutions must have been applied in a unique way at San Damiano because the community already possessed the privilege of poverty. This suggests that daily life at San Damiano went on according to the dispositions which Francis made in the first years of the community. The constitutions were not well suited to life at San Damiano, as is proved by the fact that they were so quickly dropped.[67]

Clare's view of the collective and personal poverty to which the sisters were called demanded trust in divine providence. Like Francis, she had turned her back on material and financial security and wished to entrust herself fully to

God's promises. Ugolino, however, had assumed responsibilities for the sisters and felt that absolute penury would expose the sisters to a form of hardship uncommon among enclosed religious. His attempts to prevail upon Clare to accept some property consistently failed. While he wished to protect the sisters from destitution, he demonstrated that, despite his familiarity with both Francis and Clare, his grasp of their ideals was less than perfect. After his election as Gregory IX he visited San Damiano, where he suggested some accommodation with poverty. Concluding that Clare might have fallen prey to scruples on the matter of poverty, papal powers prepared a solution: a dispensation from her vow to allay any scruples. While the gesture undoubtedly arose from Gregory's admiration for Clare, the timing was wholly incongruous. Francis had been recently canonized and lauded as a man who had recovered the apostolic life in his voluntary poverty. While work was going forward on the new basilica to house his remains, Gregory was offering Francis's most faithful disciple a dispensation from the vow of poverty. Clare's retort was magisterial, insisting that she did not wish to be absolved from following the Son of God.[68] The episode reveals the way in which Ugolino was sometimes slow to comprehend the full meaning of the insights of both Clare and Francis; it also highlights the difference between canonical and ascetical considerations. The irony of this position was that within two years of Francis's death Clare was being constrained to defend the Franciscan ideal, as it was practised at San Damiano, and to do so against the person who had recently claimed to be a familiar of Francis in *Quo elongati*. Sister Philippa reported that Clare could never be persuaded by the pope or the bishop of Ostia to receive any possessions.[69]

Not long after his visit to San Damiano the pope renewed the privilege of poverty on 17 September 1228 in similar, though abbreviated, terms to the version of Innocent III. He confirmed it and ensured that Clare should not be obliged to accept material possessions.[70] Bartoli points out that the privilege was the final document to witness the friendship between the two old friends of Francis and that thenceforth the rapport between Clare and Gregory seemed to cool.[71] Sister Beatrice believed that part of Clare's holiness consisted in her love of the privilege of poverty. Sister Philippa testified that the privilege granted to Clare was honoured with great reverence and kept well and with great diligence because she feared she might lose it. At the end of her life she entrusted the privilege of poverty to the sisters.[72]

One of the questions on which the friars sought papal guidance was on their responsibilities towards the sisters. The verdict was delivered in *Quo elongati*, with its interpretation of chapter 11 of Francis's Rule. Gregory pointed out that the friars had been accustomed to believe that they were permitted to enter the monasteries of the Poor Clares, assuming that the faculty arose from a decision taken by the general chapter. The pope interpreted this text as applying to all monasteries of women. The pope's judgement was restrictive: the friars were forbidden to have any dealings with women's communities without the direct authorization of the Holy See. While the declaration seems to have been widely accepted, the only dissenting voice was raised by Clare. In a display of defiance she dismissed the friars who were dwelling at San Damiano to provide the spiritual and material needs of the sisters. At once she sent them back to the minister, not wanting to have the questors who acquire corporal bread for them when they could not have the questors for spiritual bread. When Gregory heard this, he immediately mitigated the prohibition into the hands of the minister general.[73] Just as in 1228 Clare had to defend her choice of poverty, so in 1230 she had to fight for the free and fruitful spiritual union which bound San Damiano to the whole minorite movement.

Towards the approval of the Rule

The inspiration for the constitutions drawn up by Ugolino came from the venerable Rule of St Benedict rather than the vision jointly shared by Francis and Clare. Had this Rule satisfied Clare's deepest yearnings, she would have entered one of the established monastic communities in Umbria without much protest from her family. The nub of her resistance to various papal measures was that she wished to preserve Francis's teaching and her own close link with the friars. He had been her mentor and she repaid his encouragement and trust many times over by labouring to uphold his teaching and insights in their pristine purity. Thus, when the friars began to accept papal interpretations of the Rule and produce their own commentaries on it, Clare clung all the more insistently and tenaciously to the founding inspiration. Although popes offered the friars dispensations and permissions, Clare remained a beacon of hope for those who cherished the simple form of the Franciscan vocation.

Throughout the 1230s and 1240s Clare persevered in the hope of eventually gaining approval for her own Rule. The years following Francis's death were very difficult for her and she entered into a series of struggles with popes who wished to temper the rigour of her poverty. The 18 years after Francis's death brought innumerable anxieties, especially when she witnessed the growing polarization among the friars on the question of how evangelical poverty should be observed. At the same time there were moves afoot among the friars to distance themselves from the sisters. A glimmer of hope began to emerge with the pontificate of Innocent IV, who had begun by insisting that the sisters should profess the Benedictine Rule. On 6 August 1247 he promulgated his own Rule, *Cum omnis vera religio*. This document added considerably to that of his predecessor, and omitted references to the Rule of St Benedict. Nonetheless, this Rule was not widely accepted, even though he himself insisted on its acceptance in *Quoties a nobis*, issued on 23 August 1247.[74] One of its benefits was the recognition that the friars should be the sisters' visitators and chaplains, but on the debit side it mitigated the obligations of fasting and even allowed possessions.[75] Three years later it lost its binding force when Innocent declared in another bull, *Inter personas*, 6 June 1250, that no sister could be forced to accept this Rule. Encouraged by signs of papal flexibility, Clare began to write her own Rule, based on that of Francis and accepted passages from the earlier Rules of Ugolino and Innocent. Her poor health injected a note of urgency because Francis, Guido and Ugolino had all been dead for some years. Even though there were signs that the tide was beginning to turn in her favour, Clare wondered whether she would ever complete her life's work before Sister Death visited San Damiano. She was the first woman to write a Rule for religious women. During a period of forty years her ideals were becoming more clearly defined, especially as the Rules of Ugolino and Innocent forced her to reflect upon the uniqueness of the Franciscan vision.[76]

In this period Clare also had to battle with increasing infirmity. The papal court, which had its own political problems, moved from Lyon to Perugia. Hearing about Clare's illness, Rainaldo, the cardinal protector, hurried from Perugia to see her. Her biographer comments on the paternal role which he played towards the sisters. Clare tearfully besought him to take care of the Poor Ladies and, above all, she asked him that the privilege of poverty should be confirmed by the pope and cardinals.[77] The cardinal protector's approval of her Rule was granted on 16 September 1252 and the text was incorporated into the papal preamble to approval of her Rule. Particular attention was paid to the poverty which Francis had taught them:

> we approve your holy way of life in the Lord and we desire with fatherly affection to impart our kind favour upon your wishes and holy desires, because you have rejected the splendours and pleasures of the world and, following the footprints of Christ Himself (cf. 1 Peter 2:21) and His most holy Mother, you have chosen to live bodily enclosed and to serve the Lord in the highest poverty that, in freedom of soul, you may be the Lord's servants ... and we ratify by the protection of this document the manner of holy unity and highest poverty which your blessed Father St Francis gave you for your observance in word and writing.[78]

Innocent IV, together with the cardinals, moved from Perugia to Assisi and hastened to see Clare, whom he regarded as an extraordinary woman. Entering the monastery, he went straight to Clare, who kissed his hand and asked that she might also kiss his feet. When she asked pardon for all her sins, Innocent replied that he was in greater need of forgiveness.[79]

Clare continued to press for the papal approval which Innocent finally granted on 9 August 1253, when the officials of the papal court realized that she was dying. On 10 August 1253 a friar was dispatched from the Sacro Convento in Assisi to San Damiano with the text of the Rule approved by the pope. Sister Philippa, whose testimony was disappointingly brief, disclosed that Clare's great desire was to have the Rule of the order confirmed with a papal bull, to be able to kiss the papal seal and then die on the following day. Her wishes were fulfilled when she learned that a friar had come with letters bearing the papal bull. She reverently took it even though she was very close to death and kissed it. She died on the following day, on the feast of San Rufino, creating a further link between the foundation of Christianity in Assisi and its medieval revival by Francis and Clare.

In the turbulent 1230s and 1240s Clare not only protected Francis's ideals, but also acted as a magnet for those who had been close to her friend. She served as a focal point of unity for the fraternity at a time when the feelings of some were becoming hardened. Francis's close friends Leo, Giles and Angelo seem to have been in contact with her, particularly in the later years. Juniper, Angelo and Leo were also present at her death on 11 August 1253.[80] Their respect for her was mirrored in the reminiscences which they compiled in response to the general chapter of 1244. Although the chroniclers catalogue the failings of Elias as minister general, Clare was aware of Elias's strong friendship with Francis and her second letter to St Agnes of Prague urges her to follow the counsel of Elias, her venerable father, the minister general, so that she might walk more serenely in the commands of the Lord. This letter is assigned to the year 1235, the period when the opposition to Elias was mounting. No word of bitterness or disapproval was attributed to Clare and it is conceivable that she had seen Elias from time to time during the construction of the basilica in honour of their friend. Despite the numerous failings attributed to him, it is significant that he incurred the wrath of the minister general for visiting the monasteries of Poor Clares in defiance of a general instruction.[81]

CONCLUSION

Clare and Francis belonged to the same generation in Assisi, though he was her senior by a few years. Their lives became closely intertwined and were moving along parallel lines before the one had heard of the other. Clare was the product of the feudal world, whose overthrow had captured the imagination of the young Francis; the civil war set them on opposite sides. Ortolana went on pilgrimage several times and later joined her daughters at San Damiano. In such a small city Clare quickly learned about the events surrounding Francis's very public break with his father, the excitement caused by the public renunciation of property belonging to the first recruits of the fraternity, which soon gained an initial approval from Innocent III. She was acutely aware that Francis was a man through whom God was working; he was a prophetical voice who was drawing men of different ages and background to a closer following of the Gospel.

Francis was a key figure in Clare's discernment of her own vocation; the sources repeatedly refer to him as her father in God. He was involved in the discussions and arrangements for her flight from her family home and her profession at the Portiuncula. Later he established her and Agnes at San Damiano, where he played a prominent role as the sisters' guide and mentor. His influence persuaded Clare to overcome her reluctance and accept the position of abbess. The same influence was invoked to restrain her excessive asceticism. In later years, however, the tables were turned and Francis, who was drawn into the consideration of administrative and canonical questions for his own fraternity, turned increasingly to her for encouragement and advice. Despite the valiant efforts of the fraternity's 'official historians', Francis was becoming increasingly distressed by the discussions about its direction. In the midst of this turmoil he found in Clare a support and encouragement that was often lacking among his confrères. She became a source of strength and consolation in his declining years, when disappointment and illness were taking their toll. By this stage she was widely recognized as a woman of immense spiritual stature, who was attracting women to a life of asceticism and contemplation. Recruits arrived quickly and sisters were sent out from San Damiano to establish new foundations.

Clare was one of the earliest witnesses to the reform which grew around Francis and, like Guido, she had witnessed the gestation of the Franciscan adventure from its outset. While Francis and Guido were both dead by the summer of 1228, Clare lived for another two and a half decades. She had witnessed the halcyon days of the fraternity, when Francis was young and the friars were few and renowned for their admirable level of religious observance. The 1220s brought the remarkable expansion of the community into most parts of western Europe and beyond as well as the death of the founder. The years that followed Francis's canonization brought strain upon the fraternity and some deeply rooted ideological disputes about his inheritance. When the friars fought over the soul of the founder, Clare bore a dignified and heroic witness to the ideals of her mentor and friend. Some friars were inclined to accept permissions and relaxations which distanced them from the intention and spirit of the saint. All compromise was steadfastly refused by Clare, who for 27 years after the death of Francis, kept the flame of evangelical poverty burning and in the process resisted the good, but misguided, efforts of a series of popes who tried to persuade her to accept some form of material security. Many of Francis's companions regarded Clare as the emulator of her mentor in preserving always the poverty of the Son of God. They looked to San Damiano as the place where the encroachment of money and gifts was being stoutly resisted. Clare emerges as the trustworthy custodian of Francis's understanding of the apostolic life and the champion of evangelical poverty. She and the sisters provided the spiritual basis for the apostolate of preaching carried out by both Francis and the friars, and to that theme we now turn.

Notes

1.   *Compilatio Assisiensis*, c. 13. For a stimulating collection of studies on Clare see *Spirit and Life: A Journal of Contemporary Franciscanism*, 1: *Clare of Assisi: Model for Franciscan Women* (1991).
2.   P. Sabatier, *Life of St Francis of Assisi* (London, 1899), pp. 166-7.
3.   M. Bartoli, *Clare of Assisi*, trans. from Italian Snr Frances Teresa (London, 1993), p. xii.
4.   LSC, n. 1.
5.   Process, 1, nn. 2, 4; 19.1.
6.   Ibid., 1, n. 4; 20, n. 3.
7.   NV, 2, pp. 221-3, 343.
8.   J. Riley-Smith, *What Were the Crusades?* (Basingstoke, 2nd edn, 1992), p. 29.
9.   Process, 1, n. 4.
10.   LSC, n. 1.
11.   Process, 2, n. 2.
12.   Ibid., 3, n. 2.
13.   LSC, n. 3.
14.   Process, 1, n. 3.
15.   Ibid., 17, n. 1; 20, n. 3.
16.   Ibid., 17, n. 7.
17.   1 C, nn. 23, 36.
18.   LM, c. 4, n. 4; LSC, n. 37.
19.   Ibid., n. 4.
20.   Process, 19, n. 2.
21.   Ibid., 18, n. 2.
22.   1 C, n. 95.
23.   LSC, n. 5.
24.   Process, 12, nn. 1, 2.
25.   Ibid., 17, n. 3.
26.   Sr Frances Teresa, *This Living Mirror* (London, 1995), p. 31.
27.   LSC, nn. 5-6; 1 C, n. 18.
28.   LSC, n. 13.
29.   Process, 12, n. 3; 19, n. 2.
30.   LSC, n. 7.
31.   Process, 13.1.
32.   LSC, n. 8.
33.   Ibid., n. 9.
34.   A. Fontini, 'Nuove notizie intorno a Santa Chiara di Assisi' in AFH, 46 (1953), pp. 3-43, 29-36.
35.   LSC, n. 10.
36.   Process, 12, n. 5.
37.   Sr Frances Teresa, *This Living Mirror*, p. 38, argues that it was not a monastery, but the home of a Beguine-type group, living just down the slope from the Carceri.
38.   LSC, nn. 24-26.
39.   Bartoli, *Clare of Assisi*, p. 57.
40.   LSC, nn. 10, 12; Process, 1, n. 6.
41.   R. J. Armstrong, *Clare of Assisi: Early Documents* (New York, 1988), p. 69.
42.   LSC, n. 18, Process, 10, n. 7.
43.   J. Dalarun, *Francesco: un passaggio. Donna e donne negli scritti e nelle leggende di Francesco d'Assisi. Postfazione di Giovanni Miccoli* (I libri di Viella, 2; Rome, 1994), pp. 75-6.
44.   Armstrong, *Clare of Assisi: Early Documents*, p. 55.
45.   LM, c. 12, n. 2.
46.   LSC, n. 32.
47.   Sr Frances Teresa, *This Living Mirror: Reflections on Clare of Assisi*, p. 93.
48.   R. J. Armstrong and I. C. Brady, *Francis and Clare: The Complete Works* (New York, 1982), pp. 40-1.
49.   *Compilatio Assisiensis*, c. 85.
50.   Ibid., c. 13.
51.   1 C, nn. 116-17. Dalarun, *Francesco: un passaggio*, p. 74, refers to a similar passage in the life of St Martin of Tours.
52.   Ibid., p. 71.
53.   1 C, nn. 18-20.

54. Dalarun, *Francesco: un passaggio*, p. 148.
55. 2 C, nn. 204-7.
56. Salimbene, *Cronica*, pp. 95-6, illustrates the type of allegations that might be raised about the friars' dealings with the Poor Clares. In 1229 the whole city of Lucca was up in arms against the friars, who had been slandered by Gattaiola, abbess of the Poor Clares, who claimed that the friars, were trying to remove her from office because she prevented them from having sinful relations with the sisters. Salimbene was quick to describe this as a barefaced lie, adding that she was eventually removed from office by the friars on account of various irregularities and that the friars quickly regained their good reputation.
57. D. L. Douie and D. H. Farmer (eds), *The Life of St Hugh of Lincoln*, II (NMT; 1961), repub. in OMT (1985), p. 55.
58. 2 C, nn. 112-14; Angelo da Clareno, *Expositio Regulae*, ed. L. Oliger (Quaracchi, Florence, 1912), p. 217.
59. Bartoli, *Clare of Assisi*, p. 68.
60. C. H. Lawrence, *The Friars* (The Medieval World; London, 1994), p. 78.
61. *The Register of Walter Giffard, Lord Archbishop of York 1266-1279*, ed. W. Brown (Surtees Society, 109; Durham, 1904), n. 305, p. 53.
62. LSC, n. 14; Armstrong, *Clare of Assisi: Early Documents*, pp. 83-4.
63. Ibid., pp. 97-8.
64. LSC, n. 27.
65. 1 C, n. 122.
66. Armstrong, *Clare of Assisi: Early Documents*, pp. 87-96, for an introduction to the text and a translation.
67. Bartoli, *Clare of Assisi*, p. 94.
68. LSC, n. 14.
69. Process, 3, n. 14.
70. Armstrong, *Clare of Assisi: Early Documents*, pp. 103-4.
71. Bartoli, *Clare of Assisi*, p. 134.
72. Process, 12, n. 6; 3, nn. 14, 32.
73. LSC, n. 37.
74. Armstrong, *Clare of Assisi: Early Documents*, p. 109.
75. Ibid., pp. 27, 23.
76. Ibid., p. 23.
77. LSC, nn. 39-40.
78. Armstrong, *Clare of Assisi: Early Documents*, pp. 61-2.
79. LSC, nn. 40, 41.
80. Ibid., n. 45; Process, 3, n. 32.
81. Thomas of Eccleston, *Tractatus de adventu*, p. 69.

8

❧❧❧❧❧❧❧❧❧❧❧

Francis as the herald of the great king

It was for Christ's sake that he [Francis] had … worked so hard to preach and to exemplify the Gospel[1]

Accounts of Francis's earlier years focus on his attractive and flamboyant personality. While he underwent a spectacular change of lifestyle, his innate qualities of leadership and dramatic instincts found a new outlet in his tireless search for deeper communion with God and his neighbour. In this transitional phase there was little indication that he would become one of the most imaginative and successful preachers in the history of the western Church. His biographers did, however, seize upon one incident in the transitional phase of his life and treated it as a foretaste of his vocation. When he was walking through the woods in the winter and singing God's praises in French, a band of robbers suddenly fell upon him, demanding some form of identification. His response was that he was the herald of the great king, a declaration which proclaimed a truth about the way in which he intended to spend the remainder of his life. The conviction that God had sent him to proclaim the Gospel in the cities of Umbria and beyond became the dynamo of his life. The whole of God's creation was his enclosure and all people, whatever their tradition, were recognized as God's creatures and invited to share in the same truths and insights which inspired him. His sermons, which were preached wherever there were people, stirred the whole of creation, people and animals, to unite in the praise of their common Creator.

AN ENLARGED CLOISTER

The traditional perception that life outside the cloister was not always conducive to the pursuit of Christian perfection was voiced by Walter Daniel, the biographer of St Aelred of Rievaulx. Writing of the 1140s, he comments that it was hard for people to lead the good life unless they were monks or members of a religious order.[2] Some people took the monastic habit rather later in life — a process more recently interpreted as an act of 'fugitive piety'.[3] In the twelfth-century chronicles there are many such examples. For instance, Ansold explained to his wife

Odeline that the end of his life was approaching and that he wished to retire to a monastery; he died three days after his clothing in the monastic habit at Maule.[4] R. B. Brooke and C. N. L. Brooke contrast the prospects of a lay person's chances of salvation in the eleventh-century spirituality of Urban II with the twelfth-century view. The former, reared on monastic spirituality, doubtlessly believed that the population of heaven was small, and consisted largely of monks. Many people in the twelfth century began to believe that the population of heaven increased substantially, partly because of a greater optimism, partly because God seemed more humane, less severe and harsh, than he had been and partly because the doctrine of purgatory was elaborated and popularized.[5] The changing climate of the late twelfth century was exemplified by Hugh of Avalon's advice to lay people who lamented the hindrances of life in the world. He proclaimed that the kingdom of God was not confined to monks, hermits and anchorites and that on judgement day everyone would be examined according to their observance of Christian, rather than monastic, principles.[6] In this period the Gospel gradually came to be seen as a manual of advice for all the faithful and not something which primarily belonged to a cloistered élite making intercession for those detained in society.

Francis was born in this period of change, although he retained traces of the more traditional view about the retreat from society and the thirst for sanctity. Nonetheless, his vocation and mission to evangelize every creature constituted a significant departure from the traditional form of the religious life with its narrower invitation to holiness, which had traditionally been the preserve of monastic communities. While the monk was perceived as one who sought deeper communion with God and made intercession for those outside the stability and haven of the cloister, his focus was the monastery and his own quest for sanctification through the discipline and support of community life. Francis's personal vocation was to seek the sanctification of the entire human family and the new and global dimensions of his vocation were exemplified in his meeting with Lady Poverty recounted in the allegorical *Sacrum commercium*. She agrees to eat with Francis and the friars and asks him to show her his cloister, enumerating the marks of a monastery: the oratory, chapter room, refectory, kitchen, dormitory, stable, fine chairs and polished tables and great houses. When she repeated her request, Francis and the friars led her to a hill and showed her the whole world as far as she could see: that was his extensive friary.[7] Similarly Jacques de Vitry comments that the dimensions of the friars' cloister were world-wide.[8] Although Francis's vision of his fraternity shared some common ground with the traditional lexicon of the religious life, it was not confined by the normal spatial understanding.

Knowles notes that all previous founders of religious reforms had led men away from the world and set before them monastic life as the norm. Francis, though escaping in spirit from everything worldly as thoroughly as Bernard, wished his friars to go about in the world working, reaching others and helping them.[9] Lawrence explains that the mendicant orders broke free from one of the most basic principles of traditional monasticism by abandoning the seclusion and enclosure of the cloister in order to engage in an active pastoral mission to the society of their time. Preaching and ministering to the people was their *raison d'être*. He draws attention to the changing expectations and assumptions of the laity, whose assurance of salvation need no longer be sought by flight from the human hive or by attachment to the shirt-tails of a spiritual élite: those who lived in society, whatever their status, could fulfil the demands of the Christian life by sanctifying the humdrum duties and tasks of their estate; all that was required was that they repent and believe the Gospel.[10] Southern observes that Francis and his friars brought the monastic piety of Sts Anselm and Bernard to the market place, and that this became the common property of the clerical and lay world alike.[11]

Francis's preaching reflects the more optimistic outlook that the Gospel was to be followed by his hearers, regardless of their religious or social status. With a characteristic flourish the *Vita prima* claims that in a short space of time the face of Umbria was changed and took on a more cheerful aspect. Thanksgiving and the voice of praise resounded everywhere so that many put aside cares and gained knowledge of themselves from Francis's life and teaching and they longed to attain love and reverence for their Creator. People of all ranks, social and ecclesiastical, began to approach Francis for advice and leadership. Each of them received a norm of life from him and they were shown the way to attain salvation, whatever their position in society.[12] An insight into the lives of these followers of Francis was provided by his preaching at Greccio. Many men there joined the friars and numerous women preserved their virginity, wearing the garments of religion while dwelling in their own homes. Although they all remained in their own homes and continued their own occupations, they seemed to be more like religious, giving themselves to fasting and prayer. Francis was overjoyed by this level of observance in the town and proclaimed that there were not so many converted to penance from any one great city as there were from the small town of Greccio. Often in the evening, when the friars were praying, the men of the town, small and great alike, were accustomed to stand in the road in front of the town, making responses to the friars in loud voices. Even children would praise God as best they could when they saw the friars.[13]

FRANCIS'S PREACHING

The passage from the Gospel which revolutionized Francis's life was the set of instructions issued to the disciples. My initial response is to consider this passage within the context of the Church's missionary endeavour, especially at a time when its missionary enterprise was expanding. The disciples of Jesus Christ were being groomed to carry the Gospel throughout the entire world. While at a later date Francis cherished the ambition of going as a missionary to foreign lands, he did not immediately interpret this passage from the Gospel in such a global manner and instead became a missionary to the cities and towns of western Europe, where people needed instruction and guidance on how they should apply Christian principles to the changing economic climate. There is no indication that Francis paused to think of where the Gospel was directing him and it was abundantly clear to him that his place was in the city from which he had so recently retreated. This may be the result of his reflections on the condition of Christianity in his native Umbria. It may equally have come from an awareness that the work of evangelization should be carried out on the spot, especially because the bishops had provided little preaching and were running the risk of alienating the growing urban population. Thus Francis's biographers report that, as soon as he had heard the passage from the Gospel, he returned to his native city to preach.

Obedience to this vocation required the friars to live as the apostles had done and they believed that they had been entrusted with the responsibility of carrying the Gospel throughout the world; the growing urban population could not be excluded from their sermons. The cloistered life, with its round of the divine office, the *opus Dei*, and prayerful intercession for the world, did not satisfy the wider responsibility placed on Francis's shoulders. He felt that he was being commissioned to preach the Gospel to the whole of creation, making an immediate beginning in Assisi. His message was hopeful when compared with the pessimism of the traditional monastic spirituality, which identified the monk as the only complete Christian and offered only a tenuous hope of salvation to the married laity. Fleming observes that the early friars thought of themselves as missionaries in their own native lands and their evangelical techniques expressly addressed the vernacular culture in which they lived.[14] The detachment of the friars was such that their Rule directed them to pass through the world as pilgrims and strangers. They were schooled to become itinerant evangelists in the apostolic pattern.

Lawrence points out that because medieval parishes and collegiate bodies generally resisted any subdivision of their territories for the purpose of creating new parishes, many settlers in outlying areas were left without adequate pastoral care. Some cities had only a single church of parochial status. To lay people, dissatisfied with their role as passive spectators of religious observances and hungry for guidance in personal religion, the friars brought new possibilities of active participation.[15] Francis's special achievement was to reconcile the Church's hierarchy to ordinary, humble folk. His call was to the urban poor of Umbria, and beyond that to the whole of Italy, to the whole of humanity, Christian and pagan, Catholic and Cathar, rich and poor; the special genius of his teaching was to put his message to the ordinary people among whom he lived by example, by vivid lessons and by informal preaching.[16] Jessopp comments that the friars, the poor, took the Gospel to the poor in the cities of Italy.[17]

Francis's preaching began in the period after hearing the Gospel at the Portiuncula, though his message at this stage was exhortatory. When the small group of friars had obtained papal approbation, they were commissioned to preach penance. Doubts about the form of the friars' vocation surfaced from time to time, even as early as their return journey to Umbria. On their way back to the valley of Spoleto they discussed whether they should dwell in towns and cities or retire to solitary places. After committing their dilemma to prayer, they came to understand that they were being sent to centres of population. This corroboration of the Gospel passage which Francis had heard at the Portiuncula defined the friars' lifestyle as itinerant evangelists: he wanted the friars to go through the world preaching and praising God.[18] While he preached throughout Umbria, his native city was the venue for many of his sermons, the first of which he delivered in the church of San Giorgio in Assisi. A series of Lenten sermons followed in the cathedral of San Rufino and he probably preached in many of the parish churches in the city and environs. His sermons, preceded by prolonged prayer and reflection, contained a fire and energy which moved his hearers.

The biographers conjured up apostolic images to depict Francis, now hailed as the most valiant knight of Christ, as one who revived or continued the work of the apostles. In an era which saw little orthodox preaching, the Gospel was proclaimed by Francis and his followers. Peace was preached and salvation was taught along with penance for the remission of sins in towns and villages (Matthew 9:35). Thomas of Celano, whose desire to establish parallels with the early Church was barely camouflaged, distinguishes carefully between the persuasive words of human wisdom and the message delivered in Francis's challenging sermons, which were marked by the learning and power of the Holy Spirit; vanity, ostentatious displays of learning, flattery and seductive blandishments found no place in the sermons. His preaching exposed the shortcomings of his hearers and, like a skilled physician, he excised blemishes of character and he did not mince his words with those mired in sin. His powerful message sprang from his own convictions about the Gospel; there was no visible dichotomy between his own conduct and the truth which he proclaimed in his sermons. This sure basis played no small part in his convincing others to follow his exhortations. The purpose of such instruction was to identify and eradicate the faults which brought dishonour upon the Christian name. Francis's conduct was regulated by the Scriptures and he spoke with a fire and a passion rarely heard in the sermons of that age. In showing the effectiveness of his preaching, Thomas of Celano attests that even the most learned men wondered at his words and were struck with wholesome fear by his presence.

Francis's commitment to this apostolate was such that he allowed his body little or no rest while he travelled indefatigably. The *Vita prima* offers a rare glimpse into his mobility, adding that, often in one day, he made a circuit of four or five villages and even cities, preaching to everyone.[19] His sermons were shaped in order to touch people in all situations and at Ascoli the people trampled on one another in their eagerness to see and hear him; so often he preached the word of God to thousands and looked upon the greatest multitude of people as one person, addressing one person as he would speak to a large crowd. This remarkable gift gave an extra dimension to his homilies, which were not dry expositions of various theological and philosophical questions. Indeed, his educational background did not equip him to address such great questions. He spoke with passion and fervour, communicating his own excitement. When he preached at the papal court, he was so unable to contain his joy that he moved his feet as though he were dancing.[20] He was an extraordinarily gifted communicator, who tailored his materials to the tastes and understanding of those present. He did not confine himself to words of reproof and exhortation: words were accompanied and supplemented by signs and gestures. He was not ashamed to confess his faults in public.[21] He preached to unlearned people through visible and simple things in as much as he knew that virtue was more necessary than words. Among spiritual people and those of greater capacity he spoke enlivening and profound words.[22]

Francis's preaching generated a great deal of enthusiasm, which was manifest in the large numbers of people who hastened to hear him. Such powerful and stimulating preaching provoked a large amount of excitement which expressed itself in the universal appeal of these sermons, drawing people of every age and condition: men and women, clerics and religious. In order to emphasize the vitality and energy of Francis's sermons the *Vita prima* refers to a pervasive indifference to the Christian message in Umbria and other parts of Italy. This carelessness and lack of interest in Christianity, accompanied by an attachment to bad habits and vices, was contrasted with the power and vigour of Francis's words.[23]

At a later stage Francis's sermons were followed by the admission of candidates to the fraternity. For instance, the example and preaching of Francis and the friars at Greccio drew many men to the order[24] and, after preaching at Ascoli, he received 30 clerics and laymen to the fraternity. Writing in the spring of 1220, Jacques de Vitry gave a vivid account of the impact created by Francis, who visited the Crusaders. The friars were spreading rapidly throughout the world and enrolling great numbers of recruits because they expressly followed the life of the twelve apostles and the early Christian communities. Francis, the founder of the fraternity, was loved by God and venerated by all people. The prelate alludes to the appeal of the nascent order, which had recently admitted Rainerio, the prior of St Michael. The friars' zeal had also made inroads on the bishop's own household, from which he had lost Colin, the English clerk, along with Master Michael and Dom Matthew, to whom he had entrusted the parish of Holy

Cross. The bishop was also in danger of losing the services of the chanter, Henry, and a few others.[25]

FRANCIS THE TEACHER AND ACTOR

In the late eleventh century St Anselm wrote a series of prayers and meditations on some of the major themes in Christian piety in a manner which led the reader to reflect upon those events more closely. These beautiful texts were intended to arouse the mind of the reader, who was to be drawn increasingly into the events narrated in the Gospel. This form of devotional writing, with its emphasis upon affective piety, was devised to enable readers to discard weariness and indifference and to develop a heightened sense of awareness and fervour. Its aim was to reconstruct the biblical events and to translate their readers to the side of the crib or the cross, helping them to analyse the emotions of the principal players; the devout readers were encouraged to associate themselves with the dispositions and virtues of the major players in these scenes. Anselm and other such writers flourished in a monastic context and composed prayers and meditations designed to stimulate the piety of readers outside the monastery. Francis composed no such prayers, but his talents enabled him to draw mental pictures, allowing his hearers to imagine that they were witnesses to various scenes from the Gospels and to identify themselves with the friends of their divine master.

In spite of the limitations of Francis's formal education at the school of San Giorgio and his incomplete grasp of Latin, he was an immensely gifted and successful communicator. The genius of his teaching was to present his message to ordinary people by example, by vivid lessons and by informal instruction. His early biographers drew attention to his gifts as a communicator and his capacity to present the Gospel in an attractive and immediately intelligible manner. Francis's whole body was drawn into the wish to promote the Gospel and the dramatic way in which he couched his teaching was noted by the *Vita prima*: he edified his hearers not less by his example than by his word; he made a tongue out of his whole body so that all manner of gestures might proclaim the principles enunciated in the Gospels.[26] His early companions confirm that he strove to become a sign of the divine, likening himself to a painting which pointed to its creator, rendering honour and glory to God alone.[27] R. B. Brooke and C. N. L. Brooke comment that the way in which Francis presented the call to the Christian life was fresh and original. He was a highly gifted and imaginative teacher; he demonstrated, by living it with all his energy, that the Christian life was no fairy tale, but a challenge. Paramount importance was attached to example and he did not just tell people what they ought to do, but did it all himself, exaggerating even, and dramatizing, to drive home his lessons.[28] The Franciscan ideal was a simple one, to live by the Gospel text, which Francis taught in parables, by example, by exaggeration and paradox, by dramatization. He used the literature of the day, the *Chansons de geste* and the Arthurian cycle, and projected his vision of poverty in the language of romance and chivalry. He tried to sanctify song and the strumming of the guitar by composing songs to God in the vernacular. He was a subtle, self-conscious, imaginative teacher.[29] D. L. Jeffrey explains that Francis, the proto-poet of the order, wrote hymns and songs in Provençal and in Umbrian rather than Latin. He came to believe that the Christian life was not based on a detailed imitation of the *vita apostolica*, but upon the call to a life of identification with Jesus Christ and that this belief found its fulfilment in the stigmata.[30] Three examples illustrate the way in which he was determined to keep the teaching of the Gospel before the eyes of his contemporaries.

First, in his attempts to deflect the widely held belief in Assisi that he was a saint, Francis proceeded to demonstrate the truth of the Gospel, regardless of personal cost. While the citizens came to regard him as an ascetical figure, his primary concern was to justify himself in his Creator's eyes and he had no interest in the good opinion of his contemporaries, as he confirms in his own writings:

> Blessed is the servant who esteems himself no better when he is praised and exalted by people than when he is considered worthless, simple and despicable; for what a man is before God, that he is and nothing more.[31]

His scruples about eating meat during a bout of fever moved him to declare his laxity before the people of Assisi. Even though he had not recovered from a quartan fever, he got up and arranged for the people to be summoned to a piazza for a sermon. He delivered his sermon and then proceeded with a display of weakness and humility. At the end of the sermon he asked the people to wait for some time. He went to confession in San Rufino and then ordered Peter Catanii to do as he said. He removed his tunic and put his cord around his neck, ordering Peter to lead him naked before the people. Another friar was instructed to follow with a bowl full of ashes, which he was to scatter over Francis's head at the place where he had preached; this friar did not obey. Peter, who was weeping bitterly, led the saint back to the stone where criminals were punished in full view of the people in the piazza. The saint then protested to the people that they regarded him as a holy man and that men, moved by his example, had entered the fraternity. He then announced that during his illness he had relaxed the rigour of his usual abstinence and had eaten meat and broth.

Those present were amazed at the extraordinary spectacle and realized how austere a life he led; they were deeply moved. Nearly everyone began to weep with pity and compassion for him, especially because it was bitterly cold. This expression of humility led them to contrast the saint's rigour and abstinence with their own conduct and they made no secret of the fact that they thought that his humility was to be admired rather than imitated. Bonaventure, who presented Francis as the exemplar of the virtues proper to the Christian, concludes that the saint offered a lesson in true humility, indicating that the follower of Jesus Christ was bound to disregard all earthly praise and subdue displays of bloated pride.[32] Even when Francis wished to discourage the belief that he was a saint, his symbolic teaching confirmed both the Gospel and the popular conviction that he was an extraordinarily holy man. This dramatic lesson demonstrates his skills as a communicator, who revived the simple message of the Gospel.

Secondly, a similar desire impelled Francis on his long eagerly awaited return to San Damiano. He had been the source of inspiration for Clare and the first sisters at San Damiano and made arrangements to preach there. The homily was given at a time when his visits to the monastery were less frequent than they had been. His much awaited visit was the occasion of a certain expectancy, as the sisters looked forward to his sermon. With a scarcely concealed sense of anticipation and delight the community gathered for their mentor's sermon. Thomas of Celano explains the sisters were anxious to see their teacher once again. The homily began in a conventional enough style, with Francis raising his eyes to heaven in deep prayer. However, convention was discarded when he asked for ashes to be brought to him and he made a circle with them around himself on the pavement and sprinkled the rest of them on his head. Francis remained silently in the circle, while the sisters wondered when the homily was to commence. The silence was broken only by Francis's recitation of the penitential psalm, *Miserere mei Deus* (Psalm 51). The biographer states that the psalm was recited in place of the sermon and, when he had finished the psalm, he quickly left. This eloquent display of his own penitence and contrition had a profound effect upon the sisters. His symbolic sermon had shown them that they should regard themselves as dust and ashes.[33] This sermon, whose silence was broken only by the penitential psalm, instructed the sisters that he was a man, circumscribed by human frailty, and that they, too, should regard themselves as pilgrims in this world, where they were in need of divine strength and mercy.

Thirdly, Francis was fully immersed in the teaching of his divine master, which had directed his steps since the Mass at the Portiuncula. He reflected so deeply on the Gospel that its message seemed to fill his mind and mould his behaviour. His first biographer testifies that the focal points of his prolonged meditations were the crib and the cross, two of the major events in the redemption of humanity. The humility of the incarnation and the charity of the passion occupied his memory to the extent that he scarcely wanted to think of anything else. Leo and companions underlined his devotion to the feast of the Nativity, asserting that he had a greater regard for Christmas than for any other festival on account of the divine concern to save wayward humanity. This was summed up by the *Vita prima*'s declaration that Francis's highest intention, chief desire and uppermost purpose was to observe the Gospel in all things. He longed to follow the teaching and footsteps of his divine master and it was not sufficient for him to ponder the mystery. He wished to share with his neighbours his own sense of wonder. He was impelled by a strong desire to communicate to them the riches which he had unearthed in the Gospel.

The Rule had been confirmed by Honorius III and the constitutional status of the fraternity was secured. The friars were expanding throughout Christendom and Francis now enjoyed a greater liberty to devote himself to contemplation and communion with his Creator. Indeed, the last phase of his life was marked by an intensification of his own reflections on the Gospel, which culminated in the celebration of Christmas at Greccio in 1223 and the reception of the stigmata in September 1224. His protracted meditation on the Nativity inspired him to re-create the scene of the mean, impoverished manger. A fortnight before the feast he sent for John, a nobleman of Greccio whom he had influenced, and announced that he wished to do something to recall the child born in Bethlehem and the circumstances of that event, focusing on his poverty. The nobleman then departed to carry out the saint's instructions.

On Christmas night the people of the locality came in numbers, as did the friars. Thomas of Celano could not resist the parallel between the candles and torches carried by those present and the dawning of the light of the world on that night of the Nativity. The manger was prepared, the hay had been brought and the ox and the ass were led in. During the liturgical celebration those present were transported to the side of the crib. The drama of the incarnation was re-enacted in a novel and moving manner. The *Vita prima* attests that simplicity was honoured, poverty was exalted and humility was commended: Greccio became a new Bethlehem. Just as some medieval theologians depicted sin as something that disturbed the created order, so the liturgical celebration at Greccio had cosmic ramifications. The woods rang with the prayers of joyful thanksgiving and the rocks responded to their jubilation. The whole night resounded with harmony and the note of rejoicing. Francis stood before the manger, uttering sighs, overcome with love, and filled with an indescribable happiness. Mass was celebrated beside the manger and the celebrant experienced a new intensity of devotion. Francis exercised his office as deacon and sang the Gospel in a strong and sonorous voice. His clear and sweet voice invited those present to the highest rewards and he spoke fervently of the birth of the poor king and the little town of Bethlehem. His mouth was filled more with sweet affection than words and the warmth of his devotion was shared by others. The scene was one of religious fervour which momentarily restored the harmony of creation and the outpouring of God's gifts. For instance, one man saw a lifeless little child lying in the manger as Francis approached it, rousing the child as from a deep sleep.

Francis is frequently identified with the origins of devotion to the crib. However, E. A. Armstrong believes that he must have seen the crib in churches, especially in Rome; he might have visited the cribs at Santa Maria in Trastevere and Santa Maria ad Praesepe. Thomas of Celano closed his account by commenting that this vision of the divine child being awakened from sleep by the saint was appropriate because the divine child, who had been forgotten by many, had been brought to life again through the saint. Francis was the chosen instrument through which devotion to the infant king had been reborn. The hay from the manger was used by mothers to ensure the safe delivery of their children at birth and saved animals from different ailments. To his credit this biographer displayed little interest in making any claims on behalf of Francis and devotion to the crib. A greater priority was to present the saint as one whose dramatic sense renewed personal devotion to the mystery of the Nativity. Mindful of the complaints of the friars' critics, Bonaventure treats Francis as an innovator, explaining that he obtained papal permission for his epoch-making celebration of Christmas.

FRANCIS'S PRAISE OF GOD IN SONG AND MUSICAL INSTRUMENTS

Francis's biographers emphasize the element of continuity whereby his former tastes and talents were harnessed in the service of the Gospel. In his youth he had enjoyed the tales narrated or sung by poets, minstrels and others and these had been instrumental in the evolution of his romantic view of the world and his ambitions to become a famous knight. For instance, once his ambition to become a knight had been abandoned, his biographers depicted him as the most outstanding and courageous knight in the army of Jesus Christ. Similarly, his love of song and musical instruments were converted for the praise of the Creator. French, the lingua franca of merchants and the language of chivalry, became the medium for his prophecies and songs of spiritual joy. It was Francis's view that the legends of the Christian heroes should not be left in the pages of history. They should be brought to life to inspire people anew with the purest and highest ideals.

In the period following his rift with his father his use of French was a vehicle for his spiritual pleasure and intoxication. Thomas of Celano makes a number of such references in the period following Francis's dramatic change of life. He was singing the praises of God in French when he was apprehended by robbers in the woods and styled himself as the 'herald of the great king'.[34] When the sweetest melody of spirit would bubble up in him, he would give expression to it in French, and the breath of the divine whisper which his ear perceived in secret would burst forth in French in a song of joy. Going through the motions of playing, he would sing in French about his Lord.[35] In a kind of spiritual intoxication, he begged in French for oil and got it and, on his return to San Damiano, he fervently stirred up everyone for the work of that church. In a loud voice he used French to prophesy that there would be a monastery there of holy virgins. The *Vita secunda* proclaims that, whenever he was filled with the ardour of the Holy Spirit, he burst forth into French.[36]

Just as French served Francis as the language of prophecy and spiritual joy, so he wished to reclaim the whole universe to love of its Creator. At Rieti the ailing Francis spoke with a friar who had been a lute player before entering the order, and lamented that his contemporaries did not understand the hidden things of God. Musical instruments, which had once been destined for the praises of God, had been converted into a means of pleasure for the ears by lust. In his desire to restore the natural order to its Creator, Francis asked the friar to borrow a lute for him secretly so that he might give him some comfort in his sickness. The friar voiced his fears about what people would say, suspecting him of giving himself to frivolity. This stricture was accepted by Francis, perhaps more reluctantly than the biographer suggests. But consolation was not to be denied for much longer and the following night the sound of a lute of wonderful harmony and very sweet melody was heard by the saint during his prayers and meditations. No one was visible, but the volume of the sound marked the going and coming of the lute player as he moved backwards and forwards. The music was so enjoyable and stirring that Francis thought that he was in heaven. The following morning he recounted this episode to the former musician, explaining that, although he could not hear this instrument played by men, he had heard a far sweeter lute. Sometimes he would pick up a stick from the ground, and putting it over his left arm, would draw across it, as across a violin. Going through the motions of playing, he would sing in French about his Lord. His whole ecstasy of joy would often end in tears and his song of gladness would be dissolved in compassion for the passion of Christ.[37]

Francis imitated the habits of the minstrels and visualized the friars as the knights of the round table united in their allegiance to their divine master.[38] Their role as divine minstrels was to preach and praise God throughout the world. A properly instructed friar should preach to the people and, after the sermon, he and his companions would sing the praises of God as minstrels. After the praises the preacher should inform the people that they were the Lord's minstrels whose sole reward was that people should live in penance. The friars were to be the divine minstrels seeking to move the hearts of contemporaries and rousing them to spiritual joy. Their responsibility was to awaken people from the sleep of indifference and to engender within them a profound sense of regret for sin and a strong desire of amendment with a burning love of God and neighbour. His wish was that in the morning when the sun rises, everyone would praise God who created it, because through it the eyes are lighted by day. In the evening when it grows night, everyone would praise God for his other creature, brother fire, which lights the night. He maintained that in creatures the human race greatly offends the Creator and daily people are ungrateful for such grace, because they do not praise their Creator and giver of all good things as they should. Sitting down, he began to meditate and afterwards began: 'most high, omnipotent, good Lord'. He composed his *Canticle of Brother Sun* and taught his companions to recite it. His spirit was then in such sweetness and comfort that he wanted Brother Pacifico, who had been known as the king of verses and who had been a courtly doctor of singers before entering the fraternity, to be sent for and given some good and holy friars that they might go through the world preaching and praising God. Francis regarded his followers as divine minstrels, who were to be sent forth to proclaim the liberating truths of the Gospel. After the sermons the friars were to sing the praises of God as minstrels of the Lord and after the praises he wanted the preacher to say to the people: 'we are the Lord's minstrels and as our reward we want you to live in true penitence',[39] that is, the conversion and lifelong penitence of those who hear the sermon and take it to heart. This was a peculiar stipend, but one which reflects the friars' rationale.

SERMONS IN PARISHES

Francis, as already pointed out, had a strong respect for bishops and priests and perceived himself as their helper. He instructed his friars to preach by example and speak briefly about vices and virtues. At a time when clerics had numerous eloquent critics, his respect for the priestly office and the parish priest's primary responsibilities towards his parishioners was unwavering. He declared that, if he were as wise as Solomon and met the poorest priests in the world, he would still refuse to preach in their parishes without their approval. That respect informs the early biographies and Francis frequently preached in parishes at the instigation of the local clergy. His Rule stipulated that no one should preach against the form and institution of the Church and he was insistent that the friars should not preach in the dioceses without episcopal consent. His wishes were generally respected in the early ministry of the friars and Franciscan chroniclers provide plentiful examples of friars preaching within the parochial framework, particularly from the 1220s. It was the decision to enlarge the initially small oratories and to build churches which marred the friars' relations with their secular and monastic neighbours. Thus the *Vita secunda* reiterates Francis's wish that the friars should neither compete with nor rival the ministry of the parochial clergy. Reflecting the growing friction between the secular clergy and the friars in the 1240s, it affirms that Francis wanted the friars to be at peace with everyone; he taught them by word and example to be especially humble towards clerics. His wish was that friars should be a support for the clergy for the salvation of souls and he exhorted them to conceal the lapses of the clergy and to supply for their many defects.[40] His own practice, on entering a city, was to present himself to the bishop or priests. This practice is illustrated by his visits to Cardinal Ugolino in Florence and the bishop at Imola, a city in the Romagna, where he asked permission to preach.[41]

Francis and his followers were styled as *viri poenitentes de civitate Assisi*, penitents from Assisi.[42] Their ministry was so beneficial to the Church that it triggered off a revival of religious observance at all levels within the Christian community; their contribution was acknowledged by both secular and monastic historians. Francis took the values and some of the practices of the monastic tradition and adapted them to the lives of his contemporaries, imparting instruction on both devotional and ascetical practices. Thomas of Celano attests that it seemed that a new light had been sent from heaven, shattering the widespread darkness that had filled almost the whole of Umbria. He discloses that in that part of Italy people had become oblivious of God and his commandments. He undoubtedly exaggerated the level of indifference in order to underline the saint's remedial apostolate. The fruit of Francis's preaching was the fervour and devotion experienced by many of his hearers, who were aroused to seek a greater Christian perfection.

The third order, now known as the secular Franciscans, also took its origin in the response to Francis's preaching. Many of the people of all positions in society were inspired to approach Francis; they were anxious to have him as their guide and leader. Prudent advice was dispensed by Francis, who led his clerical and lay disciples to a fuller understanding and observance of the faith. He provided them with a norm of life and showed them how they might advance to salvation.[43] Bonaventure adds that great numbers of people adopted the new rule of penance, according to the form instituted by Francis, who decreed that they should be known as the 'order of the brothers of penance'. He opened the path of penance to all, drawing people from diverse backgrounds and positions.[44] While he was doing something revolutionary for the men and women dwelling in the new urban centres, it is significant that his teaching was welcomed by some secular priests who looked for a more disciplined form of ministry. In the course of the thirteenth century the third order spread with the friars and attracted widespread support across society in most parts of western Europe, and some of their members, like Elizabeth of Hungary (1207-31) and Margaret of Cortona (*c.* 1247-97), were canonized.[45]

The vitality and vigour of the fraternity were captured by Jacques de Vitry. Writing in 1216 he reports that, amidst the corruption of the age, he had received consolation from the great number of men and women who had renounced all their possessions and left the world for the love of Jesus Christ. They were held in high esteem by the pope and the cardinals. Totally detached from temporal things, their one passion was to snatch souls from the vanities of the world, which imperil souls. Four years later he comments that the friars were spreading rapidly throughout the world and enrolling great numbers of recruits because they expressly followed the life of the twelve apostles and the early Christian community. He asserted that the Franciscans were lesser and more humble than all contemporary religious in their habit, poverty and contempt of the world.

With great solicitude they reproduced in themselves the religion, poverty and humility of the primitive Church. They were sent two by two to preach as precursors to prepare for the second coming of Christ, travelling about with neither purse, haversack, bread, nor money in their belts. They had nothing to do with furs and linen, but used only woollen tunics with a capuche.[46] Many of the friars' sermons were preached in parochial churches, where they were welcomed by the clergy. But, in keeping with Francis's mission to preach to all comers, their sermons were not confined to churches.

SANCTIFICATION OF THE PIAZZA

Lawrence explains that the friars set out to evangelize the new world of the cities. Themselves the product of a new urban society, they preached to people whose language and mental habits they knew and understood. Their friaries were most numerous in those areas where urban density was greatest. Initially they made for the larger and long-established cities, the major centres of commerce and exchange. It was there that the size of the population offered a ripe field for the evangelist.[47] Although there were several hermitages in thirteenth-century Italy, the friars made the city the main focus of their preaching. While the friars frequently preached in the churches of the secular clergy and monks, there was another focus for their preaching and this reflected the new outlook. Just as Francis envisaged a universal cloister, so his preaching was not confined to churches.

In Assisi, as in many other Italian cities, the market place had been established around the ancient forum. The merchants also had their houses close to the piazza and shops, showrooms and storerooms for merchandise were attached to them. For Francis and his first followers the piazza, or market place, was the place of trade and commerce, which they had rejected in favour of a more fulfilling quest for union with God and their neighbours. However, it acquired associations with revelation and renunciation as Francis and the friars reclaimed it for the Creator's service. The message which Francis had heard at the Portiuncula was reinforced by the texts on which his eyes fell at the church of San Nicola in the main piazza of Assisi. These passages formed the kernel of the friars' lives and thus the piazza was a place where the friars' vocation was clarified. It was there that the first recruits had fervently demonstrated their profession of love for their divine master. Both Francis and Bernard turned their backs on the allurement of riches and devoted their lives to the pursuit of Christian perfection.

The excitement generated by Bernard's public display of fidelity to Jesus Christ rather than to material things evoked scenes from the New Testament, when the disciples discarded everything to follow the Son of God and the faithful pooled their resources. Such a spectacle in medieval Assisi showed that the renewal of the Church was under way and such spectacles served as a recruiting sergeant. Bernard's renunciation of his goods was a public event, and in a town as small as Assisi news of the exciting event spread speedily. Among the witnesses was the secular priest Sylvester. When he saw Bernard distributing his goods and giving them to the poor, he was moved to a ravenous avarice and complained to Francis that he had not received a fair price for some stones which he had sold to Bernard. To the astonishment of the secular priest, Francis filled his greedy hands with coins.[48] This event was undoubtedly instrumental in shaming the priest, who was initially delighted by Francis's liberality, and drawing him to the fraternity. On at least one occasion Francis solicited his prayers to resolve doubts about his own vocation. Reports of Bernard's renunciation and his generosity to the poor in Assisi were carried to the ears of Giles, who soon joined Francis. Although earlier generations of ascetics had turned their backs on the centres of habitation, the friars treated the piazza as a place in which they might pursue their own vocation; the dichotomy between the countryside and the city was breaking down. The piazza was in the process of being sanctified anew because the new friars chose it as the venue for the renunciation of their material possessions. Francis and his followers sought sanctification wherever they were, just as they carried the spirit of their founder into the lecture halls of the schools and universities.

The next stage was to turn it into the place where sermons were preached. Christian values, instead of being confined to the churches, were boldly and imaginatively proclaimed in the place of commerce and recreation. Inspired by the conviction that everything was created by God, Francis did not discern any separation between the material and the spiritual. While he preached in churches, sermons in the piazza were frequent; his biographers mentioned sermons at Assisi, Terni, Perugia[49] and Bologna. These references to his sermons can no doubt be multiplied. A description of Francis's sermon in Bologna was provided by Thomas, archdeacon of Spalato. He confirms Thomas of Celano's testimony to the extraordinary power of the saint's words and the excitement caused by his presence in the cities of Italy. On 15 August 1222 Thomas was a student at Bologna where he heard Francis preach in the piazza before almost the entire city. He contrasted the saint's clothing and person with the power of his words, which restored harmony and peace. He spoke so well and with such wondrous clarity about angels that the way in which this untutored man developed his subject impressed the scholars present. His sermons did not belong to the great genre of sacred eloquence: they were harangues and throughout his discourse he spoke of putting an end to hatred and arranging a new treaty of peace. The people showed him as much respect as they did devotion; men and women flocked to him. It was a question of who would at least touch the fringe of his clothing or who would tear off a piece of his poor habit.[50]

Just as he readily preached in the piazza of many cities, Francis was content to preach elsewhere in the open air. He preached on the seashore at Gaeta with the crowds pressing round to touch him. At Bevagna he preached to a huge flock of birds of various kinds and at Alviano he climbed up to a higher place so that he could be seen by all.[51] This example was followed by other friars. When Anthony of Padua was preaching in the diocese of Limoges, the multitude of hearers was such that no church could contain them. Consequently, he betook himself to the vast piazza with the crowd. On another occasion at Limoges, he had gathered the people for a solemn sermon and the crowd was so large that no church was large enough to contain them. Accordingly he led them to a spacious place in which the palaces of the pagans once stood. The churches of Padua were unable to hold the large crowds which flocked to Anthony's daily sermons in Lent 1231 and a decision was taken to withdraw to the wide spaces of open meadows.[52] On Sundays and holy days the friars in England preached in parish churches and other places where the people were assembled.[53]

MINISTRY OF PEACE AND RECONCILIATION

The landscape for the birth of the fraternity was the strife to be found in numerous Italian cities in the early thirteenth century. An incidental reference in the biographies of Anthony of Padua mentions the activities of the papal legates, who were busy re-establishing peace among the northern cities of Lombardy and the March of Treviso.[54] From the beginnings of his vocation Francis was called to be a herald of peace in Assisi, a society which was slowly recovering from the wounds inflicted by the recent civil war; the responsibility of proclaiming peace was noted in the early reports of his preaching in Assisi and elsewhere. Moreover, the centrality of this vocation was underlined by the fact that, at the end of his life, the saint recalled that God had revealed to him the greeting of peace which he was instructed to proclaim in a fragmented home city and country. A crucial dimension of the friars' ministry was to bring reconciliation to the urban centres of Italy and to inculcate there a heightened awareness of their common responsibility to live in peace and harmony.

Francis's insistence on such a greeting, based on the words of 2 Thessalonians 3:16, was considered by some of the early biographers. The risen Christ's greeting of peace was to be extended to the entire human family. Francis perceived himself as one summoned to carry on the ministry of reconciliation and peace. In the early days of the movement he was travelling with a friar, one of the first twelve, who greeted men and women on the road and in the fields. The people were taken aback by such an unheard-of greeting given by religious; they were very much surprised and some almost indignant, asking what the greeting might mean. The friar became perplexed and began to feel ashamed. In his consternation he suggested to Francis that another greeting might be employed.

The friar was advised to continue and was assured that even nobles and princes would show him and his confrères reverence on account of this greeting.[55]

Francis was accustomed to begin his sermons by praying for peace and he announced peace to all people; the same good wish was extended to all whom he met. The *Vita prima* announces that one of the benefits of his early preaching was that many who had hated peace, and salvation also, embraced peace.[56] Another local example was his personal intervention to break the deadlock between the bishop and the *podestà*, as already explained in the second chapter. Indeed, his reputation as a promoter of peace reached England, where Matthew Paris records the tradition that for many years the saint had preached the Gospel of peace.[57] This was one of the clearest signs of the persuasiveness and power of his preaching. He had found a peace which he wished to share with others and his salutation was particularly significant in a society which was beginning to recover from civil war. Peace and reconciliation were basic dispositions for the people of the city. Any instruction in that environment would be expected to concentrate upon the moves towards social tolerance and cohesion. By proclaiming peace Francis shows himself to be a true herald of Christ.

One of the most salient features of Francis's sermon in the piazza at Bologna was his capacity to heal the wounds of suspicion, division and bloodshed. Such results from his preaching were interpreted as a manifestation of the power which God bestowed upon his words in a divided society. Throughout his sermon he spoke of the duty of putting an end to hatred and to arranging a new peace treaty. His words restored peace in many a seignorial family which had been torn apart by old, cruel and furious hatreds, even to the point of assassinations. Once, when he visited Arezzo in Tuscany, Francis found the city bitterly divided between two factions, which had hated each other for a long time; there was the greatest scandal and fighting throughout almost the whole city day and night. The saint, who was lodged in a hospice in town outside the city, saw that the demons were exulting over the citizens and provoking them to destroy the city with fire and other perils. Moved by compassion, he called Sylvester and directed him to go before the gate of the city. On the part of God, he was to command the devils to leave as quickly as they could. The friar carried out the command and, praying the psalms of praise before the face of the Lord, he cried out loudly before the city gate. He commanded the devils, on the part of God and Francis, to depart. Soon afterwards the city returned to peace and the people preserved their civic rights in tranquillity. Whenever Francis preached there in later years, he reminded the citizens of Arezzo that they had once been subjected to the devil and in the bonds of the devils. They had, however, been liberated by the prayers of a poor man.[58]

The town of Greccio, where the saint had inspired many to a fuller observance of the Gospel, had been afflicted by large wolves which devoured men and each year hailstones devastated their fields and vineyards. Francis promised the people that, if they made amends for their sins and returned to God, they would be freed from these scourges and abound in spiritual goods. They were, however, admonished that, if they returned to their former habits, they would suffer more grievously. The spirit of penitence issued in a period of peace and prosperity, but after fifteen or twenty years of good fortune, they began to grow proud and to hate each other, to fight with each other with swords to the death, to kill animals secretly, to plunder and steal by night and to perpetrate many other wicked deeds. When God saw that they had not observed Francis's teaching, the hand of mercy was withdrawn: the plague of hail and wolves returned and many other tribulations worse than before. The whole town was burned.[59] The tensions between neighbouring cities and towns in Italy form the context for Francis's words of reproof to the knights who interrupted his sermon in the piazza at Perugia, as explained in the first chapter.

Social teaching looms large in the preaching of the friars, who were keen to apply the teaching of the New Testament to the commercial life of cities in the thirteenth century. For instance, the first biographer of Anthony of Padua notes that the saint called back to peace those who were in disagreement. He gave freedom to those who had been unjustly imprisoned. Whatever was taken in usury or by violence was to be restored. The impact of this preaching was such that many, having mortgaged houses and fields, placed the money at the feet of Anthony, and, with his advice, restored them to those whom they had cheated through extortion and bribery. Prostitutes were liberated from their profession and thieves were restrained. In the aftermath of Anthony's death zeal and fervour for the saint put an end to hatred and old enmities.[60] In the fifteenth century outstanding preachers of the Observant reform within the Franciscan order, such as Bernardine of Siena and John of Capistrano, carried a similar message of regional and civic reconciliation to the cities of Italy.

ECUMENICAL RECONCILIATION

There are signs to suggest that Francis had initially absorbed many of the contemporary assumptions about society and the world order, although this evidence comes from biographers whose own understanding of the saint was found to be limited. The process of conversion, however, opened new perspectives for Francis and enabled him to take a more objective view of the norms and beliefs prevailing in medieval society. He is reported to have gone to the East in the hope of preaching to the Muslims and gaining martyrdom. His independent outlook was expressed in the freshness of his response to the Crusades. In the midst of a simmering violence he sought dialogue and gentle persuasion. This courteous and respectful attitude towards those who did not share his Christian faith is one of the reasons why Francis is held in such admiration and affection in ecumenical circles.

Francis was born within the first century of the Crusades and brought up on narratives of that remarkable success, which resulted in the recapture of Jerusalem in July 1099. In the twelfth century the Crusaders experienced several reverses and lost territory, culminating in the conquest of Jerusalem by Saladin in 1187, a defeat which inflicted a deep wound on the consciousness of Christians in the West. Francis's own military ambitions had been confined to Italy and the references to the East occur within the context of his desire to preach the Gospel and earn martyrdom. He made three attempts to reach the Holy Land. The first was about 1212, but contrary winds drove the ship to Slavonia. The desire for martyrdom did not abate and a second effort was made some years later, when he got no further than Spain, where illness overtook him. In 1219 he eventually achieved his long-standing ambition and set out for Syria at a time when great battles were raging daily between the Crusaders and the Muslims.

As Francis met the leaders of this Crusade his mind turned back two decades to his own involvement in the civil war in Assisi and the death and destruction caused by such conflict. In the intervening 17 years his mind had turned more to the peace offered by the risen Christ and there are hints that he was displeased by the Crusaders' conduct. A hagiographical veil was, however, cast over anything which implied disapproval of a movement which had been launched by the papacy in the last years of the eleventh century and sustained by successive popes. Soldiers, regarded as pilgrims, had gone there to fight a holy war, but Francis went there to win the hearts of the Muslims.

The earliest account of Francis's contact with the Crusaders' armies was written in the spring of 1220 by Jacques de Vitry. He captures the breath of fresh air which the saint's visit brought to the camp, when the Crusaders were laying siege to Damietta; a later report of this visit was incorporated into the *Vita secunda*. When he learned that the Crusaders were preparing to go into battle, he was deeply grieved and prophesied to one of his companions that, if the battle took place on a particular day, the Crusaders would not meet with success. He was aware that this was an unwelcome prediction and debated whether he should disclose it. He was persuaded to utter the admonition, forbidding the battle and denouncing the reason for it. These unwelcome prophecies and warnings fell on deaf ears. Nonetheless, he was in great suspense at the time of the battle, and made his companion go watch it. The Crusaders were turned to flight, and the battle ended in shame, not triumph, for them. So great was the number of soldiers lost in the disaster that 6,000 were among the dead and captured and Francis mourned especially over the loss of the Spaniards, who had displayed a greater impetuosity in the battle; few of them survived. The biographer concludes with the mildly critical observation that, if victory was to be hoped for from God, battles must be entrusted to the spirit of God.

Both the bishop of Acre and Thomas of Celano draw attention to a more remarkable feature of his visit. In the midst of a highly charged and dangerous atmosphere Francis, accompanied by Illuminato, decided to open a dialogue with the Muslim leaders. His warning that the crusading forces should not go into battle had earned him only abuse and his proposal to enter the Muslim camp seemed the height of folly to the soldiers. To the astonishment of the Crusaders he took the most direct route, walking into the Muslims' camp and preaching to them. His thoughts were not on the destruction or annihilation of an adversary, but on the pursuit of truth in a peaceful and respectful manner. The bishop affirmed that for several days Francis had preached the word of God, but with little success. While he had ostensibly entered the camp with the intention of seeking the conversion of their leader, his gentleness and courtesy created a rather different impression from that given by other Christian leaders. The *Vita prima* affirms that Francis was taken by the Muslim soldiers, who insulted and beat him. Despite such a reception, he was not frightened and threats of torture and death failed to deter him. Bonaventure adds that the Sultan had announced a reward of a Byzantine gold piece for any of his men who brought him the head of a Christian. Thomas of Celano articulates the prejudices of the West in reporting that Francis was treated shamefully by many, who were quite hostile and hateful towards him. His persistence in seeking an interview with the Sultan eventually carried the day, although Bonaventure reports that the two friars were providentially dragged before the Sultan.

Jacques de Vitry provides the earliest testimony to Francis's influence on the Sultan, who entreated the saint to pray for him so that he might be guided in his choice of religion. Thomas of Celano explains that Francis made a very favourable impression upon the Sultan, who was shown to have initially misunderstood his mission and offered him rich gifts. The refusal of such gifts filled the Sultan with admiration for Francis, whom he regarded as an outstanding individual. He was deeply moved by his words and listened to him very willingly. In this passage the biographer seems to have been referring to the respect in which Herod held John the Baptist (Mark 6:19-20). Francis, claims Bonaventure, offered to remain in the Muslim camp in the hope of converting them to Christianity. Had his proposal been accepted, he would have preached the Gospel in the Muslim camp which was under attack from the Crusaders. The report of this visit found no place in the *Vita secunda*, which confined itself to the progress of the battle. This biography was composed when the western Church was renewing its call for Crusaders and the friars were taking a more active part in preaching the Crusade and generating funds for it. By the later 1240s, however, some friars were beginning to question the validity of such enterprises.

In some of the later biographies the question of an ordeal by fire was introduced. The *Legenda maior* furnishes details of an ordeal which was arranged for Francis, who informed the Sultan that, if he was afraid to abandon the law of Islam for Jesus Christ, he himself would undergo an ordeal by fire with the Muslim religious leaders in order to ascertain the true faith. The Sultan doubted whether any of his religious leaders would be willing to expose themselves to the flames, or suffer any torture, to defend their faith; he had just caught sight of one of the esteemed leaders slipping away, as Francis was laying down the challenge. Undaunted, Francis then offered to go into the flames alone, provided that the Sultan attributed his being burned to his own sins or his emerging unscathed to the glory of God. The Sultan replied that he did not dare accept such a challenge lest his people revolt. He was lost in admiration at the sight of such a perfect disregard for worldly wealth and he felt greater respect than ever for the saint. Illuminato, Francis's companion, describes another challenge which the Sultan addressed to the saint. His report concludes with the saint's plea that the Sultan embrace Christianity.

COMMUNION WITH ALL CREATION

Many of Francis's admirers, myself among them, first encountered him in the context of his unusually close relations with the animal kingdom and the created order. Since the late thirteenth century artists have rightly focused upon the gentleness and courtesy which characterized his communication with the whole of God's creation. In an age which has seen several environmental disasters and the maltreatment of animals, the protectors of the earth and of animals look to him as their patron. Moreover, the contemporary world is becoming increasingly conscious of the heritage which it receives from God and the need to preserve this for future generations. Francis was moved by a profound respect for everything created by God and creation supplied him with abundant examples of divine benevolence and providence. His strongly developed sacramental sense led him to find reflections of the Creator and Saviour in diverse parts of the created order. Animals aroused his sympathy and, as an itinerant evangelist, he strove to rouse the whole of creation to unite in praise of the Creator.

Animal stories were afforded more space than teaching on poverty in the *Vita prima* and this gives an important insight into the way in which Francis was perceived by his contemporaries. A close bond with the rest of the created order appears in the lives of many saints of the Celtic Church, such as Kevin at Glendalough and Cuthbert at Lindisfarne. This is a further illustration of Francis's *revival* of an earlier strand of the tradition, even though he and his biographers probably had no knowledge of Christianity in Ireland and Northumbria. He saw no dichotomy between the material and spiritual and believed that God was the source of all life and goodness. He confidently proclaimed God as the single Creator of everything in the universe, in accordance with the teaching of the first canon of the Fourth Lateran Council. He was perfectly at home in a world which was teeming with the sacramental signs of his divine master and he viewed the whole world in terms of a fraternity which was to be united in praise of its Creator.

Some animals evoked biblical imagery in Francis, who had a special affection for them, especially those which reminded him of the virtues of Jesus Christ. For instance, little worms won his affections because they reminded him of Psalm 21:7, which speaks of fallen humanity as a worm. He was accustomed to pick them up from the road and put them in a safe place, lest they be crushed by the feet of passers-by. The humility of the Son of God was more frequently likened to lambs and this gave Francis a special affection for them. For instance, he was travelling towards Osimo when he found a shepherd feeding a herd of goats in the fields. Among the great number of these goats there was a little lamb going along and feeding humbly and quietly. When Francis saw it, he commented on how it walked so meekly among the goats, seeing in it a symbol of the humble redeemer. He often rescued lambs which were being led off to slaughter, in memory of the Lamb of God, who willed to be put to death to save sinners. On occasion he intervened to save sheep from maltreatment.[61]

God, the origin of all creatures

The conviction that the whole of creation springs from the same source filled Francis with greater affection than ever and he called even the most insignificant creatures his brothers and sisters. The *Vita secunda* summarizes his reverential response to the whole of creation, announcing that in every work of the artist the saint praised the artist and rejoiced in everything created by God. In everything beautiful he recognized the source of beauty and detected the divine footprint. The whole of creation became a ladder by which he might rise to communion with the Creator. The evidence supplied by the *Vita secunda* was incorporated into Bonaventure's rich theological outlook. The Parisian master explains that Francis sought occasion to love God in everything. In everything beautiful he saw the divine source of beauty and he followed his beloved everywhere by the likeness imprinted upon creation. From the whole of creation he fashioned a ladder by which he might mount up and embrace the Creator. By the power of his extraordinary faith he tasted the goodness, which is the source of all, in each and every created thing, as in so many rivulets. He seemed to perceive a divine harmony in the interplay of powers and faculties given by God to his creatures and like the prophet Daniel he exhorted them all to praise God.[62]

Francis's compassion was extended to reptiles, birds and other creatures, sensible and insensible. He would ensure that the bees were provided with honey in winter, or the best wine, lest they die from the cold. He used to praise in public the perfection of their works and the excellence of their skill, for the glory of God, with such litanies of their praises that he would often spend a whole day in praising them and the rest of the creatures.[63] Near Bevagna he found that a very large number of birds of various kinds had congregated, namely doves, crows and some others popularly called daws. His tenderness towards animals was such that he left his companions on the road and ran eagerly towards the birds. The birds were waiting expectantly for him and he greeted them in the usual way.[64]

Animals which were trapped or in pain aroused Francis's sympathy and they, in turn, recognized a protective spirit in him. For instance, when he was staying at Greccio, a little rabbit caught in a trap was brought to him by a friar. He was moved to pity and saluted it as his brother. And as soon as the rabbit had been released by the friar, it fled to Francis; without being forced by anyone, it lay quietly in his bosom as the safest place possible. After he had rested there a little while, Francis, caressing it with maternal affection, released it so it could return free to the woods. The rabbit was given its freedom several times, but on each occasion it returned to the saint. Fish, too, moved the saint to tender affection. Sometimes he took those which had been caught and threw them back into the water, urging them to be more careful lest they be caught again. When he was sitting in a boat near a port in the lake of Rieti, a fisherman offered him a big fish popularly called a *tinca*. He accepted it joyfully and kindly, beginning to call it brother. Then, placing it in the water outside the boat, he began devoutly to bless the name of the Lord. And while he continued in prayer for some time, the fish played in the water beside the boat and did not go away from the place until his prayer was finished and Francis gave it permission to leave.[65]

The solemnity of the Nativity filled Francis with a profound sense of joy and he regarded it as a festival with cosmic consequences. For this reason he wished the animal kingdom to share in the benefits. On more than one occasion he declared that, if he could gain access to the emperor, he would implore him for the love of God to make a constitution so that no man should trap larks, whom he regarded as his sisters, or do them any harm whatsoever. His wish was that every *podestà* of cities and lords of towns and villages should be required each Christmas Day to compel the people to scatter corn and grain on the roads outside cities and towns so that the birds might have something to eat, especially the larks. Similarly, the feast should be marked by an obligation to provide oxen and asses with a good meal in memory of the animals present at the nativity. He wished that Christians should be filled with a spirit of exultation on that feast and be bountiful not only to the poor, but also to animals and birds.[66]

Inanimate objects were treated with respect and reverence. These, too, were associated with biblical imagery. For instance, stones were treated with a due respect by Francis, who walked reverently upon them, because of Him who is called the rock (1 Corinthians 10:4). When he used the versicle 'you have exalted me on a rock' (Psalm 60:3), he would say for the sake of greater reverence 'you have exalted me at the foot of a rock'. He used to consider immediately the beauty of that flower that comes from the root of Jesse (Isaiah 11:1) and gives light in the days of spring and by its fragrance has raised innumerable thousands from the dead.[67] When the friars were cutting wood, they were admonished not to cut down the whole tree, so that it might have hope of sprouting again. Similarly, gardeners were instructed to leave the border around the garden undug, so that in their proper times the greenness of the grass and the beauty of the flowers might announce the beauty of their Creator. While the *Vita secunda* maintains that such reverence for the creation was a new element in the early thirteenth century,[68] it is another example of Francis recovering an earlier element in the Christian tradition.

Francis loved and respected fire and other creatures and found so much joy in them; he was moved to such concern over them. He chatted to them and spoke to them about the things of God. He was reluctant to extinguish a candle or a lamp and did not wish the friars to throw out smoking timber, but wanted it to be laid flat on the ground out of reverence for God, the source of light. His companions remarked that it was not surprising that fire and other creatures, which he respected and loved, returned his affection. If anyone did not treat them well, he was upset. When he was sitting near the fire, his habit was caught by a flame. A friar rushed to put out the fire and was rebuked. Instead, the saint instructed him not to harm 'brother fire'. When his eyes were being cauterized at Fonte Colombo, the doctor made a fire to heat the iron. Francis prepared himself for this ordeal by prayer and then exhorted the fire to be courteous to him and to reciprocate his affection. At the sight of the iron, his terrified companions fled. On their return they were rebuked by Francis, who claimed that he had felt no pain.[69]

Sermons to animals

Francis's sermons were addressed to different members of society and the Church. His respect for the created order was such that he placed a literal interpretation on the closing words of St Mark's Gospel (16:15) that the disciples should preach to every creature. Thus from the *Vita prima* onwards the biographers recount numerous occasions when Francis urged the created order to unite in praise of its Creator. They are careful to note that there was a response to the saint's warm words of exhortation. When Francis found an abundance of flowers, he preached to them and invited them to praise the Lord as though they were endowed with reason.[70] Near Bevagna he came across a large group of birds of different kinds and humbly begged them to listen to the word of God. Saluting them as brothers, he exhorted them to praise and always love their Creator. They were reminded of the manifold blessings which God had bestowed upon them: feathers for their clothing and wings for flight and whatever else was necessary for them; they had received a nobility in the created order and a home in the purity of the air. Though they neither sowed nor reaped, they were protected and governed without any solicitude on their part. At these words the birds, rejoicing in a wonderful way, began to stretch their necks, extend their wings, open their mouths and gaze at Francis. Finally, he blessed them and gave them permission to fly to some other place. He began to blame himself for negligence in not having preached to the birds earlier, seeing that they had listened to the word of God with such reverence. From that day on he solicitously admonished all birds, all animals and reptiles, to praise and love their Creator.

The way in which animals responded to Francis's instructions was illustrated by two stories in which they served as exemplars of piety. At the Portiuncula he accepted a sheep, which he then instructed on how to praise God and avoid offending the friars. The sheep, moreover, was careful to follow its instructions, as if it realized the affection he had for it. If it was entering the church and heard the friars singing in the choir, it would go down on one knee spontaneously and bleat before the altar of our Lady, the Mother of the Lamb, as if it were trying to greet her. During the celebration of Mass, at the elevation of the consecrated host, it would bow profoundly on bended knees and its devotion reproached those who were less devout, while giving the faithful an example of respect for the Body of Christ. On another occasion, at Rome, the saint had a lamb with him, which he kept out of reverence for the Lamb of God. When he was leaving, he gave it to Lady Jacoba di Settesoli to keep. The lamb accompanied its mistress to church and stayed there with her, refusing to leave until she left, just as if the saint had trained it in its spiritual exercises. When she was late getting up in the morning, the lamb nudged her with its horns and roused her with its bleats, urging her to hurry to church. She was amazed and became very fond of the animal, which had been a disciple of Francis, from whom it learned respect for the religious life.[71]

Celebration of creation

Francis's respect for the created order was rooted in the belief that the whole of creation was created by God and should return due praise to its Creator. The Scriptures contained the divine truths necessary for the redemption of God's creation and they should be respectfully heard and obeyed. For this reason Francis was prepared to rebuke both human beings and animals when their conduct left something to be desired. For example, just as he rounded on the knights interrupting his homily in Perugia, so he castigated the animals which impeded or marred the apostolate of preaching. When he was preaching from a high place to the people at Alviano, he asked for silence. However, a flock of swallows was chattering and making a loud noise as they built their nests there. Their noise drowned out Francis's words and accordingly he exhorted them to listen to the word of the Lord and be silent until he had finished. To the astonishment of those present, the swallows immediately fell silent and did not move from their place until the sermon was finished.[72] His burning desire was to awaken the whole of creation to a greater awareness of its indebtedness to its Creator and this found classical expression in his *Canticle of Brother Sun*:

> Praised be You, my Lord, through Sister Moon and the stars,
> in heaven You formed them clear and precious and beautiful.
> Praised be You, my Lord, through Brother Wind,
> and through the air, cloudy and serene, and every kind of weather
> through which You give sustenance to Your creatures.
> Praised be You, my Lord, through Sister Water,
> which is very useful and humble and precious and chaste.
> Praise be You, my Lord, through Brother Fire,
> through whom You light the night
> and he is beautiful and playful and robust and strong.
> Praise be You, my Lord, through our Sister Mother Earth,
> who sustains and governs us,
> and who produces varied fruits with coloured flowers and herbs.[73]

Francis was very often filled with a wonderful and indescribable joy in looking upon the sun, the moon, the stars and the firmament. Just as the three youths in the fiery furnace invited all the elements to praise and glorify the Creator of the universe (Daniel 3:51-90), so Francis, filled with the spirit of God, never ceased to glorify, praise and bless the Creator and Ruler of all things in all the elements and creatures. In the same way and with the sincerest purity he exhorted the cornfields and vineyards, stones and forests and all the beautiful things of the fields, fountains of water and the green things of the gardens, earth and fire, air and wind, to love and serve God willingly. Finally he called all creatures 'brother', and in a most extraordinary way, a manner never experienced by others, he discerned the hidden things of nature with his sensitive heart, as one who had already escaped into the freedom of the glory of the sons of God.[74]

Holiness and the restoration of harmony in creation

Animals found in Francis a man of tranquillity and peace. The absence of malice and aggression, which medieval theologians identified as the consequences of Adam's rebellion, made him approachable to the animals, who loved to linger in his company. His biographers found a theological dimension in the wealth of stories about his easy relationship with the whole of God's creation. The *Vita prima* establishes a causal link between the obedience which Francis showed to the Gospel and, in turn, received from animals[75] and this paved the way for the more mature theological reflection of biographers such as Bonaventure. This was illustrated by their report that one day he went down from his cell at the Portiuncula and he saw a cicada on the branch of the nearby fig tree and was still able to touch her. Stretching out his hand, he invited her to approach him and immediately she jumped on to the fingers of his hand and with the finger of his other hand he began to stroke her and encouraged her to sing. She obeyed him and he was much comforted and praised God. For a good hour he held her thus in his hand before putting her back on the branch of the tree, from which he had taken her. Then, for eight days running, when he left his cell, he found her in the same place, and every day he took her in his hand. As soon as he said to her that she should sing and stroked her, she sang. Afterwards he gave her leave to depart and his companions marvelled that she obeyed him and was so tame with him. He had so much joy in creatures through his love of the Creator that God made tame to him the creatures which were wild.[76]

This theme was cloaked in more explicitly theological language by Bonaventure, who taught that animals have souls.[77] In the eighth chapter of the *Legenda maior* this exploration is sandwiched between a chapter dealing with poverty and another exploring Francis's passionate love, culminating in his desire for martyrdom. The saint's poverty, his positive response to the created order and his passionate love and desire to die for his Lord were perceived in complementary terms as essential ingredients in the return to the life of grace. Rehearsing the animal stories narrated by the earlier biographies, Bonaventure concludes the chapter with the following summary:

> therefore, we should respond piously to the piety of this blessed man, which had such remarkable sweetness and power that it subdued ferocious beasts, tamed the wild, trained the tame and bent to his obedience the brute beasts that had rebelled against fallen mankind. Truly this is the virtue that unites all creatures in brotherhood and is helpful *for all things since it has the promise of the present life, and of the life to come* (1 Timothy 4:8).[78]

This theme was made more explicit by the same master in the lecture halls of the Franciscan school at Paris within a quarter of a century of Francis's death. Francis's unusual level of communication with animals was attributed to his personal devotion, which resulted in his return to the innocence forfeited by Adam and Eve. This carried forward the sense of harmony and delight which he had experienced at Greccio two and a half years before his death. In response to the question about the virtue which makes a person love creatures, because they come from God and exist for him, Bonaventure replied that it was compassion and a sort of natural affection. This was illustrated by the fondness which a person may feel towards a dog because it obeys him faithfully. In the same way humanity in its pristine condition had a natural inclination to love animals and even irrational creatures. Thus the greater the progress people make and the nearer they approach the state of innocence the more docile these creatures become towards them, and the greater the affection they feel for them. This principle was exemplified by Francis who overflowed with tender compassion even for animals, because to some extent he had returned to the state of innocence. This was made clear by the way irrational creatures obeyed him.[79]

CONCLUSION

Despite his fairly modest level of education, Francis had outstanding abilities as a persuasive preacher and an imaginative communicator. He preached in a compelling and moving manner about the Gospel and drew very large groups of listeners. He spoke in a form which was accessible to people in Umbria and his vernacular sermons were both colourful and direct. Moreover, they were firmly rooted in prayerful preparation and stamped by a passion and fervour which were lacking from those whose sermons sought to impress with a display of erudition. His divine master had been an immensely effective teacher and so Francis strove to be the same. His flair enabled him to conjure up scenes from the Gospel in which he led the bystanders more deeply into the mystery of the redemption. His continual reflection upon the Gospel enabled him to re-enact the sacred drama in a way which caught the attention and sympathy of his contemporaries. He was an actor whose talents were employed for the propagation of the Christian message.

In a society recovering from civil war Francis took to the streets with a message of peace and reconciliation. He preached not only in churches, but also in public squares and his followers did the same. The friars' vocation was to take the Gospel back to the cities, reminding the local population that Christianity was not confined to the monasteries and the parochial churches: it was a positive and life-enhancing message that was to inform every human decision. Francis lived in a world which was bristling with sacramental signs and the more fully he entered into communication with God the more he caught glimpses of the divine in the created order. Acting on the divine directive to take the Gospel to all creatures, he excluded no creature. He behaved in a courteous manner towards all sections of the created order and invited it to join him in praise of their common Creator. His rapport with the animal world was interpreted as a mark of his return to innocence and the restoration of the harmony lost by Adam and Eve. His purpose as an evangelist to the cities and surrounding countryside was to reunite the human family in praise of its wise and benevolent Creator. Contemporaries revered him as a herald of his divine master and turned to him for direction in life and for prayerful intercession after his death on the evening of 3 October 1226.

Notes

1. J. R. H. Moorman, *Saint Francis of Assisi* (London, 1950), p. 104.
2. *The Life of Ailred of Rievaulx by Walter Daniel*, ed. F. M. Powicke (NMT; 1950), p. 28.
3. C. H. Lawrence, *The Life of St Edmund by Matthew Paris* (Oxford, 1996), p. 2.
4. Orderic Vitalis, *The Ecclesiastical History*, III, ed. Chibnall (OMT; 1972), pp. 196-8.
5. C. N. L. Brooke and R. B. Brooke, *Popular Religion in the Middle Ages* (London, 1984), p. 59.
6. *The Life of St Hugh of Lincoln*, II, ed. D. L. Douie and D. H. Farmer (OMT; 1985), pp. 46-7.
7. *Sacrum commercium sancti Francisci cum domina Paupertate*, ed. S. Brufani (Medioevo Francescano, 1; Assisi, 1990), pp. 170, 173.

8. Jacques de Vitry, 'Histoire de l'Orient', c. 32, pp. 8-10.
9. D. Knowles, *From Pachomius to Ignatius: A Study in the Constitutional History of the Religious Orders* (Oxford, 1966), p. 46.
10. C. H. Lawrence, *The Friars* (London, 1994), p. 121; *Medieval Monasticism* (London, 2nd edn, 1989), p. 238.
11. R. W. Southern, *The Making of the Middle Ages* (London, 1953), p. 229.
12. 1 C, n. 37.
13. *Compilatio Assisiensis*, c. 74.
14. J. V. Fleming, *An Introduction to the Franciscan Literature of the Middle Ages* (Chicago, 1977), p. 16.
15. Lawrence, *The Friars*, p. 121.
16. Brooke and Brooke, *Popular Religion in the Middle Ages*, p. 127.
17. A. Jessopp, *The Coming of the Friars and Other Historic Essays* (London, 1889), pp. 20-1.
18. *Compilatio Assisiensis*, c. 83.
19. 1 C, n. 97.
20. Ibid., nn. 62, 72-3.
21. Ibid., nn. 52-4.
22. 2 C, n. 107.
23. 1 C, n. 36.
24. *Compilatio Assisiensis*, c. 74.
25. *Lettres de Jacques de Vitry*, ed. R. B. C. Huygens (Leiden, 1960), pp. 131-3.
26. 1 C, n. 97.
27. *Compilatio Assisiensis*, c. 10.
28. Brooke and Brooke, *Popular Religion in the Middle Ages*, pp. 127-8.
29. *Scripta Leonis*, p. 22.
30. D. L. Jeffrey, 'St Francis and medieval theatre', *Franciscan Studies*, 43 (1983), pp. 321-46, 324-6.
31. R. J. Armstrong and I. C. Brady, *Francis and Clare* (New York, 1982), p. 33.
32. 1 C, n. 54; 2 C, n. 213; *Compilatio Assisiensis*, c. 80; LM, c. 6, n. 2.
33. 2 C, n. 207.
34. 1 C, n. 16.
35. 2 C, n. 127.
36. Ibid., n. 13.
37. Ibid., nn. 126-7.
38. *Compilatio Assisiensis*, c. 103.
39. Ibid., c. 83.
40. 2 C, n. 146.
41. 1 C, n. 75; 2 C, n. 147.
42. LTS, c. 10, n. 37, p. 117.
43. 1 C, nn. 36-7.
44. LM, c. 4, n. 6.
45. Cf. J. R. H. Moorman, *A History of the Franciscan Order* (Oxford, 1968), pp. 216-25, for an introduction to the early history of this part of the Franciscan movement.
46. *Lettres de Jacques de Vitry*, pp. 75-6, 131-3. In spite of his admiration for all that the friars were achieving, the bishop did not hesitate to criticize them for the practice of sending out some friars who had been neither sufficiently prepared nor schooled in conventual discipline. Cf. Jacques de Vitry, 'Histoire de l'Orient', c. 32, pp. 8-10.
47. Lawrence, *The Friars*, p. 102.
48. 2 C, n. 109.
49. *Compilatio Assisiensis*, cc. 10, 75.
50. Thomas of Spalato, *Historia pontificum Salonitanorum et Spalatensium* (MGH SS, 29; 1892), p. 580.
51. 1 C, nn. 58-59; LM, c. 12, nn. 4, 6.
52. Rigaldina, c. 9, nn. 17, 42; Assidua, c. 13, n. 1.
53. Matthew Paris, *Historia Anglorum*, II, ed. F. Madden (RS 44, ii; London, 1866), pp. 109-10.
54. Assidua, c. 27, n. 15.
55. *Compilatio Assisiensis*, c. 101.
56. 1 C, n. 23.
57. Matthew Paris, *Chronica majora*, III, ed. Luard (RS 57, iii; London, 1876), p. 134.
58. *Compilatio Assisiensis*, c. 108; 2 C, n. 108.
59. Ibid., c. 74.
60. Assidua, c. 13, nn. 11-12; c. 21, n. 4.
61. 1 C, nn. 77-80.

62.   2 C, n. 165; LM, c. 8, n. 6; c. 9, n. 1.
63.   1 C, nn. 77, 80.
64.   Ibid., n. 58. Cf. R. D. Sorrell, 'Tradition and innovation, harmony and hierarchy in St Francis of Assisi's Sermon on the Birds', *Franciscan Studies*, 43 (1983), pp. 396-407 and *St Francis of Assisi and Nature: Tradition and Innovation in Western Christian Attitudes towards the Environment* (Oxford, 1988).
65.   1 C, nn. 60-61.
66.   *Compilatio Assisiensis*, c. 14.
67.   1 C, n. 81.
68.   2 C, n. 165.
69.   *Compilatio Assisiensis*, c. 86.
70.   1 C, n. 81.
71.   LM, c. 8, n. 7.
72.   1 C, n. 59.
73.   Armstrong and Brady, *Francis and Clare*, pp. 38-9.
74.   1 C, nn. 80-81.
75.   Ibid., n. 61.
76.   *Compilatio Assisiensis*, c. 110.
77.   *S. Bonaventurae opera omnia*, V (Quaracchi, Florence, 1891), p. 300.
78.   Bonaventure, *The Soul's Journey into God; the Tree of Life; the Life of St Francis* (New York, 1978), p. 261.
79.   *S. Bonaventurae opera omnia*, III (Quaracchi, Florence, 1887), p. 622.

9

꧁ꕥ꧂ꕥꕥꕥꕥꕥꕥꕥꕥ

St Francis's death, burial and posthumous influence on the fraternity

Brother William told us that we must always consider the mind and intention of
St Francis in the Rule[1]

The events surrounding Francis's death may puzzle those who have become familiar with the details of the life of the *poverello*, the saint who recovered the emphasis on the poverty experienced by his divine master. Preparations for his death and burial were shaped by the deeply held conviction that he was an extraordinarily holy man. His canonization within two years of his death confirmed his immense appeal and necessitated the construction of a basilica to enshrine his body. His influence and authority did not cease with his death on the evening of 3 October 1226. Instead, they were enhanced by his canonization and thenceforth his words carried the halo of sanctity. His body was translated to the majestic basilica in Assisi and he remained a powerful figure in the history of his fraternity, as the flurry of biographies and the reform movements testify. Just as the source of spiritual power in the medieval diocese of Assisi was San Rufino, so the friars treated Francis as the highest authority in the order. For instance, the minister general saw himself as being responsible to the saint for the guidance and appropriate development of the fraternity. As the fraternity continued to expand, the friars became increasingly concerned about their fidelity to the teaching of the founder. From the early 1220s voices were raised in protest about some of the developments and excesses which tarnished the fraternity's good name. Internal calls for reform were matched by the complaints made by the secular clergy, who protested that their dealings with their parishioners were being undermined by the friars' preaching and hearing confessions. The friars were challenged to reform their lives and to model themselves on their founder. Like the medieval promoters of the cult of San Rufino in Assisi, the friars employed hagiography to provide a more authentic portrait of the founder and to provoke a deeper commitment to his teaching.

MEDIEVAL CONVENTIONS REGARDING THE BURIAL OF SAINTS

Those who visit Assisi for the first time, travelling along the plain by road or train, are astonished by a vast fortress-like structure which towers above the city and overshadows the plain. The basilica of San Francesco rises above the Sacro Convento, the adjacent friary built for the friars who have served the shrine since 1230. The impression of enormous strength and security in the complex of buildings stands in stark contrast to the simplicity and poverty of one of the most popular saints in Christendom. There is a seeming incongruity between the imposing edifice, with its grandeur and security, and the gentleness of the saint, who was open to all people. While Francis spent his last twenty years firmly resisting any material encroachments, his basilica was constructed on a grand and massive scale to receive pilgrims from both Umbria and all parts of Europe. A popular cult could be a major source of income,[2] as the people of Assisi knew very well from the medieval flowering of devotion to San Rufino. A popular shrine brought pilgrims from both the locality and other regions and, in its wake, commercial prosperity to Assisi. The early biographies glow with a legitimate pride in their saint and project an image of Francis, who had taken his rightful place among the leading figures in the hierarchy of saints. He could join the company of such widely popular saints such as Martin of Tours, and for that reason his shrine had to conform to certain criteria, such as security, appropriate art to celebrate his life and ample space for the pilgrims. The decision to place the bones of the *poverello* in such secure surroundings, adorned with artistic opulence, cannot be understood without reference to the value which medieval men and women placed on saints' relics and the necessity of preserving them in a safe and fitting place. The rediscovery of the relics of San Rufino in 1212, with the renewal of miracles, ensured that both the bishop and the civic officials were aware of their responsibility in the later summer of 1226.

Preparations for the death and burial of Francis were governed by the medieval conventions governing saints' shrines and the desire to promote a cult. The friars, the bishop and the commune of Assisi laid thorough plans for Francis's return to Assisi, where he was nursed in his last days and eventually buried. The death and burial of the saint were presented in a routine manner by the first biographers, who do not indicate that there was any disagreement on this matter; despite occasional flashes of suspicion between the people and the friars, events ran smoothly. There was no hint of disagreement, obstruction or violence and this was to the credit of those who had laid careful plans for the saint's death. An illustration of what might happen on such occasions was provided by the biographers of Edmund of Abingdon and Anthony of Padua. These two saints died away from home and the opportunity to lay claim to such relics proved too tempting to some towns and villages through which the saints' bodies were transported. These narratives highlight the value which people in the

Middle Ages placed upon saints' bodies, the conventions surrounding their burial and the rival claims upon these bodies, with the simmering threat of violence.

The burial of Edmund of Abingdon

Edmund of Abingdon, archbishop of Canterbury (1234-40), spent some days in the Cistercian monastery at Pontigny, perhaps on his way to the papal court in Rome. He sought some of the spiritual privileges and benefits of the monks and these were granted by the abbot. For the remainder of his stay he played an active part in the liturgical life of the community and shared in its spiritual benefits. A short time afterwards he fell ill and, on medical advice, sought a place of convalescence. He found lodgings in the house of the Canons Regular at Soisy. After three days there his condition deteriorated and he died on 16 November 1240. The following day the body of the archbishop was carried from Soisy to Trainel and followed by large crowds which witnessed miracles. The indiscipline of the followers, some of whom tried to touch Edmund's body, was vividly described by the biographers. Monks were in the procession and they were joined by the abbot of Pontigny, who went out to meet the body. By virtue of Edmund's spiritual association with that monastery, the abbot admonished him not to perform any more miracles until he had arrived at his place of rest. An armed guard was mounted, while the abbot and the members of Edmund's household discussed where the burial should take place. The abbot pressed his claims and reminded the deceased prelate's household that Thomas Becket, the martyred archbishop of Canterbury (1164-70), had spent part of his exile at Pontigny. Nonetheless, he had returned to England shortly before his death and was buried in Canterbury cathedral, whose shrine was visited by pilgrims from many parts of western Europe to the advantage of both the monastic community and the city. The abbot's remarks indicated that the monastery had already been deprived of one canonized archbishop of Canterbury. He was determined that this should not happen for the second time within a century, countering any suggestion that the saintly archbishop should be carried back to Kent.

On 18 November Edmund's body was being carried through Villeneuve-l'Archevêque, where a crowd greeted it with reverence and devotion. Although the body was guarded in a tightly wedged procession, the people forcibly removed it to the high altar of their church. At length the elders of the town were persuaded to disperse the people with clubs. The procession continued and then halted at the church of the Templars at Coulours, where they spent the night. During the night Edmund's escort overheard the Templars' conversations and feared that there might be another attempt to snatch the body. The Templars were warned not to use force in this matter lest they should incur the anger and vengeance of God and the saint. The party managed with difficulty to get away and continue their journey to Pontigny. Large crowds came to meet the funeral procession. One of the Englishmen, amazed at the excitement generated by the procession, cynically attributed it to the monks' desire to derive vast profits from the shrine of Edmund in their monastic church. Another questioned Edmund's sanctity on the élitist grounds that all the glorious saints were buried in the Benedictine churches, while few or none were interred in Cistercian churches. Once these disputes had been settled, the cortège finally arrived at Pontigny, where the saint was buried on 23 November in the presence of prelates, monks, clerics and the people.[3]

The burial of Anthony of Padua

A much more violent reaction followed the death of Anthony on 13 June 1231. The dying saint, perhaps sensing the approach of death, expressed a wish to return from Camposampiero to the friary in Padua. On his way back to the city he stayed at the friary in Arcella, where he died. Although the friars tried to conceal his death, lest the friary be overrun by those flocking to see him, the news leaked out and people rushed there, surrounding the friary. The first there were the people of Capo di Ponte, a suburb which was around the Molino bridge, north of Padua. Among them were many strong young men, who quickly placed an armed guard around the friary. The Poor Clares, whose monastery was next to the friary in Arcella, also staked a claim for his body. Meanwhile the friars of Padua, who had gone to Arcella to make plans for the transfer of the body to their friary, were appalled at the prospect of Anthony being buried in any place other than the one which he himself had indicated; the language resembles that of the *Vita prima* on Francis's affection for the Portiuncula. It emerged that Anthony had bound a companion to ensure that he was buried in the friary at Padua. The friars' claims did not persuade the people of Capo di Ponte, who strengthened their armed guard over the body to frustrate the friars' scheme; the sacred corpse was to be watched day and night. In their dismay the friars turned to the bishop of Padua, who consulted each of the canons. By this stage some of the canons had already been won over by the claims of the Poor Clares and accordingly criticized the friars' case. When the argument seemed to be tilting in favour of the Poor Clares, the friars appealed to the wishes of the saint and sought to influence the bishop by the strength of their arguments. The bishop decided in favour of the friars and ordered the magistrate of the city to give them whatever assistance they required.

While these friars were enlisting ecclesiastical support, the people from Capo di Ponte were stiffening their own resolve to claim the saint for themselves and denied the magistrate access to Arcella. When night fell and the crowds were made to leave, the friars closed the doors of the friary and reinforced them with bars and bolts to prevent a possible raid. Toward midnight, however, while the guards were still keeping watch, an excited crowd, anxious to see the body, broke down all the bars, together with the doors, and violently rushed against the house where the saint was lying; there were three such attacks. Because of the heat and delayed arrival of the minister provincial, the friars quickly placed Anthony's body in a wooden coffin and buried it in a shallow and temporary grave. This was no sooner done than a rumour circulated that the friars had spirited the body away. The people dashed to the friary and laid siege to it with swords and clubs; barricades and doors were swept aside and the people hurried to where the body had been buried. They dug until they found the coffin, but they could not prevail upon the friars to open it. The arrival of the minister provincial raised the level of excitement. When the inhabitants of Capo di Ponte saw him, they quickly convoked their council and insistently asked for the body; the petition was accompanied by intimidation. The minister tried to temper their excesses, and announced that he would take the friars' advice. In the interim he permitted the people of Capo di Ponte to guard the body of the saint.

The minister was aware of the difficulties and decided to approach the magistrate. When the urban council was convoked, he asked them for advice and help. With the consent of all, the city magistrate ordered that the place where the body lay be guarded and forbade, under a fine of one hundred pounds, that anyone should carry arms to the place, until it was known what had been decided by the bishop and clergy of the city. On the fourth day after Anthony's death, the bishop entered into counsel with the clergy: major considerations, according to the Franciscan source, were the preservation of peace and the protection of the friars' rights. The bishop ascertained that the majority of the more influential clergy had been swayed by the arguments of the Poor Clares. The minister, acknowledging the zeal of the contending parties, emphasized that Anthony was a friar and had remained one until his death. He asked that one who had entrusted himself to the order should be restored to the fraternity in death. Hearing the reasons of both parties, the bishop decreed that everything was to be done according to the minister's will.

The bishop instructed his clergy that the next day they should prepare themselves as usual and gather early in the morning at Arcella in orderly procession. He commanded the city's magistrates to offer help to the friars and to hasten, with prepared groups of people, to Arcella at the appointed time to transport the saint's body. The magistrate ordered that a bridge of boats and wooden planks should be built across the river which flowed through Arcella. He feared that, if the procession passed through the centre of Capo di Ponte, there would be a civil disturbance. As soon as the bridge was built, the people of Capo di Ponte ran to the spot with axes and swords and hacked it to pieces. The whole city was in uproar. While they were still shouting, it was learned that the people in the southern part of the city were coming with arms. Hearing of this reaction, the people of Capo di Ponte took up a defensive position and were ready for battle, in the event of the approaching group touching their houses or carrying away the body of the saint. The friars saw that the complete ruin of the city was imminent and feared lest thousands perish in defence of their cause. The Poor Clares, feeling that they had contributed to the impasse and looming carnage, repented and prayed that bloodshed be averted. The city magistrate called the people to the palace through the town crier. When the council had been assembled, he confined to the southern part of the city those who had destroyed the bridge and forbade by edict, under oath and threat of confiscation of all their goods, that they return to their homes that day. Later the bishop with all the clergy and the magistrate with a large crowd went to Arcella and a funeral cortège was formed amid hymns, praises and spiritual canticles. They transported the body of Anthony through the centre of Capo di Ponte to the friars' church in Padua; the nobles among the people and the leading citizens carried the bier on their shoulders. People wished to touch the coffin and many people carried candles. When the cortège reached the church of the Blessed Virgin Mary, the bishop solemnly celebrated Mass and then buried Anthony's body. That very day miracles occurred at the tomb.[4]

ARRANGEMENTS FOR THE DEATH AND BURIAL OF FRANCIS

Plans for the construction of the basilica and the adjacent friary mirror the tensions between Francis's own view of himself and his contemporaries' perception of him. While he regarded himself as an insignificant man, beset by weakness and a prey to temptation, the citizens of Assisi and other Italian cities revered him as a prophet. They recognized him as a man of God and a saint sent by God in the last days to revive Christianity and to make his contemporaries more aware of the benefits which they received from God and their responsibilities for sharing such abundant goodness with their neighbours.

Counsels of prudence in Assisi

Francis was seen to belong to the city of his birth as much as to the fraternity which he had founded. Thus the place of his death and the site of his tomb were viewed as matters of civic importance; such decisions could not be left entirely in the friars' hands. Events following the death of Anthony of Padua suggest that the friars had to negotiate with the local ecclesiastical and civic officials. It was expected that pilgrims would flock to Assisi and a secure tomb was a priority. The conventions regulating the burial of the saints ruled out the romantic notion that Francis might be given a pauper's grave in the countryside in accordance with his own lifestyle. Francis's early biographers remain surprisingly reticent about his own wishes for burial and even the circle associated with Leo did not attribute to the saint a desire for burial at the Portiuncula; instead, they contented themselves with the frequently reiterated statements about Francis's love for the place which he regarded as sacred. It was left to the chronicler Jordan of Giano to recount the tradition that Francis wished to be buried at the Portiuncula, though he adds that tensions with Perugia precluded this.[5] There were other more conventional factors to be taken into account. The absence of comment may be the result of the hagiographers' acceptance, albeit reluctant in some cases, of the truth that the saints' bodies had to be secured against the threat of theft.

Preparations for the death of Francis were meticulous and sprang from the assured conviction that he would be canonized. Although Francis stoutly resisted any suggestion that he was a holy man, his contemporaries were determined that his native city of Assisi should be blessed by his powerful presence and intercession in death. A group of friars, of which Elias was a key member, had already opened discussions with Guido and the *podestà*. Bulletins of Francis's deteriorating health were communicated to Assisi at regular intervals, especially during his stay at Siena, and contingency plans were laid. Decisions crucial for the city of Assisi had to be taken in this period and an armed guard had to be assembled in readiness for the pauper's return to his native city. The final decision on when to dispatch the guard to escort Francis back to Assisi remained to be taken.

The friars cannot have been indifferent to the plans being formulated in Assisi for the glorification of their founder. The lustre of their saint brought enormous benefits to the young fraternity, which was beginning to take its place in the ecclesiastical landscape. Devotees of the saint, including cardinals and bishops, were eager to demonstrate their gratitude by both embellishing the shrine and supporting the nascent order, which had received the firm backing of the popes from Innocent III to Gregory IX. Francis's magnetic personality and perspicacious teaching brought thousands of young men to the fraternity, whose ranks began to swell, enabling them to reach the large centres of western Europe within a decade of his death. There is no hint that the friars attempted to resist the plans to ensure that their founder was buried in a secure and fitting monument. Instead, they energetically promoted Francis's cult, which would bring so many benefits to them. The ministers seem to have accepted the inevitability of such plans, which were being promoted by Elias in conjunction with Gregory IX, who sometimes used the Sacro Convento as a papal residence.

An armed escort for the dying saint

When Francis and Elias were staying at Foligno, a white-garbed priest of a very great age with a venerable appearance stood before Elias and prophesied that Francis would die within two years. Elias was instructed to communicate this news to Francis.[6] R. Brown speculates on the identity of the aged figure, believing that this might have been San Feliciano.[7] This identification, despite its limitations, associates Francis with the origins of Christianity in his native city. Francis's early biographies attest that for the last year of life his health was being closely monitored by a group of interested figures in Assisi. Guido, who reached the conclusion that Francis was likely to be declared a saint, was a pivotal figure in the preparations. His knowledge of the conditions for a successful cult was an essential element in the plans being formed by such interested parties. Francis's condition may have deteriorated quite suddenly in the last months, because he returned to Assisi when Guido was on pilgrimage. Guido may have expected Francis to live for some time and with this knowledge he set out for the shrine of St Michael the Archangel. Elias, a figure excessively vilified in Franciscan writings from the 1240s, was undoutedly devoted to Francis. The strength of that friendship, however, did not blind him to the immense potential for the expansion of the fraternity. The *podestà*, another devotee of the saint, acted on behalf of the commune, which was fully conscious of the commercial advantages which another successful cult would bring to the city. The commune wished to strengthen itself against its overbearing neighbour in Perugia and regarded Francis as an immensely attractive patron saint, who himself had taken up arms on behalf of Assisi. In the closing months of Francis's life there were many meetings at which Guido, Elias and the *podestà* drew up their plans for the last act in the saint's life. This helps to explain the speed with which Elias and the commune responded to news of Francis's failing health.

During the last year of his life Francis had accepted the advice of Elias and Ugolino that he should seek medical assistance. He had been nursed for some weeks at San Damiano and had then gone to Rieti in search of treatment for his eyes. Later he moved to Siena, where he succumbed to other ailments and was afflicted with pains in the stomach six months before his death. One evening he vomited blood throughout the night and his companions feared that death was close. This news brought Elias, who hurried from a great distance, to Francis's side. On arrival he found that the saint had rallied sufficiently to be taken to Le Celle near Cortona. There, however, he suffered a relapse; his abdomen began to swell along with his feet and legs; he could hardly take any food. He then asked Elias to take him back to Assisi; Thomas of Celano depicts him as longing to return to his native city.[8]

On his way from Siena and Celle di Cortona Francis returned briefly to the Portiuncula. Despite the earlier anxieties, it was deemed safe to permit him to leave for a short period, which he spent at the friary of Bagnara, above the city of Nocera. He remained there for many days, during which his feet and legs swelled with dropsy and he began to feel very ill. Concern, however, was mounting in Assisi that death was closing in on Francis. When the citizens ascertained that he was ill at Bagnara, they speedily dispatched some soldiers to conduct him home. The companions of Francis are quite explicit about the source of this concern by the citizens of Assisi: they were afraid that the saint might die outside Assisi and that another city might lay claim to his sacred remains. On their way back they rested at Satriano, a town belonging to the commune of Assisi. While the party was staying there, an event occurred which exemplified Francis's role as a teacher, even in the last weeks of his life.

Despite the good intentions of Elias, Guido and the *podestà*, Francis experienced a certain amount of frustration, possibly anguish, at being unable to direct events; he was becoming increasingly the prisoner of the preparations made by others. He did not relish the prospect of returning to Assisi with an armed guard, which would accompany him until his burial at San Giorgio in Assisi. He, who had preached peace for twenty years and lived in apostolic poverty, acknowledging that possessions sometimes lead to violence, had the indignity of being taken back to his own city of Assisi under armed guard. The former soldier was now under an armed escort; he may have foreseen that he would be buried in a vast fortress-like basilica. Eternal life offered the only release from the tightening grip of the allied forces in search of a famous cult for the city and the fraternity. As so often in his life, Francis's objectives differed from those of his neighbours. He was intent on living according to the Gospel, while the armed guard and the friars dreamed of a highly successful cult in Assisi. Chilled by these thoughts, Francis was determined that the claims of the Gospel should be heard once more amidst all the plans dictated by expediency. He was determined to assert his own principles and offer guidance to the soldiers, who were more inclined to place their trust in their own efforts. The soldiers had passed through the town in a vain search for supplies. They returned to Francis, saying to him in jest that he should supply them with alms. In one of his last defences of his ideal he retorted that the soldiers had placed more trust in their money than in God and that this had prevented them from obtaining anything. They were commanded to return to the houses where they had attempted to purchase food, and to seek alms for the love of God. Francis's personal authority was such that they went out and begged and, as he had predicted, they received abundant alms. This was taken for another miracle by the soldiers, who returned to Francis to give him an excited account of what had transpired.[9]

Francis nursed at the episcopal palace

When the group of soldiers and friars eventually reached the outskirts of Assisi, numerous thoughts vied for Francis's attention. He was acutely aware that he was returning to the city of his birth for the last time. Did he recollect other occasions when he had returned to his beloved city, such as after gaining the pope's approval for the fraternity or after his pilgrimage to the East to face division within the fraternity? Countless memories, mingled with hopes and anxieties for the welfare of the fraternity, filled his mind. News that Francis was nearing the city brought people to the streets. In a rich hagiographical vein Thomas of Celano speaks of Francis's return in messianic terms: the whole city rejoiced and all gave themselves to the praise of God and hoped that the saint would die nearby. Even the biographer could not exclude the people's hopes that the saint would die in their midst and confirms that the cause of such joy was that Francis would die in Assisi.[10] Guido's involvement in the plans for the passing of the saint is mirrored in the decision to have Francis nursed in the episcopal palace. Following his return from the friary at Bagnara, the ailing Francis lay at the bishop's palace at Assisi. A friar, with a reputation for piety and sanctity, predicted that the saint's body, which wore a sackcloth, would be clothed in rich brocades and silks; Francis acknowledged that this would be so.[11]

The level of worry lest Francis be buried outside Assisi placed some strains on the alliance between the bishop, the *podestà* and the friars; some of the local populace cast doubt on the friars' loyalty to the city. Once the party had returned to Assisi, the citizens remained anxious: they were afraid that the saint might die during the night without their knowing and be buried secretly by the friars in another city; five years later the people of Capo di Ponte entertained similar suspicions about the friars' plans regarding Anthony of Padua. Despite his illness, Francis often caused his companions to sing by day the *Praises of God*, which he had composed to console his spirit in illness, lest it fail him on account of his numerous different ailments. The friars were also instructed to sing by night for the edification of the guards, who had mounted a round-the-clock watch outside the palace. While the *Vita prima* presents Elias as the good son of the saint in arranging to have him carried back to Assisi, Leo and companions offered a much more critical account, styling him as one who did not understand the saint's teaching. Elias was familiar with hagiographical models and expectations and this prompted him to deliver a mild reprimand to the saint, who rejoiced in the midst of infirmity. Francis was told that the people of Assisi already venerated him as a saint and that the singing of such praises might occasion scandal at the eleventh hour. Francis, who cared so little for this popular acclaim, reminded him of the prediction of his death two years earlier and that he had long pondered upon his death. Elias was dismissed by the saint, who wished to give himself to praising God.

FRANCIS'S DEATH AT THE PORTIUNCULA AND BURIAL AT SAN GIORGIO

John, a doctor from Arezzo and Francis's friend, visited him as he lay dying at the *vescovado*. Asked by Francis how long his illness of dropsy would last, he initially gave an evasive answer, saying that with God's grace he would recover. This reply did not satisfy the saint, who pressed him for a more honest answer. Exhorting him to tell the truth, he assured him that death held no terrors for him. John then responded that his friend would die either at the end of September or the beginning of or on 4 October; the accuracy of the second date looks like careful editorial work! The news was greeted by Francis who joyfully welcomed Sister Death.[12] The final confirmation that death was near quickened the discussions between the friars and the civic authorities. The saint himself seems to have pressed his dying wish to be permitted to return to the Portiuncula once more. The exchanges were lengthy and the decision to allow him to return to Santa Maria degli Angeli was taken with some reluctance, although conditions were imposed. Nonetheless, contingency plans were made for his transfer and an armed guard was dispatched to the Portiuncula. Francis's illness was so serious that he could not go on horseback and he had to be carried on a litter. When those who were carrying him crossed the road by the hospital, he asked them to put his bed on the ground. Because he was almost blind, he had the litter turned so that he faced Assisi for the last time and entreated God to remember his mercy towards the city so that it might become the home of those who acknowledged their Creator. After this prayer the party of friars and soldiers completed the short journey to Francis's beloved Portiuncula. The biographers make no mention of an armed escort at this stage, but it is highly improbable that the guards ever let Francis out of their sight until his mortal remains were safely interred at San Giorgio. A guard was probably posted on the roads leading to Perugia in order to provide early news of any attack from that quarter, especially because the Portiuncula was very vulnerable to such raids.

The biographers unite in their observation that the Portiuncula was a place of special importance to Francis and his first followers; it was undoubtedly his wish to die there. In the church which he had restored with his own hands he had heard the Gospel directing him to live and preach as an apostle. The friars made their home beside the renovated chapel, where he received Clare and countless others to the community of those pledged to imitate their divine master. He loved the chapel above all others and implored the friars never to abandon it. He wished this friary to be preserved as a model of humility and highest poverty for the order and disclosed that God had revealed to him that the Blessed Virgin loved this church with a special love and for that reason he nurtured a special devotion towards it. The most rigid discipline obtained there in everything regarding silence, work and the other ordinances of the Rule. He did not want the friars there, whose number was strictly limited, to be distracted by news of worldly things, lest their meditation on heavenly things be disturbed. Friars of proven virtue were to be appointed so that a model observance might reign there. Near his death he wanted to have it written in his *Testament* that the friars should always have the greatest reverence and devotion for the house.[13]

There is a sharp contrast between the rather stiff and ecclesiastically correct biographies compiled by Thomas of Celano and the more spontaneous reminiscences assembled by Leo and companions. His exceedingly circumspect version of the saint's dealings with women was balanced by the materials assembled by Leo and companions, who provide two cherished anecdotes about Francis's friendship with two women in his last days, suggesting a more refreshingly open disposition.

For many years Francis had enjoyed the friendship of Lady Jacoba of Settisoli, a pious and wealthy Roman widow; she had also become the friars' benefactor. She had derived great benefit and grace from Francis's preaching. On his death bed he wished to see her again and had a letter sent to inform her of the deterioration in his health and to ask her to bring some cloth for a tunic and marzipan. He particularly asked that she might send the friars a tunic, the colour of ashes, and some marzipan, which he had enjoyed on many trips to Rome. Just as the letter was about to be dispatched she arrived at the Portiuncula with her son and others. The friar who received her hurried to inform Francis and to ask him what should be done about the monastic enclosure, which effectively barred women from entering the inner part of the friary. Francis showed no signs of conforming to the expectations of those who regarded him as a saint and waived the ban on the cloister. Jacoba told the friars that she had received a premonition of the saint's death and hastened to Assisi carrying those items requested as well as additional gifts. Some marzipan was prepared for Francis who could eat very little. The tunic became his burial garment, over which he had sackcloth sewn as a token of humility and poverty. She also brought numerous candles, which would burn before his body.

Similarly in the week before Francis's death Clare was very ill and afraid that she would die before him. She wept and was inconsolable because she could not see Francis, her mentor, who had first established her in God's grace. She had sent a friar to him with news of her illness. Francis was moved with pity and reflected on the origins of the fraternity and the conversion of Clare at his advice. When he pondered that it was impossible to fulfil her request for a meeting, he wrote her a blessing to comfort her and absolved her from all her failings, if she had any, in obeying his commands. The same friar was sent back to Clare with the instruction that she should lay aside all sorrow and sadness that she could not see him. She was assured that before her death she and the sisters would see him and receive the greatest consolation from him.[14]

In the middle of his infirmities Francis praised God fervently and gladly, knowing that death was approaching. He had Angelo and Leo summoned that they might sing to him of Sister Death. These friars tearfully approached him and sang the *Canticle of Brother Sun* and the other creatures of God, which he had composed in his illness. In this song he inserted before the last verse the following words about Sister Death:

> be praised my Lord for our sister the death of the body, which no man living can escape. Woe to those who die in mortal sin, blessed those who find it in your most holy will, for a second death will not harm them.[15]

He himself burst forth in the psalm of David (Psalm 142) and went forward to meet Sister Death with a song on his lips. His joyful spirit was contrasted with the grief of the friars, one of whom bewailed the fact that they would soon be orphaned and asked Francis to forgive the friars' failings.

There was no spirit of presumption in Francis who was about to enter his last battle with the devil. He had himself placed naked upon the earth so that in that final hour he might wrestle naked with a naked enemy. In these last moments he was armed with poverty and, laying aside his garment of sackcloth, he raised his face to heaven and announced to the friars that he had accomplished his work and asked God to teach his followers what they should do. Giving away even his clothes, Francis rejoiced to have kept faith with Lady Poverty to the very end. In his zeal for poverty he had carried out his work and shown himself a true imitator of Jesus Christ. The friars were summoned and for a long time he spoke about practising patience and poverty, setting the evangelical counsels and the Gospel before all other prescriptions. He invited all God's creatures to love and bless their Creator. The friars present were then blessed in turn, beginning with his vicar. Francis blessed some bread and broke it and gave a small piece of it to each one. His last act was one which was deeply symbolic of the previous twenty years: he called for the book of the Gospels and commanded that the Gospel of John be read from the beginning of the thirteenth chapter. This passage had also appeared at the first opening of the book two years earlier at La Verna and might indicate that Thomas of Celano perceived the saint's death as the fulfilment of the process which had been revealed at La Verna. In his last moments Francis was eager to be faithful to the Gospel and to return to the dust from which he had come. Accordingly, he asked that a hair shirt be put on him, and that he be sprinkled with ashes, symbolizing that he would soon become dust and ashes.

Francis's biographers, following conventions of that genre, delight in recording the extraordinary events which marked the moment of Francis's death. One of the friars saw the founder's soul rise like a star to its celestial home. Thomas of Celano explains that larks love the noonday light and shun the darkness of twilight. But on the night of Francis's death they approached the roof of the Portiuncula, though twilight had already fallen; they flew about the friary for a long time amid a great clamour, showing perhaps their joy or their sadness. The city watchmen who guarded the friary carefully were astonished at the spectacle and called others to witness it.[16] News of Francis's death spread like wild fire throughout the area, quickly reaching the city. People from the city and beyond hurried to the Portiuncula to revere the body of the saint. The friars who assembled with a vast multitude of people from nearby cities spent the night of the saint's death singing the praises of God. In the morning a large crowd of people from Assisi assembled with all the clergy and carried Francis's body into the city with hymns, praises and the sound of trumpets. They all took up branches of olive trees and of other trees and carried him to San Damiano, where the coffin was opened. On arrival at San Giorgio, they laid his body to rest amidst great rejoicing and exultation.[17] The celebrant at the requiem Mass is not named, although in the absence of Guido, the minister provincial may have presided. Cardinal Ugolino, who had taken part in St Dominic's funeral in 1221, may have travelled to Assisi to pay his respects to his deceased friend. Francis's body was laid to rest honourably with hymns and praises in his native city.[18]

THE PROCLAMATION OF FRANCIS'S STIGMATA

Rumours about Francis's health were probably rife throughout the spring and summer of 1226. Within a few hours of his death or shortly afterwards Elias sent a letter to all members of the order, informing them of the saint's death at the Portiuncula. This was presented in conventional terms of bereavement: each ordained friar was required to offer three Masses, clerics were to recite the Psalter and the lay brothers were to recite the Lord's Prayer five times. Elias then proceeded to announce in triumphal terms that a new kind of miracle had been worked in the flesh of Francis, a miracle unprecedented in the history of the world. For two years before his death the saint's body had borne the wounds of the crucified Christ: his hands, feet and side had been pierced. Thomas of Celano, too, proclaimed this unheard-of miracle, which provided the friars with an additional reason for promoting their saint. Those who had dashed to the Portiuncula to venerate his body were thrilled by the singular privilege accorded to him. They saw his flesh, which had hitherto been dark, gleaming with a dazzling whiteness.[19]

Devotion to the cross assumed a central place in Francis's piety. He regarded the cross as a symbol of the divine generosity towards wayward humanity and the recollection of the passion suffered by the Son of God reduced him to tears; his mourning also moved others to weep at the thought of the pain endured by the Son of God in reconciling humanity. This devotion was summarized by Bonaventure, who enumerates the manifestations of the cross in the saint's life, culminating in the stigmata. The seal of the cross had been impressed upon his heart from the beginning of his religious life; he wished to carry it in his body too. He had clothed himself with the cross, donning the habit of penance, which was in the form of a cross. He had put on the person of Christ crucified in his heart and his body was clothed in the armour of the cross. A love of the cross had seized him from the beginning and it was the honour of bearing the cross which made him a cause of admiration for the world.[20] Just as the Crusaders had the cross sewn on to their tunics, Francis was eager to manifest his commitment to the Gospel. Elias triumphantly announced the fact of the stigmata, but it fell to Thomas of Celano to give a detailed description of the miracle.

In the late summer of 1224 Francis had withdrawn from the crowds and sought out a quiet and secret place in order to spend time with God and to renew himself. With a small group of companions he went to the hermitage at La Verna in the province of Tuscany in search of deeper communion with his Creator. What took place there may be seen as a fulfilment of the earlier stages of his vocation, when he had entered the church of San Damiano near Assisi and heard the message from the crucified Christ, directing him to restore the Church. Francis had resolved his earlier uncertainty about his lifestyle by hearing the Gospel read at the Portiuncula and, when he was joined by Bernard, he had had the Gospel opened thrice at San Nicola. In this last phase of his life he did the same and prayed before an altar in the hermitage of La Verna. Taking the book of the Gospels, he fervently asked God to make known his will to him. The first passage on which his eye fell described the passion. This message was reinforced by the second and third readings. This random opening of the Gospels convinced Francis that he was to enter the kingdom of heaven through many tribulations, trials and struggles; the first text to appear on that occasion was later identified as the beginning of the thirteenth chapter of St John's Gospel.

As Francis prayed on the side of the mountain he saw a vision of a man standing above him, like a seraph with six wings, his hands extended. Two of the wings were above his head, two were extended as if for flight and two were wrapped around the whole body. As Francis struggled to comprehend the meaning of this vision, the marks of the nails began to appear in his hands and feet, just as he had seen in the crucified man above him. His hands and feet seemed to be pierced through the middle by nails, whose heads appeared in the inner sides of the hands and on the upper sides of the feet and their pointed ends on the opposite sides. The marks in the hands were round on the inner side, but on the outer side they were elongated; and some small pieces of flesh took on the appearance of the ends of the nails, bent and driven back and rising above the rest of the flesh. In the same way the marks of the nails were impressed upon the feet and raised in a similar way above the rest of the flesh. Furthermore, his right side was as though it had been pierced by the lance and had a wound, which frequently bled and covered his tunic and trousers with his sacred blood. He made every effort to conceal this miracle from both friars and those outside the order; very few friars were privileged to see the wounds and among these were Elias and Rufino.[21]

The *Vita prima* was content to herald the new and wondrous miracle of the stigmata. In the 1230s and 1240s the hagiographical tradition, however, began to speak of confessors in the language of martyrs and this enters the biographies and sermons on Anthony of Padua and Matthew of Paris's biography of Edmund of Abingdon. The archbishop's indomitable faith and extraordinary austerity of life led his monastic biographer to claim that he endured a prolonged and almost insupportable martyrdom and received the martyr's palm, even though he did not die by the sword.[22] The theme of substitute martyrdom was explored in Bonaventure's account of the stigmata:

Francis's body had been weakened by the austerity of his past life and the fact that he had carried the cross without interruption. Eventually he realized that God had shown him this vision in his providence, in order to let him see that, as Jesus Christ's lover, he would resemble the Crucified perfectly not by physical martyrdom, but by his fervour.

A more theological reflection on the miracle was given by Bonaventure, who affirms its reality. He emphasizes that Francis bore a representation of the Crucified which was not the work of an artist in wood or stone, but had been reproduced in the members of his body by the hand of the living God.[23] The concern to verify the miracle played a prominent role in later descriptions and a list of eyewitnesses was compiled in Assisi before the middle of the thirteenth century.[24] Bonaventure confirms that some friars saw the stigmata and gave evidence under oath, although they were worthy of credence. The stigmata were witnessed not just by two or three, but by a whole multitude, including some of the friars who lived in the same friary as Francis. Some of the cardinals, who were close friends of the saint, also saw his wounds and celebrated them in hymns and antiphons; Alexander IV was among those who testified that he had seen the wounds. Similar testimony was received from more than fifty Poor Clares and several lay people.[25]

In the 1240s and 1250s the friars were keen to verify the stigamta and to record as much detail as possible from the living witnesses. Leo, confirming the truth of the miracle, subsequently testified that the Seraph appeared to the saint who was rapt in contemplation. He disclosed that the saint had directed Rufino to wash the stone on which the angel had stood and to anoint it with oil. During the general chapter at Genoa John of Parma, the minister general, instructed Boniface, a companion of the saint, to tell the friars the facts about the stigmata because many doubted its truth. The friar tearfully confirmed that his own eyes and hands had born witness to this miracle.[26] Paintings of the saint with the stigmata also feature in the miracles recounted by Thomas of Celano. For example, a woman in Rome had chosen Francis as her advocate and had a painting of him in her room, where she was accustomed to pray. In her prayers one day she was surprised and upset to notice that there was no sign of the stigmata; the artist had, in fact, omitted this miracle. She pondered the absence of the stigmata for some days, when the saint's wounds suddenly appeared in the painting. The startled woman called her daughter to ascertain whether the wounds had been missing from the painting and her daughter confirmed that they had been omitted. The woman began to doubt once more and to think that the stigmata had been there from the outset. Bonaventure's catalogue of miracles concerning the stigmata concludes with the declaration that there could be no doubt about this miracle.[27]

TOWARDS CANONIZATION

From the day of his burial numerous miracles occurred at Francis's tomb in the church of San Giorgio in Assisi. With hagiographical licence Thomas of Celano claimed that Francis was honoured by the whole world, which venerated, glorified and praised him; God deigned to work miracles through his intercession. Particular attention was paid to the evidence of devotion and miracles in France, the country for which Francis had such deep respect and affection. The king and queen were among the powerful people who hastened to kiss and venerate the pillow used by the saint in his illness. Even the University of Paris joined the ranks of the pious and the city of scholars humbly and devoutly venerated, admired and honoured the saint. While Francis was working miracles throughout the world, he was particularly active at his tomb, where countless cures were reported. Thomas of Celano relates that miracles were constantly taking place there and that a large number of petitions was addressed to Francis. Sight was given to the blind, hearing to the deaf and the handicapped were enabled to walk. Francis's beloved lepers were not abandoned at his death and benefited from his celestial intercession. The miracles were properly recorded, perhaps at Guido's instigation, for use in the inquiry into Francis's sanctity. The friars, possibly in conjunction with the civic officials, built up a dossier of miracles, which was then handed over to the papal officials to open the process of canonization.

The miracles mirror the dissemination of Francis's fame and the practices of pilgrims at his tomb. One such miracle occurred on the day of his burial. A girl was brought to the tomb: for a year her neck had been monstrously bent and her head had gone down to her shoulders so that she could look up only sideways. When she had placed her head on the tomb for a little while, she raised up her neck and her head was restored to its proper position. She was astonished by the sudden change in herself and began to run away and weep. A man from Foligno had a crippled left leg and suffered great pain. He had spent vast sums of money – more than he could afford – on seeking medical assistance. He eventually vowed to go to Francis's tomb, where he spent the whole night in prayer. He was cured and returned home joyfully, having cast aside his cane. A girl from Gubbio, who had been unable to use her hands for a year, was carried by her nurse to Assisi with a waxen image, in search of healing. She remained there for eight days and recovered the use of all her limbs.[28] While the majority of those who were cured had travelled to the tomb, others were healed in their own towns and cities. Initially the cures concerned people from Umbria, though a leper at San Severino in the Marches of Ancona made a vow to the saint and was healed.

Goodich has observed that the first stage in the process of canonization was the receipt by Rome of petitions from leading lay and ecclesiastical figures;[29] the same procedure was followed in the process of Anthony of Padua's canonization.

In Assisi the bishop, friars and *podestà* drew up a formal petition for the canonization of Francis. At an early stage Gregory IX decided to go to Assisi, where he received a warm reception. His first act was to visit the tomb of his friend and there can be little doubt that he sought Francis's intercession for the dangers confronting the papacy at that time. Thomas of Celano reports that the pope sighed deeply, struck his breast, shed tears and bowed his head with great devotion. The universality of the saint's appeal was underlined by his first biographer: at the pope's approach the whole region rejoiced, Assisi was filled with exultation and a large crowd of people. Many who had been healed by the new saint were present; a large number of miracles was reported. On this visit there was a solemn discussion about the canonization and several other meetings were held by the cardinals, who received testimony from those who had been freed from their illnesses through Francis's intercession. Further miracles were reported in this period: these were approved, verified, heard and accepted.

The urgency of papal business carried Gregory to Perugia, where there were further meetings between him and the cardinals on the matter of Francis's canonization. A decisive session was held in the papal rooms and it was unanimously agreed to proceed with the canonization and the date was set. The miracles were read and treated in a reverent manner, commending the life and conduct of the saint. One of Francis's companions referred to his testimony before the pope and cardinals in Assisi.[30] Another witness was Guido, who almost two decades earlier had so decisively given Francis his backing first at the episcopal tribunal and then at the papal court. In the process of canonization his testimony was equally important on account of his long association and friendship with Francis. In addition to his knowledge of Francis and his fraternity from its inception, he had also been personally involved in the miraculous incident at the Portiuncula. Did his carefully recorded and verified account of the saint's appearance to him form part of the process of canonization? In enrolling Francis among the saints of the Church, Gregory IX expressly mentioned that he had sought the prelates' advice and visited Assisi to pray at Francis's tomb and to discuss the canonization.

The ceremony of canonization took place on 16 July 1228 in the piazza in front of the church of San Giogrio. The contemplative Giles, one of Francis's first companions, was undoubtedly present and reflected on his own renunciation of goods on that very piazza twenty years earlier to follow a man who was about to be formally declared a saint. The broad appeal of the new saint was reflected in the ecclesiastical and social status of those present: cardinals, bishops, abbots, prelates, some of whom had travelled from the most remote parts of the world, priests, nuns, counts, princes, including John of Brienne, king of Jerusalem. In short, people of every age and condition, a microcosm of the universal Church, assembled to pay their respects to the poor man of Assisi. The pope, who was arrayed in vestments ornamented with jewels set in gold and graven by the work of a lapidary, preached to the people and praised Francis in a noble eulogy, recalling his purity of life. Cardinal Octavian Ubaldini of Mugello read out the miracles and then Raynerius Canocius of Viterbo, a cardinal deacon, spoke about them. This was followed by the pope's decree, enrolling Francis among the catalogue of the saints and decreeing that his feast should be observed on the day of his death, 4 October. The proceedings were closed with the intonation of the *Te Deum* and the celebration of Mass by the pope.[31]

BASILICA OF ST FRANCIS AND THE SACRO CONVENTO

The combined influence of Elias with the ministers and the ecclesiastical and civic authorities had supervised Francis's return to Assisi and his death and burial in the city of his birth. They also planned the construction of a basilica which would honour their saint and bring spiritual protection to their city as well as the trade and prosperity associated with a popular shrine. Added to these united forces was the support of the new pope, Gregory IX, Francis's former friend. The friars' plans for the construction of a basilica benefited from the valuable experience gained in the recovery and translation of the relics of San Rufino, an event over which Guido had presided in 1212.

San Giorgio, a small church, was unable to provide a lasting resting place for a very popular saint; it was unsuitable for the stream of pilgrims who flocked to seek the intercession of the new saint. Elias, Guido and the *podestà* regarded Francis's burial in this church as no more than a temporary measure until the time when they could plan and build a more appropriate shrine to receive the flood of pilgrims who wished to pay homage to the *poverello*. In the period before the canonization Elias had devoted his energies to finding a site appropriate for the basilica to be constructed in honour of his friend. On 29 March 1228 Gregory IX granted an indulgence of 40 days to those who assisted in the construction of the new basilica to be built in honour of Francis. On 30 March 1228 the piece of land on the 'hill of hell' was granted by Simon de Pucciarello in favour of Elias, who received it through Gregory IX for the use of the friars and particularly for the construction of an oratory or church to receive the saint's body. This gave a certain urgency to his plans for the completion of the project. Elias imposed levies upon all the provinces to finance the building of the basilica.[32]

On Monday 17 July 1228, the day after the canonization, Gregory IX laid the foundation stone of the new basilica, and some days later he blessed the new high altar in the cathedral of San Rufino. Thus, even in death there is the symbolic juxtaposition between Francis and the church of Assisi. Special privileges were bestowed upon the new basilica by Gregory IX, who pronounced it to be the head and mother of the entire fraternity, a title which Francis had already conferred on the Portiuncula. In letters of 2 October 1228, 21 February 1229, 23 July 1229 and 22 April 1230 Gregory extolled the new saint and extended papal privileges to those whose donations assisted in the construction.[33] His own contribution to the buildings was noted by Salimbene, who records that the pope built a magnificent palace not only for the friars to honour Francis, but also as a residence for him whenever he was in Assisi; there were a large number of rooms and separate apartments.[34] Mockler observes that Elias built the new basilica on the model of the Crusaders' fortress-churches which he had known in Outremer.[35] This was not intended to appeal to idealists, but it paid handsome dividends for both the city and the friars when the Perugians sacked Assisi in 1442, but were unable to steal Francis's body. This vindicated the friars' wisdom in hiding the coffin and putting it a church that was also a strategically placed fortress.[36]

When the first phase of the building of the new basilica was completed, Elias finalized arrangements for the translation of the saint's relics. Although the friars attending the general chapter had been invited for the translation, Elias was afraid lest the ceremony be marked by dangerous outbursts of piety, which might endanger the saint's body. His anxiety was such that, in conjunction with civic officials, he decided to bring forward the translation, which took place on 25 May 1230.[37] As the sacred relics were being carried through the town a number of miracles were worked.[38] Bonaventure's testimony was corroborated by Salimbene, who furnishes details of one of these miracles. James da Yseo, a friar, who had been seriously wounded in the groin and genitals, was completely restored to health. Instead of enumerating the miracles which took place, Salimbene points the reader to the life and legend of the saint. The peaceful and successful translation, accompanied by miracles, was interpreted as a mark of divine favour by Elias and those responsible. Just as the arrangements for the saint's death four years earlier had been planned with an admirable precision, his relics were safely translated to the new basilica without incident. There were some influential friars, however, who were highly critical of Elias's plans, although the collaborating civic officials escaped the friars' censure.

Thomas of Eccleston, Jordan of Giano and Salimbene were united in their vigorous criticism of Elias as minister general, focusing on his policies and personal faults. Eccleston reports the premature translation and then goes on to portray the unruly scenes involving Elias's followers at the ensuing general chapter, where they tried to have him acclaimed as minister general. Although the ministers were undoubtedly disappointed, if not angered, by Elias's decision, some of them may have overcome their personal disappointment and viewed the translation as necessary. After the general chapter the disgraced Elias was seen to embrace a penitential life, which earned him the respect of many friars. His rehabilitation was so complete that in 1232 the general chapter of Assisi elected him as minister general. Later accounts of his ministry, which were significantly embroidered, link the aggravation caused by the covert translation and the disorder at the chapter. In his catalogue of the minister general's twelve major faults, Salimbene discloses that under the tyranny of Elias the ministers provincial bore the full expense of having a splendid great bell cast and indeed five more like it to be hung in the basilica at Assisi, although the chronicler admits that their delightfully sweet tones filled the whole valley.[39] Papal dispensations, overriding the statutes of the order, were granted for the completion of the basilica. On 10 July 1253 Innocent IV authorized Master Philip de Campello, the friar in charge of the construction of the basilica, to accept money in the form of alms for altars and other furnishings.[40]

While the friars seem to have accepted the basilica as a necessary consequence of the cult of a very attractive saint, it represented a retreat from the earliest days of the friars who lived in poverty and simplicity.[41] There was a similar process following the death of St Clare. The compromises which she had fiercely rejected in her own lifetime were symbolized by the fine Gothic basilica that was built in Assisi during the decade after her death.[42] The basilica of St Francis symbolized the changes which were taking place in the fraternity during the 1230s and the collections for the building works rankled with some friars, who recalled Francis's own warnings against the divisiveness of money. The friars were still determined to follow their founder and, like Clare, the splendour of the basilica did not dispense them from observing his ideals. The basilica was the venue of one of the miracles associated with the ailing Clare on Christmas Eve in 1252. R. B. Brooke comments that there is no contemporary evidence that Francis's first companions had any conscientious objections to the basilica and that Bernard, Masseo, Angelo, Rufino and Leo chose to be buried there. Leo also bequeathed to it the blessing which Francis had written out for him at La Verna. The first criticisms of its size and decoration were made in the fourteenth century,[43] although they were attributed to the saint's companions. When he had been shown around the convent, Giles retorted that the friars had need of nothing except wives and he complained that it was as wrong to violate the vow of poverty as that of chastity.[44] Leo publicly expressed his displeasure at the construction of a large and sumptuous church. He was so displeased by what he saw that he smashed one of the collecting jars. Elias had him flogged and driven from Assisi.[45] These anecdotes may have been circulating among the spiritual friars, who were protesting against the development of the fraternity in the later thirteenth century. They also resemble the charges of cruelty which those same reformers levelled against Bonaventure for presiding at the trial of his predecessor, John of Parma, who resigned as minister general in 1257.

Thomas of Celano closes his biography with a brief account of the miracles carried out through Francis's intercession and charts his transition from founder to patron or advocate of the fraternity. He reflects that the friars would never find anyone like him on earth and contrasts Francis's spirit of justice and holy simplicity with the plight of the penitent who sought his intercession.

Addressing the saint as the most holy father, the biographer entreats his intercession for sinners, reminding the saint that he loved sinners. He asks Francis to use his celestial influence to raise up those lying ensnared in sin. In his death Francis was hailed as the light of the world, shining in the universal Church more splendidly than the sun. He had withdrawn the rays of his light and had entered the world of light, exchanging the company of sinners for saints. He was entreated not to put aside the care of his sons, even though he had put off his flesh, which he shared with his brethren. At the end of the second book of the *Vita prima* the biographer voices his unworthiness for the task of honouring the saint by his biography and asks Francis to intercede for him that he might follow him in this life in order to be admitted to a place alongside him in eternity. The gracious father was entreated to remember his poor and grieving sons and to show to God the Father the marks of the stigmata in order that his disciples might be admitted to eternal life.[46] These petitions and prayers reveal that Francis, now enrolled among the saints, was exercising a new and broader influence. As celestial patron he was a support and guide to the friars individually and collectively, and in the period of transition between 1230 and 1260 his intercession was frequently sought. The saint had been assured that the fraternity would continue, with God as its chief protector and himself as its shepherd.[47]

FRANCIS'S POSTHUMOUS INFLUENCE ON AN EXPANDING FRATERNITY

The tensions within the fraternity were visible in Francis's lifetime and afterwards they increased sharply. He had served as a focal point of unity, attracting and inspiring such diverse followers as Giles and Elias. After his death the friars experienced a great deal of difficulty in resolving these internal differences and disputes. Within four years of Francis's death, the general chapter at Assisi could not provide authoritative guidance and papal intervention was sought. In the 1230s and 1240s friars, intent on following the letter and the spirit of the founder, looked backwards to the simplicity and poverty of the early fraternity. There was a sense of nostalgia for a golden age in the life of the community and these reflections gave a new edge to the internal disagreements and the external criticisms, which focused on how the founder's teaching should be adapted to ever-changing situations within the Church and society. The friars' desire to be faithful to Francis's ideals expressed itself in their own attempts to maintain high standards of observance and the collective and individual comments on the Rule. They turned more and more to consider the intention of the saint and how his inspirational teaching might be applied to changing circumstances.

Internal tensions and the demand for reform

The friars' zeal and dedication captured the popular imagination and were instrumental in bringing large numbers of zealous men to the order. Initially the friars were few and they were content with cramped quarters on their first arrival in cities. Their voluntary poverty, bare feet, poor habits and the practice of begging for alms gained them immense respect and admiration. However, that level of popularity and the consequent expansion made the friars the victims of their own broad appeal. The small and impoverished rooms were no longer able to house the increased numbers of friars: the fraternity which had forsworn ownership was in need of more space for their many and varied apostolates. The question on the friars' lips was: what type of accommodation would Francis select? How should the founder's ideals be applied to the various pastoral situations in which the friars found themselves?

Friction about building appears in the chronicles compiled by friars in the thirteenth century and the founder's wishes were invoked by those who promoted a development consonant with poverty. Francis was depicted as intervening in these controversies and reasserting his own teaching. Within two years of his death the friars in Paris found that it was no longer feasible to remain on the outskirts of the city as the guests of the monks of Saint-Denis. When Henry of Burford arrived at the friary in Paris there were only about thirty friars in the community. It was decided to build a friary and church at Vauvert, near the Luxembourg gardens, but the plans for the new building produced tensions between those who wanted to build a suitable friary as a base for their apostolate in the city and those who measured such plans by the teaching of Francis. Thomas of Eccleston observes that the new friary was so large and lofty that many of the friars deemed it to be contrary to the order's rule of poverty. The style of the new buildings so dismayed a group of friars that they entreated the founder to destroy the friary. As they were about to take possession of the new buildings, the roof and the walls collapsed and on the site were found words of rebuke for the ministers, that God teaches by this ruin that man should be content with a humbler place. The chronicler sympathized with Angelus, who judged that by divine decree no friars were to reside there.[48] Robert of Slapton informed the same chronicler that, while the friars were living in a borrowed house, the guardian dreamed that Francis visited the place. The founder was welcomed by the friars, who led him into a living room, where he sat a long time looking around him. The friars were surprised at this and the guardian asked the saint about his thoughts. Francis directed the guardian to look at the house, which was entirely built of laths and rubble, plastered with clay. He then declared that all friars' houses should be built like that. After this the guardian took water and washed Francis's feet and kissed the stigmata.[49]

Within a decade of the Franciscans' arrival in England there were complaints about the way in which they forced their way into monastic centres. They were beginning to rely more on papal letters than on Francis's co-operative disposition towards his monastic and clerical neighbours. In 1233 the friars wished to settle at Reading and showed their papal letters to the abbot of Reading and the bishop of Winchester. Their insistence and their settlement close to the town's bridge were recorded as the cause of a scandal. This conduct dismayed Albert of Pisa and, in the spirit of the founder, he returned the charter or agreement made between the monks and the friars on 14 July 1233, whereby the monks could not eject them, and he offered to remove the friars, if the monks so desired. The style and decoration of the friars' chapel there, which had been built by Henry III, also displeased Albert. Because he was not permitted to pull it down, he expressed the hope that heaven might destroy it.[50] By 1235 Matthew Paris accuses the friars of barging into the old, respected monasteries, claiming a papal licence to erect their own altars and hear confessions, to the detriment of the monastic and parochial clergy alike.[51]

Interpretation of the Rule

The discussions on the way in which the founder's Rule should be interpreted led to the promulgation of *Quo elongati*. While the pope addressed various vexed points of interpretation and offered an authoritative ruling, statutes were added, sometimes by the minister general and at other times by the general chapters. Elias's conduct as minister general resulted in further examination of the application of the Rule to diverse areas of the friars' lives. William of Nottingham urged the friars to consider the mind and intention of the saint in the Rule lest superfluous things arise within the fraternity. In his letter of 23 April 1257 Bonaventure called the friars to a more rigorous interpretation of the Rule and declared that the founder was crying out for it. The series of constitutions were another medium for the interpretation of Francis's teaching and the constitutions of Narbonne applied the letter and the spirit of the Rule to each part of the friars' life.

The publication of the general constitutions of the order at the general chapter at Rome in 1239 did not bring an end to the debates about the Rule,[52] which also surfaced at the general chapter of definitors at Montpellier in 1241. It was decreed that each province should establish a commission to explore disputed passages of the Rule and then send in their findings to Haymo of Faversham, the minister general (1240–44). The report of the French province was the only one to survive and this sought a resolution of the disputed points by focusing on the founder's intention in drafting the Rule.[53] On the night of his appointment the founder appeared to John Bannister and showed him a deep pit. John notified the founder that the ministers wished to interpret the Rule and suggested that the former should give the exposition. The saint replied that John should have the

Rule expounded by the lay friars; this was clearly a snub to the more learned friars, some of whom were serving on the commission. When the commission had completed its task, they sent their report to the minister general in a little casket without a seal and implored him by the blood of Jesus to preserve the Rule unaltered as it had been given them by the saint under the inspiration of the Holy Spirit. This petition gladdened the heart of the cardinal protector of the order as well as the friars in other provinces across the channel.[54]

By the late 1230s anecdotes about learning were being told to the discomfort of theologians in the fraternity, although the lectors were prominent among those who worked to depose Elias. Nonetheless, reports of visions were in circulation and were stamped with the founder's authority. Richard Rufus of Cornwall, who spent his life as master in the schools at both Paris and Oxford, informed a chapter at Oxford that a friar at Paris had seen a vision of Giles. The celebrated contemplative was sitting in a chair and expounding the seven petitions of the Lord's Prayer to an audience of lectors. During that address Francis entered the room in silence, and told the lectors that they should be ashamed that their merits were exceeded by the lay brother. He added that, while learning breeds pride, charity builds up and predicted that highly regarded friars would be counted as nothing in the kingdom of God.[55]

THE BIOGRAPHIES AND THE PORTRAIT OF THE EXEMPLARY FRIAR

The first biography by Thomas of Celano announced the deeds of a newly canonized saint whose followers were sweeping throughout Christendom and impressing their contemporaries. In contrast the subsequent biographies appear to have a more domestic agenda, as they mirror the tensions surrounding the fraternity toward the middle of the thirteenth century. The tone of the biography reflects the priorities of the writer as sectarian elements come to the fore. At a time when both popes and friars, collectively and individually, were beginning to expound Francis's teaching, the biographers set about explaining the founder's wishes. The materials assembled by Leo, Rufino and Angelo contain a call to return to the excellence and vitality of the early fraternity. They were wary of learning and all its ramifications, such as schools and libraries, with their challenge to the founder's simplicity and poverty. Thomas of Celano's second biography made use of the companions' writings, but offered more support to the direction which the fraternity was taking in the 1240s, although numerous reservations were made about aspects of the friars' lives. By the end of the 1250s the divisions within the fraternity were on the increase and the *Legenda maior*, drawing much of its contents from the *Vita secunda*, presented Francis as the exemplary friar. All three texts demonstrate that the biographies were being used as extensive commentaries on the founder's Rule. In the prologue to the *Vita secunda* the biographer announces his intention to portray and declare with careful zeal what was 'the good and acceptable and perfect will' (Romans 12:2) of the founder both for himself and his followers.[56]

Leo, Rufino and Angelo, who pay particular attention to Francis's intention regarding the Rule, locate examples of his teaching during the last phase of his life. When the friars at Siena thought that he was going to die, they pressed him for what they thought would be his last message to the fraternity. Francis exhorted the friars to remember his blessing and testament; they should always love one another and treasure holy poverty; they should always be faithful and submissive to bishops and priests. A curse was directed at those whose depraved and bad example provoked people to blaspheme against the order.[57] The companions recognized the order's success in attracting vocations as a source of danger and attributed to the saint the teaching that large communities of friars imposed a strain on poverty. They were much more familiar with large communities and the organizational problems associated with them than Francis was. Their teaching was concluded with the observation that throughout his life Francis had wished to live in holy poverty. While Francis was at the bishop's palace, he received some of his familiars and expounded his own ideas about the observance of the Rule. One of his visitors was Richer of the March of Ancona, a man whom the saint held in great affection. The first question raised was the thorny issue of books used by the clerical friars. Richer, who conceded that some friars had many books, sought permission for their retention on condition that they were not recognized as personal property; such books were distributed by the minister in accordance with the friar's apostolate and needs. A short response was made by the saint, who declared that the friars should have only a habit, cord and breeches, in accordance with the Rule. Another friar reflected on how the order flourished in its early days, observing poverty in buildings, implements, clothes and books; the friars were also united in their love of God and neighbour. He explained that many friars took the view that the people were edified more by the new way than the old, thereby compromising humility and poverty. Francis replied that, while he had held office, the friars had remained true to their vocation. In those days his teaching and example had been sufficient. Although the multiplication of friars had been achieved by God, the friars had deviated from his teaching. Having renounced the office of minister himself, he endeavoured to teach the friars.[58]

The *Vita secunda*, following the ruling of Gregory IX's *Quo elongati*, affirms the priority of the founder's Rule over his *Testament*, which had been quoted freely in the earlier biography. Thomas of Celano displays the greatest respect for the Rule, devoting a whole section to the founder's commendation of it. A very special blessing was bestowed by the founder on those who were zealous for the Rule, which he called the friars' book of life, the hope of salvation, the marrow of the Gospel, the way of perfection, the key of paradise and the covenant of an eternal alliance. He wanted it to be known by all. Thomas of Celano wishes to avoid any suggestion that the Rule was merely a juridical document which the saint had compiled with the canonical help of Cardinal Ugolino. The spiritual character of the document was reflected in the founder's wish that it should be perceived as a vehicle to address the inner man for his comfort in weariness and a remembrance of the vows already taken. Francis taught them to keep it ever before their eyes as a reminder of the life they were to live and that they should die with it. The second half of this advice was fulfilled to the letter by the friar who died in mission territory clutching the Rule and seeking pardon for any infringement against it. The biographer takes issue both with those who complain about the severity of the Rule and those who succumb to laziness. This contrast provided him with an opportunity to appeal to the origins of the fraternity, echoing the traditional appeal to the apostolic Church. Thus the zeal and devotion of the first generation of friars reproved contemporary friars who quibbled about various aspects of religious observance. The earlier friars were faithful to their profession and eager to go beyond what was required; they did not consider the Rule to be difficult or harsh. Neither was there any place for laziness or idleness, because the stimulus of love urged them on to even greater things.[59]

Intermittent outbursts of rivalry and tension marred relations between the Franciscans and the Dominicans in the 1220s and 1230s. In 1243 controversy had broken out regarding the observance of poverty and the movement of aspirants from one order to the other, with each order securing papal letters. In the later 1230s and early 1240s efforts were made at an official level to foster good relations by Albert of Pisa, minister general about 1239, and John of Wildeshausen, master general in 1246.[60] The same conciliatory spirit informs Thomas of Celano's recollections of the links between the canonized founders, their united opposition to plans to raise friars to the episcopate and the good relations which had prevailed between the orders in an earlier age. Emphasizing the humility, charity and respect which united the founders, Celano fulminates against the sons of these distinguished saints who yield to jealousy, envy, ambition and hatred; the discontent between the orders was generated by friars whose concupiscence produced conflict and strife. He regrets that the two orders, which had been sent to combat a common enemy, wasted their time in attacking each other. The example of the first generation of friars, the *patres*, demonstrates that friars of the two orders were both wise and God-fearing and on good terms with each other. If the friars of the 1240s were charitable towards each other, the teaching of piety would progress more fruitfully throughout the world; the virtuous in each fraternity were exempted from these charges, but the bad should be rooted out lest they infect the holy. This stinging rebuke is concluded with the prayer that the friars should return to the paths of humility and an account of the mutual respect which the two founders had for each other.[61]

Elected as minister general on 2 February 1257, Bonaventure continued the policies of his predecessor.[62] His reforming credentials were set out in a letter of 23 April 1257 in which he listed ten practices which were tarnishing the order's good reputation. His letters to the ministers, his biography and the general constitutions of Narbonne in 1260 were vehicles for disseminating the reforms which he wished to introduce. His interpretation of the vow of poverty was uncompromising, leaving the friars in no doubt about their responsibilities to safeguard what had become one of the hallmarks of their vocation. His *Legenda maior*, composed by 1263, was adopted as the official biography of the founder by the general chapter of Paris in 1266. Other biographies were withdrawn from circulation in a decision resembling the one taken by the general chapter of the Dominicans at Strasbourg in 1260.[63] What this biography lacks in original material it gains in a devotional and ascetical manner, whereby Francis was depicted as the model for all friars and the general principles of his life could also be applied to all Christians. For instance, the tenth chapter focuses on Francis's prayer and provides instruction for all Christians intent on closer union with God.

Bonaventure treats Francis's love for absolute poverty, *altissima paupertas*, as a gift from God and a special privilege, which enabled him to grow rich in spiritual wealth. From the opening words of chapter 7 he expatiates on the founder's convictions about the centrality of evangelical poverty and its value to the friars. The memory of the poverty experienced by the Son of God and his mother often reduced Francis to tears, and he called poverty the queen of the virtues because it was so evident in the life of the king of kings and of the queen, his mother. Firmly believing that the Son of God had embraced a life of poverty, Francis left home and cast aside his possessions to follow his divine master in a virtue which was scorned by the whole world. No one was so greedy for gold as he was for poverty. When the friars asked him privately which virtue made one dearest to Jesus Christ, he replied that it was poverty, which he regarded as the special way of salvation. His love of evangelical poverty was such that he used to be particularly offended if he ever saw anything contrary to poverty among the friars. From the first moment of his religious life until his death, his sole wealth consisted in a habit, a cord and a pair of trousers, and he was content with that.

Francis gave orders that friaries should be small, resembling the houses of the poor. Bonaventure does not shy away from recording instances of the founder venting his wrath on those whose buildings infringed the principle of the poverty which they had voluntarily espoused. Francis had taught that poverty was the basis of the whole order; the whole structure of the friars' lives was founded on it. Bonaventure believed that high standards of poverty were essential for the harmony and prosperity of the order, arguing that the fraternity's future depended upon its fidelity to evangelical poverty. The founder warned the friars that, as long as they remained firm in their commitment to this vow, the order would flourish. Conversely, the undermining of the central vow would have catastrophic consequences for the fraternity, which would be demolished.[64] The rest of the seventh chapter applies the founder's teaching to different aspects of the friars' lives, frequently using ideas and phraseology from the recently approved constitutions of the fraternity.

CONCLUSION

The ideological struggles within the fraternity in the early 1220s sharpened divisions among the friars. There was some internal criticism of developments within the order even before Francis's death and external criticism followed quickly. As early as 1217 Cardinal Ugolino had warned Francis that the nascent community had opponents in the papal court and in the *Vita prima* the cardinal was celebrated as the friars' defender and protector. Even supporters of the friars, such as Jacques de Vitry, drew attention to deficiencies in their preparation for the ministry. By the later 1230s the friars' academic profile was rising and there were already regrettable excesses, although they seem to have had an inferiority complex in relation to the Dominicans in academic terms. The simple and humble sons of the *poverello* poured scorn on the monastic orders, which had not opened houses at the University of Paris. They also insisted on establishing themselves in some monastic towns against the wishes of their Benedictine and Cistercian neighbours. Perhaps the most persistent complaint arose from the secular clergy and bishops, who resented the extensive pastoral powers granted to the friars by a succession of popes. They maintained that the friars were undermining their relationship with the parishioners by preaching and hearing confessions. By the middle of the thirteenth century the secular masters at the University of Paris had joined the ranks of the friars' critics and advanced penetrating arguments against the mendicants' rationale.

Many of these critics maintained that the friars had deviated from the teaching of their founder, who had embraced evangelical poverty and sought to assist the secular clergy in their ministry, living in peace with everyone. These external complaints were matched by tension within the fraternity, as the friars strove to uphold the ideals of their canonized founder. The concern for a high level of observance expressed itself in the early constitutions of the order. As early as 1230 the friars had turned to Gregory IX for an authoritative ruling on aspects of Franciscan observance and afterwards popes felt justified in their interventions, some of which were deemed to be relaxations. The battle for the soul and inheritance of the founder was being played out by friars, who began to give much thought to the way in which the Rule of the founder should be observed. Commentaries on the Rule appeared from the early 1240s and were produced at regular intervals throughout that century. The differing interpretations and emphases were well ventilated in the biographies of Thomas of Celano and the reminiscences of Leo, Rufino and Angelo. It should be noted that there is a measure of agreement between these texts as well as differences of emphasis. The general constitutions of the thirteenth and fourteenth centuries shared some common ground with the commentaries on the Rule, as successive general chapters endeavoured to apply Francis's teaching to the new situations in which the friars found themselves.

In their concern for the order, generations of friars have turned to the saint at his tomb in Assisi for support and direction. When the number of recruits soared, some adaptation was necessary and on that very decision the harmony and unity of the fraternity depended. The years following Francis's death were turbulent for the fraternity, which was faced with crucial decisions about its own future and its contribution to the medieval Church. Francis's vision had been ideally suited to a small fraternity over which he presided in his own inimitable and inspirational style. As they grappled with these decisions the friars turned to their saint at his tomb in the majestic basilica in Assisi. They went there on pilgrimage in the knowledge that they were going close to the saint, who would be attentive to their prayers. Since 1230 numerous general chapters of the fraternity have been celebrated at Assisi, where the friars have pledged themselves anew to preserve the ideals of their founder; many general chapters have been held in Assisi in the present century. Francis's teaching was the criterion by which all new developments were measured and he was seen to be governing and directing the fraternity from his tomb, where he remained the ultimate source of authority for the friars.

This examination of Francis's life began with a consideration of the role played by the martyred bishops of Assisi in the life of the medieval Church. It concludes with Francis, the devotee of the city's patron saints, enthroned in a basilica, which is visited daily by thousands of people at the height of the pilgrimage season in the spring and summer. He has taken his place along with Rufino, Vittorino and Savino, the martyred bishops of the ancient diocese of Assisi, as the protector of his native city. These martyred bishops provided the authority which was entrusted to the bishops of Assisi. Similarly, Francis's heritage was placed in the hands of the ministers general and provincial, especially at a general chapter. The cults of the martyrs of Assisi were, however, largely local in character. In contrast Francis, who was ever open to God's goodness in the created order, is a saint with a global reputation and, to some extent, this reflects his travels throughout Italy and beyond. His fame was carried far and wide by his followers, who were present in most parts of Christendom. The breadth of Francis's appeal is mirrored in the people of various cultures and religious traditions who visit his shrine. While his heritage remains the driving force of the Franciscan vocation, he is a most attractive saint whose appeal is universal.

Notes

1. Thomas of Eccleston, *Tractatus de adventu*, p. 99.
2. C. N. L. Brooke and R. B. Brooke, *Popular Religion in the Middle Ages* (London, 1984), p. 14.
3. C. H. Lawrence, *St Edmund of Abingdon: A Study in Hagiography and History* (Oxford, 1960), pp. 264-78.
4. *Assidua*, cc. 17-25.
5. *Chronica Fratris Jordani*, n. 50, pp. 45-6.
6. 1 C, n. 109.
7. R. Brown, *The Roots of St Francis* (Chicago, 1982), pp. 86-7.
8. *Compilatio Assisiensis*, cc. 58-59; 1 C, n. 105.
9. Ibid., c. 96; 2 C, n. 77.
10. 1 C, n. 105.
11. *Compilatio Assisiensis*, c. 4.
12. Ibid., cc. 99, 100.
13. 1 C, nn. 88, 106; 2 C, nn. 18-19, 57; *Compilatio Assisiensis*, c. 56.
14. Ibid., cc. 8, 13.
15. *Scripta Leonis*, pp. 264-5.
16. 1 C, nn. 109-10; 2 C, nn. 214-17; 3 C, n. 32.
17. 1 C, nn. 112-14, 116-18.
18. Ibid., n. 88.
19. Elias of Cortona, 'Epistola encyclica de transitu S. Francisci' in AF, 10, pp. 525-8, where the letter was printed. *Chronica Fratris Jordani*, n. 50, pp. 45-6, refers to the consolatory letters which Elias, the vicar, sent to the friars on this occasion; 1 C, nn. 112-15.
20. LM, miracula, I, 1.
21. 1 C, nn. 91-95, 110.
22. Julian of Speyer, *Officio Ritmico e Vita secunda*, ed. V. Gamboso (FAA, 2; Padua, 1985), pp. 394-5; Lawrence, *St Edmund of Abingdon: A Study in Hagiography and History*, p. 247.
23. LM, c. 13, nn. 2-3, 5.
24. M. Bihl, 'De quodam elencho Assisano testium oculatorum S. Francisci Stigmatum', in AFH, 19 (1926), pp. 931-6.
25. LM, c. 13, nn. 8-9.
26. Eccleston, *Tractatus de adventu*, pp. 74-5.
27. 3 C, nn. 8-9; LM, miracula, I, n. 6.
28. 1 C, nn. 118, 120-21, 127, 129, 132.
29. M. Goodich, 'The politics of canonisation in the thirteenth century' in S. Wilson (ed.), *Saints and their Cults* (Cambridge, 1983), p. 173.
30. *Compilatio Assisiensis*, c. 72.
31. 1 C, nn. 123-26.
32. *Chronica Fratris Jordani*, n. 61, pp. 54-5.
33. BF, I, pp. 46, 48, 50, 60; J. R. H. Moorman, *The Sources for the Life of S. Francis of Assisi* (University of Manchester, Historical Series, 79; 1940), p. 61.
34. Salimbene, *Cronica*, p. 235.
35. A. Mockler, *Francis of Assisi* (Oxford, 1976), p. 21.
36. R. B. Brooke, *Early Franciscan Government* (Cambridge, 1959), p. 142; A. Fortini, *Assisi nel medioevo* (Rome, 1940), pp. 451-76.
37. Eccleston, *Tractatus de adventu*, p. 66.
38. LM, c. 15, n. 8; cf. A. Fortini, *Assisi nel medioevo*, pp. 111-15.
39. Salimbene, *Cronica*, pp. 96, 151-2. At the instigation of the minister provincial in Hungary, the king of that country sent a great golden cup to Assisi adorned with a striking portrait of Francis.
40. BF, 1, p. 666.
41. P. Sabatier, *Life of St Francis of Assisi* (London, 1899), p. 345, exhorts his readers to visit the basilica, which was proud, rich and powerful, and contrasts it with the Carceri and San Damiano. He envisages it as a symbol of the ideal which separated Francis from the pope who canonized him.
42. C. H. Lawrence, *The Friars* (London, 1994), p. 42.
43. Brooke, *Early Franciscan Government*, p. 149.
44. 'Chronica XXIV generalium ordinis minorum' in AF, III (Quaracchi, Florence, 1897), p. 90.
45. E. Lempp, *Frère Élie de Cortone* (Collection d'études et de documents sur l'histoire religieuse et littéraire du moyen âge, 3; Paris, 1901), pp. 76, 163-4.
46. 1 C, nn. 50, 83, 111, 118.

47. 2 C, n. 158.
48. Eccleston, *Tractatus*, pp. 47, 28; D. Vorreux, 'Un sermon de Philippe le Chancelier en faveur des Frères Mineurs de Vauvert', in AFH, 68 (1975), pp. 3-22. The sermon was preached on 1 September 1228. Cf. L. Beaumont-Maillet, *Le Grand Couvent des Cordeliers de Paris* (Bibliothèque de l'école des hautes études, IV section, sciences historiques et philologiques, 325; Paris, 1975).
49. Eccleston, *Tractatus*, p. 46.
50. *Annales Monastici*, III, ed. Luard (RS; London, 1866), p. 134; Eccleston, *Tractatus*, pp. 79-80.
51. Matthew Paris, *Chronica majora*, III (RS 57, iii; London, 1876), pp. 332-4.
52. Salimbene, *Cronica*, pp. 145-7. Cf. C. Cenci, 'De fratrum Minorum Constitutionibus Praenarbonensibus', in AFH, 83 (1990), pp. 50-95.
53. *Expositio quatuor magistrorum super regulam fratrum minorum (1241-1242)*, ed. L. Oliger (Storia e Letteratura raccolta di studi e testi, 30; Rome, 1950), pp. 31-2.
54. Eccleston, *Tractatus*, p. 71.
55. Ibid., pp. 51-2.
56. 2 C, n. 2.
57. *Compilatio Assisiensis*, cc. 58-59; 1 C, n. 105.
58. Ibid., cc. 57, 101, 106.
59. 2 C, nn. 208-209.
60. Eccleston, *Tractatus*, p. 82; 'Litterae encyclicae magistrorum generalium' in MOPH, V, ed. Reichert (Rome, 1900), pp. 7-9.
61. 2 C, nn. 148-50.
62. D. V. Monti, *Works of St Bonaventure*, V (New York, 1994), p. 28, who retreats from the earlier view of Bonaventure as the 'second founder' of the fraternity and regards him as continuing the policies of John of Parma.
63. 'Acta capitulorum generalium ordinis praedicatorum, I' in MOPH, III, ed. Reichert (Rome), p. 105.
64. LM, c. 7, nn. 1–3.

Bibliography

1. PRIMARY SOURCES

'Acta capitulorum generalium ordinis praedicatorum, I' in MOPH, III, ed. Reichert (Rome).

Alan of Lille, *Summa de arte praedicandi* in PL, 210.

Ambrose, *Epistola* 22 in PL, 16.

Angelo da Clareno, *Expositio Regulae*, ed. L. Oliger (Quaracchi, Florence, 1912).

Angelo da Clareno, 'Historia de septem tribulationibus' in ALKG, II.

Angelo da Clareno in *Rendiconti della Reale Accademia dei Lincei, Classe di Scienza morali, storiche e filologiche*, serie 5a, XVII (Rome, 1908).

Annales Monastici, III, ed. Luard (RS; London, 1866).

L'Anonyme de Pérouse: Un témoin de la fraternité franciscaine primitive, trans., intro. and notes B. Beguin (Textes franciscains; Paris, 1979).

Anthony of Padua, *Sermones Dominicales et Festivi*, I, ed. B. Costa, L. Frasson, and I. Luisetto (Padua, 1979).

Armstrong, R. J. and Brady, I. C., *Francis and Clare: The Complete Works* (The Classics of Western Spirituality; New York, 1982).

Augustine, *Confessiones* in PL, 32 and in *Corpus Christianorum, Series Latina*, 27, ed. L. Verheijen (1981).

Bartholomew of Pisa, 'De conformitate vitae Beati Francisci ad vitam Domini Iesu' in AF, IV (Quaracchi, Florence, 1906).

Bede, *Ecclesiastical History of the English People*, ed. B. Colgrave and R. A. B. Mynors (OMT; 1969).

Bede, *Historiam Ecclesiasticam, gentis Anglorum, Historiam Abbatum, Epistolam ad Ecgberctum una cum Historia Abbatum auctore anonymo*, I, ed. C. Plummer (Oxford, 1896).

S. Bernardi opera, II, ed. J. Leclercq, C. H. Talbot and H. M. Rochais (Rome, 1958).

S. Bernardi opera, III, ed. J. Leclercq and H. M. Rochais (Rome, 1963).

S. Bernardi opera, VIII, ed. J. Leclercq and H. M. Rochais (Rome, 1977).

Bihl, M., 'Statuta generalia Ordinis edita in Capitulis generalibus celebratis Narbonae an. 1260, Assisii an. 1279 atque Parisiis an. 1292. (Editio critica et synoptica)' in AFH, 34 (1941), pp. 13-94, 284-358.

Bonaventure, 'Legenda maior S. Francisci' in AF, 10, pp. 555-652.

Bonaventure, *The Soul's Journey into God; the Tree of Life; the Life of St Francis*, trans. E. Cousins (The Classics of Western Spirituality; New York, 1978).

Works of Saint Bonaventure: Writings concerning the Franciscan Order, V, trans. with intro. D. V. Monti (New York, 1994).

S. Bonaventurae opera omnia, III (Quaracchi, Florence, 1887).

S. Bonaventurae opera omnia, V (Quaracchi, Florence, 1891).

S. Bonaventurae opera omnia, VII (Quaracchi, Florence, 1895).

S. Bonaventurae opera omnia, VIII (Quaracchi, Florence, 1898).

The Book of St Gilbert, ed. R. Foreville and G. Keir (OMT; 1987).

Buchardi Praepositi Urspergensis Chronicon (MGH SS; 2nd edn, 1916).

Cenci, C., 'De fratrum Minorum Constitutionibus Praenarbonensibus' in AFH, 83 (1990), pp. 50-95.

Chronica Fratris Jordani, ed. H. Boehmer (Collection d'études et de documents sur l'histoire religieuse et littéraire du moyen âge, 6; Paris, 1908).

'Chronica XXIV generalium ordinis minorum' in AF, III (Quaracchi, Florence, 1897).

The Chronicle of Bury St Edmunds 1212-1301, ed. A. Gransden (NMT; London, 1964).

Clare of Assisi: Early Documents, trans. with intro. R. J. Armstrong (New York, 1988).

'Communitatis Responsio "Religiosi Viri" ad Rotulum Fr. Ubertino de Casali', ed. A. Chiappini in AFH, 7 (1914), pp. 654-75; 8 (1915), pp. 56-80.

Compilatio Assisiensis dagli Scritti di fra Leone e compagni su S. Francesco d'Assisi, ed. M. Bigaroni (Pubblicazioni della biblioteca francescana chiesa nuova – Assisi, 2; Assisi, 1992).

Constantine of Orvieto, 'Legenda Sancti Dominici' in MOPH, 16.

Dante, *The Divine Comedy*, 3: *Paradiso*, ed. and trans. J. D. Sinclair (Oxford, 1971).

David, C. W. (ed.), *De expugnatione Lyxbonensi* (New York, 1936).

'De finibus paupertatis auctore Hugone de Digna, O.F.M.', ed. C. Florovsky in AFH, 5 (1912), pp. 277-90.

'Declaratio fratris Ubertini de Casali' in ALKG, III.

The Deeds of the Franks and the other pilgrims to Jerusalem, ed. R. Hill (NMT; 1962); republished in OMT (1972).

Delorme, F. M., ' "Diffinitiones" Capituli Generalis O.F.M. Narbonensis (1260)' in AFH, 3 (1910), pp. 491-504.

Delorme, F. M., 'Textes franciscains', *Archivo italiano per la storia della pietà*, 1 (1951), pp. 179-218.

Denifle, H. (ed.), *Chartularium Universitatis Parisiensis*, II (Paris, 1891).

Dicta Beati Aegidii Assisiensis (BFAMA, 3; Quaracchi, Florence, 1905).

Einhard and Notker the Stammerer: Two Lives of Charlemagne, trans. L. Thorpe (Penguin Classics; London, 1969).

Elias of Cortona, 'Epistola encyclica de transitu S. Francisci' in AF, 10, pp. 525-8.

The Epistolae Vagantes of Pope Gregory VII, ed. H. E. J. Cowdrey (OMT; 1972).

Expositio quatuor magistrorum super regulam fratrum minorum (1241-1242), ed. L. Oliger (Storia e Letteratura raccolta di studi e testi, 30; Rome, 1950).

Fra Tommaso da Celano, Vita di S. Chiara Vergine d'Assisi, trans. Casolini (Assisi, 3rd edn, 1976). See Thomas of Celano, below.

Fratris Johannis Pecham quondam archiepiscopi Cantuariensis Tractatus tres de Paupertate, ed. C. L. Kingsford, A. G. Little and F. Tocco (BSFS, 2; Aberdeen, 1910).

Geoffrey of Auxerre, *S. Bernardi vita prima* in PL, 183.

Gerald of Frachet, 'Vitae fratrum', ed. B. M. Reichert in MOPH, 1 (Rome, 1897).

Gibson, S. (ed.), *Statuta Antiqua Universitatis Oxoniensis* (Oxford, 1931).

Gieben, S., 'Robert Grosseteste on preaching, with the edition of the sermon "Ex rerum initiatarum" on redemption', *Collectanea Franciscana*, 37 (1967), pp. 100-41.

Giraldi Cambrensis opera, II, ed. Brewer (RS 21, ii; London, 1862).

Golubovich, G., *Biblioteca Bio-Bibliografica della Terra Santa e dell'Oriente Francescano*, I (Quaracchi, Florence, 1906).

Gregory of Tours, *Liber in gloria martyrum* (MGH SS; 1885).

Gregory the Great, *Homilarium in evangelia* in PL, 76.

Les registres de Grégoire IX, ed. L. Auvray, I (Paris, 1896).

Grudundmann, H., 'Die Bulle "Quo elongati" Papst Gregors IX' in AFH, 54 (1961), pp. 3-25.

Henry d'Avranches, 'Legenda S. Francisci versificata' in AF, 10.

Regesta Honorii Papae III, ii, ed. P. Pressutti (Rome, 1895).

Hugh of Digne's Rule Commentary, ed. D. Flood (Spicilegium Bonaventurianum, XIV; Quaracchi, Grottaferrata, 1979).

Hugh the Chanter, *The History of the Church of York 1066-1127*, ed. and trans. C. Johnson, rev. M. Brett, C. N. L. Brooke and M. Winterbottom (OMT; 1990).

Jacopone da Todi, *The Lauds*, trans. S. and E. Hughes (The Classics of Western Spirituality; London, 1982).

Jacques de Vitry, 'Histoire de l'Orient' in Golubovich, above.

John Chrysostom, *The Gospel of St Matthew* in PG, 58.

Jordan of Saxony, 'Libellus de principiis Ordinis Praedicatorum' ed. M. H. Laurent, in MOPH, 16 (Rome, 1935).

Jordan of Saxony, *On the beginnings of the order of Preachers*, trans. S. Tugwell (Dominican Sources, new edns in English; Dublin, 1982).

Julian of Speyer, *Officio Ritmico e Vita Secunda*, ed. V. Gamboso (FAA, 2; Padua, 1985).

Julian of Speyer, 'Vita Sancti Francisci' in AF, 10.

Lazzeri, Z., 'Il Processo di canonizzazione di S. Chiara d'Assisi' in AFH, 13 (1920), pp. 403-507.

'Legenda Monacensis' in AF, X, pp. 694-719.

Legenda Sanctae Clarae Virginis, ed. F. Pennacchi (Società internazionale di studi francescani in Assisi; Assisi, 1910).

'Legenda trium Sociorum Édition critique', ed. T. Desbonnets in AFH, 67 (1974), pp. 38-144.

'Leggende e culto di S. Rufino in Assisi', ed. A. Brunacci, *Bollettino della Deputazione di Storia Patria per l'Umbria*, 45 (1948), pp. 5-91.

Leo the Great, *Sermon on the Beatitudes* in PL, 54.

The Letters and Poems of Fulbert of Chartres, ed. F. Behrends (OMT; 1976).

The Letters of John of Salisbury (1153-1161), I, ed. W. J. Millor and H. E. Butler, rev. C. N. L. Brooke (NMT; 1953), and repr. in OMT (1986).

The Letters of John of Salisbury, II: *The Later Letters (1163-1180)*, ed. W. J. Millor and C. N. L. Brooke (OMT 1979).

Lettres de Jacques de Vitry, ed. R. B. C. Huygens (Leiden, 1960).

The Life of Ailred of Rievaulx by Walter Daniel, ed. F. M. Powicke (NMT; 1950).

The Life of St Hugh of Lincoln, II, ed. D. L. Douie and D. H. Farmer (NMT; 1961), repub. in OMT (1985).

'Litterae encyclicae magistrorum generalium' in MOPH, V, ed. Reichert (Rome, 1900), pp. 7-9.

Lynch, K. F., 'Three Sermons on The Doctor Evangelicus, by John de la Rochelle', *Franciscan Studies*, 23 (1963), pp. 213-37.

Marston, Roger, *Quodlibeta quatuor ad fidem codicum nunc primum edita*, ed. G. F. Etzkorn and I. Brady (BFSMA, 26; Florence, 1968).

Matthew Paris, *Chronica majora*, III, ed. Luard (RS, 57, iii; London, 1876).

Matthew Paris, *Chronica majora*, IV, ed. Luard (RS, 57, iv; London, 1877).

Matthew Paris, *Chronica majora*, V, ed. Luard (RS, 57, v; London, 1880).

Matthew Paris, *Historia Anglorum*, II, ed. F. Madden (RS, 44, ii; London, 1866).

Opuscula Sancti Patris Francisci Assisiensis, ed. C. Esser (BFAMA, 12; Grottaferrata, Rome, 1978).

Orderic Vitalis, *The Ecclesiastical History*, II, ed. Chibnall (OMT; 1969).

Orderic Vitalis, *The Ecclesiastical History*, III, ed. Chibnall (OMT; 1972).

Orderic Vitalis, *The Ecclesiastical History*, IV, ed. Chibnall (OMT; 1973).

Paul the Deacon, *Historia Langobardorum* (MGH SS; 1878).

Peter Damian, *Sermo 36* in *Corpus Christianorum, continuatio mediaevalis*, 57, ed. J. Lucchesi (1983), pp. 217-22.

The Prayers and Meditations of Saint Anselm, trans. B. Ward (Penguin Classics; Harmondsworth, 1973).

The Register of Walter Giffard, Lord Archbishop of York 1266-1279, ed. W. Brown (Surtees Society, 109; Durham, 1904).

Roberti Grosseteste episcopi quondam Lincolniensis Epistolae, ed. H. R. Luard (RS, 25; London, 1861).

Rosemann, P. W. (ed.), 'Tabula magistri Roberti Lincolniensis episcopi cum additione fratris Adae de Marisco' in *Opera Roberti Grosseteste Lincolniensis*, gen. ed. McEvoy (Corpus Christianorum, continuatio mediaevalis, 130; Steenbrugge, 1995), pp. 235-320.

Roger Bacon, *Opera quaedam hactenus inedita*, v. 1, ed. J. S. Brewer (RS, 15; London, 1859).

Roger of Wendover, *Flores historiarum*, II, ed. H. G. Hewlett (RS, 84, ii; London, 1887).

Sacrum commercium sancti Francisci cum domina Paupertate, ed. S. Brufani (Medioevo Francescano, 1; Assisi, 1990).

Salimbene de Adam, *Cronica*, ed. G. Scalia (Scrittori d'Italia, 232-33; Bari, 1966).

Selected Letters of Pope Innocent III concerning England (1198-1216), ed. C. R. Cheney and W. H. Semple (NMT; 1953).

Tanner, N. P. (ed.), *Decrees of the Ecumenical Councils*, I (London, 1990).

Thomas Gallus, *De ecclesiastica hierarchia*, III, 5, from cod. lat. 695 of the Nationalbibliothek, Vienna. c.135r.

Thomas of Celano, 'Tractatus de miraculis B. Francisci' in AF, 10 (1926-41), pp. 269-330.

Thomas of Celano, 'Vita prima S. Francisci' in AF, 10, pp. 1-117.

Thomas of Celano, 'Vita secunda S. Francisci' in AF, 10, pp. 127-268.

Thomas of Eccleston, *Tractatus de adventu fratrum minorum in Angliam*, ed. A. G. Little (Manchester, 1951).

Thomas of Spalato, *Historia pontificum Salonitanorum et Spalatensium* (MGH SS; 1892).

Ubertino da Casale, 'Incipiunt articuli accepti de regula, contra quos sepe transgressiones fiunt' in ALKG, III.

Vita del 'Dialogus' e 'Benignitas', ed. V. Gamboso (FAA, 3; Padua, 1986).

Vita prima o Assidua, ed. V. Gamboso (FAA, 1; Padua, 1981).

Vite 'Raymundina' e 'Rigaldina', ed. V. Gamboso (FAA, 4; Padua, 1992).

The Writings of Leo, Rufino and Angelo Companions of St Francis, ed. R. B. Brooke (OMT, 1970), repr. with corrections (1990).

2. SECONDARY SOURCES

Armstrong, E. A., *St Francis: Nature Mystic: The Derivation and Significance of the Nature Stories in the Franciscan Legend* (Berkeley, 1973).

Armstrong, R. J., 'Pope Gregory IX's view of St Francis of Assisi', *Analecta Tertii ordinis regularis Sancti Francisci*, 21 (1989), pp. 261-89.

Barraclough, G., *The Medieval Papacy* (London, 1968).

Bartoli, M., *Clare of Assisi*, trans. from Italian Sister Frances Teresa (London, 1993).

Beaumont-Maillet, L., *Le Grand Couvent des Cordeliers de Paris* (Bibliothèque de l'école des hautes études, IV section, sciences historiques et philologiques, 325; Paris, 1975).

Bennett, H. S., *The Pastons and Their England* (Cambridge, 1922).

Bihl, M., 'De Iohanne de S. Paulo, Cardinali episcopo Sabinensi, primo S. Francisci in Curia Romana an. 1209 fautore' in AFH, 19 (1926), pp. 282-5.

Bihl, M., 'De quodam elencho Assisano testium oculatorum S. Francisci Stigmatum' in AFH, 19 (1926), pp. 931-6.

Bihl, M., 'De canonizatione S. Francisci' in AFH, 21 (1928), pp. 468-514.

Biller, P., 'Heresy and literacy: earlier history of the theme' in P. Biller and A. Hudson (eds), *Heresy and Literacy, 1000-1530* (Cambridge Studies in Medieval Literature, 23; 1994), pp. 1-18.

Bolton, B., 'Innocent III and the Humiliati' in J. M. Powell (ed.), *Innocent III: Vicar of Christ or Lord of the World?*, pp. 114-20.

Bracaloni, L., *Storia di San Damiano in Assisi* (Todi, 2nd edn, 1926).

Brady, I., 'The authenticity of two sermons of St Bonaventure', *Franciscan Studies*, 28 (1968), pp. 4-26.

Brooke, C. N. L. (ed.), *David Knowles Remembered* (Cambridge, 1991).

Brooke, C. N. L. and R. B., *Popular Religion in the Middle Ages* (London, 1984).

Brooke, R. B., *Early Franciscan Government: Elias to Bonaventure* (Cambridge Studies in Medieval Life and Thought; Cambridge, 1959).

Brooke, R. B., *The Coming of the Friars* (Historical Problems, Studies and Documents, 24; London, 1975).

Brooke, R. B., 'Recent work on St Francis of Assisi', *Analecta Bollandiana,* 100 (1982), pp. 653-76.

Brown, P., *The Cult of the Saints* (Chicago, 1981).

Brown, R., *The Roots of St Francis: A Popular History of the Church in Assisi and Umbria before St Francis as Related to his Life and Spirituality* (Chicago, 1982).

Brunacci, A., 'Il messale consultato da San Francesco all'inizio della sua nuova vita', *San Francesco Patrono d'Italia*, 58 (1978), pp. 80-8.

Callebaut, A., 'Autour de la rencontre à Florence de S. François et du Cardinal Hugolin (en été 1217)' in AFH, 19 (1926), pp. 530-58.

Canonici, L., 'Guido II di Assisi. Il vescovo di san Francesco', *Studi Francescani*, 77 (1980), pp. 187-206.

Carney, M., 'Francis and Clare. A critical examination of the sources', *Laurentianum*, 30 (1989), pp. 25-60.

Casolini, F., *Nell'anno 750 della vestizione di Santa Chiara d'Assisi (1211-1961)* (Assisi, 1961).

Chibnall, M., *The World of Orderic Vitalis* (Oxford, 1984).

Clasen, S., *St Anthony, Doctor of the Church*, trans. from German I. Brady (Chicago, 1973).

Da Gama Caeiro, F., 'Fonti portoghesi della formazione culturale di sant'Antonio' in A. Poppi (ed.), *Le fonti e la teologia dei sermoni Antoniani* (Padua, 1982), pp. 145-69.

Dalarun, J., *Francesco: un passaggio. Donna e donne negli scritti e nelle leggende di Francesco d'Assisi. Postfazione di Giovanni Miccoli* (I libri di Viella, 2; Rome, 1994).

D'Alatri, M., 'Antonio, martello degli eretici?', *Il Santo*, 5 (1965), pp. 123-30.

De la Bedoyère, M., *Francis: A Biography of the Saint of Assisi* (London, 1962).

De la Marche, L., *Anecdotes historiques* (Paris, 1877).

Di Fonzo, L., 'L'Anonimo Perugino tra le fonti francescane del sec. XIII. Rapporti letterari e testo critico', *Miscellanea Francescana*, 72 (1972), pp. 117-483.

Documents relating to the University and Colleges of Cambridge, I (1852).

Emery, R. W., *The Friars in Medieval France* (New York, 1962).

Faloci-Pulignani, M., 'Il più antico documento per la storia di San Francesco', *Miscellanea Francescana*, 2 (1887), pp. 33-7.

Faloci-Pulignani, 'Il messale consultato da S. Francesco quando si convertì', *Miscellanea Francescana*, 15 (1914), pp. 33-43.

Faloci-Pulignani, 'La passio S. Feliciani e il suo valore storico', *Archivio per la storia ecclesiastica dell'Umbria*, 4 (1917), pp. 137-274.

Figueredo Frias, A., 'Lettura ermeneutica di sant'Antonio di Padova', *Il Santo*, 35 (1995), pp. 279-458.

Fleming, J. V., *An Introduction to the Franciscan Literature of the Middle Ages* (Chicago, 1977).

Fonti Francescane (Padua, 3rd edn 1980).

Fortini, A., *Assisi nel medioevo* (Rome, 1940).

Fortini, A., 'Nuove notizie intorno a Santa Chiara di Assisi' in AFH, 46 (1953), pp. 3-43.

Fortini, A., *Francis of Assisi*, trans. from NV, H. Moak (New York, 1981).

Fortini, G., *Francesco d'Assisi Ebreo?* (Assisi, 1978).

Frances Teresa, Sister, *This Living Mirror: Reflections on Clare of Assisi* (London, 1995).

Freed, J. B., *The Friars and German Society in the Thirteenth Century* (Cambridge, MA, 1977).

Frugoni, C., *Francesco e l'invenzione delle stimmate: Una storia per parole e immagini fino a Bonaventura e Giotto* (Turin, 1993).

Gamboso, V., *St Anthony of Padua: His Life and his Teaching*, trans. from Italian H. Partridge, rev. L. Poloniato (Padua, 1991).

Gardner, J., 'Patterns of papal patronage circa 1260-circa 1300' in C. Ryan (ed.), *The Religious Roles of the Papacy: Ideals and Realities, 1150-1300* (Pontifical Institute of Mediaeval Studies, Papers in Mediaeval Studies, 8; Toronto, 1989), pp. 439-56.

Gieben, S., 'Robert Grosseteste and the evolution of the Franciscan Order' in J. McEvoy (ed.), *Robert Grosseteste: New Perspectives on his Thought and Scholarship* (Instrumenta Patristica, XXVII; Turnhout, Brepols, 1995), pp. 215-32.

Gilson, E., *La philosophie de saint Bonaventure* (Études de philosophie médiévale, 4; Paris, 1943).

Goodich, M., 'The politics of canonisation in the thirteenth century: lay and mendicant saints' in S. Wilson (ed.), *Saints and their Cults: Studies in Religious Sociology, Folklore and History* (Cambridge, 1983), pp. 169-87.

Gratien de Paris, *Histoire de la fondation et de l'évolution de l'ordre des frères mineurs au xiiie siècle* (Rome, 1926), repr. with updated biblio. by M. D'Alatri and S. Gieben (Bibliotheca seraphico-Capuccina cura instituti historici ord.Fr.Min.Capuccinorum, 29; Rome, 1982).

Jeffrey, D. L., 'St Francis and medieval theatre', *Franciscan Studies*, 43 (1983), pp. 321-46.

Bibliography

Jessopp, A., *The Coming of the Friars and Other Historic Essays* (London, 1889).

Kempers, B., *Painting, Power and Patronage: The Rise of the Professional Artist in the Italian Renaissance*, trans. from Dutch B. Jackson (London, 1992).

Knowles, D., *From Pachomius to Ignatius: A Study in the Constitutional History of the Religious Orders* (Oxford, 1966).

Lawrence, C. H., *St Edmund of Abingdon: A Study in Hagiography and History* (Oxford, 1960).

Lawrence, C. H., *Medieval Monasticism: Forms of Religious Life in Western Europe in the Middle Ages* (London, 2nd edn, 1989).

Lawrence, C. H., The Friars: The Impact of the Early Mendicant Movement on Western Society (The Medieval World; London, 1994).

Lawrence, C. H., ed. and trans., *The Life of St Edmund by Matthew Paris* (Oxford, 1996).

Le Goff, J., *Medieval Civilisation 400-1500*, trans. from French J. Barrow (Oxford, 1988).

Lempp, E., *Frère Élie de Cortone* (Collection d'études et de documents sur l'histoire religieuse et littéraire du moyen âge, 3; Paris, 1901).

Little, A. G., 'Brother William of England, companion of St Francis, and some Franciscan drawings in the Matthew Paris manuscripts' in A. G. Little et al. (eds), *Collectanea Franciscana*, 1 (BSFS, 5; Aberdeen, 1914), pp. 1-8.

Little, L. K., *Religious Poverty and the Profit Economy in Medieval Europe* (London, 1978).

Longpré, E., 'Guillaume d'Auvergne et l'école franciscaine de Paris', *France Franciscaine*, 10 (1922), pp. 5-45.

Maccarrone, M., *Vicarius Christi: storia del titolo papale* (Rome, 1952).

Maier, C. T., *Preaching the Crusades: Mendicant Friars and the Cross in the Thirteenth Century* (Cambridge Studies in Medieval Life; Cambridge, 1994).

Mockler, A., *Francis of Assisi: The Wandering Years* (Oxford, 1976).

Moorman, J. R. H., *The Sources for the Life of S. Francis of Assisi* (University of Manchester, Historical Series, 79; 1940).

Moorman, J. R. H., *A History of the Franciscan Order From its Origins to the Year 1517* (Oxford, 1968).

Moorman, J. R. H., *St Francis of Assisi* (London, 1950).

Moorman, J. R. H., *The Grey Friars in Cambridge 1225-1538* (Cambridge, 1952).

Morris, C., *The Papal Monarchy: The Western Church from 1050 to 1250* (Oxford History of the Christian Church; Oxford, 1989).

Paolini, L., 'Italian Catharism and written culture' in P. Biller and A. Hudson (eds), *Heresy and Literacy, 1000-1530* (Cambridge Studies in Medieval Literature, 23; 1994), pp. 83-103.

Paschini, P., 'Il cardinale Giovanni di San Paolo' in *Studi di Storia e Diritto in onore di Carlo Carlisse*, III (Milan, 1940), pp. 109-18.

Pasztor, E., 'San Francesco e il cardinale Ugolino nella "questione francescana"', *Collectanea Franciscana*, 46 (1976), pp. 209-39.

Peters, E., 'Restoring the Church and restoring churches: event and image in Franciscan biography', *Franziskanische Studien*, 68 (1986), pp. 213-36.

Powell, J. M. 'The papacy and the early Franciscans', *Franciscan Studies*, 36 (1976), pp. 248-62.

Powell, J. M. (ed.), *Innocent III Vicar of Christ or Lord of the World?* (Washington, DC, 2nd edn, 1994).

Powell, J. M., 'Innocent III and the Crusade' in *Innocent III: Vicar of Christ or Lord of the World?*, pp. 121-34.

Purcell, M., *St Anthony and his Times* (Dublin, 1960).

Riley-Smith, J., *What Were the Crusades?* (Basingstoke, 2nd edn 1992).

Riley-Smith, L. and J., *The Crusades: Idea and Reality 1095-1274* (Documents of Medieval History, 4; London, 1981).

Robson, M., 'Assisi, Guido II and St Francis', *Laurentianum*, 34 (1993), pp. 109-38.

Robson, M., 'Saint Anthony of Padua in medieval Cambridge', *Il Santo*, 34 (1994), pp. 341-8.

Robson, M., 'Saint Anselm and his Father, Gundulf', *Historical Research: The Bulletin of the Institute of Historical Research*, 69 (1996), pp. 197-200.

Rubin, M., *Charity and Community in Medieval Cambridge* (Cambridge Studies in Medieval Life and Thought; Cambridge, 1987).

Sabatier, P., *Life of St Francis of Assisi*, trans. from French L. S. Houghton (London, 1899).

Sayers, J. E., *Innocent III: Leader of Europe, 1198-1216* (London, 1994).

Schmucki, O., *The Stigmata of St Francis of Assisi*, trans. C. F. Connors (Franciscan Institute Publications, History Series, 6; New York, 1991).

Smalley, B., 'The Gospels in the Paris Schools in the late 12th and early 13th centuries', *Franciscan Studies*, 40 (1980), pp. 298-369.

Smalley, B., 'The use of Scripture in St Anthony's "Sermones"' in A. Poppi (ed.), *Le fonti e la teologia dei sermoni Antoniani*, pp. 285-97.

Smith, J. M. H., 'Oral and written: saints, miracles, and relics in Brittany, c. 850-1250', *Speculum*, 65 (1990), pp. 309-43.

Sorrell, R. D., 'Tradition and innovation, harmony and hierarchy in St Francis of Assisi's Sermon on the Birds', *Franciscan Studies*, 43 (1983), pp. 396-407.

Sorrell, R. D., *St Francis of Assisi and Nature: Tradition and Innovation in Western Christian Attitudes towards the Environment* (Oxford, 1988).

Southern, R. W., *The Making of the Middle Ages* (London, 1953).

Southern, R. W., *Western Society and the Church in the Middle Ages* (London, 1970).

Thomson, W. R., 'The earliest cardinal-protectors of the Franciscan Order: a study in administrative history, 1210-1261', *Studies in Medieval and Renaissance History*, 9 (1972), pp. 21-80.

Thomson, W. R., *Friars in the Cathedral: The First Franciscan Bishops 1226-1261* (Pontifical Institute of Mediaeval Studies, Studies and Texts, 33; Toronto, 1975).

Thomson, W. R., 'The image of the Mendicants in the Chronicles of Matthew Paris' in AFH, 70 (1977), pp. 3-34.

Tini, A. P., 'La culla delle Damianite e Guido vescovo', *Miscellanea Francescana*, 14 (1912), pp. 33-7.

Trexler, R. C., *Naked before the Father: The Renunciation of Francis of Assisi* (Humana Civilitas 9; New York, 1989).

Tugwell, S., 'Notes on the life of St Dominic', *Archivum Fratrum Praedicatorum*, 65 (1995), pp. 5-169.

Tugwell, S., *Saint Dominic* (Strasbourg, 1995).

Van Dijk, S. J. P. and Walker, J. H., *The Myth of the Aumbry* (London, 1957).

Van Dijk, S. J. P. and Walker, J. H., *The Origins of the Modern Roman Liturgy* (London, 1960).

Vicaire, M.-H., *Histoire de Saint Dominique: au coeur de l'Église* (Paris, 1957).

Voorvelt, G. C. P. and Van Leeuwen, B. P., 'L'evangéliaire de Baltimore', *Collectanea Franciscana*, 59 (1989), pp. 261-321.

Vorreux, D., 'Un sermon de Philippe le Chancelier en faveur des Frères Mineurs de Vauvert' in AFH, 68 (1975), pp. 3-22.

Bibliography

Waley, D., *The Italian City-Republics* (London, 3rd edn, 1988).

Watt, J. A., *The Theory of Papal Monarchy in the Thirteenth Century: The Contribution of the Canonists* (London, 1965).

Index